# THE NEW CAMBRIDGE SHAKESPEARE

GENERAL EDITOR
Philip Brockbank, *Professor of English Language and Literature, University of Birmingham*

ASSOCIATE GENERAL EDITORS
Brian Gibbons, *Professor of English Literature, University of Zürich*
Robin Hood, *Senior Lecturer in English, University of York*

## THE SECOND PART OF KING HENRY IV

Giorgio Melchiori offers a new approach to the text of *The Second Part of King Henry IV*, which he sees as an unplanned sequel to the *First Part*, itself a 'remake' of an old, non-Shakespearean play. The *Second Part* deliberately exploits the popular success of Sir John Falstaff, introduced in *Part One*; the resulting rich humour gives a comic dimension to the play which makes it a unique blend of history, Morality play and comedy.

This approach throws new light on the Falstaff/Oldcastle tangle, and on Elizabethan theatrical practice in general. A thorough textual analysis also counteracts some recent theories on the extent and timing of the revisions of both parts.

Among modern editions of the play this is the one most firmly based on the quarto. Professor Melchiori presents an eminently actable text, by showing how Shakespeare's own choices are superior for practical purposes to suggested emendations, and by keeping interference in the original stage directions to a minimum, in order to respect, as Shakespeare did, the players' freedom.

Extracts from Shakespeare's historical and literary sources are printed at the back, including substantial quotations from Holinshed's *Chronicles* and *The Famous Victories of Henry the Fifth*.

# THE NEW CAMBRIDGE SHAKESPEARE

# THE SECOND PART OF KING HENRY IV

*Edited by*
GIORGIO MELCHIORI
*Professor of English Literature, University of Rome*

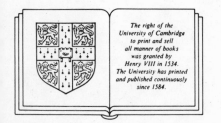

The right of the
University of Cambridge
to print and sell
all manner of books
was granted by
Henry VIII in 1534.
The University has printed
and published continuously
since 1584.

CAMBRIDGE UNIVERSITY PRESS

Cambridge
New York   Port Chester
Melbourne   Sydney

Published by the Press Syndicate of the University of Cambridge
The Pitt Building, Trumpington Street, Cambridge CB2 1RP
40 West 20th Street, New York, NY 10011, USA
10 Stamford Road, Oakleigh, Melbourne 3166, Australia

© Cambridge University Press 1989

First published 1989

Printed in Great Britain at
the University Press, Cambridge

*British Library cataloguing in publication data*

Shakespeare, William
[Henry IV. Part 2.] The second part of King Henry IV. – (The New Cambridge Shakespeare).
I. [Henry IV. Part 2]  II. Melchiori, Giorgio
822.3′3

*Library of Congress cataloguing in publication data*

Shakespeare, William, 1564–1616
[King Henry IV. Part 2]
The Second part of King Henry IV / edited by Giorgio Melchiori.
p.  cm. – (The New Cambridge Shakespeare)
Bibliography: p.
ISBN 0 521 25695 X  ISBN 0 521 27652 7 (pbk.)
1. Henry IV, King of England, 1367–1414 – Drama.  I. Melchiori, Giorgio.  II. Title.
III. Series: Shakespeare, William, 1564–1616. Works.
1984. Cambridge University Press.
PR2811. A2M4  1989
822.3′3 – dc19  88-39402

ISBN 0 521 25695 X hard covers
ISBN 0 521 27652 7 paperback

# THE NEW CAMBRIDGE SHAKESPEARE

The *New Cambridge Shakespeare* succeeds *The New Shakespeare* which began publication in 1921 under the general editorship of Sir Arthur Quiller-Couch and John Dover Wilson, and was completed in the 1960s, with the assistance of G. I. Duthie, Alice Walker, Peter Ure and J. C. Maxwell. *The New Shakespeare* itself followed upon *The Cambridge Shakespeare*, 1863–6, edited by W. G. Clark, J. Glover and W. A. Wright.

*The New Shakespeare* won high esteem both for its scholarship and for its design, but shifts of critical taste and insight, recent Shakespearean research, and a changing sense of what is important in our understanding of the plays, have made it necessary to re-edit and redesign, not merely to revise, the series.

The *New Cambridge Shakespeare* aims to be of value to a new generation of playgoers and readers who wish to enjoy fuller access to Shakespeare's poetic and dramatic art. While offering ample academic guidance, it reflects current critical interests and is more attentive than some earlier editions have been to the realisation of the plays on the stage, and to their social and cultural settings. The text of each play has been freshly edited, with textual data made available to those users who wish to know why and how one published text differs from another. Although modernised, the edition conserves forms that appear to be expressive and characteristically Shakespearean, and it does not attempt to disguise the fact that the plays were written in a language other than that of our own time.

Illustrations are usually integrated into the critical and historical discussion of the play and include some reconstructions of early performances by C. Walter Hodges. Some editors have also made use of the advice and experience of Maurice Daniels, for many years a member of the Royal Shakespeare Company.

Each volume is addressed to the needs and problems of a particular text, and each therefore differs in style and emphasis from others in the series.

PHILIP BROCKBANK
*General Editor*

# CONTENTS

# Contents

# ILLUSTRATIONS

Illustrations 8, 9, 10 and 13 are reproduced by courtesy of the Shakespeare Centre Library, Stratford-upon-Avon

# PREFACE

It is unusual to entrust the two parts of *Henry IV* to different editors, but the splendid results of this policy in the Variorum edition of half a century ago, when *Part One* was edited by H. B. Hemingway (1936) and *Part Two* by M. A. Shaaber (1940), give warrant for adopting it. Concentrating on only one of the two plays an editor is forced to examine with greater care the question of its relationship with the other (and, in the case of *Henry IV*, with *Henry V* and *The Merry Wives of Windsor* as well), so that it becomes a vantage point from which to survey the elusive play of interrelations in the whole sequence of Shakespeare's histories. Besides, the two parts posit such widely divergent textual problems that a single editor may find it difficult to disentangle them.

In tackling the *Second Part* I had the advantage of exchanging notes with the editor of the *First*, Herbert Weil, as well as of enjoying the constant friendly guidance of the General Editor, Philip Brockbank. My greatest debt is to him, while the existence of Shaaber's edition made my basic task much easier. I have learnt a lot from the more recent editors of the play, notably P. H. Davison and the late A. R. Humphreys, from Harold Jenkins and from a host of scholars whose contributions are at times inadequately recorded in the Introduction and Textual Analysis, or mentioned in the Reading List. But I am particularly grateful to the editors of the play in the new Oxford Shakespeare, John Jowett and Gary Taylor, who kept me informed of the progress of their work: though I was unable to share their views on several points in textual and other matters, their communications have always been extremely stimulating.

My task was made very pleasant by my repeated stays in Cambridge during the last seven years, in the hospitable atmosphere of Clare Hall, to whose President, members and staff I wish to express my thanks for making me welcome at all times. I enjoyed the same warm and friendly welcome at the Shakespeare Institute in Stratford-upon-Avon, whose guest I was in the spring of 1981. I was greatly helped by the constant amicable interest in the progress of my work shown by Muriel Bradbrook, and by her generous hospitality, and I am grateful to Kenneth Muir and the British Academy for offering me, together with the honour, the opportunity of testing some of the ideas resulting from the work on this edition in the Annual Shakespeare Lecture of 1986. Without the constant help over the years of my old friend and colleague Vittorio Gabrieli I would have lost myself in the meanders of British historiography.

I could not have embarked on this enterprise without the facilities and the help offered by the staff of the Cambridge University Library, and especially by Janice Fairholm who hunted up several things for me, of the English Faculty Library in Cambridge, of the Shakespeare Institute and of the Shakespeare Centre in Stratford-upon-Avon. Finally I am grateful for the constant help from the Press, especially Sarah Stanton and Victoria

Cooper, who spared me the heavy task of procuring the illustrations. Walter Hodges was delightfully co-operative in producing his admirable drawings. Paul Chipchase went through the typescript with a very fine comb; I lay a personal claim to the mistakes left in it.

G.M.

*Clare Hall, Cambridge*

# ABBREVIATIONS AND CONVENTIONS

Shakespeare's plays, when cited in this edition, are abbreviated in a style modified slightly from that used in the *Harvard Concordance to Shakespeare*. Other editions of Shakespeare are abbreviated under the editor's surname (Holland, Davison), or, in some cases, under the series title (Cam., Globe). When more than one edition by the same editor is cited, later editions are discriminated by a raised figure (Dyce²). All quotations from Shakespeare, except those from *The Second Part of King Henry IV*, use the lineation, though not necessarily the spelling, of *The Riverside Shakespeare*, 1974, on which the *Harvard Concordance* is based.

## 1. Shakespeare's plays

| | |
|---|---|
| *Ado* | *Much Ado About Nothing* |
| *Ant.* | *Antony and Cleopatra* |
| *AWW* | *All's Well That Ends Well* |
| *AYLI* | *As You Like It* |
| *Cor.* | *Coriolanus* |
| *Cym.* | *Cymbeline* |
| *Err.* | *The Comedy of Errors* |
| *E3* | *Edward the Third* |
| *Ham.* | *Hamlet* |
| *1H4* | *The First Part of King Henry the Fourth* |
| *2H4* | *The Second Part of King Henry the Fourth* |
| *H5* | *King Henry the Fifth* |
| *1H6* | *The First Part of King Henry the Sixth* |
| *2H6* | *The Second Part of King Henry the Sixth* |
| *3H6* | *The Third Part of King Henry the Sixth* |
| *H8* | *King Henry the Eighth* |
| *JC* | *Julius Caesar* |
| *John* | *King John* |
| *LLL* | *Love's Labour's Lost* |
| *Lear* | *King Lear* |
| *Mac.* | *Macbeth* |
| *MM* | *Measure for Measure* |
| *MND* | *A Midsummer Night's Dream* |
| *MV* | *The Merchant of Venice* |
| *Oth.* | *Othello* |
| *Per.* | *Pericles* |
| *R2* | *King Richard the Second* |
| *R3* | *King Richard the Third* |
| *Rom.* | *Romeo and Juliet* |
| *Shr.* | *The Taming of the Shrew* |
| *Temp.* | *The Tempest* |
| *TGV* | *The Two Gentlemen of Verona* |
| *Tim.* | *Timon of Athens* |

| *Tit.* | *Titus Andronicus* |
| *TN* | *Twelfth Night* |
| *TNK* | *The Two Noble Kinsmen* |
| *Tro.* | *Troilus and Cressida* |
| *Wiv.* | *The Merry Wives of Windsor* |
| *WT* | *The Winter's Tale* |

## 2. Other works cited and general references

| AAEB | *Analytical and Enumerative Bibliography* |
| Abbott | E. A. Abbott, *A Shakespearian Grammar*, 1869 (references are to numbered paragraphs) |
| Alexander | *The Complete Works of William Shakespeare*, ed. Peter Alexander, 1951 |
| Berger–Williams | Thomas L. Berger and George Walton Williams, 'Notes on Shakespeare's *2 Henry IV*', *AAEB* 3 (1979), 240–53 |
| Bulloch | John Bulloch, *Studies on the Text of Shakespeare, with Numerous Emendations*, 1878 |
| Bullough | *Narrative and Dramatic Sources of Shakespeare*, ed. Geoffrey Bullough, IV, 1962 |
| Cam. | *The Works of William Shakespeare*, ed. William George Clark, John Glover and William Aldis Wright, 9 vols., 1864, IV (Cambridge Shakespeare) |
| Capell | *Mr William Shakespeare his Comedies, Histories, and Tragedies*, ed. Edward Capell, 10 vols., 1767–8, V |
| conj. Capell | Edward Capell, *Notes and Various Readings to Shakespeare*, 2 vols., 1779 |
| Collier | *The Works of William Shakespeare*, ed. John Payne Collier, 8 vols., 1842–4, IV |
| Collier² | *Shakespeare's Comedies, Histories, Tragedies, and Poems*, ed. J. Payne Collier, 6 vols., 1858, III |
| Collier³ | *The Plays of Shakespeare*, ed. J. Payne Collier, 8 vols., 1876, IV |
| conj. | conjecture |
| corr. | corrected state |
| Cowl | *The Second Part of King Henry the Fourth*, ed. R. P. Cowl, 1923 (Arden Shakespeare) |
| CQ | *Critical Quarterly* |
| Craig | *The Complete Works of William Shakespeare*, ed. W. J. Craig, 1892 (Oxford Shakespeare) |
| Daniel | Samuel Daniel, *The First Fowre Bookes of the Ciuile Wars between the two Houses of Lancaster and Yorke*, 1595 |
| Davison | *The Second Part of King Henry the Fourth*, ed. P. H. Davison, 1977 (New Penguin) |
| Dent | R. W. Dent, *Shakespeare's Proverbial Language: An Index*, 1981 (references are to numbered proverbs) |
| Dering MS. | *The History of King Henry the Fourth as revised by Sir Edward Dering, Bart.* (1623), a facsimile edition, ed. G. Walton Williams and G. Blakemore Evans, 1974 |
| Douce | Francis Douce, *Illustrations of Shakespeare, and of Ancient Manners*, 2 vols., 1807 |
| Dyce | *The Works of William Shakespeare*, ed. Alexander Dyce, 6 vols., 1857, III |

| | |
|---|---|
| Dyce² | *The Works of William Shakespeare*, ed. A. Dyce, 9 vols., 1864, IV |
| EETS | The Early English Text Society |
| *ELN* | *English Language Notes* |
| *ELR* | *English Literary Renaissance* |
| F | *Mr. William Shakespeares Comedies, Histories, & Tragedies*, 1623 (First Folio) |
| F2 | *Mr. William Shakespeares Comedies, Histories, and Tragedies*, 1632 (Second Folio) |
| F3 | *Mr. William Shakespeares Comedies, Histories, and Tragedies*, 1664 (Third Folio) |
| F4 | *Mr. William Shakespeares Comedies, Histories, and Tragedies*, 1685 (Fourth Folio) |
| Furnivall | *The Works of William Shakespeare*, ed. F. J. Furnivall, 1877 (Leopold Shakespeare) |
| *FV* | *The Famous Victories of Henry the fifth . . . Printed by Thomas Creede, 1598.* A facsimile . . . by Charles Praetorius, with an introduction by P. A. Daniel, 1887 |
| Globe | *The Works of William Shakespeare*, ed. W. G. Clark and W. A. Wright, 1864 (Globe Shakespeare) |
| Golding | *Shakespeare's Ovid: being Arthur Golding's Translation of the Metamorphoses* (1565–76), ed. W. H. D. Rouse, 1961 |
| Hall | [Edward Hall,] *The Vnion of the two noble and illustre famelies of Lancastre & Yorke . . .*, 1550 |
| Hanmer | *The Works of Shakespeare*, ed. Thomas Hanmer, 6 vols., 1743, III |
| Harpsfield | *The life and death of Sr Thomas Moore, knight, . . . written in the tyme of Queene Marie by Nicholas Harpsfield, L.D.*, ed. Elsie Vaughan Hitchcock, EETS OS 186, 1932 |
| Holinshed | *The Third volume of Chronicles . . . beginning at duke William the Norman . . . first compiled by Raphaell Holinshed, and by him extended to the yeare 1577. Now newlie recognised, augmented and continued . . . to the yeare 1586*, 1587 (page/column/line refs. are to this edn) |
| Holland | *The Second Part of King Henry IV*, ed. Norman N. Holland, 1965 (Signet) |
| Hudson | *The Complete Works of William Shakespeare*, ed. Henry N. Hudson, 20 vols., 1880, XI (Harvard Shakespeare) |
| Humphreys | *The Second Part of King Henry IV*, ed. A. R. Humphreys, 1966 (Arden Shakespeare) |
| Jenkins, *Structural Problem* | Harold Jenkins, *The Structural Problem in Shakespeare's 'Henry IV'*, 1956 |
| Johnson | *The Plays of William Shakespeare*, ed. Samuel Johnson, 8 vols., 1765, IV |
| Jonson | *The Collected Works of Ben Jonson*, ed. C. H. Herford and P. Simpson, 1925 |
| Jowett–Taylor | John Jowett and Gary Taylor, 'The three texts of *2 Henry IV*', *SB* 40 (1987), 31–50 |
| Keightley | *The Plays of William Shakespeare*, ed. Thomas Keightley, 6 vols., 1864, III |
| *KM80* | *KM80 A Birthday Album for Kenneth Muir*, 1987 |
| Knight | *The Pictorial Edition of the Works of Shakspere*, ed. Charles Knight, 7 vols., 1839, I |

| | |
|---|---|
| *L&H* | *Literature and History* |
| Malone | *The Plays and Poems of William Shakespeare*, ed. Edmond Malone, 10 vols., 1790, V |
| conj. Maxwell | James C. Maxwell, '*2 Henry IV*, II.iv.91 ff.', *MLR* 42 (1947), 485 |
| Melchiori, 'Corridors' | Giorgio Melchiori, 'The corridors of history: Shakespeare the re-maker', *PBA* 72 (1986), 67–85 |
| Melchiori, 'Jealousy' | Giorgio Melchiori, 'The role of jealousy: restoring the Q reading of *2 Henry IV*, Induction, 16', *SQ* 34 (1983), 327–30 |
| Melchiori, 'Umfrevile' | Giorgio Melchiori, 'Sir John Umfrevile in *Henry IV*, Part 2, I.i.169–79', *REAL* 2 (1984), 199–210 |
| Melchiori, 'The ur-*Henry IV*' | Giorgio Melchiori, 'Reconstructing the ur-*Henry IV*', in *Essays in Honour of Kristian Smidt*, ed. P. Bilton, L. Hartveit, S. Johansson, A. O. Sandved, B. Tysdahl, Oslo, 1986, pp. 59–78 |
| *MLR* | *Modern Language Review* |
| More | *The Booke of Sir Thomas Moore*, ed. W. W. Greg, MSR 1911 (the hand responsible for different additions is indicated) |
| MSR | Malone Society Reprints |
| Munro | *The London Shakespeare*, ed. John Monro, 6 vols., 1957, IV |
| *N&Q* | *Notes and Queries* |
| ODEP | *The Oxford Dictionary of English Proverbs*, 3rd edn, rev. F. P. Wilson, 1970 (references are to numbered proverbs) |
| OED | *The Oxford English Dictionary*, 13 vols., and 4 vols. *Supplement*, 1933–86 |
| *1 Oldcastle* | *The first part Of the true and honorable historie, of the life of Sir John Oldcastle, the good Lord Cobham*, ed. P. Simpson, MSR 1908 |
| Oxford | *William Shakespeare: The Complete Works*, ed. Stanley Wells and Gary Taylor, 1986 (Oxford Shakespeare) |
| *PBA* | *Proceedings of the British Academy* |
| *PMLA* | *Publications of the Modern Language Association of America* |
| Pope | *The Works of Shakespear*, ed. Alexander Pope, 6 vols., 1723, III |
| *PQ* | *Philological Quarterly* |
| Prosser | Eleanor Prosser, *Shakespeare's Anonymous Editors: Scribe and Compositor in the Folio Text of '2 Henry IV'*, 1981 |
| Q | *The Second part of Henrie the fourth* ... Written by William Shakespeare ... Printed by V.S. for Andrew Wise and William Aspley, 1600 |
| Qa | The first issue of the 1600 quarto |
| Qb | The second issue of the 1600 quarto, with a cancel quire E |
| Rann | *The Dramatic Works of Shakespeare*, ed. Joseph Rann, 6 vols., 1786–94, III |
| *REAL* | *The Yearbook of Research in English and American Literature* |
| *RES* | *Review of English Studies* |
| Ridley | *Henry IV, Second Part*, ed. M. R. Ridley, 1934 (New Temple Shakespeare) |
| Riverside | *The Riverside Shakespeare*, ed. G. Blakemore Evans, 1974 |
| Rowe | *The Works of Mr William Shakespear*, ed. Nicholas Rowe, 6 vols., 1709, III |
| Rowe[3] | *The Works of Mr William Shakespear*, ed. N. Rowe (third edn), 8 vols., 1714, IV |
| *SB* | *Studies in Bibliography* |
| SD | stage direction |
| *SEL* | *Studies in English Literature 1500–1900* |

| | |
|---|---|
| SH | speech heading |
| Shaaber | *A New Variorum Edition of Shakespeare, The Second Part of Henry the Fourth*, ed. Matthias A. Shaaber, 1940 |
| Singer | *The Dramatic Works of William Shakespeare*, ed. Samuel Weller Singer, 10 vols., 1826, V |
| Singer² | *The Dramatic Works of William Shakespeare*, ed. S. W. Singer, 2nd edn, 1855–6, V |
| Sisson | *William Shakespeare: The Complete Works*, ed. Charles Jasper Sisson, 1954 |
| conj. Sisson | C. J. Sisson, *New Readings in Shakespeare*, 2 vols., 1956 |
| Smidt, *Unconformities* | Kristian Smidt, *Unconformities in Shakespeare's History Plays*, 1982 |
| *SP* | *Studies in Philology* |
| Spevack | Marvin Spevack, *A Complete and Systematic Concordance to the Works of Shakespeare*, 9 vols., Hildesheim, 1968 ff. |
| *SQ* | *Shakespeare Quarterly* |
| *S.St.* | *Shakespeare Studies* |
| *S.Sur.* | *Shakespeare Survey* |
| Stow, *Annales* | *The Annales of England, faithfully collected ... from the first inhabitation vntill this present yeere 1592, by Iohn Stow citizen of London*, 1592 |
| Stow, *Chronicles* | *The Chronicles of England, from Brute vnto this present yeare 1580. Collected by Iohn Stow Citizen of London*, 1580 |
| subst. | substantively |
| Taylor | Gary Taylor, 'The fortunes of Oldcastle', *S.Sur.* 38 (1985), 85–100 |
| Theobald | *The Works of Shakespeare*, ed. Lewis Theobald, 7 vols., 1733, III |
| Tilley | Morris Palmer Tilley, *A Dictionary of the Proverbs in England in the Sixteenth and Seventeenth Centuries*, 1950 |
| Tito Livio | *The First English Life of Henry V*, ed. C. L. Kingsford, 1911 |
| *TLS* | *The Times Literary Supplement* |
| *TSLL* | *Texas Studies in Literature and Language* |
| uncorr. | uncorrected state |
| *UTQ* | *University of Toronto Quarterly* |
| Vaughan | Henry Halford Vaughan, *New Readings and New Renderings of Shakespeare's Tragedies*, 2 vols., 1878–81 |
| Walker | Alice Walker, *Textual Problems of the First Folio*, 1953 |
| Warburton | *The Works of Shakespear*, ed. William Warburton, 8 vols., 1747, IV |
| White | *The Works of William Shakespeare*, ed. Richard Grant White, 12 vols., 1859, VI |
| Williams | George Walton Williams, 'The text of *2 Henry IV*: facts and problems', *S.St.* 9 (1976), 173–82 |
| Wilson | *The Second Part of the History of Henry IV*, ed. John Dover Wilson, 1946 (New Shakespeare) |
| Wilson, *Fortunes* | John Dover Wilson, *The Fortunes of Falstaff*, 1953 |
| Wilson, 'Origins' | John Dover Wilson, 'The origins and development of Shakespeare's Henry IV', *The Library* 4th ser. 24 (1945), 2–16 |

All biblical references are to the Geneva version, 1560.

# INTRODUCTION

*The First Part of King Henry IV* ran to no fewer than six editions between 1598 and its inclusion in the Shakespeare Folio of 1623, a sure token of its constant appeal on the stage. The *Second Part*, however, was never reprinted in the 23 years following its first publication in 1600. The fact is rather puzzling since there is no doubt about the extraordinary popularity of Falstaff, who dominates it from beginning to end, to a larger extent than either the *First Part* – where the combined forces of Prince Hal and Hotspur could steal the show – or even *The Merry Wives of Windsor*, where he had to compete with a number of other comic humours. Perhaps its more limited appeal to the readers of plays was due to its being Falstaff's play rather than the History promised by the title. When it was revived at the Theatre Royal, Drury Lane, in 1720, the adapter (supposed to have been the late Thomas Betterton) presented it as *The Sequel of Henry the Fourth, with the Humours of Sir John Falstaffe, and Justice Shallow*, and dignified the fifth act by 'completing' it with extracts from the first two acts of *Henry V*, up to the arrest of Cambridge, Scroop and Grey, ending with Henry's triumphant claim 'For I will be – No King of *England*, if not King of *France*.'[1]

The *Second Part* is merely a 'sequel', and Richard David is justified in saying that it 'has pot-boiler written all over it'.[2] In fact it bears all the marks of the time-honoured technique, still practised nowadays especially by the film industry, for concocting a sequel: the introduction of a host of new characters to support the central figure responsible for the success of the original play, the parallelism in structure with the 'parent' production, and even the explicit promise at the end of further instalments: 'our humble author will continue the story with Sir John in it . . .'[3] There is no doubt about the casual nature of the play, born and bred as a commercial product to exploit the humours of Sir John Falstaff – but its richness and strength reside precisely in this casualness. They give the play a metadramatic quality, forcing a new approach to the job of playwriting, and making it a reconsideration of the nature of the dramatic event.

*Part Two* is first and foremost an exploration of the ways in which a play comes to be conceived, a re-elaboration from different angles of pre-used theatrical materials. As such, it affords an extraordinary plurality of readings: a Morality version of the subject matter of *Part One*;[4] a psychodrama on the father–son relationship; a comedy of

---

[1] *The Sequel of Henry the Fourth by Thomas Betterton*, 1721. Facsimile (1969) from the copy in Birmingham Shakespeare Library. See p. 37 below, n. 2.
[2] Richard David, 'Shakespeare's history plays: epic or drama', *S.Sur.* 6 (1953), 129–39. In *Shakespeare in the Theatre*, 1978, p. 203, David adds that *Part Two* is 'a pot-boiler of genius'.
[3] Epilogue 21. For the parallelism in structure between the two parts see G. K. Hunter, '*Henry IV* and the Elizabethan two-part play', *RES* ns 5 (1954), reprinted in his *Dramatic Identities and Cultural Tradition*, 1978, pp. 303–18; R. A. Law, 'The composition of Shakespeare's Lancastrian trilogy', *TSLL* 3 (1961–2), 321–7.
[4] *Part One* has also been read in terms of Morality; see, for instance, J. Dover Wilson, *The Fortunes of Falstaff*, 1943, pp. 15 ff.; but a distinction should be made between the two parts; see pp. 15–18 below.

humours; a country as opposed to a city comedy; a series of variations on the theme of time; an enquiry into the nature of policy. All these readings are perfectly legitimate and by no means mutually exclusive. The play acquires in this way an exceptional density and pregnancy of meaning, so that L. C. Knights could rightly speak of its different tone from the earlier plays, and single it out as 'markedly a transitional play' that 'looks back to the Sonnets and the earlier history plays, and ... forward to the great tragedies'.[1] Its originality must be assessed within the context of the other histories, and more precisely of what has been called, perhaps deceptively, the Henriad or second tetralogy,[2] from *Richard II* to *Henry V*, as well as of the 'Falstaff plays', including *The Merry Wives*.

## Publication and date

While the *First Part* had been entered in the Stationers' Register on 25 February 1598 and published as *The History of Henry the Fourth*, the entry to the booksellers Andrew Wise and William Aspley for *Part Two* on 23 August 1600 reads:

Entred for their copies vnder the hands of the wardens Two bookes. the one called *Muche a Doo about nothing.* Thother *the second parte of the history of kinge Henry the iiii*[th] *with the humours of Sir IOHN FFALLSTAFF:* Wrytten by master Shakespere. xij[d]

Publication followed shortly afterwards, as the title page of the quarto edition makes clear:

*THE* Second part of Henrie the fourth, continuing to his death, *and coronation of Henrie* the fift. With the humours of sir Iohn Fal-*staffe, and swaggering* Pistoll. *As it hath been sundrie times publikely* acted by the right honourable, the Lord Chamberlaine his servants. *Written by William Shakespeare. LONDON* Printed by V. S. for Andrew Wise, and William Aspley. 1600.

The peculiarities of this printing are discussed in detail in the Textual Analysis but one or two points relevant to the dating of the play must be noted now. There is general agreement that the copy for the printer was Shakespeare's own foul papers (the original manuscript which was handed over to the company book-keeper who would prepare from it the prompt-book for use in performance), so that it reflects as fully as possible the author's original intentions. But accidents happened in the course of printing, the most obvious being the omission from the first issue of the quarto (known as Qa) of a whole scene – 3.1, the night musings of the king – which was promptly restored in the second issue of the same (Qb). Besides, eight more passages of some length, present in the 1623 Folio, are not in the quarto. Though it has been recently suggested that they may be later additions,[3] the confused state of the text surrounding some of them in the quarto shows

---

[1] L. C. Knights, 'Time's subjects: the Sonnets and *King Henry IV, Part II*', in *Some Shakespearean Themes*, 1959, p. 63.
[2] The notion of tetralogy, so persuasively advocated by E. M. W. Tillyard, *Shakespeare's History Plays*, 1944, is dangerous because it suggests that Shakespeare's histories were planned in advance as continuous cycles. This is far from being proven, as appears from the current discussion on the order of composition of the three parts of *Henry VI*, as well as on the origin of *Henry IV*; see pp. 9–13 below.
[3] John Jowett and Gary Taylor, 'The three texts of *2 Henry IV*', *SB* 40 (1987), 31–50. I am grateful to the authors for letting me have in typescript an ampler version of their paper before publication. Their detailed account of

that they had been marked for deletion – theatrical expediency, possibly not unconnec-
ted with political caution, discouraged their transfer from the foul papers to the prompt-
book which was being prepared for the early performances of the play. The title page
assures us that these had taken place before 1600, while the reference in Ben Jonson's
play *Every Man out of his Humour* (1599) to the character of Justice Silence[1] is evidence
that *Part Two* was well known to London audiences before that date. On the other hand,
the fact that *Part One* was registered and published, as we saw, in 1598 as a play complete
in itself, with no indication of a possible sequel, suggests that by then *Part Two* was as yet
unperformed if not unwritten.

It can be safely assumed, therefore, that *Part Two* appeared on the stage after March
1598 but before 1599, and its composition must be dated late 1597/early 1598. The
fairly unanimous agreement over this – in the whole Shakespeare canon perhaps only
*Henry V* can be dated more precisely – is far from solving the problem of the relationship
of *Part Two* to the other 'Falstaff plays'. On the contrary, the problem is rendered more
complex by several other signals coming from the quarto text itself – not only the already
noted omissions and partial restorations, but the presence in it of a greater number of
what have been called by Kristian Smidt 'unconformities'[2] than in any other
Shakespearean history.

## Unconformities

*Henry IV Part Two* can be placed in its proper historical and theatrical context, the
plurality of readings it offers can be accounted for, and the richness of its texture can be
fully appreciated, only if satisfactory answers can be found to the problems posed by the
original quarto text, only a few of which the Folio edition of 1623 has endeavoured to
iron out. Here is a list of the major ones:

1. The omission of Act 3, Scene 1 from the first issue of the quarto may well be a case
of inadvertency on the printer's part: if the scene was on a separate manuscript leaf, the
printer may have overlooked the mark in the foul papers at the end of 2.4 requiring its
insertion at that point. But it has been observed that the repetition of 'come' in the
Hostess's last speech in 2.4 and in Shallow's opening speech in 3.2 suggests that 2.4 and
3.2 had been originally conceived as consecutive,[3] in which case the insertion of 3.1
would be an afterthought. The scene is irrelevant to the development of the action: we
know already of the king's illness from 1.2 and 2.2, and the only new piece of information
we gather here is the news of Glendower's death. But on the other hand the scene,

---

the insertion of 3.1 in the 1600 quarto has now been incorporated in Taylor's general introduction to *William
Shakespeare: A Textual Companion*, ed. S. Wells and G. Taylor with J. Jowett and W. Montgomery, 1987, pp.
49–50. Their arguments in connection with the omissions in the quarto are discussed in the Textual Analysis,
pp. 192–9 below.

[1] Ben Jonson, *Every Man out of his Humour* 5.2.20–2 (ed. Herford and Simpson, III, 567): 'Saviolina. What's hee,
gentle Monsieur Briske? not that gentleman? Fastidius. no ladie, this is a kinsman to iustice *Silence*.'

[2] Smidt, *Unconformities in Shakespeare's History Plays*, 1982, *passim*.

[3] Jowett and Taylor, in a passage omitted from the printed version of their paper. But see Wells and Taylor,
*Textual Companion*, p. 360, note to 2.4.392/1420.

# THE
# Second part of Henrie

the fourth, continuing to his death,
*and coronation of Henrie*
the fift.

With the humours of fir Iohn Fal-
*staffe, and swaggering*
Piſtoll.

*As it hath been sundrie times publikely*
acted by the right honourable, the Lord
Chamberlaine his feruants.

*Written by William Shakespeare.*

## LONDON
Printed by V.S. for Andrew Wife, and
William Afpley.
1600.

1 Title page of the 1600 quarto, from the copy at Trinity College, Cambridge

identifying the country's sickness with the king's, is absolutely central to the theatrical and ideological structure of the play as a whole. Now, granting that 3.1 was introduced at that point of the play as an afterthought, was the scene newly written for the purpose, or was it a scene, which at first had been considered expendable, salvaged from an earlier version of the play?

2. The 'goodly dwelling' of Justice Shallow is located in Gloucestershire in 4.1.431 and 475 (as in *The Merry Wives of Windsor* 1.1.5 F), with confirmation from allusions in 5.1 and 5.3. But the enrolment scene in which the Justice makes his first appearance (3.2) suggests somewhere on the Great North Road, a much more logical situation since Falstaff is pressing soldiers on his way from London to York, and a detour through Gloucestershire[1] is at least as absurd as the notion that 'a Justice of Peace and Coram in the County of Gloucester' should have a manor and deer park at Windsor (*Wiv.* 1.1.111–12). The inconsistencies open up a double problem: one connected with the stages of composition of *Part Two* and the other with the date of *Merry Wives*, assigned by many to the spring of 1597,[2] before our play.

3. The presence in the play of two characters with practically the same name: Bardolph, an 'irregular humorist' already figuring as one of Falstaff's followers in *Part One*, and the 'new' historical character of Lord Bardolph out of Holinshed's *Chronicles*. The question is: if the two Parts were conceived from the beginning as a single play in ten acts, why should the author, when forced by circumstances to change the names originally assigned to the prince's companions, replace that of Sir John Russell (or Rossill) with Bardolph,[3] if he already expected to introduce the historical Lord Bardolph in the *Second Part*?

4. The presence in the quarto of the speech heading *Old.* at 1.2.96, and of 'Sir Iohn Russel' in the entrance stage direction at 2.2. These are obvious fossils of the original version of the Henry IV play(s), in which, as it appears from several signs in *Part One*, Falstaff's name was Sir John Oldcastle, and Bardolph and Peto were Rossill (a nickname

---

[1] For a discussion of the different suggestions on this point see 'Justice Shallow and Gloucestershire', Appendix IV in A. R. Humphreys (ed.), *2H4*, 1966, pp. 235–6. The location of 5.1 in Gloucestershire is discussed in the first note to that scene in the present edition.

[2] The case for considering *The Merry Wives of Windsor* as a play written for the Garter Feast of 1597 was first advanced by Leslie Hotson, *Shakespeare versus Shallow*, 1931, and was strongly supported by William Green, *Shakespeare's 'Merry Wives of Windsor'*, 1962. Though the weakness of several of their arguments has been pointed out since, notably by H. J. Oliver in his edition of *Wiv.*, 1971, pp. xliv–lii, the dating finds credit in several editions of the complete plays, such as *The Riverside Shakespeare*, ed. G. Blakemore Evans, 1974, and the new Oxford *Complete Works*, ed. S. Wells and G. Taylor, 1986. I find much more convincing George R. Hibbard's suggestion in his New Penguin edition of *Wiv.*, 1973, pp. 47–50, that the play was written later, incorporating 'with the economy so characteristic of [Shakespeare]' the earlier Garter entertainment. See my note 'Which Falstaff in Windsor?' in *KM80*, 1987, a tribute to Kenneth Muir on his eightieth birthday.

[3] There is a curious misapprehension about the replacement of the names of 'Haruey' and 'Rossill' which appear in all early editions of *Part One* at 1.2.162. Since the Dering MS. changes the list of the participants in the Gad's Hill robbery to 'Falstaffe, Harvay, Peto and Bardolff', it has been assumed that Peto was substituted for Rossill, and consequently Bardolph must be the new name for Harvey. I believe the substitution took place the other way round: the nickname Rossill for Russell was chosen deliberately in order to play on the Italian *rosso* for red – the formidable red nose of this particular 'knight' was to be his main feature in the play, and this is exactly the feature inherited after the name change not by Peto but by Bardolph. See Melchiori, 'The ur-*Henry IV*', pp. 64 ff.

for Russell) and Harvey respectively. Two explanations have been offered for their presence also in *Part Two*: (a) the name changes were forced on Shakespeare when he was already busy writing *Part Two* and had reached the second act; he went over his foul papers correcting the names, but missed these two out;[1] (b) the name changes had already taken place, but the author was still thinking in terms of the old designations, and he reverted to them by an oversight in these two instances.[2] Neither explanation is fully satisfactory. There must be a third that takes a wider view of the origin and development of the play, and it suggests itself when the last of the major unconformities is examined.

  5. The question of Sir John Oldcastle. He is actually mentioned in the Epilogue to *Part Two*, in what has been taken as an apology for the use of the name in the original version of the play:

our humble author will continue the story with Sir John in it, and make you merry with fair Katherine of France, where, for anything I know, Falstaff shall die of a sweat, unless already a be killed with your hard opinions; for Oldcastle died martyr, and this is not the man.

(Epilogue 21–5)

This part of the Epilogue has been recognised as a later addition to the original one, which was limited to the first thirteen lines, and the protests that prompted it are seen in the Prologue to the Admiral's Men play *The First Part of Sir John Oldcastle*, which claims that Sir John 'is no pamperd glutton... / Nor aged Councellor to youthfull sinne, / But one, whose vertue shone aboue the rest'.[3] From Henslowe's *Diary* the date of completion and performance of *Oldcastle* can be fixed with certainty in November 1599. So the addition to the Epilogue of *Part Two* could have been written only after that date. But by then *Henry V* had already been performed at the new Globe playhouse, and the promise to show Falstaff in it, made in the same breath with the 'apology' for Oldcastle, was not kept. Either the apology is not motivated by the new Admiral's Men's play, or it is not an apology.

  A number of other inconsistencies could be pointed out, such as the mention of the prince having been committed to prison for striking the Lord Chief Justice (1.2.42–3), an episode never mentioned in *Part One* though much emphasised in the sources of the plays; the transformation of the Hostess from a 'most sweet wench' and 'an honest man's wife' in *Part One* (1.2.40 and 3.3.119; the prince is gracious enough to enquire 'How doth thy husband? (3.3.92–3), and Falstaff enjoins her to 'love thy husband' (3.3.171)) into the superannuated 'poor lone woman' of *Part Two*, who has developed a genius for equivocal 'Quicklyisms' and is not above favouring Falstaff's intimacy with her younger friend Doll Tearsheet – not to mention her further metamorphosis into Doctor Caius's housekeeper in *Merry Wives*, while from *Henry V* we learn that she has married Pistol, the 'fustian rascal' that she wanted 'thrust downstairs' in *Part Two*. And surely the Falstaff of *Part Two* is a much older man than the Falstaff of *Part One*.

---

[1] This explanation was first offered in Theobald's edition of 1733.
[2] The suggestion was first made by Capell, *Notes and Various Readings to Shakespeare*, 1779, I, 170, in connection with the '*Old.*' speech heading.
[3] *The first part Of the true and honorable historie, of the life of Sir John Oldcastle, the good Lord Cobham*, 1600, sig. A2. Edited by Percy Simpson for the Malone Society, 1908.

**The sources and *The Famous Victories***

A reappraisal of the materials on which Shakespeare based his Henriad is an indispensable premise to any attempt at solving these contradictions. The main sources of *Part
Two* obviously coincide with those of *Part One*, and largely with those of *Richard II*,
discussed by Herbert Weil and Andrew Gurr respectively in their editions of those
plays.[1] A distinction must be made between those works that were used to construct and
support the main story line – books that one imagines as constantly at the author's elbow
for reference during composition – those in which he simply dipped for information on
particular episodes, and finally those that he happened to have read at some time or other
and stored in his memory, to provide occasional hints, suggestions or turns of phrase.
Holinshed's *Chronicles of England, Scotland and Ireland*, in the posthumous 1587 edition
enlarged by the antiquarian Abraham Fleming and by Grafton to include new material
from Stow and other historians and further extracts from Hall, undoubtedly belongs to
the first category: most of the historical scenes in the play echo Holinshed at times
verbatim, apart from the manipulations and transpositions usual in the construction of
dramatic plots. Holinshed may also have suggested some new dramatic inventions such
as the introduction of Rumour as the presenter.[2] The 1592 edition of John Stow's
*Annales of England* may have been consulted, too, especially for the report of the king's
advice to Prince Hal and of the Lord Chief Justice's firmness with the prince who had
threatened him in the place of judgement – an episode that may have made the dramatist
look also into Stow's source, *The Boke named the Gouernour* (1531) by Sir Thomas Elyot.

Shakespeare certainly knew also the recently published poem of Samuel Daniel, *The
first fowre bookes of the ciuile wars between the two houses of Lancaster and Yorke* (1595), which
versified much of the historians' subject matter, presenting it in a form more suitable for
dramatic speech.[3] Two other works at least can be pointed out in the third category: as
J. W. Lever[4] has shown, Shakespeare remembered the character of the Braggart in John
Eliot's *Ortho-epia Gallica* (1593) when devising the language of Pistol, while the
Hostess's peculiar interjections are strictly modelled on those reported of Lady More in
Sir Thomas More's biography written before 1557 by Nicholas Harpsfield,[5] a forbidden
book circulating in manuscript in the houses of Roman Catholic recusants, such as those
in which, according to E. A. J. Honigmann, Shakespeare had spent part of his 'lost
years'.[6]

As for the stories of the 'wild prince', they are to be found mainly in the much

---

[1] In the New Cambridge Shakespeare. See Bullough, III, 353–491, for *Richard II*, and IV, 155–346, for the two parts of *Henry IV*.

[2] See Commentary to Induction o SD. The likelihood that the conception of Rumour was suggested by a passage near the beginning of Holinshed's chronicle of the reign of Henry IV seems to have escaped previous editors.

[3] Daniel suggests a direct confrontation between Prince Hal and Hotspur (which is not mentioned by other historians), but does not attribute to the prince the killing of Hotspur.

[4] 'Shakespeare's French fruits', *S.Sur.* 6 (1953), 79–90. See Appendix I, item 6, in Humphreys (ed.), *2H4*, pp. 231–2.

[5] *The life and death of Sr Thomas Moore, knight, sometymes Lord high Chancellor of England, written in the tyme of Queene Marie by Nicholas Harpsfield, L.D.*, ed. Elsie Vaughan Hitchcock (EETS, OS 186), 1932, pp. 93–9.

[6] E. A. J. Honigmann, *Shakespeare: 'The Lost Years'*, 1985.

amplified English version (1513) of Tito Livio's Latin *Vita Henrici Quinti* (c. 1437), but it would be idle to speculate on the possibility that Shakespeare had access to a work that remained in manuscript till 1911.[1] Its contents, already reported in Stow's *Chronicles of England* (1580) and partly in Holinshed, are the main source of another dramatic work which stands in a peculiar relationship to Shakespeare's.

*The famous Victories of Henry the fifth: Containing the Honourable Battell of Agin-court: As it was plaide by the Queenes Maiesties Players* was printed by Thomas Creede only in 1598,[2] though it had been entered in the Stationers' Register four years earlier. As is well known, Creede's quarto is an extremely poorly-put-together memorial report of an old play, possibly in two parts, which had enjoyed wide popularity as, among other things, a vehicle for the famous clown Richard Tarlton, who died in 1588.[3] By 1594 the Queen's Men, in a phase of rapid decline, were selling off their plays in partial compensation for their losses. It looks as if no decent text of *Famous Victories* was readily available at the time of the entry in the Stationers' Register, and they were induced to hand in a wretched summary reconstruction only in 1598, to cash in on the current success of the Shakespearean Henry plays that the Chamberlain's Men had started staging at the time. Though there is no real evidence of the fact, the text we have falls so neatly into two halves, one concerned with Prince Hal's youthful misbehaviour and reformation, and the other with his exploits as a wise warrior and sovereign, that the likelihood that the original play was in two parts is very strong.[4]

What interests us is to establish the special relationship between Shakespeare's three Henry plays and *Famous Victories*, normally regarded as one of their main sources. Surely at the time of writing *Part One*, and possibly *Part Two*, Shakespeare could not have known Creede's unprinted quarto. But he or some of his fellow actors must surely have seen the original version of the play (or plays) at some earlier time, and they may even have had access to the full text of *Famous Victories* in prompt-book or some other form. The relationship between the Henriad and Creede's text of *Famous Victories* is, on the face of it, non-existent, or rather vicarious. What counts is the relationship between Shakespeare's plays and the lost original of which Creede's quarto is no more than a distorted and reduced reflection. Bad as it is, it must all the same convey a fair idea of the general conception, dramatic structure and individual characterisation of the original.

[1] *The First English Life of Henry V*, ed. C. L. Kingsford, 1911.
[2] See P. A. Daniel's facsimile in Praetorius Shakespeare Quartos, 1887. Now more readily available in Bullough, IV, 299–343.
[3] It has been maintained that the well-known anecdote in *Tarltons Iests* (1638; see Bullough, IV, 289–90) of the Clown's joke about the box on the ear of the Lord Chief Justice must refer to a different play because it implies the doubling of the Clown and the Justice, which is impossible in the version of *Famous Victories* that has reached us. But Creede's text is merely the summary of an original which may well have allowed for such doubling; if not, the players may have altered the original to meet an emergency.
[4] There is no definitive proof that the original version of *Victories* was in two parts, but most recent scholarship is inclined to believe so. Wilson, 'Origins', sees *Victories* as 'a much abridged and debased version of two plays belonging to the Queen's company'. As for the authorship of the lost original, the most attractive suggestion is that advanced by Philip Brockbank, 'Shakespeare: his histories, English and Roman', in *English Drama to 1710*, ed. C. Ricks, 1971, p. 168: Robert Greene had written the Henry V play(s), and his jealousy of Shakespeare is accounted for by the fact that the new *Henry VI* plays had replaced his work on the London stage.

So it affords something more than mere speculation, and the relationship must be seen in the light of current theatrical practice.

## The Henriad as remake

A fairly common practice in the theatre business was what could be called, borrowing a term from the present-day film industry, the remake. When a play (nowadays a film) proves successful, a rival company sets up after some years not a new production of the same, but a complete reworking of it with a new script as well as a different cast and possibly a new slant to the story.[1] A remake has the advantage of offering a chance to 'improve' the original not so much on the formal level as on the ideological one. The new script updates the original by taking into account the audience response to new attitudes in the social or, as the case may be, political and religious fields. This becomes the more important at times when such response is controlled by massive censorial interventions. It is known that the 1590s were exactly such a time: the Master of the Revels, after a period of remarkable tolerance, had started watching much more closely than in previous years what was going to be performed on the public stage.[2] It was a time, therefore, particularly suited to the remaking of plays that offered a historical perspective which did not conform to the new Tudor orthodoxy.

Apart from these considerations, the evidence of such plays as *Hamlet, Troilus and Cressida* and *King Lear* shows that by the beginning of the seventeenth century Shakespeare was an expert at remakes of old plays for the Chamberlain's/King's Men. But his career as a remaker must have begun earlier, and the popular chronicle plays of the 1580s and 1590s were surely the most suitable material for remakes that would readjust their political focus in accordance with the stricter rulings of the Master of the Revels. The original – probably double – play of *Famous Victories* successfully acted in the 1580s by the Queen's Men was an obvious choice for remaking by the Chamberlain's Men, especially after their production in 1595 of *Richard II*, which had so markedly readjusted the historical focus of the earlier *Woodstock*.[3] The subject matter of the two halves of the old play lent itself naturally to a new treatment in two separate history plays, one, *Henry IV*, mainly concerned with the youthful exploits and reformation of Prince Hal at the death of his father, and the other, *Henry V*, with the 'famous victories' of the new sovereign. The history planned by the Chamberlain's Men for 1596 – a logical continuation of the 1595 *Richard II* – was a remake of the original first part of *Famous Victories* under the title *Henry IV*, presumably to be followed in the next theatrical season by *Henry V* as a remake of the second part of the earlier play.

Though 1596 is generally recognised as the date of composition of the original Shakespearean *Henry IV*, there is considerable difference of opinion on whether this was

[1]  See on this subject Melchiori, 'Corridors'.
[2]  See David Bevington, *Tudor Drama and Politics*, 1968, pp. 230 ff.
[3]  For different views on the relationship between *Woodstock* and *Richard II* see A. P. Rossiter (ed.), *Woodstock, A Moral History*, 1946, as well as Bullough, III, 358–62, and the latest reassessment by Andrew Gurr (ed.), *King Richard II*, 1984, pp. 11–16.

a one-play version of what are now the two parts, or just a version of *Part One*.[1] It is, however, universally accepted that in this version the fat knight accompanying the young prince was not called Falstaff but Sir John Oldcastle, a name found in an equivalent role in *Famous Victories*, and that two of his companions (collectively designated 'knights' in the old play) had been named by Shakespeare Harvey and Rossill instead of Peto and Bardolph.[2] It is also agreed that the name changes in the final version were occasioned by the protest of the Brooke family, direct descendants of the historical Sir John Oldcastle, who had been celebrated at great length by John Foxe in his *Acts and Monuments* as a Protestant protomartyr.[3] The protest would have carried particular weight when in August 1596 William Brooke, Lord Cobham, took over from Henry Carey, Lord Hunsdon, the patron of Shakespeare's company who had just died, the office of Lord Chamberlain, which gave him control over public entertainments.[4] Though Lord Cobham himself died shortly after in March 1597 and the new Lord Hunsdon became Lord Chamberlain, those seven months in office must have been enough to enforce the elimination of Oldcastle's name from Shakespeare's play.

The Oldcastle question and the timing of the name change is basic to any discussion of *Part One*, but another point is more relevant for deciding the real nature and origin of *Part Two*, and there is as yet no agreement among scholars about it. Did the name changes take place before or after the Oldcastle version of *Henry IV* was actually performed on the public stage? More important: was the Oldcastle version a single instead of a two-part play, or did it correspond exactly to the present *Part One*, apart from a few name changes?[5] With regard to the first question, it is difficult to think that Shakespeare's plays were still referred to with the name of Oldcastle as late as 1639 if the early version had never been performed.[6] The second question is harder to answer. If the early version coincided fully with *Part One*, the implication is that, as many believe, Shakespeare's *Henry IV* was conceived from the beginning as a two-part play or,

[1] The notion of a one-play Shakespearean version of *Henry IV* is implicit in Dover Wilson, 'Origins', especially pp. 15–16, when he states: 'I myself would date *1 Henry IV* in the Autumn or Winter of 1597; but I think that twelve months or more earlier Lord Hunsdon's men were playing another *Henry IV*, in which Oldcastle spoke comic blank verse', and adds that this earlier version was 'probably a one-part play like its Queen's company original', but 'in the end Falstaff, grown "out of all compass", needed a double drama to contain him'. The notion got somehow obscured or ignored in later criticism but is revived by Kristian Smidt, *Unconformities*, pp. 109–20.

[2] The companions are called knights, for instance, in the stage direction at line 700 (Bullough, IV, 319). For the new names see p. 5 above, n. 3.

[3] See 'A Defence of the Lord Cobham, Against Nicholas Harpsfield', in J. Foxe, *Acts and Monuments*, ed. J. Pratt, 1874, III, 348–402. On the whole question see Alice-Lyle Scoufos, *Shakespeare's Typological Satire: A Study of the Falstaff–Oldcastle Problem*, 1979.

[4] The best argument for believing that the protest came from William Brooke, Lord Cobham, in 1596 and not, as Chambers and others maintain, from his son and successor in the title Henry Brooke, is put forward by Dover Wilson, 'Origins', pp. 12–15.

[5] The latter view is vigorously propounded by Gary Taylor, 'The fortunes of Oldcastle', *S.Sur.* 38 (1985), 85–100. He applied it to his edition of *1 Henry IV* in the new Oxford *Complete Works* by replacing Falstaff's name throughout with that of Oldcastle. In my view, the mechanical substitution of names, far from restoring Shakespeare's original uncensored version, gives us a completely new play.

[6] See the bill for payment to the King's Men in 1639: 'At the Cocpit the 29th of May the princes berthnyght – ould Castel' (E. K. Chambers, *William Shakespeare*, 1930, II, 353). The reference cannot be to the *Oldcastle* plays originally presented by the Admiral's Men.

according to another definition, a single play in ten acts.[1] In other words, it was planned as part of a tetralogy, from *Richard II* to *Henry V*, parallel to the earlier foursome including the three parts of *Henry VI* and *Richard III*. In this case some of the unconformities in *Part Two* listed earlier, such as the duplication of Bardolph, the ambiguous location of Justice Shallow's home, the mention of the prince having struck the Lord Chief Justice, must remain unexplained.

All these difficulties are solved if we accept that *Henry IV* was not only conceived but also written and performed in 1596 as a one-play remake of the first part of *Famous Victories*, partly intended to ground the legend of the wild prince more firmly in history and to reassess the extent of such wildness. While in *Famous Victories* there is hardly any mention of the continual state of civil strife and even open war that beset the unquiet reign of Henry IV, Shakespeare, drawing heavily on Holinshed, stressed in the remake the theme of rebellion and of the inner conflicts in the sick king, and, developing a mere hint in Daniel's *Civil Wars*, anticipated the wild prince's reformation by his triumph at Shrewsbury.[2] The emphasis placed on the youthful gallantry of Hotspur makes the prince's triumph greater. The prince's generosity is stressed by his not taking personal credit for the killing of Hotspur – a subtle way of justifying the fact that the chronicles do not record the event. There are other significant changes in the remake: while in *Famous Victories* the prince devises in his own person the robbing of his father's receivers, in *Henry IV* he only pretends to organise the robbery, but in fact he robs the robbers and returns the booty, and the main responsibility for his wildness is attributed to an older 'abominable misleader of youth'.[3]

It was only natural to give the latter character the name of the most authoritative (though also the most sedate) of the prince's followers in *Famous Victories*: Sir John Oldcastle. And since in the parent play the other companions, with the exception of the professional 'setter' Gadshill,[4] are referred to as 'knights', Shakespeare chose for them good English family names: Sir John Russell, Harvey, Pointz.[5] The remake alternated the new historical material drawn from Holinshed with 'comic' scenes drawn from the first part of *Famous Victories*. By keeping in mind the version we have of the latter play,

---

[1] For a recent discussion of this issue see Sherman H. Hawkins, '*Henry IV*: the structural problem revisited', *SQ* 33 (1982), 279–301, which is a careful survey of all that has been said on the subject so far; but his single-minded refutation of Harold Jenkins's fundamental essay of 1956, *The Structural Problem in Shakespeare's 'Henry IV'*, prevents him from reaching any helpful positive conclusion. Among earlier papers which are still relevant to this question, R. A. Law, 'Structural unity in the two parts of *Henry IV*', *SP* 24 (1927), 223–42, and M. A. Shaaber, 'The unity of *Henry IV*', in *John Quincy Adams Memorial Studies*, 1948, pp. 217–27, consider *Part Two* as a more or less unpremeditated sequel, while Clifford Leech, 'The unity of *2 Henry IV*', *S.Sur.* 6 (1953), 16–24, takes the impression of disunity within the second play to be a feature common to all Elizabethan drama.

[2] The key reference is found in stanza 110 of Book III of Daniel's poem (Bullough, IV, 214): 'There lo that new-appearing glorious starre / Wonder of Armes, the terror of the field / Young *Henrie*, laboring where the stoutest are, / And euen the stoutest forces back to yeild, / There is that hand boldned to bloud and warre / That must the sword in wondrous action weild.' There is no hint, though, that Prince Henry killed 'furious Hotspur'.

[3] The prince's definition of Falstaff in *Part One* 2.4.462–3.

[4] See Bertrand H. Bronson, 'A note on Gadshill, *Our Setter*', *PMLA* 45 (1930), 749–53.

[5] Stokes, reported in the Variorum edition of *The Second Part of Henry the Fourth*, ed. M. A. Shaaber, 1940, p. 4, speaks of 'the family of Poyntz, one of high antiquity, in Gloucestershire'.

bad as it is, and the implications of the unconformities noted in the two parts of *Henry IV*, it is possible to reconstruct the outline of the ur-*Henry IV*,[1] that is to say the Shakespearean one-play version staged in 1596 which had to be withdrawn under pressure from the new Lord Chamberlain, William Brooke, Lord Cobham, and presumably also from the Russell and Harvey families. The first half of the ur-*Henry IV* must largely have corresponded to *Henry IV Part One* up to 4.1 included, with substantial differences mainly in the comic scenes. These were generally much shorter than in the present version, and the differences were by no means limited to the changes in the names of the prince's companions. Prince Hal's famous soliloquy at the close of 1.2, 'I know you all', has the air of being an afterthought, introducing from the start the theme of policy, central to the rewriting of the play. The same is true of the 'play extempore' at 2.4.280–481, obviously prefiguring the rejection of Falstaff. In the ur-*Henry IV* the scene must have been much shorter: after the exposure of the Gadshill cheat, the Lord Chief Justice coming to arrest one of the companions was boxed on the ear by the prince, and proceeded to commit him to prison. This accounts for the repeated mention of the episode in *Part Two*. There was, of course, no searching of the sleeping knight's pockets at the end of the scene, and consequently the earlier version of 3.3 was much shorter, with no complaint by Oldcastle about having been robbed, but only his initial dialogue with Rossill (Bardolph), and the marching order to York given by the prince, who had procured for him a 'charge of foot'.[2]

The second half of the ur-*Henry IV* differed much more markedly from the rewritten text or texts. The Coventry scene (*1H4* 4.2) was preceded by an introductory part showing Oldcastle in the act of recruiting his ragamuffins on his way from London to the Midlands, with the help of a local Justice of the Peace. This accounts for the use of Gloucestershire as the home county of Justice Shallow, a character conceived as the counterpart of the Lord Chief Justice.[3] The episode, left out in the rewriting of the ur-*Henry IV* as *Part One*, was to be revived and very much extended to fill up *Part Two*. The original Shakespearean one-play version did not end with the battle of Shrewsbury. It was followed by an interview between Oldcastle and the Lord Chief Justice, the substance of which (one page of the foul papers) was reutilised in *Part Two*, becoming 1.2.74–*c*. 135. This accounts for the survival of the speech heading *Old*. at 96.

The king's illness was mentioned in this scene, which closed with the arrival of a messenger for the Lord Chief Justice, and the rest of the dialogue may have been echoed in *Part Two* 2.1.105–7 and 130–53. The king was then presented monologising on his sick condition, reflected in the state of the country. The scene, filling a separate leaf in the foul papers, was at first omitted in the rewriting, but later introduced in *Part Two* as 3.1. This explains the first of the unconformities listed above.

---

[1] See Melchiori, 'The ur-*Henry IV*'. Most of the rest of this section of the Introduction and the whole of the next are summaries of that paper.

[2] *Part One* 3.3.186. Significantly in *Part Two* there is no intimation before 3.2 (the first Shallow scene) that Falstaff must enrol soldiers. After the prince's sudden summons to court, there is only the rather incongruous announcement that Falstaff must go too, because 'A dozen captains stay at door for you' (2.4.304).

[3] I am not sure that in the ur-*Henry IV* the Justice of the Peace (who must have put in only a brief appearance) bore the name of Shallow: it is a name that fits too well the new Morality pattern of *Part Two*; see 'The Morality structure', p. 15 below.

The king's illness was also discussed by the prince with Pointz and Rossill in a scene which ended with the summons of the prince to court. The first page of the ur-*Henry IV* version of this survives in *Part Two* 2.2.1–52, thus accounting for the presence of the name of Sir John Russell in the entrance stage direction, while the summons is echoed with many changes in *Part Two* 2.4.287–98.

The next scene, up to the death of the king, was to provide the basis for the amplified version in *Part Two* 4.2. As for the closing section of the ur-*Henry IV*, the first part of it must have been practically identical with *Part Two* 5.2: Warwick, coming straight from the Jerusalem chamber, announced to the Lord Chief Justice the death of the king; he was followed by the other princes and eventually by the new king, who confirmed the Justice in his office and called his first parliament. The entrance of Oldcastle with the other companions (obviously not Justice Shallow or Pistol) occurred at this point, with no intervening coronation ceremony, and the rejection took place in the terms now echoed in *Part Two* 5.5.39–67.

One thing at all events is fairly certain: in integrating the framework provided by *Famous Victories* with historical events out of Holinshed, there was never any intention of including the second rebellion culminating in the Gaultree episode; the ur-*Henry IV* moved on directly from Shrewsbury to the king's illness and death.[1]

## Rewriting the remake

In spite of the fact that the role allotted to Sir John Oldcastle in the ur-*Henry IV* must have been considerably smaller than that of Sir John Falstaff in either of the two parts of the play as it stands now, the stage creation of the fat misleader of youth must have proved immediately very popular with London audiences. Forced to withdraw the play by the shocked reaction of the descendants of the martyred Oldcastle, the Chamberlain's Men could not afford to renounce altogether such a box office draw. Changing the offending name – or rather names, since similar reactions must have come from the Russells and the Harveys – was not enough. The play had to be rewritten by expanding rather than reducing the comic parts, now that the main comic character was no longer identified with the Protestant martyr. There were dangers in the expansion. The prince might appear too firmly enrolled on Oldcastle's – now Falstaff's – side in the expanded comic scenes, making less credible his revulsion from youthful wildness. The solution to this problem was to show from the beginning the prince's awareness of his difference from Falstaff's wanton crew. This was done in several ways:

1. By reducing the 'knights', except for Falstaff, to the status of commoners; Bardolph was a striking name found in the chronicles but much less identifiable than Sir John Russell, and Peto (the Italian for 'fart') would suit a vulgarian much better than Harvey.

2. By introducing the prince's soliloquy in the first scene in which he appears, stating from the outset that his association with Falstaff and the rest was mere pretence.

3. By leaving out altogether the episode of the box on the ear of the Lord Chief Justice.

[1] For a more detailed account of the structure of the ur-*Henry IV* see Melchiori, 'The ur-*Henry IV*'.

4. By introducing the 'play extempore' (*Part One* 2.4.280–481) in which Falstaff takes the part of the prince, and the prince that of his father – a masterly device that only a professional man of the theatre could have thought of, prefiguring the rejection of Falstaff not only in his role as misleader of youth, but also as surrogate father-figure.

The last addition served another purpose, too. As Harold Jenkins shrewdly surmised,[1] at a fairly late stage in the writing – or rather rewriting – of *Henry IV*, Shakespeare must have realised that all the additional 'comic' material could not be fitted into a single play. There would be no room left for the last section of the original Shakespearean play, from the death of the king to the rejection scene. Its absence would be compensated for by such a scene as the 'play extempore'. In other words, what we know as *The First Part of King Henry IV* was rewritten in 1597 as a self-sufficient play with an open ending. Thus, if the new play was not very successful, some of the historical scenes left over from the ur-*Henry IV* could be conflated into the opening part of the projected remake of the second part of *Famous Victories* as *Henry V*. In fact it is difficult to assign to either half the central scene of *Famous Victories*, since it includes the coronation, the rejection of the companions, the declaration of war against France, and finally the confirmation in office of the Lord Chief Justice. If instead the new play – presented simply as *Henry IV* and not as *The First Part*[2] – went well, the left-over material, with the addition of fresh episodes, could be incorporated in a newly devised straight sequel to it.

In all likelihood, therefore, *Part Two* had not been planned in advance: it was not intended as the second half of a ten-act play, but it was thought of at most as an open option. This option had in fact to be taken when the 1597 *Henry IV* proved, thanks to Falstaff as well as Hotspur (the two names figuring in the 1598 quarto title page), a resounding success. To see *Henry IV Part Two* as the unplanned sequel to the rewriting of a remake entails no diminution in appreciation of its theatrical qualities. On the contrary, it allows us to savour to the full its author's craftsmanship and sense of the stage, while at the same time it justifies the already noted unconformities.

What was left over from the ur-*Henry IV* could fill at most one act with historical material and a couple of scenes with comedy. While the comedy could be extended *ad libitum* by devising a very much amplified version of the recruiting scene as well as other Shallow scenes, and by introducing new comic characters (see Pistol, Doll Tearsheet and the new personality given to Hostess Quickly), the same could not be said for the historical side; and it was indispensable to keep some sort of balance between history and comedy. There was no alternative to going back to Holinshed and using that part of the chronicle of the unquiet reign of Henry IV which had been, as I think, deliberately left out of the original one-play version. The inclusion of the second rebellion, culminating in the deception practised on the rebels at Gaultree, entailed some major readjustments. In the first place it meant that the only military action presented in the play was a victory by policy and not by a 'just and honourable' fair fight or loyal combat (Shrewsbury style). This implied a remarkable shift of focus, which must be kept in mind when dealing with the treatment of history in *Part Two*.

[1] Jenkins, *Structural Problem, passim*. Jenkins, though, does not contemplate an ur-*Henry IV* as an intermediate stage in the process.
[2] See the title pages of the quartos.

There was also another difficulty: in the hurried replacement of the offending names in the ur-*Henry IV*, Shakespeare had picked on that of Bardolph for Russell, finding it in those pages of Holinshed that he did not mean to utilise, in the same way as he had earlier found Russell's name in another unused passage of the chronicles.[1] But the historical Lord Bardolph had played a major role in the second rebellion in the north, and the decision to present the episode in the sequel forced Shakespeare to introduce him as a new character in the play. This accounts for the awkward duplication of names noted as one of the main unconformities in *Part Two*. It was in fact impossible to change again the name of the most strongly characterised of the prince's companions in *Part One*, always excepting Falstaff. It accounts also for the fact that in the sequel Bardolph is partly overshadowed by the introduction of a new 'irregular humorist': the swaggering Pistol, a revival of the traditional comedy figure of the Braggart. On the other hand, the role of the historical Lord Bardolph is limited to only two appearances in the first act, so that they do not overlap with those of his namesake. Besides, Lord Bardolph's first entrance right at the beginning of the play upon the heels of Rumour, the allegorical 'presenter' of the sequel to *Henry IV*, suggests that he, as the bringer of the false tidings that Rumour had announced, is the incarnation in the world of history of a moral allegory.

## The Morality structure

The opening of a play with an Induction is a rare occurrence in Shakespeare's work. We must assume that the first stage direction of the quarto, *Enter Rumour painted full of tongues*, is directly derived from Shakespeare's own foul papers. He meant that Rumour – the only allegorical figure appearing in any of his plays, apart from Time in *The Winter's Tale* – should wear the traditional costume of Fame or Report in sixteenth-century pageants, masques or interludes: a cloak or herald's coat all painted over with tongues (in the case of Fame, with eyes and ears also). The coat, incidentally, could be removed in no time at all, so that the actor impersonating Rumour could reappear a moment later on the stage as Lord Bardolph. But the really striking feature, in this case, is Shakespeare's deliberate choice, to open his sequel to the history of Henry IV, of a figure that would immediately remind the audience of the popular Moralities.[2]

John Dover Wilson, referring to both parts of *Henry IV*, described them as 'Shakespeare's great morality play',[3] and evidence for the definition is provided by the author himself when, in *Part One*, at 2.4.453, Falstaff is referred to as 'that reverend Vice'. There is no doubt that the first of the two parts (and surely also the ur-*Henry IV*, if it ever existed) is modelled on the most common of the Morality patterns, that of the

---

[1] Russell's name seems to have been suggested by the report of the capture and execution at Bristol of Scroope, Green and Bushy, in Holinshed's chronicle of the reign of Richard II (1587 edn, III, 498–9), a report that may have been recalled also in *2 Henry IV*; see Commentary to 4.1.95. Holinshed's passage quoted there goes on: 'Sir Iohn Russell was also taken there, who feining himselfe to be out of his wits, escaped their hands for a time.' The marginal heading at this point reads: 'A politike madnesse'. Earlier on the same page 'Iohn Bushie, William Bagot, Henrie Greene, and Iohn Russell knights' were described as 'other of the kings priuie councell'.

[2] See illustration 2 (p. 16) which shows the likely original staging of the Induction and the entrances for 1.1, as reconstructed by C. Walter Hodges.

[3] Wilson, *Fortunes*, pp. 14 ff.

2 A possible Elizabethan staging of the opening scene, by C. Walter Hodges. Booted Rumour may exit after speaking the prologue and re-enter immediately, having removed his coat 'full of tongues', as Lord Bardolph

Prodigal Son, presented in a number of Interludes, from *The Marriage of Wit and Wisdom* to the *Wit and Science* plays, *The Trial of Treasure* and *Lusty Juventus*.[1] In fact such a Morality pattern is implicit in the subject matter of the play, as was the case with its predecessor, the first half (or the whole) of *Famous Victories*: the Shakespearean remake simply brings it out by placing a stronger emphasis on the character of Oldcastle/Falstaff as the Vice – a natural development out of the *miles gloriosus* of classical comedy, combined with the *capitano* figure in the *commedia dell'arte*.

But if *Part One* is Hal's Morality play, *Part Two* presents a much more complex Morality structure. The first fell naturally into the Morality pattern, while the second – since all the outer events of the reign of King Henry IV had already been enacted in the rewritten play of 1597 – is a deliberate revisitation of the same situations in a shifted key: that of the secular, partly political, Morality or moral Interlude, englobing and compounding the simpler pattern of *Part One*. The tone is set by the Induction spoken by Rumour – the Presenter, in his own speech, of a concentrated little Interlude in which the other two actors (the only two abstract nouns capitalised in the quarto as personifications) are War and Jealousy – that is to say, the deadly sin of Envy, the originator of all rebellion and civil strife.[2] And another little mental drama is enacted between Time, Spite (Envy again), Nature and Order in Northumberland's speech in the very first scene of the play (see the Commentary to 1.1.150–60). In fact, besides Lord Bardolph, who is cast from the beginning as Rumour or Bad Counsel, the other historical characters inherited from *Part One* are built much more closely on Morality models. The stress placed on the king's illness from his first appearance in 3.1 makes of him a penitential figure, while the prince's role is shifted from that of Lusty Juventus to that of Good Government. The Lord Chief Justice is, of course, defined in Morality terms by his title. A much subtler transformation takes place in the character of Falstaff. He is no longer the generic 'reverend Vice' appearing in *Part One*: his role as braggart is transferred to the newly created character of Pistol. Falstaff, as it appears from the interview with the Lord Chief Justice in 1.2, is 'written down old with all the characters of age'; in other words he is the type of Old Mortality.

The introduction of a number of new 'comic' characters, though suggested in the first place by the practical need of filling up the sequel with fresh inventions in view of the lack of primary historical material, is particularly significant. While the names of the irregular humorists in the ur-*Henry IV* were those of known (in some cases too well known) English families, and the changes made in the rewriting (Bardolph, Peto) added at most an ironic quality to them, all the characters appearing for the first time in *Part Two* bear deliberately allusive names. It was, of course, common practice in comedy, but those chosen in this case savour very much of the tradition of the moral Interludes. The Shallow Justice and the Silent Justice of the two country magistrates are the counterparts of the Right Justice (5.2.101) of the Lord Chief Justice; 'Pistol' describes the explosive quality of the Braggart; 'Doll Tearsheet' refers not only to the activities that she shares

---

[1] Alan C. Dessen, *Shakespeare and the Late Moral Plays*, 1986, pp. 55–112, provides an exhaustive treatment of the distinct Morality elements in the two parts of *Henry IV* with parallels from many sixteenth-century Interludes.

[2] See Melchiori, 'Jealousy'.

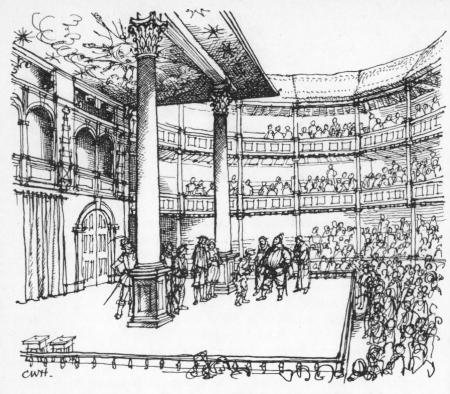

3   Act 3, Scene 2: Falstaff interviews his recruits. An Elizabethan staging, by C. Walter Hodges

with that Jane Nightwork alluded to by Justice Shallow (3.2.163–77), but also to disease and mortality; she is a fitting partner for Falstaff in his new role. There is no need to comment on Fang and Snare as the two sergeants, while the significance of the names of the five unhappy recruits in 3.2 is amply illustrated in the dialogue.

It is mainly this use of the new names that gives to *Part Two* the imprint of a moral Interlude. At the same time the new characters form a gallery of carefully observed human types that seem a prelude to Jonson's technique of building character through humours.

### The comedy of humours

The title page of the 1598 quarto of *Part One* pointed out as one of the attractions of the play 'the humorous conceits of Sir John Falstaff'. That of the 1600 quarto of *Part Two* boasted instead of 'the humours of Sir John Falstaff and swaggering Pistol'. The distinction between 'humorous conceits' and simply 'humours' is not irrelevant. It should be remembered that in between the publication of the two quartos, more precisely between July and September 1598, a new play by Ben Jonson had been performed: *Every Man in his Humour*. Shakespeare was one of the cast,[1] and therefore was sure to have heard Piso's definition of 'humour' in that play: 'it is a monster, bred in a man by self-love and affectation, and fed by folly', to which Cob replied 'Humour, avaunt, I know you not', taking the word as the designation not simply of one aspect in the nature of man, but of the whole man.[2] This explains the different uses to which 'humorous' and 'humour' are put in the two title pages. In the first case the term is the equivalent of 'witty', 'amusing', 'in a particular mood'. In the second 'humour' is short for 'character', 'human type'. The sequel to *Henry IV* written at the same time as Jonson's *Every Man* is advertised two years later on its title page in terms of *Every Man*, as, at least in part, a comedy of humours – the two main humours being Falstaff and Pistol, but the definition is obviously meant also for all the other characters with allusive names. *Henry IV Part Two* reveals that the new comedy of humours born at the end of the sixteenth century is the direct descendant of the moral Interludes which had flourished in the middle of that century.

In Shakespeare's treatment, though, the humours become charged with a much more complex humanity because of their connection with universal themes running through the whole play and forming its basic texture. Time, Nature, War affect the single humours, so that Justice Shallow is not only the type of Shallow Justice but a formal representative of the foibles and involuntary pathetic hypocrisy of decaying age, while Justice Silence embodies the more genial side of dotage. Pathos and farce mingle together in the way in which the recruits face the impositions of the war lords with half-witted cunning; and perhaps the most subtle feat of characterisation, apart from the many-sided Falstaff, is Doll Tearsheet. From her first appearance on the stage half-drunk she undertakes a desperate fight against the degradation of Love through Disease and Mortality. Her sad fate, reported in *Henry V* (5.1.81–2: 'News have I that my Doll is dead i'th'spittle of a malady of France'), is prefigured in *Part Two*, but at the close of this play we can still admire her bravery in her encounter with the Beadle (5.4 – a scene frequently cut in performance).

The extraordinary invention of Doll is the reason for the transformation of the character of the Hostess. Her name, Mistress Quickly, an allusion to professional briskness in *Part One*, is no longer appropriate for the pathetically gullible old bawd whose delusions of respectability are reflected in her new language. The Hostess too has to pay her tribute to the dominating theme of Time, but she remains somewhat outside the characterisation derived from the moral Interludes, and her humour is based exclusively on linguistic exploits. The other comic characters inherited from *Part One* cannot be fitted into the comedy of humours scheme. Peto is a mere shadow putting in a brief appearance as messenger – possibly instead of Poins.[3] Poins himself is more than

---

[1] Shakespeare's name is the first in the list of the 'principall Comoedians' who acted *Every Man in his Humour* in 1598, as reported in the 1616 Folio edition of Jonson's *Works*.

[2] *Every Man in his Humour*, a parallel-text edition of the 1601 quarto and the 1616 Folio, ed. J. W. Lever, 1971; quarto text, 3.1.146–54.

[3] 2.4.287–99, a passage showing signs of patching up. There is actually no room for Peto in *Part Two*, and the role of court messenger is certainly more suited to Poins. In his conflation of the two parts into one Dering did

4    Act 2, Scene 4: Falstaff, Doll Tearsheet, the prince and Poins. Engraved by W. Leney, after the painting by Henry Fuseli, 1789

ever the private confidant of the prince rather than an irregular humorist, and the only distinctive feature of Bardolph (now merely Falstaff's assistant) is not a moral attribute but the picturesque redness of his nose and complexion.

## City and country comedy

The reading of the play as a comedy of humours raises another question. Mainly in view of the Eastcheap scenes, both parts of *Henry IV* have frequently been hailed as harbingers of the *genre* of city comedy that developed out of the comedy of humours at the turn of the century, at first as a celebration of citizen values and later, in the hands of the children's companies, as a satire of teeming city life. The claim is partially justified especially in the case of *Part One* by references to city locations and *mores*, but the representation is restricted to tavern life, without the variety and richness of city types from all arts and trades that were to characterise not only Jonson's *Every Man* plays, but also those of Dekker and Chapman, and later Middleton's, Massinger's and those of a host of other playwrights. All the same, the Eastcheap scenes in *Part One* suggest a contrast between city, court and battlefield, which are the three settings of the play, so that the first of these locations receives a definite emphasis.

If this is enough to qualify that play as city comedy, then we must acknowledge in *Part Two* the emergence of another *genre*. In fact there the life of the city is evoked more vividly in Justice Shallow's nostalgic reminiscences than in direct on-stage presentation. True, Doll and Pistol, Fang and Snare, and the Beadle in 5.4 – the newly created characters – are more representative of the city than the prince's and Falstaff's companions in the earlier play. But Shallow, Silence, Davy and the recruits outnumber them. The two scenes in Eastcheap (2.1 and 2.4, possibly with the addition of the very short 5.4 between Doll, the Hostess and the Beadle) are counterbalanced by the three in Shallow-land (3.2, 5.1 and 5.3). The basic contrast is no longer, as in *Part One*, between court and city, but rather between city and country. The recruiting scene and the moderate revels in Justice Shallow's orchard sanction the birth of what could be called country comedy, a *genre* that breaks down the traditional and conventional, more or less bucolic view of country life, which Shakespeare himself seemed to restate shortly after in *As You Like It*. The note of warning that Jacques sounds even in that 'romantic' comedy is anticipated in this play, where the country is threatened by city and court interference. But in *Henry IV* the uncertainly placed countryside of Gloucestershire or Lincolnshire is under a darker threat: it is overshadowed by History.

not hesitate to transfer the lines to the latter, but there is no authority for the change. As G. Walton Williams and G. Blakemore Evans show in the introduction to their facsimile edition of *The History of King Henry the Fourth as revised by Sir Edward Dering*, 1974, the text does not reflect a possible earlier one-play version, but is a late compilation based on quarto editions of the two parts. Possibly in the ur-*Henry IV* a somewhat similar announcement was entrusted to Poins, but the introduction, in the rewriting of the new scene, of the prince and Poins in disguise watching Falstaff's behaviour prevented the later entrance of Poins with the news, so the author had no alternative but to revive for a moment Peto as the messenger. See also Commentary to 2.4.294–9.

## Language

The transition from city comedy in *Part One* to country comedy in *Part Two* accounts in some measure for the marked difference in the language of the two plays. It emerges most clearly in the prose or 'comic' sections which are in fact predominant: *Part Two* is the only Shakespearean history for the greater part in prose, though the predominance of verse over prose in *Part One* is very slight.[1]

Indeed the variations are not so conspicuous in the verse language of the historical characters, even those introduced for the first time in the second play. All the same, Northumberland's speech at 1.1.136–60, some of the Archbishop's speeches in 1.3 and 4.1, Lady Percy's in 2.3, the king's monologue at 3.1.1–31, and the deathbed exchanges between king and prince in 4.2 mark an extraordinary advance in Shakespeare's use of oratorical rhetoric. There is a new assurance in the creation of complex patterns of thought sustained by vigorous imagery that fully conveys a sense of the power of words. In the case of the prose we can speak of change rather than advance. In comparison with *Part One*, the prince's witticisms are more subdued and at the same time more elaborate, as when he comments on Poins's shortage of linen (2.2.9–22). Falstaff's language is affected by the change of his sparring partners: no longer the prince but by turns the Lord Chief Justice, the Hostess, Pistol, Doll, Justice Shallow, and even Sir John Colevile. His humorous conceits in *Part One*, which frequently took the form of paradoxical exercises in formal logic, with ample use of rhetorical questioning, are replaced by the practice of evasion through broad jokes, jocular self-commiseration, games with true or fictitious memories, and lengthy soliloquies in which the criticisms addressed to Justice Shallow or Prince John are in fact half-hearted attempts at self-justification or at keeping up a flagging morale.

The language of the other irregular humorists appearing in *Part One* was not particularly distinctive, and the same is true of *Part Two*, where Peto practically disappears, Bardolph, as we have noted, is individualised not by style but by his red nose, and Poins is not Falstaff's but the prince's partner in witty repartee. The real transformation is that of Mistress Quickly, who in *Part One* was content to repeat from time to time her interjection 'Jesu, Jesu', while in *Part Two* she is endowed with the most original linguistic inventions in the play, both in her choice of ejaculations and in her vivid narrative and evocative speeches. From her first appearance in the company of Fang and Snare in 2.1 she exhibits the new Shakespearean technique of character construction through language, which is later applied to all the new comic characters introduced in the play. Hence Doll Tearsheet's speeches are distinguished by an original manipulation of strong abuse alternating, in tender moments, with paradoxical endearment ('Thou whoreson little tidy Bartholomew boar-pig' (2.4.187–8)). Pistol's swaggering relies on the nonsensical use of irregular verse rhythms evocative of heroic poetry. The trick of repetition characterises Justice Shallow from his first entrance as a man most of whose life is in the past, while Justice Silence's economy of speech transforms his breaking into song in 5.3 into the sudden revelation of unsupected depths of

---

[1] Statistical data are derived from M. Spevack, *A Complete and Systematic Concordance to the Works of Shakespeare*, vols. 1–6, 1968–70.

personality. Even each of the recruits and Shallow's servant Davy in their brief appearances are individualised by personal linguistic quirks.

The difference in the language, or rather languages, between the two parts is confirmed by quantitative measuring of the plays' characteristics. The much firmer separation in *Part Two* between the historical and the comic scenes is exemplified in the figure of Prince Hal, who in *Part One* acted as a kind of link between the two linguistic registers of the play, the prose of comedy and the verse of history. There he spoke over 18 per cent of the total number of words in the play, but the prose speeches which he exchanged with Falstaff and his companions prevailed over the verse he used in the court and battle scenes (60 per cent prose as against 40 per cent verse). In *Part Two* the prince's overall role is practically halved (he speaks only 9.5 per cent of the total number of words in the play), but the proportion between his verse (59.5 per cent) and his prose (40.5 per cent) is completely reversed. In a play in which comedy prevails, he has moved to the side of history. His separation from Falstaff is further marked by the fact that most of the prince's prose speeches are exchanged not with him but with Poins or are comments made behind Falstaff's back. The only direct exchanges between the two, in 2.4.230–85, take the form of deliberate abuse: 'Thou globe of sinful continents . . . you whoreson candle-mine'; more significantly, when the two meet next (and last) in 5.5 the prince, now King Henry V, addresses Falstaff not in prose but in verse.

The sharp distinctions in the individual linguistic features of each character and humour in the play turn it into a comedy of languages, anticipating the use of different national linguistic structures in *Henry V* and, with broader effects, in *The Merry Wives of Windsor*.

## History

The original *Famous Victories* must have contained more historical matter than appears in the wretched 1598 version, where it figures only as a series of anecdotes. There is no doubt, though, that the Shakespearean version, going back directly to the historical sources, greatly expanded those parts of the play. Any treatment of historical events in fictional form entails a measure of manipulation. What emerges from a consideration of both parts of *Henry IV* as we have them now is that, in comparison with *Part One*, the manipulation of history for dramatic and ideological purposes in *Part Two* appears basically different if not contradictory. In *Part One* the quarrelsome alliance of Glendower with Mortimer, Worcester and Hotspur, for instance, is presented in a grotesque light, so as to discredit it; what is more, at Shrewsbury Prince Hal is given the triumphal distinction of killing Hotspur in person, taking a liberty with historical facts that not even the enthusiastic Daniel had dared to take in his *Civil Wars*. In *Part Two*, on the other hand, the meeting of the Archbishop of York with Mowbray and the Lords Hastings and Bardolph is treated as the war council of level-headed men with a real grievance and even the sense of a mission. It is significant that all eight major omissions in the text of the 1600 quarto are from speeches pronounced by the rebels – Morton, Lord Bardolph, the Archbishop, Lady Percy, and Mowbray (two passages in Westmoreland's speeches in 4.1 are omitted because they are addressed to Mowbray). The omissions seem intended to weaken the case so eloquently put by the rebels. Again, the responsibility for devising the Gaultree trap, which Holinshed is at pains to attribute only to Westmoreland, exonerating the members of the royal family,[1] is placed squarely in *Part Two* on Prince John – and Prince John himself appears as a projection of Prince Hal, who in 2.4.294–9 had prepared us for his participation in the northern campaign, so that his absence is unaccountable in dramatic though not in historical terms.[2]

It would be mistaken to take this seeming reversal of attitude from *Part One* to *Part Two* as the result of the author's change of heart. *Part One* (and presumably even more the original one-play version of *Henry IV*) was the story of the transformation of wild prince into wise ruler. *Part Two* instead is in the nature of a reconsideration of the subject matter and leading themes of *Part One* in a Morality key. Hence among other things the introduction of the prince's soliloquy on redeeming time upon his first appearance on the stage in 1.2, which is a statement of policy: he plays Falstaff's game in order to show his own wisdom and uprightness by throwing him off in the end. Policy is an ambiguous term: the equivalent of deceit in ordinary usage but an indispensable instrument of government for the wise statesman. Within its Morality framework, *Part Two* becomes an exploration of the nature of policy in all its aspects. The theme resounds from one end to the other of the play. Rumour's policy in the Induction is that of spreading false news, Northumberland is 'crafty-sick', Prince Hal's policy in 2.4 is that of the disguised ruler spying on the behaviour of his subjects, finding out the opinion they have of him. And after Prince John's supreme act of policy in order to conquer the rebels, the king himself, in his deathbed advice to the prince, recognises that in planning a penitential expedition to the Holy Land he was pursuing a deliberate policy:

> and had a purpose now
> To lead out many to the Holy Land,
> Lest rest and lying still might make them look
> Too near unto my state. Therefore, my Harry,
> Be it thy course to busy giddy minds
> With foreign quarrels...                    (4.2.337–42)

This piece of advice is going to be punctually acted upon in *Henry V*, as we are reminded by Prince John in the very last words of *Part Two*:

> I will lay odds that, ere this year expire,
> We bear our civil swords and native fire
> As far as France. I heard a bird so sing
> Whose music, to my thinking, pleased the king.                    (5.5.98–101)

*Part Two* is the triumph of Policy with a capital P – state policy as contrasted with the

---

[1]  Holinshed (III, 529) goes to the length of offering two separate accounts of the event, a longer one which hardly mentions Prince John while it speaks of Westmoreland 'vsing more policie then the rest', and a brief second version stating that 'the lord Iohn ... was present there in the field with banners spred, redie to trie the matter by dint of sword if they refused [Westmoreland's] counsell'.

[2]  The fact that Prince Henry is never mentioned in any of the chronicles in connection with the second rebellion is a sure token that Shakespeare, like the author of *Famous Victories* before him, had not planned to include the Gaultree episode in the original version of the play(s).

inept plotting of the rebels as well as with Falstaff's naïve idea of the prince's (now the king's) policy after his rejection, when he tells Justice Shallow:

Do not you grieve at this. I shall be sent for in private to him. Look you, he must *seem* thus to the world ... This that you heard was but a colour.                                          (5.5.72–80)

Shallow's reply could not be more apt:

A colour that I fear you will die in, Sir John.

One wonders whether the subtlest piece of policy in the whole play, this time neither the prince's nor his companions', but the author's own, is not to be found in the conclusion of the Epilogue, where the disclaimer that Falstaff dying of a sweat[1] is not Oldcastle who 'died martyr' is a perfect reminder for the audience that Sir John Falstaff was born at 'about three of the clock in the afternoon' (the time when performances in public theatres began) as Sir John Oldcastle.

## Psychodrama

The Oldcastle allusion and the Policy theme favour what has been called a 'political' reading of the play – in radical terms if the Gaultree episode and the rejection of Falstaff are taken as ferocious exposures of the cynicism of power politics, in conservative terms if they are interpreted as examples of political wisdom. Perhaps in view of this insoluble ambiguity, the rejection has been more frequently considered on the level of personal psychology, as a statement about the father–son relationship. The basic data are there: the prince seems to recoil from his natural father – the usurper king – and be in quest of another father-figure. Who better suited for this role than the aged counsellor of youthful sin? Seen in this light, the rejection of Falstaff is, of course, the rejection of the father, or, more drastically, the ritual killing of the father/king. The case was beautifully put by J. I. M. Stewart: 'I suggest that Hal, by a displacement common enough in the evolution of ritual, kills Falstaff instead of killing the king, his father. In a sense Falstaff *is* his father; certainly is a "father-substitute" in the psychologist's word; and this makes the theory of a vicarious sacrifice the more colourable.'[2]

All this is fine, but only in terms of the original one-play version, the ur-*Henry IV* we postulated earlier, which culminates in the rejection as the final twist to the Prodigal Son parable. But in the texts we have now the situation is already reversed in the 'play extempore' scene of *Part One* (2.4), when the prince rejects the role of son to Falstaff by playing the king himself and thus assuming the role of father, condemning once and for all the man who pretends to father him. The last scene of *Part Two* is in a way merely the official sanctioning of a statement made at the close of the play extempore in *Part One*. 'I know thee not, old man' is the equivalent of the prince's reply to Falstaff's plea 'banish plump Jack and banish all the world' in *Part One* 2.4.479–80: 'I do, I will.'

In fact by the beginning of *Part Two* the relationship between the prince and Falstaff is

---

[1]  See G. Melchiori, 'Dying of a sweat: Falstaff and Oldcastle', *N&Q* ns 34 (1987), 210–11.
[2]  'The birth and death of Falstaff', in J. I. M. Stewart, *Character and Motive in Shakespeare*, 1949, pp. 138–9.

already severed. The only time they are seen together on the stage (apart from the rejection scene) is 2.4, where there is no question of a father–son relationship between Falstaff and the prince. The latter appears in it in the role of the ruler in disguise who has 'come to draw out by the ears' a disloyal subject.[1] There is no longer any question of a single psychodrama involving the prince and Falstaff. The interlocutors in Falstaff's mental drama are now the Lord Chief Justice on the one hand and the country Justices of the Peace on the other. In the case of the prince, the father–son relationship is explored instead in real terms: the father-figure represented by Falstaff in *Part One* is replaced by the natural father, King Henry IV.

This development has been somewhat obscured in the transition from the one-play version of *Henry IV* to the present arrangement. The casual origin of *Part Two* has forced the author to introduce into it a duplication of the same dramatic curve that governed *Part One*. According to the reconstruction of the ur-*Henry IV* that I have suggested above, in that version the battle of Shrewsbury, in which the prince kept the vow made to his father to 'redeem all [past offences] on Percy's head' (see *Part One* 3.2.132), was followed by the mention of the king's illness in the dialogue between Oldcastle and the Lord Chief Justice. Straight after it the sick king was presented on the stage in a revealing soliloquy reflecting the country's state as well as his own, and between this and the deathbed scene (now *Part Two* 4.2) there would be only the brief discussion with Poins of the prince's feelings for his father before he is summoned to the king's bedside, where the episode of the removal of the crown from the pillow would take place.

This sequence presents a continuous pattern of development of the father–son theme that the transposition of one scene (the king's night musings, now *Part Two* 3.1) and the redistribution of parts of other scenes (now included in 1.2, 2.2, 2.4) make hard to follow. The initial point, the so-called first reconciliation scene in *Part One* 3.2, showed a relationship which was still largely formal, involving the natural duty of son to father and of subject to sovereign. But the acknowledgement on the king's part of his own responsibilities and even of his own faults sets in motion a process of identification between son and father which takes at first, in the dialogue with Poins (2.2.1–52), the form of committed acceptance of the role of son ('my heart bleeds inwardly that my father is so sick'). Emblematically, Falstaff's only part in all this is that of conveying not to the prince but to the audience the information that the king is sick: his father-role is cancelled. The culmination of the process, from acceptance to identification, is magnificently achieved in Shakespeare's treatment of the ambiguous anecdote found in the sources[2] of the prince taking the crown from the king's pillow. The monologue that accompanies the gesture (4.2.151–77) is much more than a statement of the right of succession. The prince takes over full and comprehensive responsibility for the sins of the father together with those of the diseased state. As such, it is an act of redemption. The son redeems his father by identifying with him.

---

[1] William Empson in 'They that have power' (in *Some Versions of Pastoral*, 1935, pp. 89–118) connects Prince Hal – and Henry V – with Angelo in *Measure for Measure*. Surely the analogy is rather with the 'Duke of dark corners' in the same play; see Melchiori, 'Corridors'.

[2] The episode is in *Famous Victories*, but Shakespeare's wording suggests that he was relying on Holinshed's account (III, 541), conflating it with the king's dying advice to his son in Stow, *Annales*, p. 545.

5   Act 4, Scene 2: the taking of the crown. Engraved by R. Thew, after the painting by John Boydell

The scene establishes a symbolic pattern which was to be reaffirmed more emphatically in the Gloucester–Edgar relationship in *King Lear*, emblematically reflected in the same play in Cordelia's redemption of Lear himself. The full implications of such an act come into the open when, in the romances, the partners in the generational conflict are young girls: Marina, Perdita, Miranda. *The Tempest* has frequently been read as psychodrama,[1] and in fact the figure of Prospero lends itself easily to an interpretation in this key. But Prospero's original sin is a sin by omission: he had overlooked the duties of a ruler. Henry IV's sin was a sin of commission, even if the action was forced upon him by necessity of state (see 3.1.72–4). For this reason the history play is more the father's than the son's psychodrama, while in *The Tempest* Miranda and Ferdinand are characters in the drama acted in Prospero's mind. The final advice of the king to the prince, though couched in political terms, prefigures Prospero's wisdom at the close of his play: both represent solutions to their respective mental dramas. Falstaff instead is confined to the role of actor in the prince's private psychodrama:

> I have long dreamt of such a kind of man...
> But being awaked, I do despise my dream.                          (5.5.45–7)

## Time and disease

In the rejection speech the prince, now King Henry V, distances the figure of Falstaff not only in spatial but also in temporal terms. Falstaff is for him a dream from a past deliberately placed outside memory, because the prince has fulfilled the promise made in his first soliloquy in *Part One*, that of 'redeeming time when men think least I will' (1.2.216–17). In fact throughout *Part Two* Falstaff is the incarnation of Unredeemed Time.

The Falstaff of *Part One* is certainly no young man. But the stress is placed not on his age but on his bulk as well as his cowardice. He is agile enough to run away at Gad's Hill in spite of having refused to put his ear to the ground, arguing: 'Have you any levers to lift me up again, being down?' (*Part One* 2.2.34–5). And his 'sweating to death' on that occasion (2.2.108) is not a sign of disease but simply of fear – a motif resumed with ambiguous overtones at the very end of the Epilogue to *Part Two*:

> ...France, where, for anything I know, Falstaff shall die of a sweat, unless already a be killed with
> your hard opinions.                                              (Epilogue 22–4)

In the later play sweating is mentioned as the consequence of military exertion, in an attempt at countering the Lord Chief Justice's statement that Falstaff is 'written down old with all the characters of age' (1.2.141–2). But he himself later acknowledges his condition ('I am old, I am old') when left alone with Doll, who acts upon him as a reminder of mortality:

> Peace, good Doll, do not speak like a death's-head, do not bid me remember mine end.
>                                                                   (2.4.190–1)

The dominance of the theme of time in the play has been frequently noted and

---

[1] See, for instance, W. H. Auden's dramatic poem *The Sea and the Mirror*, 1945.

commented upon.¹ It is explored in all its aspects. The redemption of time promised by the prince is the actual subject of the whole play. Hence the constant attention in it to 'the revolution of the times', from the moment Northumberland announces, in the first scene, that 'the times are wild' to the final rejection of Falstaff, of which we have already noted the significance on the temporal level. What must be underlined, though, is the constant association of the view of time in the play with images of sickness and disease. In no other play by Shakespeare do these two words, and their compounds or derivatives, occur as frequently: 'disease' 13 times, and 'sick' or 'sickness' no less than 21, apart from a number of mentions of specific diseases and references to physical mutilation running through the play.

Shakespeare rings all possible changes on the theme of disease, beginning with Rumour's announcement in the Induction that Northumberland 'lies crafty-sick'. Northumberland's true or pretended sickness is healed only by his learning of Hotspur's death, in 1.1, but already in the second scene this crafty sickness is overruled by the mention of the king's 'discomfort', which is to become, with its wide symbolic overtones, the ruling motif of the rest of the play. At first it is introduced in passing, as part of Falstaff's strategy to divert the Lord Chief Justice's enquiries: he suffers from 'the disease of not listening, the malady of not marking' (1.2.97). But he concludes the scene with two further allusions to sickness, one metaphorical and one real:

I can get no remedy against this consumption of the purse: borrowing only lingers and lingers it out, but the disease is incurable ... A pox of this gout, or a gout of this pox, for the one or the other plays the rogue with my great toe. 'Tis no matter if I do halt: I have the wars for my colour ... A good wit will make use of anything: I will turn diseases to commodity. (1.2.186–95)

Disease and craftiness go hand in hand. Northumberland pretends sickness to avoid involvement in the rebellion, Falstaff turns what was considered a dishonourable disease to personal advantage as a means of getting a pension. Even the king's very real illness must be deliberately played down by the the the prince:

I tell thee my heart bleeds inwardly that my father is so sick; ... What wouldst thou think of me if I should weep?
POINS I would think thee a most princely hypocrite. (2.2.36–41)

In order to avoid the accusation of hypocrisy the prince is forced to further hypocrisy, that of pretending indifference towards his father's illness. Disease is tantamount to deception not only in the sufferer but also in others. When in 2.4 Doll Tearsheet enters 'sick of a calm', as the Hostess puts it, Falstaff underlines the idea of contagion:

you help to make the diseases, Doll; we catch of you, Doll, we catch of you. (2.4.36–7)

Hints like these in the 'comic' scenes prepare the ground for the basic theme of the play, on which its whole metaphoric structure is built: the king's illness and its spatial, temporal and historical implications.

Act 3, Scene 1, at the very centre of the play, develops the disease theme in full. It is stated from the beginning in visual terms, by the appearance on stage of the king 'in his

¹ Notably B. T. Spencer, '2 Henry IV and the theme of Time', UTQ 13 (1943–4), 394–9, and, more comprehensively, Knights, Some Shakespearean Themes, pp. 45–64.

nightgown', an indication of his sick state. It is the king himself who identifies his condition with that of the country:

> Then you perceive the body of our kingdom
> How foul it is, what rank diseases grow. (3.1.37–8)

The connection with time and history is made in the king's report of Richard II's prophecy:

> 'The time shall come', thus he did follow it,
> 'The time will come that foul sin, gathering head,
> Shall break into corruption.' (3.1.74–6)

And even more subtly in Warwick's words:

> There is a history in all men's lives
> Figuring the natures of the times deceased... (3.1.79–80)

The ambiguity is deliberate: the 'times deceased' evoked by each individual man to create his view of history are also inevitably 'times diseased'. The implications of the word-play are far-reaching. It involves both the nature of 'time' and that of 'history'. Time is the progress of the generations of man through disease to death – a classical conception that in Shakespeare had found its most powerful expressions in the Sonnets. History in turn is by no means the splendid record of the great events of the past, but a subjective reading, an imaginative figuration of the diseases of past times.

This is in fact the pivotal scene of the play, conveying its essential meaning. The theme of time is inextricably connected with that of disease and death, and history records decay in all men's lives, from the king's to the commoner's. The consummation is obviously 4.2, the king's deathbed scene. But already in 3.2 Falstaff and the two country Justices, evoking the good old times of their youth, acknowledge that all that is left them is but decay and death:

Jesu, Jesu, the mad days that I have spent! And to see how many of my old acquaintance are dead...
Death, as the psalmist saith, is certain to all, all shall die. (3.2.26–30)

Shallow's thoughts are diverted by worldly matters, such as the price of a good yoke of bullocks at Stamford Fair, but cannot help returning to the main theme: 'And is old Dooble dead?' he keeps asking of Justice Silence (3.2.33–43), and wistfully wonders that Jane Nightwork, remembered as a forbidding bona roba, is now, in Falstaff's report, 'old, old, Master Shallow' (3.2.162–73). Thus we learn that 55 years have passed since Shallow and Falstaff had 'heard the chimes at midnight' at Clement's Inn – Shallow must be in his seventies, while Falstaff, who was a page at the time, is surely close (in spite of giving his age in *Part One* 2.4.224–5 as 'some fifty, or... inclining to threescore') to the biblical limit of threescore and ten, double the normal life expectation for that time.

'Devouring time' is present as much in the comic as in the historical scenes. And so is history itself. The recruiting is a way of showing how history interferes in the lives of the common people, adding to their misery. Bullcalf adducing illness in order not to be pressed into service is countered by Falstaff's 'thou shalt go to the wars in a gown' (3.2.153), recalling the image of the king 'in his nightgown' in the previous scene, as an

6  'The hook-nosed fellow of Rome' (see 4.1.391): Julius Caesar, from the medallion portrait in North's
Plutarch, 1579

emblem of the diseased condition of the times and of the country. Thus, at the moment
of his rejection, Falstaff becomes the outsize representative of death-bound humanity,
when the new king reminds him:

> know the grave doth gape
> For thee thrice wider than for other men.                                    (5.5.49–50)

## Part Two on the stage

If we are correct in thinking that *Part Two* was devised as the rewriting of a remake, and
more precisely as a sequel undertaken at short notice to cash in on the success of a
previously rewritten play, it can be assumed that the circumstances of the envisaged
staging of the new production must have been particularly present to its author's mind.
As well as structuring the sequel on the pattern of the parent play, he would be thinking
all the time in terms not only of the recasting of the roles – including those newly created
– for the same actors, but also of the facilities offered by the playhouse likely to be used by
the company. This preoccupation may account, at least in part, for the difficulties met by
some modern readers of the play in regard both to the substantial omissions in the
original quarto text of the play, and of apparent imprecisions in the directions for staging,
which have entailed massive editorial interventions, from the introduction of highly
questionable new scene divisions in Act 4, to radical rearrangements of stage directions,
for instance at the beginning of 1.1 and of 2.4, as well as in several places in Act 4 itself.[1]

---

[1]  See collation and Commentary to 1.1.0 SD, 1.1.6 SD, 2.4.1–16, 4.1.0 SD, 4.1.227–8, 4.1.351 SD.2 and 4.2.132
SD.

The second category of difficulties must be examined in the light of the acting space available, while for the first an essential key to the solution may be offered by a consideration of the practice of doubling.

## DOUBLING

By their very nature, history plays, following the pattern of the chronicles that report a succession of separate episodes, entail a very large number of speaking roles of moderate length, as different historical figures appear in single episodes and then leave the stage for good. *Part One* is no exception, with about thirty speaking roles of some relevance, apart from the menial and functional ones (messengers, officers and the like). Historically important characters such as the Archbishop of York, Glendower, Mortimer, Northumberland, and even Prince John, appear and speak only in single scenes: they fulfil their historical function, but the actors impersonating them remain available to cover different short roles in other sections of the play. The writing of a sequel entailed the introduction not only of new historical characters, but also of a number of others to enliven the fictional comic scenes. The two parts have only thirteen characters in common, two of whom, Peto and Francis the drawer, are reduced in the second to insignificance,[1] while the total number of speaking roles is greatly increased in *Part Two* to well over forty. But the most striking difference is in the fact that while in *Part One* the minor fictional roles, such as Gadshill, the carriers and the like, were hardly distinguishable, in *Part Two*, besides the radical transformation of Mistress Quickly and the major creations of Doll, Pistol, Justice Shallow, Justice Silence and Davy, even the minimal roles of the Officers in 2.1, the recruits in 3.2 and the Beadle in 5.4 are very strongly characterised. The inadvertency of the printer of the quarto who, setting from Shakespeare's own foul papers, used the name of the actor Sincklo instead of 'Beadle' in the stage direction and speech headings of 5.4 is revealing: the author was thinking in terms of his fellow actors and their individual abilities as well as their availability when hurriedly writing a text that would at short notice be turned into a prompt-book. Why bother to write 'Beadle' when that bit part was in any case to be added to the acting-load of the notoriously lean John Sincklo, who had already been cast in the author's mind for Snare in 2.1 and for Shadow in 3.2, and whose appearance (like a 'starved bloodhound') had actually suggested the mood of this particular scene?[2]

As for the historical characters, Shakespeare obviously knew which of his fellow actors were best suited to take oratorical roles, but the exploitation of new material from Holinshed called for a considerable number of suitably skilled performers. It looks as if at first he was inclined to borrow from the chronicles with no regard for immediate scenic

---

[1] In the quarto Francis is given four short speeches in the very confused opening of 2.4 (see Commentary to 2.4.1–16), and for the one brief appearance of Peto at 2.4.286 ff., see p. 19 above, n. 3.

[2] For Sincklo see first note to 5.4. His mention in this scene suggests that he must have been exceptionally tall and thin (and therefore admirably suited for 'half-faced' Shadow in 3.2, who 'presents no mark to the enemy'), but Jean Robertson – reported in Brian Morris (ed.), *Shr.*, 1981, p. 158 – argues that he was, on the contrary, very small, so that the Hostess's and Doll's remarks would sound particularly sarcastic. The fact that Sincklo, in the Induction to *The Malcontent* in which he appears in his own person, is compared to a viol da gamba does not warrant this deduction. The suggestion that he doubled for Snare in 2.1 was advanced by Dover Wilson (see Commentary to 2.1.4); but in the recruiting scene (3.2) Wilson saw him as Feeble the woman's tailor rather than Shadow, and Harold Brooks agrees with him on this point.

feasibility: the survival, in the foul papers that went to the quarto printer, of entrance directions in different scenes for Falconbridge and Kent[1] bears witness to this. But in the actual writing of the scenes these characters disappear, and so does Lord Bardolph, whose entrance was marked at the opening of 4.1: he had already appeared in the first act and his presence at Gaultree would be the natural consequence of the decisions taken at the war council at 1.3. But by Act 4 the actor for whom the new role of Lord Bardolph was conceived must be engaged in another fairly exacting part, possibly on the other side of the conflict (Westmoreland? Prince John? Warwick? None of them figures in the earlier acts of the play). And it is curious that at Gaultree Prince John should be accompanied only by Westmoreland and an anonymous 'army', with no other recognisable loyal nobleman or kinsman. His two brothers, Gloucester and Clarence, appear for the first time only at the dying king's bedside, after the supererogatory Colevile scene has given the stage rebels time for 'present execution' at York as well as for changing into more princely attire. Considerations of the same nature may be partly at the root of the eight major omissions in the quarto – passages that must have been marked for deletion in the foul papers in view of the preparation of the prompt-book of the play. Political reasons, as we have seen, may explain some of the cuts (though only half of them), but four omitted passages do not seem to contain any offensive matter, such as the allusions to the deposition of Richard II. It is more likely, therefore, that the author took advantage of compulsory cuts in order to lighten the parts of some actors who were expected to shoulder heavy commitments, doubling exacting roles in later scenes. That of Lady Percy is a case in point, if the same boy-actor, immediately after his magnificent speech celebrating Hotspur, had to change into the mean clothes of Doll Tearsheet. The Textual Analysis supports this explanation (see p. 199 below).

THE ACTING SPACE

As for the acting space available to the company, it seems fairly certain that while at first the Chamberlain's Men had been using mainly the Theatre, sometime in 1597 they settled at the Curtain, while the Theatre was being torn down in preparation for the building of the Globe, which was completed in 1599. The author of *Part Two* must have had in mind the playhouse where it was going to be performed, about which unfortunately we have very little information, except for the fact that the Curtain was a polygonal structure of unspecified dimensions.[2] The directions at the beginning of 1.1 make it clear that Shakespeare was thinking in terms of three separate accesses to the stage, for Lord Bardolph 'at one door', for the Porter, and, shortly after, for Northumberland, obviously coming from a different direction (the orchard 'gate'). Several editors since Collier in 1853, including Dover Wilson, thought in terms of a stage like the one in Aarend van Buchell's sketch of the Swan with only two 'doors' and no central opening in the back wall, and postulated the entrance of the Porter 'above', but it seems significant that nowhere else in this play are there directions for the use of an upper stage, while they are fairly common both in earlier plays, such as *Titus Andronicus* and *Romeo and Juliet*, and in later Globe plays such as *Henry V* (the siege of Harfleur, for example, in 3.3). It looks as

---

[1] Falconbridge's entrance at 1.3.0 was suggested by Holinshed, and for Kent see Commentary to 4.2.0 SD.
[2] See G. E. Bentley, *The Jacobean and Caroline Stage*, 7 vols., 1941–68, VI, 131–9.

A

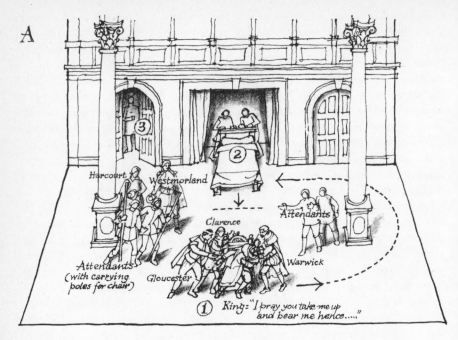

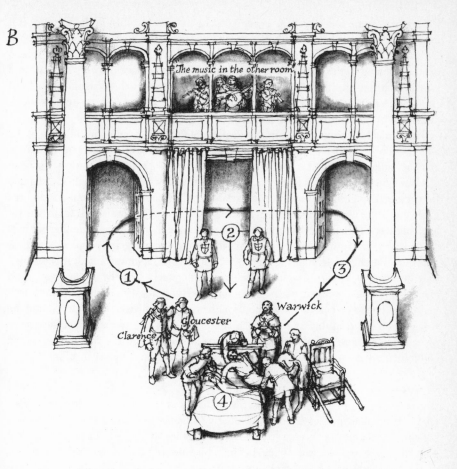

The music in the other room

Clarence
Gloucester
Warwick

7   Act 4, Scene 2: alternative ways of staging the change of location between lines 130 and 135 (where no exeunt is given), by C. Walter Hodges

Variant A (opposite): (1) The king falls sick and is carried in his chair to a new position on the stage. (2) During the move, the king's bed is brought from behind curtains. (3) The prince about to enter. (4 and 5) The prince at the king's bedside, and exit

Variant B (above) assumes an exeunt and re-entry: (1) The king is carried out in his chair. (2) The bed is brought on, replacing the chair in the original forward position. (3) The king re-enters and is carried to the bed. Warwick holds the crown, which has fallen from the king's head

if the use of some sort of gallery as acting space was not foreseen at the Curtain. If it existed at all it would be used only as a music gallery, and that would account for the call for 'music in the other room' at 4.2.136. The implication is that the Curtain had instead a central opening in the back wall, as access to a discovery place closed by a door or a curtain, figuring in the first scene as the orchard 'gate', at which significantly Lord Bardolph has no time to knock, as suggested by the Porter (1.1.5), because he is prevented by the entrance through it of Northumberland.[1]

The central opening is, of course, indispensable for trundling on in full view of the audience the bed on which the king is laid at 4.2.132, before his removal to the Jerusalem chamber at the end of that scene. Walter Hodges suggests two possible ways of staging this (see illustration 7). My feeling is that Variant A shows what was originally planned for presentation at the Curtain, while Variant B, which assumes a general exit and re-entry, may show what was used on later occasions – in court performances, for instance – as giving scope for a musical interlude at this point. In either case the beginning of a new scene at 133, first introduced by the Cambridge editors in 1864, and adopted, though at times with strong reservations, by more recent editions, is unwarranted: it is justified only in terms of Victorian concern for naturalistic staging, implying a curtain and a change of the stage-set to mark the transition from the Jerusalem chamber to the king's bedroom. The same considerations apply to the two scene divisions introduced into the first part of Act 4; in this case the Folio compilers took care to mark Colevile's mute presence from the very first entrance direction of the act to ensure that the scene would continue uninterrupted by his confrontation with Falstaff in the last part of it.

STAGING, ADAPTATIONS AND SEQUELS

The stage history of *Part Two* necessarily coincides in large measure with that of *Part One*. All the same, the fact that only one quarto edition of it survives, while *Part One* was reprinted five times between 1599 and 1622, implies that it did not enjoy the same popularity as its predecessor. When, in 1623, Sir Edward Dering prepared a conflation of the two parts into one for private theatricals, he included the substance of the historical scenes in *Part Two* and, among the comic ones, only brief extracts from 2.1, between Falstaff and the Hostess, ignoring the presence in it of Fang and Snare, and even of the Lord Chief Justice. All the other newly created characters – Pistol and Doll, Shallow and Silence – have gone, along with the Justice and the constables.[2] This was due mainly to limitations both in the number of amateur actors available to Dering and in their abilities, but surely the weeding out would not have been so drastic if any of the characters had enjoyed a popularity at all comparable with that of Falstaff.

---

[1] On the other hand, Shaaber (Variorum, pp. 18–19) comments: 'To me it seems most likely that the gate kept by the porter ... would have been represented by the entrance to the inner stage; the orchard gate, presumably smaller, would have been represented more appropriately by a side door.' Walter Hodges's drawing (illustration 2) represents the view of the present editor.

[2] In their introduction to the Dering MS. Williams and Evans establish the circumstances of the compilation and remark that Dering omitted 11 per cent of *Part One* and approximately 75 per cent of *Part Two*. Definitive evidence for the dating of the manuscript to February 1623 and for Dering's original intention to include a larger proportion of *Part Two* is provided by Laetitia Yeandle, 'The dating of Sir Edward Dering's copy of "The History of King Henry the Fourth"', *SQ* 37 (1986), 224–6.

Nevertheless, *Part Two* seems to have been one of the 'fowerteene seuerall playes' performed at Whitehall in the course of the festive season 1612–13 to celebrate the marriage of Princess Elizabeth to the Elector Palatine. In the Chamber Accounts it is listed as 'Sir Iohn Falstaffe', and it is unlikely that the title refers to *Part One*, since another payment to John Heminges for six more plays presented in the same season includes one called 'The Hotspur', a suitable designation for the first part. Besides, among the plays considered for performance at court in 1619–20, listed on slips of paper inserted in the manuscript of the *History of Richard III* by the Master of the Revels, Sir George Buck, there appears a 'Second part of Falstaff not plaid theis 7. yeres'. The time lag between performances tallies perfectly. There is no further record for performances of *Part Two* till the closing of the theatres, while 'The First Part of Sir John Falstaff' was played at Whitehall on New Year night of 1625, and 'ould Castel' (obviously *Part One*) was given at the Cockpit for the prince's birthnight on 29 May 1638.[1]

The revival of *Part Two* at the Theatre Royal, Drury Lane, in 1720 as an independent play, in an adaptation attributed to Thomas Betterton, staked all on Falstaff and the new characters by eliminating the historical scenes in the first three acts, except for 1.3 (the rebels' meeting in preparation for Gaultree) and part of the king's monologue in 3.1 (incorporated in the deathbed scene).[2] This gave scope for the antics of Pistol, a role that was taken over in 1729 by Theophilus Cibber, while the Shallow of Colley Cibber was such a success that the same actor was still playing it in 1744. By that time Betterton's version had to compete with another, first staged at Covent Garden in 1738, which claimed to be the genuine and unaltered Shakespearean text. In the second half of the century the emphasis moved from the comic to the historical parts of the play. From 1758 to 1770 Garrick at Drury Lane gave dignity to the role of the king, while the Covent Garden productions counted especially on the scenic display of the coronation, and this trend, after a lull of some thirty years interrupted by John Philip Kemble's diligent but uninspired adaptation of 1804,[3] culminated in Macready's Covent Garden production of June 1821, introducing four additional scenes 'displaying the grand Coronation'. For the performance of 19 July, the day of the coronation of George IV, 'the King commanded the theatre to be opened gratuitously to the public'. In the revival of 1834 at Drury Lane Macready introduced into the second part of *Henry IV* 'a grand Musical Festivall', with 'Airs, Duets, Trios, Chorusses &c.' Meanwhile, the coronation pageant of the Covent Garden production was introduced in the 1822 revival, at the Park Theatre in New York, of the version of the play first given there in 1820 (the only recorded earlier performance of the play in the United States was at Philadelphia in

---

[1] The relevant documents are readily available in Appendix D, 'Performances of Plays', of E. K. Chambers, *William Shakespeare: A Study of Facts and Problems*, 1930, II, 342–3, 346, 347, 353.

[2] *The Sequel of Henry the Fourth ... As it is Acted by His Majesty's Company of Comedians at the Theatre-Royal in Drury-Lane. Alter'd from Shakespear, by the late Mr. Betterton* [1721]. Facsimile reprint, 1969. The attribution to Betterton is, to say the least, surprising, since he had died in 1710.

[3] *Shakespeare's King Henry the Fourth (The Second Part), A Historical Play, revised by J. P. Kemble; and now first published as it is acted at the Theatre Royal in Covent Garden*, 1804 (in *The Folger Facsimiles: John Philip Kemble Promptbooks*, ed. Charles H. Shattuck, vol. 3, 1974). The adaptation is Falstaff-centred, along 'Betterton' lines, starting directly with 1.2, eliminating Lord Bardolph, Northumberland, his wife and Lady Percy, incorporating the king's monologue of 3.1 in the deathbed scene, and bowdlerising the comic scenes.

8    Theophilus Cibber as Pistol, Drury Lane, 1729

1815). Macready himself played his usual role of the king in *Part Two* in the New York performance of 1827.[1]

The eighteenth and early nineteenth centuries saw more radical adaptations of and further sequels to *Part Two*, centring on the figure of Falstaff. The most remarkable is the comedy *Falstaff's Wedding* by W. Kenrick, published in 1760 with a dedication to the actor James Quin, who since 1722 had been playing Falstaff, mainly in the first part of the play. The comedy is an ingenious exploitation of some hints and inconsistencies in the Shakespearean original. Falstaff, after his rejection by King Hal, makes good the intention expressed at the end of 1.2, when he gave his page a letter for 'old Mistress Ursula, whom I have weekly sworn to marry since I perceived the first white hair of my chin'. This mysterious dame, never mentioned elsewhere in the plays (see note to 1.2.189), turns out to enjoy a competence of four hundred marks a year, enough for the immediate needs of Falstaff, who is pressed for the thousand pounds he still owes to a belligerent Justice Shallow. The hint in Falstaff's letter to Hal at 2.2.97–9 – 'Be not too familiar with Poins ... he swears thou art to marry his sister Nell' – is duly taken into account: Eleanor Poins is presented as the 'quondam Mistress to the King'. But she is a loyal mistress who, in spite of having been rejected, helps to unmask the plot against Henry. In fact, Cambridge, Scroop and Grey, counting on Falstaff's resentment at *his* rejection, had hired him as the king's assassin, but at the very last moment the knight, on his knees, offers his dagger to Henry, in a scene curiously reminiscent of that in *Famous Victories* where Prince Hal behaves in the same way with Henry IV. In the preface the author protests that the play was never meant for performance, but the piece has some merit, and Garrick was right in considering it 'a very good imitation of Shakespeare', though 'there would be some risque in bringing on so many of Shakespeare's known characters [besides Shallow, there are Hostess Quickly and Doll, Bardolph, Pistol and even Master Slender from *The Merry Wives of Windsor*] in a new piece'.[2]

There is hardly an un-Shakespearean word or situation in the compilation published in 1829 by the London lawyer Charles Short under the title *The Life and Humours of Falstaff*. It puts together in sequence the Falstaff scenes in both parts of *Henry IV*, concluding with the news of his illness and death from *Henry V* 2.1 and 2.3. Apart from some bowdlerisation, the discreet addition of odd connecting lines between scenes and the substitution of the Mayor of London for the Lord Chief Justice, the adaptation is respectful and workmanlike. It avoids the temptation to borrow incongruous bits from *The Merry Wives* – as the pastiche *The Life and Death of Sir John Falstaff* edited in 1923 by Ernest Rhys was to do – and has the merit of restoring the recruiting scene in *Part Two* (3.2) to its proper place, before the Coventry and Shrewsbury battle scenes in *Part One* (4.2, 5.1–3), while the other Shallow scenes (*Part Two* 5.1 and 5.3) are placed immediately after the battle, and before the street and tavern scenes in *Part Two* (1.2, 2.1–2, 2.4). In view of this transposition, Pistol's news in 5.3 must be modified, and Short

---

[1]  See the 'Stage History' in Shaaber's Variorum edition of *Part Two*, pp. 656–9, and that by Harold Child in Dover Wilson's edition of *Part One*, 1946, pp. xxix–xlvi.

[2]  Quoted in the author's preface to *Falstaff's Wedding: A Comedy. Being a Sequel to the Second Part of the Play of King Henry the Fourth. Written in Imitation of Shakespeare, by Mr. Kenrick*, 1760 [though the preface is dated 1 January 1766]. Cornmarket Press Facsimile, 1969.

notes at this point: 'King Henry IV must live a little longer, to introduce the following scenes with effect.'[1]

The one truly successful treatment of the Falstaff saga in this century has been in film form, though retaining its essential theatrical quality: Orson Welles's *Chimes at Midnight* (1966) relies on *Part Two* more than on the other Falstaff plays in order to underline the tragic sadness in the comedy of a declining old man, impersonated with tremendous power by Welles himself.[2] In sharp contrast with it, in Robert Nye's novel *Falstaff* (1976) the figure of the fat knight becomes a mere pretext for an uproarious story in the *Fanny Hill* vein.

## PART TWO ON ITS OWN

Though dominated by Falstaff, *Part Two* is perhaps, among Shakespeare's plays, the one with the widest range of minor or even minimal roles, offering opportunities for short 'turns' to a large number of bit-part actors as well as for collective playing. As such it is suitable, with some bowdlerisation, for school and college performances and youth theatres, and in fact most of its stagings as an independent play, without *Part One*, are enterprises of this nature. The first was in 1801, when Richard Valpy, the headmaster of Reading School, produced with his pupils his own adaptation of the play.[3] Apart from obvious cuts and transpositions, especially in the last act, Valpy's text echoes the preoccupations of the time with the threat of a Napoleonic invasion of the British Isles, so that Prince John's last speech in the play is replaced by:

> Thrice happy land, with ev'ry virtue grac'd,
> Whose sons, inflam'd with gen'rous loyalty,
> Firm in their union, scorn Invasion's boast! –
> Thrice happy King, who, free from Faction's wiles,
> By wisdom guided, and with justice arm'd,
> Reveres the freedom, which supports his throne;
> Whose bliss is founded on the public good;
> Whose strongest bulwark is – his People's Love!           *Exeunt*

In the second half of the nineteenth century the professional theatre too began to appreciate the opportunities offered by *Part Two*. Samuel Phelps, who had won fame as Falstaff in *Part One* at Sadler's Wells in 1846, where he revived the play season after season, was even more successful when in 1853 he staged *Part Two*, in which he doubled the king and Justice Shallow. He repeated the same feat in 1861, and even as late as 1874 in Manchester, but his greatest achievement was in the centenary year 1864, when in March he was Falstaff in *Part One*, and in October both the king and Shallow in *Part Two*. The student dramatic societies of the two major universities each chose *Henry IV* as its

[1] *The Life and Humours of Falstaff; A Comedy formed out of the two parts of Shakespeare's Henry the Fourth, and a few scenes of Henry the Fifth. Compiled, &c. By C.S.*, 1829. Cornmarket Press Facsimile, introduction by John Russell Brown, 1971.

[2] In an interview which appeared in *Sight and Sound* 35 (1966), 158–63, when the film was shown at the Cannes Festival, Welles acknowledged that he 'lost the comedy', because Falstaff is 'the most completely good man in all drama'.

[3] See Peter Davison's introduction to the Cornmarket Press Facsimile reprint (1970) of *The Second Part of King Henry the Fourth, altered from Shakespeare, as it was acted at Reading School, in October, 1801*.

9   Pleasant Doll: Constance Benson in Frank Benson's production at the Memorial Theatre, Stratford-upon-Avon, 1894

first Shakespearean production after its foundation, the OUDS in 1885 and the Cambridge ADC in 1886, but in both cases they gave precedence to the *First Part*.[1] The OUDS made amends some forty years later, in 1926, with a memorable production of *Part Two* on its own, directed by W. Bridges-Adams. The real test of the popularity of *Part Two* with school companies was during the blitz, in 1943, when the King's Scholars of Westminster School staged it at Whitbourne Court, Worcestershire, where they had been evacuated from London. Cambridge had to wait till 1959, when John Barton as a junior don staged both parts for the ADC with student actors Derek Jacobi as Prince Hal, Clive Swift as Falstaff, and Ian McKellen as Justice Shallow.[2]

Three years earlier Michael Croft had founded the Youth Theatre with the support of the boys of Alleyn's School and Dulwich College. Their second production in 1957, after *Henry V*, was *Henry IV Part Two*, and it was so successful that it was revived in 1961 at the Apollo Theatre in London with a cast of over forty: the oldest was Richard Hampton (23) as Prince Hal; David Weston (22) was Falstaff; Paul Hill (21) doubled for Rumour, Doll Tearsheet and Prince John; and Michael Pennington (17) was Warwick.[3]

The real rediscoverer of *Part Two* as an independent play had been Frank Benson, who from 1886 to 1919 was the manager of the Memorial Theatre at Stratford-upon-Avon. *Part Two* without *Part One* was staged in April 1894, with Benson himself as Falstaff and his wife Constance Benson as Doll Tearsheet, a role that until then Victorian moralism had played down. The significance of the role was fully appreciated by the great Max Reinhardt in his famous staging of both parts of *Henry IV* at the Berlin Deutsches Theater in 1912, and again in 1914, with sets and costumes by Ernst Stern: Doll's part was taken by Else Bassermann, with Alessandro Moissi as Prince Hal, Paul Wegener as the king, and Wilhelm Diegelmann as Falstaff.[4]

Benson's production was staged in Stratford year after year, and it is significant that when Shakespeare's histories were put on as a cycle in 1901 and 1906, Benson left *Part One* out, including it instead in another historical cycle, beginning with Marlowe's *Edward II*, in 1905. By 1913 Benson had moved from the role of Falstaff (which was taken over by Louis Calvert) to that of the king.[5] The two parts of *Henry IV* remained great favourites with the Stratford companies under later managements. They were chosen as the opening productions in the newly built Stratford Memorial Theatre in 1932, under the management of W. Bridges-Adams, and distinguished by the haunting rendering of Doll Tearsheet by Dorothy Massingham, as a Nemesis rather than a *Threepenny Opera* whore. A production of both parts, directed by Trevor Nunn for the Royal Shakespeare Company, inaugurated the new Barbican Theatre in London in 1982.

---

[1] Harold Child in Dover Wilson (ed.), *1H4*, p. xli.
[2] Ian McKellen, 'An actor's life for me', *Observer*, 31 August 1986, p. 17.
[3] Information from the Apollo Theatre Shakespeare Season programme, August 1961.
[4] See the illustrated catalogue of the exhibition *Max Reinhardt und Shakespeare* at the Berlin Deutsche Akademie der Künste on the 25th anniversary of Reinhardt's death (1968).
[5] For Stratford performances see Michael Mullin with Karen Morris Muriello, compilers, *Theatre at Stratford-upon-Avon: A Catalogue-Index of Productions*, 2 vols., 1980.

10   Haunting Doll: Dorothy Massingham in W. Bridges-Adams's inaugural production at the newly built
Shakespeare Memorial Theatre, 1932

11    Laurence Olivier as Justice Shallow at the New Theatre, 1945

NEW WAYS WITH *HENRY IV*

From the 1930s onwards, *Part Two* was hardly ever performed in isolation. It was increasingly seen as part of a cycle and frequently accompanied not only by *Part One*, but also by *Henry V*. There was a tendency to underline more and more the choral qualities of these plays, as well as to offer to star performers the opportunity of 'doubling across' the plays by taking different parts in each. This was not the case in the 1935 Old Vic production, which staked everything on Robert Donat's Prince Hal, but it was eminently true of the next production, at the New Theatre in 1945, when Laurence Olivier, after a

12   Act 5, Scene 5: the rejection scene. Anthony Quayle as Falstaff and Richard Burton as the king in Michael Redgrave's production, Stratford-upon-Avon, 1951

fiery rendering of Hotspur in *Part One*, created the most memorable and endearing Justice Shallow of this century,[1] playing against the formidable Falstaff of Ralph Richardson.

The choral quality emerged when the four plays, from *Richard II* to *Henry V*, were staged as a sequence at Stratford in 1951, in a permanent setting devised by Tanya Moiseiwitsch. The Memorial Theatre was under the management of Anthony Quayle, who established himself as one of the great Falstaffs of this century – a position confirmed by his performance in the otherwise undistinguished BBC television production of the two parts of *Henry IV* directed by David Giles in 1979. But the highlight of the 1951 Stratford *Part Two*, direct by Michael Redgrave, was the deathbed scene, which revealed the talent of young Richard Burton as the prince, playing against Harry Andrews as the king.[2] The presentation of the histories as a cycle made Kenneth Tynan suspect at the time that the *Henrys* were 'great public plays in which a whole nation is under scrutiny and on trial'. The full realisation of this came to him when he saw Douglas Seale's production of the two parts of *Henry IV* at the Old Vic in 1955. Seale's

---

[1]   For Kenneth Tynan, Olivier's Shallow was 'a crapulous, paltering scarecrow of a man, withered up like the slough of a snake' but with 'quick, commiserating eyes and the kind of delight in dispensing food and drink that one associates with a favourite aunt' (Kathleen Tynan, *The Life of Kenneth Tynan*, 1987, p. 53).

[2]   Sally Beauman, *The Royal Shakespeare Company. A History of Ten Decades*, 1983, p. 209. See also Micheline Steinberg, *Flashback. A Pictorial History 1879–1979*, RSC publications, 1985.

13   Act 3, Scene 2: Falstaff (Hugh Griffith) enrols his ragamuffins; Mouldy (David Warner) sits disconsolately upstage. From the 1964 centenary production of the histories at Stratford, directed by Peter Hall, John Barton and Clifford Williams

approach to the histories (he had already directed the three parts of *Henry VI*) marks an important turning-point in Shakespearean productions. The stress moves from individual performances to the total impact of the plays as vehicles of a problematic view of history: 'A way of life is facing dissolution; we are in at the deathbed of the Middle Ages. How shall the crisis be faced?' Significantly, the actors who received most praise from Tynan were Rachel Roberts as Mistress Quickly, Paul Daneman doubling Shallow and Worcester in *Part One*, and John Neville as Pistol, but not as Hotspur.[1]

A real *tour de force* was the production by the Royal Shakespeare Company, on the occasion of the Shakespeare centenary in 1964, of both tetralogies as a single sequence, albeit the three parts of *Henry VI* were reduced to two under the titles of *Henry VI* and *Edward IV*; they had been produced the year before as 'The Wars of the Roses'. Peter Hall, John Barton and Clifford Williams joined forces to direct the seven plays in the austere, metallic movable setting devised by John Bury. It was this setting, as much as the hay-carts which were dragged on and off the stage, that made the critics speak of a Brechtian reading of English history. There was ample scope for 'doubling across': David Warner, in between his neurotic Richard II and pathetic Henry VI, was able to sketch in a melancholy Mouldy, while Ian Holm transferred the ambiguous irony of

[1]   Kenneth Tynan, 'Henry IV, Parts I and II at the Old Vic' (1955), in his *A View of the English Stage 1944–1963*, 1975, pp. 152–4.

Prince Hal/Henry to his Richard III. Within the framework of this troubled iron age, Hugh Griffith's Falstaff was crafty and aggressive, while Roy Dotrice tried to repeat Olivier's achievement by doubling Hotspur and Shallow.[1]

The new way with the histories, intended to underline their relevance to our time, was more apparent in the show devised by John Barton in 1970 for the RSC's Theatregoround under the title *When Thou Art King*. Directed by Barton himself with Gareth Morgan, it conflated the two parts of *Henry IV* and *Henry V*, with extensive rearrangements and interpolations, as well as massive cuts in the texts. The limited number of actors in the cast forced a revival of the Elizabethan art of doubling, so that, for instance, in *The Rejection of Falstaff* (Barton's title for his 75-minute adaptation of *Part Two*) Jeffery Dench was in rapid succession Snare, Pistol and the king, after having appeared as Gadshill in *The Battle of Shrewsbury* and before becoming the King of France in *The Battle of Agincourt*: Janet Key doubled Lady Percy and Doll Tearsheet, fulfilling at last what must have been Shakespeare's original intention. Brewster Mason was Falstaff, and he repeated his gentlemanly interpretation of the fat knight when the full texts of the two parts of *Henry IV*, together with *Henry V*, were staged in 1975 by another of the leading RSC directors, Terry Hands. (The previous year the same three plays, directed by Kenny McBain, had been taken on tour by the Prospect Theatre Company, which had replaced Theatregoround at the London Round House.) Hands's production was distinguished by Alan Howard's sensitive playing of Prince Hal, while an element of topicality was provided by Pistol (Richard Moore) as a long-haired ruffian out of the student demonstrations of the previous years.

In the next RSC production of the two parts, directed by Trevor Nunn for the opening of their new Barbican Theatre in London in 1982, the fact that *Henry IV* is not Falstaff's play or a private generational conflict, but represents a crisis in the values of a whole nation and age, was powerfully conveyed through the possibility offered by the multi-level permanent set designed by John Napier. It allowed for the constant presence on stage throughout both parts of the 'people', as involved witnesses or unwilling partakers of the disease that afflicted the country, while they try to carry on their usual trades.[2]

A complete break with tradition, cutting across all previous attempts at updating, or at least at showing the relevance of Shakespeare's histories to us and our times, came from the Italian eight-actor group Collettivo di Parma. Their *Enrico IV*, first staged in Parma in 1981-2 and taken to the London Riverside Studios the next year, is a rethinking of the meaning of the two plays rolled into one in contemporary terms.[3] The action takes place in a village *osteria* with jukebox, the resort of a group of *vitelloni*, haunted from the start by the pathetic whore Lola (Doll) as a constant reminder of mortality. The soldiers are partly recruited among the audience seated at the *osteria* tables, and trained in the Japanese martial arts, leading to the Gaultree ceremonial slaughter. Rejected Falstaff,

---

[1] T. F. Wharton, *Henry the Fourth Parts 1 and 2. Text and Performance*, 1983; pp. 44–80 are a comparative analysis of the leading performers in the RSC productions of 1964, 1975, and 1982, as well as in the 1979 BBC television production.

[2] See the review article by R. L. Smallwood, 'Henry IV, Parts 1 and 2 at the Barbican Theatre' (*CQ* 25 (1983)), included in D. Bevington (ed.), *Henry the Fourth Parts 1 and 2. Critical Essays*, 1986, pp. 423–30.

[3] Luigi Allegri, *Tre Shakespeare della Compagnia del Collettivo/Teatro Due*, Florence 1983; pp. 63–80 discuss in detail the staging of the play.

14 Act 5, Scene 4: Gemma Jones as Doll and Miriam Karlin as Mistress Quickly in the seldom performed confrontation with the beadles. From the opening production by the Royal Shakespeare Company at the Barbican, directed by Trevor Nunn, 1982

the ageing rowdy, tries desperately to cajole members of the audience into lending him money, while skinhead Hal, who has learnt the ways of the world, stands absolutely still under a spotlight far upstage, a monument to himself, singing under his breath Peachum's song from *The Threepenny Opera*. The effect of the whole performance has been described as 'hypnotic',[1] conveying an unequivocal message even to audiences who do not understand a word of the actors' colloquial Italian.

The Collettivo di Parma's was a radical rethinking of the play, made possible by the fact that it was performed in another language, but it was rich in suggestions for the treatment of the basic situations in later productions of the original Shakespeare texts. The motor-bicycles replacing the horses in the Gadshill robbery turned up again in the much discussed and praised production of *Part One* directed by Michael Edwards and designed by Norvid Jenkins Roos at the University of California at Santa Cruz in 1984, with Tony Church as Falstaff, the ageing leader of a gang of punks, and Paul Whitworth as a long-haired Hal in tight-fitting shiny trousers, who later turns into a crew-cut GI in

[1] From Michael Coveney's review in the *Financial Times*, quoted in Allegri's book; see Coveney in *Plays and Players*, February 1983, p. 40.

15  Act 4, Scene 1: the slaughter at Gaultree. Gian Paolo Bocelli, Roberto Abati, Bruno Stori and Marcello Vazzoler in the production by the Collettivo Teatro Due di Parma, 1981–2

combat fatigues.[1] Unfortunately, *Part Two* could not be staged: a text reduced by two-thirds was given as a studio reading, preserving most of Hal's lines, but only half of Falstaff's, though Tony Church's doubling Falstaff with the king threw new light on the father–son relationship in the play.

The new way with Shakespeare's histories, cutting across barriers of time and culture in order to see them as permanently valid statements about man's political as well as existential condition, inspired Ariane Mnouchkine's French production of *Part One* for the Théâtre du Soleil, which impressed audiences by its originality when it was staged later at the Olympic Arts Festival in Los Angeles in 1984. It is significant that the latest major venture in staging Shakespeare, the English Shakespeare Company founded in 1986 by Michael Bogdanov and Michael Pennington, should have chosen the *Henry*s (*IV* and *V*) as its first production. Though the cuts in the texts are hardly more numerous than in 'straight' performances, the whole perspective is new, and Pennington acknowledges that the main lesson comes from continental Europe: 'The most exciting work in Europe comes in re-defining classical or Shakespeare, because it's done so much more clearly there. There are no divisions between the politicians and the artist – somebody

[1]  See May Judith Dunbar's review in *SQ* 35 (1984), 475–8, and Alan C. Dessen, 'Staging Shakespeare's history plays in 1984: a tale of three Henrys', *SQ* 36 (1985), 71–9.

16  Act 5, Scene 5: Gigi dall'Aglio as Falstaff pleads with the audience, while far upstage a monumental Henry sings Peachum's song from Brecht's *Threepenny Opera*, in the production by the Collettivo Teatro Due di Parma, 1981–2

17  Jenny Quayle as Doll Tearsheet and John Woodvine as Falstaff in the English Shakespeare Company
production of the *Henry* plays, directed by Michael Bogdanov, 1986–7

who is concerned with the arts does not operate in a ghetto, but is somebody who is concerned socially, culturally, and aesthetically to the life of his country as a whole.'¹ Bogdanov's direction creates a sequence of impressive images in which what counts is not historical time but the immediacy of communication: Edwardian politicians jostle with the inevitable punks, led throughout by a spike-haired Gadshill and a leather mini-skirted Doll, and it does not seem incongruous to see among them a Falstaff in chequered trousers dating back to the 1940s. The transposition of the last two scenes of *Part One* is psychologically a master touch: Hal has to endure the king's scorn when he refrains from exposing Falstaff's lie about the killing of Hotspur. The whole of *Part Two* is conditioned by Hal's resentment at his father's and Falstaff's attitudes, and this accounts for the cold savagery of the final rejection of Falstaff, in a climate of ruthlessness prepared by the Gaultree episode, when Prince John's sinister thugs mow down the Archbishop and the other rebels on the stage. The intensive doubling, limiting the number of actors appearing in the three plays, was no mean achievement: it is revealing to see John Woodvine's superb Falstaff, 'sly as a fox and warm as a coal-fire',² turn into the correct and businesslike Chorus in *Henry V* – the natural unwilling witness of History becomes the official political commentator.

¹ Interviewed by Peter Roberts for *Plays International*, October 1986, p. 20. (I am grateful to Janice Fairholm of the Cambridge University Library for a number of reviews and other items on these plays that she procured for me from newspapers and periodicals.)
² Michael Billington, *Guardian*, 23 March 1987.

# NOTE ON THE TEXT

This edition is firmly based on the text of the 1600 quarto (Q) of the play, the only one printed before its inclusion in the First Folio of 1623 (F). It is generally acknowledged that the copy for the 1600 printing was Shakespeare's own foul papers, so that the text reflects much more closely than F the author's own choices in matters of spelling, punctuation, colloquial forms and stage practice. For this reason editorial interference especially in punctuation and in integration of stage directions has been kept to a minimum. The New Cambridge Shakespeare use of commas before vocatives is a grammatical convention and they do not require pauses in speech. The eight passages of some length present only in F have been reintegrated into the text, while the odd additions of words or half-lines for the sake of metre characteristic of the Folio text have not been accepted, and are recorded in the collation and Commentary. The present editor does not share the view of the Oxford Shakespeare editors (1986), according to whom the longer passages missing from Q were later authorial additions to the text, so that F, including the formal regularisation of certain passages, represents Shakespeare's second thoughts for an improved version of the play. The case for considering that the longer omissions in Q are the result of theatrical expediency and censorship, and for substantially accepting Prosser's view that the other 'improvements' in the Folio text are scribal or compositorial sophistications, is argued in the Textual Analysis.

The ample use of colloquial forms in Q (notably 'a' for 'he' and 'and' for 'if') has been preserved and noted in the Commentary only when it could cause misunderstandings; F variants are collated, except for the most common contractions, such as 'I'll' for 'I will'. Punctuation variants are collated only when relevant to the meaning; a separate case is represented by the compositor's misreading of the copy, taking a final 's' for a comma or vice versa, as at 1.1.44, where 'forwards' is misread 'forward,' and at 2.4.87 SD, where Q misreads *Bardolfe, boy* as *Bardolfes boy*, and F makes confusion worse confounded by improving it as *Bardolph and his Boy*.

The numerous press corrections in the extant copies of Q have been studied by T. L. Berger and G. W. Williams ('Variants in the quarto of Shakespeare's *2 Henry IV*', *The Library* 6th ser. 3 (1981), 108–18), and are collated – 'corr.' indicating the corrected and 'uncorr.' the uncorrected form – only in case of ambiguity. Qa and Qb designate the first and second state respectively of quire E of Q: out of 23 whole or fragmentary extant copies of Q only 11 include 3.1 as part of that quire. The omission of the scene from the first printing of Q entailed, in the second printing, the replacement of E3 and E4 of Qa with a new quire, signed E3–E6, that is to say a resetting of those sections of the play included in the original E3–E4 (2.4.312–20 and 3.2.1–83 in the present edition); variants in the two settings of these passages are collated, but the sigla Qa and Qb are not used elsewhere in the collation.

Original spellings have been modernised in lemmas, but retained in the section of the collation following the square bracket, including the use of 'i' for 'j' and of 'u' for medial 'v'. The same applies to quotations from other works in the Commentary, except for citations from Shakespeare and some other major dramatists, where the old spelling is retained only when necessary to emphasise particular points.

The Folio division of Act 4 into two scenes has been retained; an additional series of marginal line numbers in brackets has been introduced for ease of reference to modern editions and concordances which divide the act into five scenes.

# The Second Part of
# King Henry IV

# LIST OF CHARACTERS

RUMOUR, *the presenter*

KING HENRY IV
PRINCE HENRY, *afterwards crowned King Henry V*
PRINCE JOHN OF LANCASTER
HUMPHREY [DUKE] OF GLOUCESTER ⎫ *sons to Henry IV and brethren to Henry V*
THOMAS [DUKE] OF CLARENCE ⎭

[EARL OF] NORTHUMBERLAND
*The* ARCHBISHOP *of York*
[LORD] MOWBRAY[, *Earl Marshal*]
[LORD] HASTINGS
LORD BARDOLPH ⎬ *opposed against King Henry IV*
TRAVERS
MORTON
[*Sir John*] COLEVILE

[*Earl of*] WARWICK
[*Earl of*] WESTMORELAND
[*Earl of*] SURREY
GOWER ⎬ *of the king's party*
HARCOURT
LORD CHIEF JUSTICE
[*Sir John* BLUNT]

POINS
[*Sir John*] FALSTAFF
BARDOLPH
PISTOL ⎬ *irregular humorists*
PETO
[*Falstaff's*] PAGE

[*Robert*] SHALLOW ⎬ *both country justices*
SILENCE

DAVY, *servant to Shallow*
FANG *and* ⎬ *two sergeants*
SNARE

[*Ralph*] MOULDY
[*Simon*] SHADOW
[*Thomas*] WART ⎬ *country soldiers*
[*Francis*] FEEBLE
[*Peter*] BULLCALF

DRAWERS[: FRANCIS, WILL *and another*]
BEADLES

[*Three*] GROOMS
[*The Lord Chief Justice's* SERVANT]
[*A* PORTER]
[*A* MESSENGER]

[LADY NORTHUMBERLAND,] *Northumberland's wife*
[LADY PERCY,] *Percy's widow*
HOSTESS QUICKLY

DOLL TEARSHEET

[*The*] EPILOGUE

[*Officers, musicians, lords, a captain, soldiers, another page*]

**Note**
The list is reproduced (with additions in square brackets) from F, where it occupies a whole page at the end of the play-text. There is no list in Q.

# THE SECOND PART OF HENRY THE FOURTH, CONTINUING TO HIS DEATH, AND CORONATION OF HENRY THE FIFTH

### INDUCTION

*Enter* RUMOUR *painted full of tongues*

RUMOUR  Open your ears; for which of you will stop
    The vent of hearing when loud Rumour speaks?
    I from the Orient to the drooping West
    (Making the wind my post-horse) still unfold
    The acts commencèd on this ball of earth;       5
    Upon my tongues continual slanders ride,
    The which in every language I pronounce,
    Stuffing the ears of men with false reports:
    I speak of peace while covert enmity,
    Under the smile of safety, wounds the world;      10
    And who but Rumour, who but only I,
    Make fearful musters, and prepared defence,
    Whiles the big year, swoll'n with some other grief,
    Is thought with child by the stern tyrant War?

Title CONTINUING ... FIFTH] Q; Containing his Death: and the Coronation of King Henry the Fift. F    **Induction**]*Actus Primus.*
*Scæna Prima.* / INDVCTION. F; *not in* Q    0 SD *painted ... tongues.*] *painted ... Tongues:* Q; *not in* F    1 SH RUMOUR] *Capell; not in* Q, F
6 tongues] Q; Tongue F    8 men] Q; them F    13 Whiles] Q; Whil'st F    13 grief] Q; griefes F    14 tyrant War?] Q; Tyrant, Warre, F

### Induction

INDUCTION A variant of 'Prologue', not merely announcing the theme of the play and inviting attention, but leading directly into the action.

0 SD The allegorical figure of 'Report' in a court pageant presented in 1519 before Henry VIII entered 'apparelled in crimson sattin full of toongs' (Holinshed, III, 849), and Thomas More described 'Fame' in a pageant of his own devising, *c.* 1492 as 'with tonges compassed all rounde' (More, *English Works,* 1557, sig. iiiᵛ); the costume had become traditional by 1553, when the Revels Office paid 'for painting of a coat and cap with eyes, tongues and ears for Fame': Rumour is the male negative incarnation of Fame, who, according to Virgil (*Aeneid* IV), reported indifferently both true and false deeds. The idea of the false report seems prompted by Holinshed (III, 525)

on the Countess of Oxford's secretary spreading the rumour that Richard II was alive in 1404, in Henry IV's reign, a passage closely echoed here; see Appendix 1, p. 204 below.

3 **drooping West** Compare John Donne, 'The Good Morrow', 18: 'without declining West'.

4 **post-horse** A horse for hire at a stage inn to carry post or travellers; the proverb 'a false report rides post' (Tilley R83) is recorded only from 1659.

4 **still** ever, continually (the usual meaning at the time; see 19).

5 **acts** (1) actions, (2) divisions of a play.

12 **fearful ... defence** enrolment of soldiers and preparation of defence prompted by fear; preparations against a Spanish invasion were made in England in 1596–7.

13 **big** pregnant.

And no such matter. Rumour is a pipe                          15
Blown by surmises, Jealousy's conjectures,
And of so easy and so plain a stop
That the blunt monster with uncounted heads,
The still discordant wav'ring multitude,
Can play upon it. But what need I thus                        20
My well-known body to anatomise
Among my household? Why is Rumour here?
I run before King Harry's victory,
Who in a bloody field by Shrewsbury
Hath beaten down young Hotspur and his troops,                25
Quenching the flame of bold rebellion
Even with the rebels' blood. But what mean I
To speak so true at first? My office is
To noise abroad that Harry Monmouth fell
Under the wrath of noble Hotspur's sword,                     30
And that the king before the Douglas' rage
Stooped his anointed head as low as death.
This have I rumoured through the peasant towns
Between that royal field of Shrewsbury
And this worm-eaten hold of raggèd stone,                     35
Where Hotspur's father, old Northumberland,

15 matter. Rumour] matter Rumour Q; matter? *Rumour*, F   15 pipe] Pipe F; pipe, Q   16 Jealousy's conjectures,] *This edn, Oxford, conj. Shaaber;* Ielousies coniectures, Q; Ielousies, Coniectures, F   19 discordant wav'ring] Q; discordant, wauering F   21 My ... body] F; (My wel knowne body) Q   27 rebels'] *Theobald,* rebels Q, F, rebel's *Globe*   28 first?] F; first: Q   34 that] Q; the F   35 hold] *Theobald;* hole Q, F   36 Where] F; When Q

15 **And ... matter**. Though completing the preceding interrogative sentence, the affirmative tone suggested by Q's punctuation makes the clause dramatically more effective.

15 **pipe** recorder; a wooden instrument, contrasted with the trumpet or clarion with which Fame in its positive aspect was traditionally represented.

16 **surmises ... conjectures** Surmises, that is to say rumours, are the conjectures prompted by Jealousy – another name for Envy, a traditional 'sin' personified in Moralities and Interludes; 'surmise' and 'conjecture' (this time with 'expectation') are found again in 1.3.23, and hardly anywhere else in Shakespeare. On the restoration of Q reading here see Melchiori, 'Jealousy'.

17 **easy ... stop** i.e. the pipe's fingering is straightforward, its vents easily stopped; compare *Ham.* 3.2.70–1: 'they are not a pipe for Fortune's finger / To sound what stop she please', and the exchange between Hamlet and Guildenstern later in the scene (350–62).

18 **blunt** obtuse, stupid (*OED* sv *adj* 1).

18–19 **monster ... multitude** Proverbial (Tilley M1308); see *Cor.* 2.3.16–17: 'the many-headed multitude', and 4.1.1–2: 'the beast / With many heads'; also *R2* 2.2.129: 'the wavering commons'.

22 **my household** the playhouse audience.

23–7 A summary of the events in *1H4* 5.3–4 for the benefit of the new audience; Globe's reading 'rebel's' (= Hotspur's) is defensible but unnecessary.

29 **Monmouth** Prince Hal was born at Monmouth in Wales.

33 **peasant towns** rustic villages (derogatory; see 'peasant' in *Ham.* 2.2.550).

35 **hold** castle, fortification; the reading 'hole' of Q and F is defensible, but Theobald's emendation is sound in view of the e/d confusion in Elizabethan script, and, more, because this line aims at establishing in the audience's mind the setting for the next scene.

36 **Where** In Q 'When', another easy confusion, suggesting reduced legibility of the foul papers in these lines.

Lies crafty-sick. The posts come tiring on,
And not a man of them brings other news
Than they have learnt of me. From Rumour's tongues
They bring smooth comforts false, worse than true wrongs.　40

*Exit*

1.1 *Enter the* LORD BARDOLPH *at one door*[, *and the* PORTER *at another*]

LORD BARDOLPH　Who keeps the gate here, ho? Where is the earl?
PORTER　What shall I say you are?
LORD BARDOLPH　　　　　　　　　Tell thou the earl
That the Lord Bardolph doth attend him here.
PORTER　His worship is walked forth into the orchard,
Please it your honour knock but at the gate,　　　　　　　5
And he himself will answer.

*Enter the Earl* [*of*] NORTHUMBERLAND

LORD BARDOLPH　　　　　　　Here comes the earl.

[*Exit Porter*]

NORTHUMBERLAND　What news, Lord Bardolph? Every minute now
Should be the father of some stratagem;
The times are wild: contention, like a horse
Full of high feeding, madly hath broke loose,　　　　　　10

---

**40** SD] F; *exit Rumours.* Q　**Act 1, Scene 1**　1.1] *Scena Secunda.* F; *not in* Q　0 SD *the ... door, and the* PORTER] *the ... doore.* Q; *Lord Bardolfe, and the Porter.* F　0 SD *at another*] *This edn; not in* Q; *above.* / *Singer² (subst., conj. Collier)*　1 ho? Where] Q, *hoa?* / *Where* F, *ho?* [*Enter Porter*] *Where* Dyce　6 SD.2 *Exit Porter*] *Dyce; not in* Q, F　7 SH NORTHUMBERLAND] *Nor., North.* F; *Earle.* Q (*throughout scene*)

---

**37 crafty-sick** feigning illness; in *1H4* 4.4.16–17, where illness is given as the reason for Northumberland's absence at Shrewsbury, there is no suggestion of craftiness.

**37 tiring on** (1) exhausting their horses, (2) at tearing speed.

**40 smooth comforts false** 'false' is transposed for emphasis, to balance the oxymoron 'true wrongs'.

**Act 1, Scene 1**
**1.1** The location (Northumberland's decaying Warkworth Castle) is clear from Rumour's words in Induction 35–7.

**0 SD LORD BARDOLPH** In Holinshed, Northumberland's closest confederate, sharing his final fate (see 4.2.97–9). Presumably when changing the name of Oldcastle's companion from Sir John Russell to Bardolph in *Part One* (see pp. 5 and 15 above),

Shakespeare did not intend to use this section of Holinshed's chronicle in *Part Two*.

**0 SD at one door** Q's reading implies the nearly simultaneous entrance of a different character at another door. Most modern edns place the Porter's entrance after 'ho?' in 1, but the first six words may be shouted from 'within', especially if one actor is doubling Rumour and Lord Bardolph, so that he and the Porter would enter at the same time from opposite doors; see above, pp. 15–16 and p. 36 n. 1.

**6 SD** Northumberland's entrance from a third direction does not give Lord Bardolph time to go and knock at the gate.

**7 Every minute now** Introducing the basic Time theme; see B. T. Spencer, '2H4 and the theme of time', *UTQ* 13 (1943–4), 394–9, and L. C. Knights, *Some Shakespearean Themes*, 1959, pp. 45–64.

**8 stratagem** violent deed (*OED* sv 3).

**10 high feeding** too rich food (*OED* High *adj* 8).

And bears down all before him.

LORD BARDOLPH                                    Noble earl,
I bring you certain news from Shrewsbury.

NORTHUMBERLAND  Good, and God will.

LORD BARDOLPH                          As good as heart can wish:
The king is almost wounded to the death,
And, in the fortune of my lord your son,                                    15
Prince Harry slain outright, and both the Blunts
Killed by the hand of Douglas. Young Prince John
And Westmoreland and Stafford fled the field,
And Harry Monmouth's brawn, the hulk Sir John,
Is prisoner to your son. O, such a day,                                    20
So fought, so followed, and so fairly won,
Came not till now to dignify the times
Since Caesar's fortunes.

NORTHUMBERLAND                    How is this derived?
Saw you the field? Came you from Shrewsbury?

LORD BARDOLPH  I spake with one, my lord, that came from thence,    25

*Enter* TRAVERS

A gentleman well bred, and of good name,
That freely rendered me these news for true.

NORTHUMBERLAND  Here comes my servant Travers, who I sent
On Tuesday last to listen after news.

LORD BARDOLPH  My lord, I over-rode him on the way,                  30
And he is furnished with no certainties
More than he haply may retail from me.

---

13 God] Q; heauen F    25 SD] *Placed as* Q; *after 29,* F; *after 27,* Capell; *after 33,* Pope    28 who] Q; whom F

---

13 **and** Current at the time for 'if'; see Abbott 101.
16 **both the Blunts** The death of Sir Walter Blunt is staged in *1H4* 5.1.1–13, but Daniel (*Civil Wars*, III, st. 112) adds 'Another of that forward name [Blunt] and race / In that hotte worke his valiant life bestowes, / Who bare the standard of the king that day.' The death of *both* Blunts is intended rather as another of Rumour's lies or half-truths, since 'an English knight, one sir Iohn Blunt' is the brave defender of an English fortress in France in 1412 (Holinshed, III, 540, I, 51), and figures in the Q version of this play at 3.1.31 SD, 4.1.424 and 5.2.41 SD.
18 **Stafford** The death, not the flight, of the Earl of Stafford is reported in *1H4* 5.1.7–9.
19 **Harry … John** The first allusion to Falstaff: 'brawn' = 'fattened swine or boar' (*OED* sv *sb* 4);

'hulk' = a large merchant ship, hence 'an unwieldy person'; see 2.4.52.
21 The triple alliteration evokes Caesar's (see 23) *Veni, vidi, vici* (I came, saw, overcame), quoted by Falstaff at 4.1.391–2.
25 SD It is important that Travers's entrance should occur at this point (as in Q), in time to overhear Lord Bardolph's statements that he must contradict. His name has been linked with his task of 'traversing' Lord Bardolph's report.
28 **who** Used by Shakespeare also for the object form (Abbott 274).
30 **over-rode** overtook (*OED* Over-ride *v* 4); not, as for Wilson, equivalent of 'out-rode' at 36.
32 **haply** perhaps.

NORTHUMBERLAND Now Travers, what good tidings comes with you?
TRAVERS My lord, Sir John Umfrevile turned me back
    With joyful tidings, and, being better horsed,     35
    Out-rode me. After him came spurring hard
    A gentleman, almost forspent with speed,
    That stopped by me to breathe his bloodied horse.
    He asked the way to Chester, and of him
    I did demand what news from Shrewsbury:     40
    He told me that rebellion had bad luck,
    And that young Harry Percy's spur was cold.
    With that he gave his able horse the head,
    And bending forwards struck his armèd heels
    Against the panting sides of his poor jade     45
    Up to the rowel head, and starting so
    He seemed in running to devour the way,
    Staying no longer question.
NORTHUMBERLAND           Ha? Again:
    Said he young Harry Percy's spur was cold?
    Of Hotspur, Coldspur? That rebellion     50
    Had met ill luck?
LORD BARDOLPH         My lord, I'll tell you what:
    If my young lord your son have not the day,
    Upon mine honour, for a silken point
    I'll give my barony, never talk of it.
NORTHUMBERLAND Why should that gentleman that rode by Travers     55
    Give then such instances of loss?
LORD BARDOLPH                Who he?

---

33 with] Q; frō F   34 Umfrevile] Q; *Vmfreuill* F   36 hard] Q; head F   41 bad] Q; ill F   44 forwards] forward, Q, F   44 armèd] Q; able F   48 Ha? Again:] Q *subst.*, F; Ha! Again? *Capell*; Ha? Again. F2; Ha? Again! *Wilson*   53 honour, . . . point] F; honor . . . point, Q   55 should that] Q; should the F   56 Who he?] Q; Who, he? F

33 **comes** A singular form for the plural, common in Shakespeare (Abbott 333). 'Tidings' could be taken as singular like 'news', but at 31 'news' was treated as plural.

34 **Sir John Umfrevile** Not a 'fossil' of the name given originally to Lord Bardolph, as Wilson suggests, but a reference to the 'gentleman well bred, and of good name' mentioned by him at 26; see Melchiori, 'Umfrevile', pp. 203–4. The name was picked out at random from Holinshed, III, 336–7, where Sir Robert Umfrevill and his nephew Gilbert are mentioned in the reign of Henry IV; actually Gilbert Umfrevile's widow became the second wife of Northumberland.

36 **Out-rode me** Left me behind, taking another direction.

37 **forspent** exhausted.

38 **bloodied** covered with blood from the spurs.

43 **able** vigorous (*OED* sv 5).

44 **armèd** with spurs; F's 'able' was picked from the previous line.

46 **rowel head** The spiked wheel at the end of the spur.

48 **Ha? Again:** Exclamation and question marks are interchangeable in Elizabethan orthography; the choice is left to the actor.

49–50 The play on hot/cold is from Daniel, *Civil Wars*, III, st. 114.

53 **point** lace for tying garments; hence 'worthless thing'.

56 **instances** 'evidence' rather than 'samples'.

He was some hilding fellow that had stol'n
The horse he rode on, and, upon my life,
Spoke at a venture. Look, here comes more news.

*Enter* MORTON

NORTHUMBERLAND  Yea, this man's brow, like to a title-leaf,          60
    Foretells the nature of a tragic volume:
    So looks the strond whereon the imperious flood
    Hath left a witnessed usurpation.
    Say, Morton, didst thou come from Shrewsbury?

MORTON  I ran from Shrewsbury, my noble lord,                        65
    Where hateful death put on his ugliest mask
    To fight our party.

NORTHUMBERLAND          How doth my son, and brother?
    Thou tremblèst, and the whiteness in thy cheek
    Is apter than thy tongue to tell thy errand.
    Even such a man, so faint, so spiritless,                     70
    So dull, so dead in look, so woe-begone,
    Drew Priam's curtain in the dead of night,
    And would have told him half his Troy had burnt:
    But Priam found the fire ere he his tongue,
    And I my Percy's death ere thou report'st it.                 75
    This thou wouldst say: 'Your son did thus and thus;
    Your brother thus; so fought the noble Douglas – '
    Stopping my greedy ear with their bold deeds.
    But in the end, to stop my ear indeed,
    Thou hast a sigh to blow away this praise,                    80
    Ending with 'brother, son, and all are dead'.

MORTON  Douglas is living, and your brother, yet;

---

59 Spoke] Q; Speake F; Spake F2–4   59 a venture] a venter Q; aduenture F   59 SD] *Placed as* Q, F; *after* venture *Sisson*   62 strond]
Q, F; strand *Dyce*   62 whereon] Q; when F   64 Morton] F, Mourton Q   65 SH MORTON] F *(Mor.)*, Mour. Q *(throughout)*
68 tremblèst] Q; trembl'st F   77 Douglas – ] *Johnson subst.*; Dowglas, Q, F   79 my] Q; mine F

57 **hilding** contemptible (*OED* sv *sb* 2).
59 **at a venture** at random.
59 SD MORTON A gentleman, not a servant like
Travers. A. L. Scoufos (*Shakespeare's Typological
Satire*, 1979, pp. 122–5) sees an allusion to the failed
rising of the North against Elizabeth in 1569, led by
the Earl of Northumberland, when the priest
Nicholas Morton, described by Holinshed (III, 1361/
2) as 'an Old English fugitiue and conspirator, was
sent from Rome into the north parts of England ... to
stirre vp the first rebellion there'.
60–1 **like to ... volume** As an example of the

descriptive nature of Elizabethan title pages, see that
of the 1600 quarto of this play (p. 4 above).
62 **strond** Variant form of 'strand', shore.
63 **witnessed usurpation** evidence of the invasion
of the shore left by the retreating tide.
70–3 A confused classical reminiscence: it was not
Priam but Aeneas who had a night vision of Hector's
ghost announcing the burning of Troy (*Aeneid* II,
268–97).
74 **ere ... tongue** before the bringer of the news
had time to speak.

        But for my lord your son –
NORTHUMBERLAND              Why, he is dead?
        See, what a ready tongue suspicion hath:
        He that but fears the thing he would not know        85
        Hath by instinct knowledge from other's eyes
        That what he feared is chanced. Yet speak, Morton,
        Tell thou an earl his divination lies,
        And I will take it for a sweet disgrace,
        And make thee rich for doing me such wrong.        90
MORTON You are too great to be by me gainsaid,
        Your spirit is too true, your fears too certain.
NORTHUMBERLAND Yet for all this, say not that Percy's dead.
        I see a strange confession in thine eye:
        Thou shak'st thy head, and hold'st it fear, or sin        95
        To speak a truth. If he be slain,
        The tongue offends not that reports his death,
        And he doth sin that doth belie the dead,
        Not he which says the dead is not alive.
        Yet the first bringer of unwelcome news        100
        Hath but a losing office, and his tongue
        Sounds ever after as a sullen bell
        Remembered, tolling a departing friend.
LORD BARDOLPH I cannot think, my lord, your son is dead.
MORTON I am sorry I should force you to believe        105
        That which I would to God I had not seen,
        But these mine eyes saw him in bloody state,
        Rendering faint quittance, wearied and out-breathed,
        To Harry Monmouth, whose swift wrath beat down
        The never-daunted Percy to the earth,        110

83 son – ... Why, ... dead?] sonne: / *Earle* Why ... dead? Q, Sonne. / ... Why, ... dead. F   86 other's] *Warburton*, others Q, F;
others' *Capell*; other *Pope*   88 an] Q; thy F   96 slain,] Q; slaine, say so: F   102–3 bell Remembered,] F; bell, Remembred Q   103
tolling] Q; knolling F   106 God] Q; heauen F   109 Harry] Q; Henrie F

83 **he is dead?** Another permissive construction; see 48 n.

86 **other's** 'other' is a collective plural (Abbott 12).

87 **is chanced** has happened.

88–9 To give the lie to a nobleman is normally a bitter offence, but I consider ('take') your telling me that my prediction is false ('divination lies') as a reassuring insult ('sweet disgrace').

94 **strange** reluctant.

95 **fear** fearful act; see 4.2.323.

96 F completes the line with the unnecessary words 'say so': it is the first of many 'regularisations' introduced by the scribe in the copy for F (see Textual Analysis, p. 192 below).

98 **he ... dead** Proverbial (Dent D124.1), hence the use of generic 'that' for specific 'who'.

102 **sullen** of mournful sound; see Sonnet 71.2.

108 **quittance** return (of blows); a financial metaphor.

108 **out-breathed** Shakespeare's coinage, probably not 'out of breath' but 'shorter of breath' than his opponent.

From whence with life he never more sprung up.
In few: his death, whose spirit lent a fire
Even to the dullest peasant in his camp,
Being bruited once, took fire and heat away
From the best-tempered courage in his troops,                    115
For from his metal was his party steeled,
Which once in him abated, all the rest
Turned on themselves, like dull and heavy lead.
And as the thing that's heavy in itself
Upon enforcement flies with greatest speed,                      120
So did our men, heavy in Hotspur's loss,
Lend to this weight such lightness with their fear
That arrows fled not swifter toward their aim
Than did our soldiers, aiming at their safety,
Fly from the field. Then was that noble Worcester                125
So soon ta'en prisoner, and that furious Scot,
The bloody Douglas, whose well-labouring sword
Had three times slain th'appearance of the king,
Gan vail his stomach, and did grace the shame
Of those that turned their backs, and in his flight              130
Stumbling in fear, was took. The sum of all
Is that the king hath won, and hath sent out
A speedy power to encounter you, my lord,
Under the conduct of young Lancaster
And Westmoreland. This is the news at full.                      135
NORTHUMBERLAND  For this I shall have time enough to mourn.
In poison there is physic, and these news,

---

116 metal] mettal Q; Mettle F   126 So] Q; Too F   135 Westmoreland] *Warburton*; Westmerland Q, F *(throughout)*   137 these] Q; this F

---

112 **In few** In a few words (*OED* Few *adj* 1g).

114 **Being bruited once** As soon as the news went round.

116 **metal** (1) mettle, manly vigour, (2) the focus of the weaponry imagery beginning with 'fire and heat' at 114 and continued through 'best-tempered', 'steeled', 'abated' (= 'blunted'), 'lead', 'arrows', to 'aiming' and 'fly' at 125.

120 **Upon enforcement** When force is applied to it.

121 **heavy in** (1) weighed down (as at 119), (2) saddened by; the quibble anticipates the paradox in the next line.

125 **Then was that** A double construction: (1) It happened then that Worcester..., (2) For this reason that noble man was...

126 **So soon** The Q reading is preferable to F's 'Too soon' as linking up with 'then was' = 'It so happened'.

128 See *1H4* 5.3.1–28 and 5.4.25–8, based on Holinshed's report (III, 523/2) that Douglas 'sleu sir Walter Blunt, and three other, apparelled in the kings sute and clothing'.

129 **Gan vail** Began to abate (*OED* Vail *v²* 4a).

129 **stomach** courage.

129 **grace** excuse by sanctioning.

131 **Stumbling ... took** From Holinshed III, 523/2; 'took' = 'taken' (Abbott 343).

137 **physic** medicine; compare *Rom.* 2.3.23–4: 'Within ... this weak flower / Poison hath residence and medicine power.'

Having been well, that would have made me sick,
Being sick, have (in some measure) made me well.
And as the wretch whose fever-weakened joints,                        140
Like strengthless hinges, buckle under life,
Impatient of his fit, breaks like a fire
Out of his keepers' arms, even so my limbs,
Weakened with grief, being now enraged with grief,
Are thrice themselves. Hence therefore thou nice crutch!             145
A scaly gauntlet now with joints of steel
Must glove this hand. And hence thou sickly coif,
Thou art a guard too wanton for the head
Which princes fleshed with conquest aim to hit.
Now bind my brows with iron, and approach                            150
The ragged'st hour that Time and Spite dare bring
To frown upon th'enraged Northumberland!
Let heaven kiss earth! Now let not Nature's hand
Keep the wild flood confined, let Order die,
And let this world no longer be a stage                              155
To feed contention in a lingering act;
But let one spirit of the first-born Cain
Reign in all bosoms, that each heart being set
On bloody courses, the rude scene may end,
And darkness be the burier of the dead.                              160
MORTON   This strainèd passion doth you wrong, my lord.

143 keepers'] keepers Q, F; keeper's *Rowe*    149 fleshed] Q, F; flush'd *Capell*    151 ragged'st] Q, F; rugged'st *Theobald*    155 this]
Q; the F    161] Q; *not in* F    161 SH MORTON] *This edn; Vmfr.* Q; *L. Bard.* / *Pope, et al.; Travers.* / *Capell, et al.*

138 **Having ... that would** That, if I had been
well, would; an inverted construction to match that in
the next line.

141 **under life** under the strain imposed by living.

143 **keepers'** nurses' (*OED* sv *sb* 1e); the lack of
apostrophe in Q and F, common in Elizabethan manuscript and printing, allows for a singular or plural
genitive.

145 **nice** effeminate.

147 **coif** A close-fitting cap tied under the chin
(*OED* sv 1); together with 'crutch', a pointer to stage
costume.

148 **wanton** Like 'nice'; self-indulgent.

149 **fleshed** made eager; dogs were 'fleshed', i.e.
fed with raw meat, to prepare them for the chase.

151 **ragged'st** roughest; compare 'raggèd stone' at
Induction 35.

151 **Time and Spite** Capitalised in Q and therefore not an hendiadys (= spiteful time) but personifications in the Morality tradition; like Jealousy at
Induction 16, Spite is the Vice Envy. They introduce

the traditional metaphor of the world as stage (Tilley
w882) developed at 155–60.

156 **lingering act** (1) long-drawn-out struggle, (2)
prolonged performance (see Induction 5): the
Morality play that Northumberland is staging (155) in
his mind represents the struggle between Time and
Envy (Spite, 151) on the one hand and Nature (153)
and Order (154) on the other.

157 **one** single, all-engulfing.

159 **rude scene** (1) rough (see 'ragged'st', 151) or
violent action, (2) unpolished play.

161 The line is omitted in F, which could make no
sense of the Q SH *Vmfr.* prefixed to it. Some assign it to
Lord Bardolph, assuming 'Umfrevile' to be an earlier
name for him (see 34), others to Travers who, though
present, is mute for the rest of the scene. Both
solutions are unsatisfactory; the reasons for assigning
the line to Morton are given in Melchiori,
'Umfrevile'; see Textual Analysis, pp. 197–9 below.

161 **strainèd passion** forced, unnatural outburst
(*OED* Strained *ppl a*[1] 4, and Passion *sb* 6c).

LORD BARDOLPH  Sweet earl, divorce not wisdom from your honour,
    The lives of all your loving complices
    Lean on your health, the which, if you give o'er
    To stormy passion, must perforce decay.                                        165
MORTON  You cast th'event of war, my noble lord,
    And summed the account of chance before you said
    'Let us make head.' It was your presurmise
    That in the dole of blows your son might drop.
    You knew he walked o'er perils, on an edge,                                     170
    More likely to fall in than to get o'er;
    You were advised his flesh was capable
    Of wounds and scars, and that his forward spirit
    Would lift him where most trade of danger ranged,
    Yet did you say 'Go forth'; and none of this,                                  175
    Though strongly apprehended, could restrain
    The stiff-borne action. What hath then befallen,
    Or what hath this bold enterprise brought forth,
    More than that being which was like to be?
LORD BARDOLPH  We all that are engagèd to this loss                                    180
    Knew that we ventured on such dangerous seas
    That if we wrought out life, 'twas ten to one;
    And yet we ventured, for the gain proposed
    Choked the respect of likely peril feared,

---

162 SH LORD BARDOLPH] Q, F; *Morton. / conj. Capell, et al.*   162 honour,] Q; Honor. F   163 The] *Conj. Daniel; Mour.* The Q;
*Mor.* The F   164 Lean on your] Leane-on your F; Leaue on you Q   166–79] F; *not in* Q   166 SH MORTON] *This edn; not in*
F   170 edge,] *Capell;* edge F   178 hath … brought] F2–4; hath … bring F; did … bring *Riverside;* doth … bring *Oxford*   182
'twas] Q; was F   183 ventured, … proposed] *Capell;* venturd … proposde, Q, F *subst.*

163–5 Both Q and F assign these lines to Morton,
but the comma in Q at the end of 162 suggests that this
is a continuation of the previous speech.

163 **complices** comrades.

164 **Lean on your** The misreading in Q suggests
that the MS. was damaged here, possibly by an
'overflow' of the marks for the omission of 166–79.

166–79 Omitted in Q, though lacking those political
implications that caused the excision of most of
Morton's next speech at 189–209. Probably, since the
latter *had* to go, it seemed expedient to lighten
Morton's part so that the actor could double more
extended roles later in the play.

166 **cast th'event** (1) forecast the result, (2) cal-
culated the risk; the financial metaphor is picked up in
the next line and in 'dole' (169) and 'trade' (174).

168 **make head** raise an army; see *1H4* 3.1.64.

168 **presurmise** presupposition; a Shakespearean
coinage; see 'surmises' at Induction 16 and 1.3.23.

169 **dole** dealing out; with a possible play on
'dole' = dolour, sorrow.

170 **edge** Humphreys suggests a metonymy for
'sword', as in *Cor.* 5.6.113, and sees an allusion to the
romance tradition of magic sword-bridges across
rivers, referred to in *1H4* 1.3.192–3: 'to o'erwalk a
current roaring loud / On the unsteadfast footing of a
spear'.

172 **advised** aware.

172–3 **capable Of** open to.

177 **stiff-borne** (1) firmly pursued, (2) proudly
carried.

180–6 Resuming his argument from 162–5, Lord
Bardolph extends Morton's commercial metaphor
(166–9) to include the voyages of the Elizabethan
Merchant Venturers, referred to in many plays of the
time.

180 **engagèd** involved in (*OED* Engage *v* 13).

182 **wrought out** preserved (*OED* Work *v* 38f).

184 **respect** consideration.

And since we are o'er-set, venture again.                                185
Come, we will all put forth, body and goods.
MORTON  'Tis more than time; and, my most noble lord,
I hear for certain and dare speak the truth:
The gentle Archbishop of York is up
With well appointed powers; he is a man                                  190
Who with a double surety binds his followers.
My lord your son had only but the corpse,
But shadows and the shows of men, to fight.
For that same word, Rebellion, did divide
The action of their bodies from their souls,                             195
And they did fight with queasiness, constrained
As men drink potions, that their weapons only
Seemed on our side; but for their spirits and souls,
This word 'Rebellion' it had froze them up
As fish are in a pond. But now the bishop                                200
Turns insurrection to religion,
Supposed sincere and holy in his thoughts;
He's followed both with body and with mind,
And doth enlarge his rising with the blood
Of fair King Richard scraped from Pomfret stones:                       205
Derives from Heaven his quarrel and his cause,
Tells them he doth bestride a bleeding land
Gasping for life under great Bullingbrook,
And more and less do flock to follow him.
NORTHUMBERLAND  I knew of this before, but, to speak truth,              210

---

186 forth, body] forth; Body, F; forth body Q     188 dare] Q; do F     189–209] F; *not in* Q     192 corpse,] Corpes, F; corpse's *Dyce;*
corpses, *Collier³*     201–2 religion, ... thoughts;] Religion, ... Thoughts; F; religion; ... thoughts, *Rowe, et al., subst.*
208 Bullingbrook] Bullingbrooke F *(throughout play);* Bolingbroke *Pope et al.*

185 **o'er-set** overthrown, set back.
186 **we ... forth** (1) all of us will put forth to sea, (2)
we will stake all.
187–209 Q has only the first two lines of Morton's
speech, making nonsense of the Archbishop's reply;
for the reason see 166–79 n.
189–209 A typical compression of historical time:
the events here related took place in 1405, while the
battle of Shrewsbury was fought on 21 July 1403.
189 **gentle** (1) well-born, of noble blood, (2) of
gentle disposition.
191 **double surety** temporal and spiritual
authority.
192 **corpse** bodies; a collective plural; perhaps F's
'corpes' should be retained as the plural of obsolete
'corp' = 'body'.

202 Repunctuation by modern editors obscures the
basic meaning: the Archbishop honestly believes the
insurrection to be 'holy'; 'supposed' (= held, considered, with no negative overtone) refers to 'insurrection' (201), not to 'He' (203). That he himself is
considered to be in good faith by his followers is
implicit.
204–5 **doth ... stones** attracts followers by recalling the murder in Pontefract Castle (see *R2* 5.5)
of Richard II, whose blood is treated as a holy relic.
207 **bestride** protect; compare Falstaff asking Hal
to bestride him if he should fall down in the battle,
*1H4* 5.1.121–2.
208 **Bullingbrook** Henry IV's title in *R2*.
209 **more and less** nobles and commoners.

> This present grief had wiped it from my mind.
> Go in with me, and counsel every man
> The aptest way for safety and revenge:
> Get posts and letters, and make friends with speed;
> Never so few, and never yet more need.                                    215
>
> *Exeunt*

**1.2** *Enter Sir John* [FALSTAFF], *with his* PAGE *bearing his sword and buckler*

FALSTAFF  Sirrah, you giant, what says the doctor to my water?

PAGE  He said, sir, the water itself was a good healthy water, but for the party that owed it, he might have moe diseases than he knew for.

FALSTAFF  Men of all sorts take a pride to gird at me: the brain of this foolish compounded clay-man is not able to invent anything that    5
intends to laughter more than I invent, or is invented on me; I am not only witty in myself, but the cause that wit is in other men. I do here walk before thee like a sow that hath overwhelmed all her litter but one; if the prince put thee into my service for any other reason than to set me off, why then I have no judgement. Thou whoreson mandrake,    10
thou art fitter to be worn in my cap, than to wait at my heels. I was never manned with an agate till now, but I will inset you neither in

---

215 and] Q; nor F    Act 1, Scene 2    1.2] *Scena Tertia.* F; *not in* Q    0 SD *Enter* SIR JOHN FALSTAFF, ... *buckler*] *Enter sir Iohn alone,* ... *buckler.* Q; *Enter Falstaffe, and Page.* F    1 SH FALSTAFF] *Fal.* F; *Iohn.* Q (*also at* 4, 53, 64, 70, 147, 157, 162, 175, 179, 184, 186)    3 moe] Q; *more* F    3 knew for] Q, F; knew cure for *Capell*    5 foolish ... clay-man] Q, F; foolish-compounded clay, man, *Pope subst., Rowe, et al.*    10 judgement.] F; iudgement Q    12 inset] in-set Q; sette F

---

212 **counsel every man** let each of us consider.

**Act 1, Scene 2**

**1.2** The survival in Q of the SH *Old.* at 96 suggests that this scene incorporates a section of an earlier version of the confrontation with the Lord Chief Justice (possibly not, as here, in the public street) in which Falstaff still bore the name of 'Oldcastle' (see p.12 above and Textual Analysis, pp. 199–200).

**0** SD From the evidence of Q it can be argued that Shakespeare had originally written *Enter sir John Oldcastle alone*, then, when altering the names, he decided to add the entrance of the diminutive page in contrast with the fat knight, crossed out 'Oldcastle' to replace it with 'Falstaff', but forgot to delete 'alone'; but compare 3.1.0 SD.

**1** **water** urine.

**3** **owed** owned.

**3** **moe** 'more' was used for quantity, 'moe' for number (*OED* Mo *a* 2).

**3** **knew for** was aware of (modelled on 'care for').

**4** **gird** gibe.

**5** **foolish ... clay-man** There is no need to alter the punctuation (see collation): man, made of clay, is a compound of folly.

**6** **intends** tends to cause.

**8** **overwhelmed** crushed under her weight.

**10** **set ... off** show me to the best advantage.

**10** **whoreson** A favourite epithet with Falstaff, who uses it more for familiarity than abuse.

**10** **mandrake** A poisonous plant thought to have aphrodisiac powers because its roots resembled the lower parts of the human body.

**12** **manned** attended.

**12** **agate** Semi-precious stone, at times carved with diminutive human figures, used for seals or set (see 'inset') in brooches worn as decorations on caps. See *Rom.* 1.3.55: 'In shape no bigger than an agate-stone'.

gold nor silver, but in vile apparel, and send you back again to your
master for a jewel – the juvenal the prince your master, whose chin is
not yet fledge; I will sooner have a beard grow in the palm of my hand,    15
than he shall get one off his cheek, and yet he will not stick to say his
face is a face royal: God may finish it when He will, 'tis not a hair
amiss yet: he may keep it still at a face-royal, for a barber shall never
earn sixpence out of it; and yet he'll be crowing as if he had writ man
ever since his father was a bachelor. He may keep his own grace, but       20
he's almost out of mine, I can assure him. What said Master
Dommelton about the satin for my short cloak and my slops?
PAGE  He said, sir, you should procure him better assurance than
Bardolph: he would not take his band and yours, he liked not the
security.                                                                  25
FALSTAFF  Let him be damned like the glutton, pray God his tongue be
hotter, a whoreson Achitophel! a rascal, yea forsooth, knave, to bear a
gentleman in hand, and then stand upon security! The whoreson
smoothy-pates do now wear nothing but high shoes and bunches of
keys at their girdles, and if a man is through with them in honest        30
taking up, then they must stand upon security. I had as lief they would
put ratsbane in my mouth, as offer to stop it with security. I looked a
should have sent me two-and-twenty yards of satin, as I am a true

13 vile] Q; vilde F    15 fledge] Q; fledg'd F    16 off] Q; on F; of *Sisson*    16 and yet] & yet Q; yet F    17 face royal: God] face royal,
God Q; Face-Royall. Heauen F    17 'tis] Q; it is F    19 he'll] heele Q; he will F    21 he's] hees Q; he is F    22 Dommelton] Q;
Dombledon F    22 and my] Q; and F    23 SH PAGE] *Pag.* F; *Boy* Q *(for the rest of this scene)*    24 band] Q; bond F    26 SH FALSTAFF]
*Fal.* F; *sir Iohn.* Q *(also at 39, 44, 82)*    26 pray God] Q; may F    27 rascal, yea forsooth, knave,] rascall: yea forsooth knaue Q;
Rascally-yea-forsooth-knaue, F; rascal, yea-forsooth knave! *Holland*    29 smoothy-pates] Q; smooth-pates F    33 a true] Q; true F

**14 jewel … juvenal** Punning on the alliteration:
the page is presented as a brooch (jewel) to the young
(juvenal) prince.

**15 fledge** covered with down (used of young birds);
'fledged' (F) means 'ready to fly'.

**16 off** from; alternatively 'of' = 'on'.

**17 face royal, 18 face-royal** Punning upon (1)
princely, noble face, (2) the face on the 'royal', a coin
worth ten shillings, i.e. twenty sixpences, a sum which
no barber would get for shaving a non-existent beard.

**19 writ man** attained manhood (*OED* Write *v* 11b).

**20 grace** (1) the form of address to a prince, (2)
favour.

**22 Dommelton** Coined on 'dommel' or 'dumble',
a dumb, stupid person.

**22 slops** Baggy knee-breeches fashionable at the
time.

**24 band** bond given as security.

**26 damned … glutton** Referring to the parable of

Dives and Lazarus; see *1H4* 3.3.31–3 and 4.2.25–6.
Dives in hell asked for a drop of water to cool his
tongue.

**27 Achitophel** The Old Testament (2 Sam. 15–
16) counterpart of Judas Iscariot.

**27 rascal, … knave** 'yea forsooth' seems Falstaff's
own interjection rather than (as suggested by F's
reading) an adjectival expression for 'rascally person
too ready with the oath "yea forsooth" '.

**27–8 bear … in hand** assure a man, lead a man on
(*OED* Bear *v* 3e).

**28 stand upon** demand (*OED* Stand *v* 78m).

**29 smoothy-pates** Puritan tradesmen, wearing
their hair cropped.

**30 through** thorough, straightforward.

**31 taking up** making deals on credit.

**32–3 looked a should** expected that he should; 'a'
is the colloquial unstressed form of 'he'.

knight, and he sends me 'security'! Well he may sleep in security, for
he hath the horn of abundance, and the lightness of his wife shines          35
through it – Where's Bardolph? – and yet cannot he see, though he
have his own lanthorn to light him.

PAGE  He's gone in Smithfield to buy your worship a horse.

FALSTAFF  I bought him in Paul's, and he'll buy me a horse in Smithfield:
and I could get me but a wife in the stews, I were manned, horsed and        40
wived.

*Enter* LORD CHIEF JUSTICE *and* SERVANT

PAGE  Sir, here comes the nobleman that committed the prince for
striking him about Bardolph.

FALSTAFF  Wait close, I will not see him.

JUSTICE  What's he that goes there?

SERVANT  Falstaff, and't please your lordship.                               45

JUSTICE  He that was in question for the robbery?

SERVANT  He, my lord; but he hath since done good service at
Shrewsbury, and, as I hear, is now going with some charge to the
Lord John of Lancaster.                                                      50

JUSTICE  What, to York? Call him back again.

SERVANT  Sir John Falstaff.

FALSTAFF  Boy, tell him I am deaf.

---

34 Well he] Q; Well, he F   36 it – Where's Bardolph? – and] it: wheres Bardolf, & Q; it, and F, *Rowe*   37 him.] Q; him. Where's
*Bardolfe?* F, *Rowe*   38 in] Q; into F   40 and I] Q; if I F   40 but a] Q; a F   41 SD LORD CHIEF] Q; *Chiefe* F   41 SD *and* SERVANT] F;
*not in* Q   45 SH JUSTICE] Q; *Ch. Iust.* F   47 SH JUSTICE] *Iust.* Q (*so to 130*), F

---

34–7 for ... light him Intimating that the tradesman's wealth ('horn of abundance') is due to his
turning a blind eye on the infidelity of his wife – a
frequent multiple pun in city comedies: 'horn' = (1)
cornucopia, (2) cuckold's horn, (3) the material used
to make lanterns ('lant-horns'); 'lightness' = (1) light
(in a lantern), (2) sexual promiscuity.

36 Where's Bardolph? Q's placing of the question
in mid speech is subtler and more natural than F's
'regularisation': the idea of a lighted lantern calls to
Falstaff's mind Bardolph's scarlet face; see *1H4*
3.3.24–51: '... Thou art the Knight of the Burning
Lamp ... I never see thy face but I think upon hell-fire
and Dives that lived in purple ... Thou hast saved me
a thousand marks in links and torches, walking with
thee in the night betwixt tavern and tavern ...'

39–41 Masterless servants set up their bills for
employment in the nave of St Paul's; Falstaff alludes
to the common saying (Tilley w276, from *Choise of
Change*, 1585): 'A man must not make choice of three

things in three places: of a wife in Westminster, of a
servant in Paul's, of a horse in Smithfield, least he
chuse a quean, a knave or a jade.' Compare *More*
Add.vi (Hand B) 64–9.

40 and I if I.

42–3 The episode is in *Famous Victories* (from Hall
and Holinshed) but not in *1H4*; in earlier sources the
prince threatens but does not strike the Lord Chief
Justice (see Appendix 2, pp. 219–20 below).

44 close near.

46 and't if it (also at 82, 88, 96).

47 in question under enquiry.

49 charge military command; see *1H4* 2.4.545: 'a
charge of foot'.

49–51 to the Lord ... to York See *1H4* 5.5.35–7
and compare 159–61 here, suggesting that parts of
this scene were written for the earlier 'Oldcastle'
version of the play (see p. 12 above, and Textual
Analysis, pp. 199–200 below).

PAGE  You must speak louder, my master is deaf.

JUSTICE  I am sure he is, to the hearing of anything good. Go pluck him by      55
the elbow, I must speak with him.

SERVANT  Sir John!

FALSTAFF  What? A young knave and begging? Is there not wars? Is there
not employment? Doth not the king lack subjects? Do not the rebels
need soldiers? Though it be a shame to be on any side but one, it is      60
worse shame to beg than to be on the worst side, were it worse than
the name of Rebellion can tell how to make it.

SERVANT  You mistake me, sir.

FALSTAFF  Why, sir, did I say you were an honest man? Setting my
knighthood and my soldiership aside, I had lied in my throat if I had      65
said so.

SERVANT  I pray you, sir, then set your knighthood and your soldiership
aside, and give me leave to tell you, you lie in your throat, if you say I
am any other than an honest man.

FALSTAFF  I give thee leave to tell me? So I lay aside that which grows to      70
me! If thou gettest any leave of me, hang me; if thou takest leave, thou
wert better be hanged, you hunt counter: hence, avaunt!

SERVANT  Sir, my lord would speak with you.

JUSTICE  Sir John Falstaff, a word with you.

FALSTAFF  My good lord, God give your lordship good time of day. I am      75
glad to see your lordship abroad, I heard say your lordship was sick. I
hope your lordship goes abroad by advice. Your lordship, though not
clean past your youth, have yet some smack of an ague in you, some
relish of the saltness of time in you, and I most humbly beseech your
lordship to have a reverend care of your health.      80

JUSTICE  Sir John, I sent for you before your expedition to Shrewsbury.

58 SH FALSTAFF] *Falst.* Q *(also at 75, 85, 88, 91, 101, 107, 110, 112, 115, 121, 123, 125, 129, 131)*   58 begging?] Q; beg? F;
begging! *Dyce*   60 need] Q; want F   64 sir,] Q; Sir? F   64 man?] F; man, Q   70 tell me? So] tell me, so Q; tell me so? F; tell me so!
F4   70-1 to me! If] F4; to me, if Q; to me? If F   71 hang me; if] F; hang me, if Q   72 hanged, you] Q; hang'd: you F   72 hunt
counter:] *Cam.*; hunt counter, Q, Hunt-counter, F   75 lord, God give] Q; Lord, giue F   75 day.] day, Q; the day. F   78 have] Q;
hath F   78 of an ague] Q, *Ridley*; of age F   79 time in you, and] Q; Time, and F   81 for you] Q; you F

**61–2 were it … make it** even if that side were
worse than it is, although it is hard to see what could
be worse than to side with rebels.

**64–8 Setting … aside** It is inconceivable that
knights and soldiers should lie; see *1H4* 3.3.120:
'setting thy knighthood aside, thou art a knave to call
me so'. Tilley (T268) records the expression 'to lie in
one's throat' (= infamously) only from 1590.

**70–1 grows to me** is an integral part of me.

**72 you hunt counter** (1) you are on the wrong

scent, (2) you'll end up in the Counter (a London
prison), (3) you jack-in-office! ('hunt-counter'
= petty officer in charge of arresting offenders).

**76 abroad** out of doors, about.

**77 by advice** of the doctor.

**78 an ague** sickness; F's 'age' is probably a scribal
'improvement'.

**79 saltness of time** Perhaps with reference to the
use of salt to preserve meat.

FALSTAFF  And't please your lordship, I hear his majesty is returned with
some discomfort from Wales.

JUSTICE  I talk not of his majesty: you would not come when I sent for you.

FALSTAFF  And I hear moreover, his highness is fallen into this same     8·
whoreson apoplexy.

JUSTICE  Well, God mend him. I pray you let me speak with you.

FALSTAFF  This apoplexy, as I take it, is a kind of lethargy, and't please
your lordship, a kind of sleeping in the blood, a whoreson tingling.

JUSTICE  What tell you me of it? Be it as it is.                          9·

FALSTAFF  It hath it original from much grief, from study and perturba-
tion of the brain. I have read the cause of his effects in Galen, it is a
kind of deafness.

JUSTICE  I think you are fallen into the disease, for you hear not what I say
to you.                                                                  9·

FALSTAFF  Very well, my lord, very well. Rather and't please you, it is the
disease of not listening, the malady of not marking, that I am troubled
withal.

JUSTICE  To punish you by the heels, would amend the attention of your
ears, and I care not if I do become your physician.                     10·

FALSTAFF  I am as poor as Job, my lord, but not so patient: your lordship
may minister the potion of imprisonment to me in respect of poverty,
but how I shall be your patient to follow your prescriptions, the wise
may make some dram of a scruple, or indeed a scruple itself.

JUSTICE  I sent for you when there were matters against you for your life  10·
to come speak with me.

82 And't] Q; If it F   84 for you.] Q; for you? F   87 God] Q; heauen F   87 pray you] Q; pray F   88 apoplexy, as I take it, is]
appoplexi as I take it? is Q; Apoplexie is (as I take it) F   88–9 and't ... of sleeping in] Q; a sleeping of F   90 it? Be ... is.] F; it, be ...
is Q; it, be ... is? *Ridley*   91 hath it] Q, F; hath its F3–4   96 SH FALSTAFF] *Fal.* F; *Old.* Q   100 do become] Q; be F

82–3 returned ... Wales A conflation of the
expedition into Wales announced shortly after the
battle of Shrewsbury in 1403 (*1H4* 5.5.39–40), which
never took place for lack of funds (Holinshed, III, 524/
1), with that after Gaultree in 1405, when the king in
Wales 'found fortune nothing fauourable unto him'
(Holinshed, III, 530/2).

86 apoplexy Holinshed's definition of the king's
last illness in 1413 (III, 541/1).

91 it original its origin; 'it' was used as possessive
article (Abbott 228).

91 study, worry, anxiety.

92 Galen A famous Greek physician of the second
century AD.

96 SH For 'Falstaff' Q has *Old.*; see 1.2 n. and
49–51 n.

99 punish ... heels put you in the stocks (*OEL*
Heel *sb*¹ 18).

101 poor ... patient Proverbial, Tilley J60 (poor as
Job) and J59 (patient as Job).

102 in ... poverty in view of my inability to pay
fines or bribes.

104 scruple (1) pharmaceutical measure of weight,
like 'dram', (2) moral perplexity; compare *TN* 3.4.78–
9: 'no dram of a scruple, no scruple of a scruple, no
obstacle ...'

105 for your life entailing capital punishment;
referring to the Gad's Hill episode (*1H4* 2.1–2 and 4);
see 117–20.

FALSTAFF  As I was then advised by my learned counsel in the laws of this
    land-service, I did not come.
JUSTICE  Well, the truth is, Sir John, you live in great infamy.
FALSTAFF  He that buckles himself in my belt cannot live in less.        110
JUSTICE  Your means are very slender and your waste is great.
FALSTAFF  I would it were otherwise, I would my means were greater and
    my waist slender.
JUSTICE  You have misled the youthful prince.
FALSTAFF  The young prince hath misled me. I am the fellow with the     115
    great belly, and he my dog.
JUSTICE  Well, I am loath to gall a new-healed wound: your day's service
    at Shrewsbury hath a little gilded over your night's exploit on Gad's
    Hill. You may thank th'unquiet time for your quiet o'er-posting that
    action.                                                             120
FALSTAFF  My lord?
JUSTICE  But since all is well, keep it so: wake not a sleeping wolf.
FALSTAFF  To wake a wolf is as bad as smell a fox.
JUSTICE  What? You are as a candle, the better part burnt out.
FALSTAFF  A wassail candle, my lord, all tallow – if I did say of wax, my   125
    growth would approve the truth.
JUSTICE  There is not a white hair in your face, but should have his effect
    of gravity.
FALSTAFF  His effect of gravy, gravy, gravy.
JUSTICE  You follow the young prince up and down, like his ill angel.     130

109 infamy.] Q; infamy F; infamy – *conj. this edn*    110 himself] Q; him F    111 are] Q; is F    111 waste is] Q; wast F    112 greater] Q;
F; great *conj. Berger–Williams*    113 waist slender] waste slender Q; waste slenderer F    118–19 Gad's Hill.] Gads-hill. F;
Gadshill, Q    121 lord?] F; lord. Q; lord – *Theobald, et al.*; lord! *Craig*    127 in your] Q; on your F    130 ill] Q; euill F

108 **land-service** military service; therefore 'the
laws of war'; Falstaff points to his sword and buckler
as his lawyer ('learned counsel').
109 The absence of the final full stop in F suggests
that the Justice is interrupted by Falstaff.
111–13 The common pun on the homophones
'waste'/'waist' (see e.g. *Wiv.* 1.3.41–3) does not
require emendation of Q's reading (see collation).
115–16 **I am … dog** Perhaps an allusion to 'the
man in the moon': the spots on the moon's face were
seen as a man carrying a bush, accompanied (or led)
by a dog (see *MND* 5.1.135–6); the 'big belly' is the
full moon itself.
118 **gilded over** Compare Hal's remark to Falstaff
in *1H4* 5.4.157–8: 'if a lie may do thee grace I'll gild it
with the happiest terms I have'.
119 **unquiet time** The relevant section of Hall's
*Union* bears the title 'The vnquiete tyme of Kyng
Henry the fourthe'.

119 **o'er-posting** Shakespeare's coinage, from
'riding post', hence 'over-riding', escaping the consequences; but possibly = 'to post over', i.e. 'cover up',
as in *2H6* 3.1.255: 'His guilt should be but idly posted
over / Because his purpose is not executed.'
123 **smell a fox** be suspicious (proverbial, Dent
F652.1); Falstaff implies that the Justice is both wolf
and fox.
125 **wassail candle** An outsize candle to last
through a feast-night ('wassail' = feast).
125 **wax** Playing on (1) beeswax (contrasted with
'tallow'), (2) growth, increase, (3) handsome aspect
(see *Rom.* 1.3.76: 'a man of wax').
126 **approve the truth** confirm the statement.
129 **gravy** grease, sweat; in Elizabethan pronunciation the same long vowel was used in 'gravy' and
'gravity' as in 'grave'.

FALSTAFF Not so, my lord, your ill angel is light, but I hope he that looks
upon me will take me without weighing; and yet in some respects I
grant I cannot go. I cannot tell: virtue is of so little regard in these
costermongers' times, that true valour is turned bearherd, pregnancy
is made a tapster, and his quick wit wasted in giving reckonings; all    135
the other gifts appertinent to man, as the malice of this age shapes
them, are not worth a gooseberry. You that are old consider not the
capacities of us that are young: you do measure the heat of our livers
with the bitterness of your galls; and we that are in the vaward of our
youth, I must confess, are wags too.                                     140

JUSTICE Do you set down your name in the scroll of youth, that are
written down old with all the characters of age? Have you not a moist
eye, a dry hand, a yellow cheek, a white beard, a decreasing leg, an
increasing belly? Is not your voice broken, your wind short, your chin
double, your wit single, and every part about you blasted with          145
antiquity? And will you yet call yourself young? Fie, fie, fie, Sir John.

FALSTAFF My lord, I was born about three of the clock in the afternoon,
with a white head, and something a round belly. For my voice, I have
lost it with hallooing, and singing of anthems. To approve my youth

---

134 costermongers' times,] Q *subst.*; Costor- / mongers, F; Costor-mongers dayes F3–4    134 bearherd, pregnancy] Berod,
Pregnancie Q; Beare-heard. Pregnancie F    135 and his] Q; and hath his F    136–7 this . . . them, are] F; his . . . the one Q    138 do
measure] Q; measure F    141 SH JUSTICE] *Iust.* F; *Lo.* Q    143 eye, . . . hand, . . . cheek, . . . beard, . . . leg,] Q; eye? . . . hand? . . .
cheeke? . . . beard? . . . leg? F    144–5 broken, . . . short, your chin double, your wit single,] Q; broken? . . . short? your wit single?
F    146 antiquity? And] F; antiquitie, and Q    146 you yet] Q; you F    147–8 born about . . . afternoon, with] Q; borne with F

131 your . . . light Playing on (1) Satan as 'angel of
light' (2 Cor. 9), and (2) 'angel' as a gold coin, so
called from the Archangel Michael impressed on it;
tradesmen weighed coins to make sure they were not
counterfeit or filed.

133 go have currency, pass as genuine.

133 tell (1) know what to think, (2) be reckoned
with ('tell' = 'count money').

134 costermongers' times materialistic age; 'cos-
termonger' = 'petty tradesman', originally a street
seller of costards (apples).

134 valour (1) courage, military virtue, (2) value,
worth.

134 bearherd keeper of performing bears at
country fairs.

134 pregnancy i.e. pregnancy of wit: intelligence,
inventiveness.

137 not . . . gooseberry Compare *Tro.* 5.4.11–12:
'not proved worth a blackberry'.

138–9 measure . . . galls The liver was considered
the seat of passion (love and courage) and gall (bile)
that of anger.

139 vaward vanguard.

140 wags high-spirited.

142 characters (1) letters (in writing), (2) dis-
tinguishing features, (3) literary compositions modelled on those of Theophrastus, describing in elegant
rhetorical terms different human types. The Justice's
speech is in fact a 'Character of an Old Man', based
on the figure of antithesis.

142–5 moist eye . . . decreasing leg . . . wit single
Compare *Ham.* 2.2.198–200: 'their [old men's] eyes
purging thick amber and plumtree gum . . . they have a
plentiful lack of wit, together with most weak hams'.

147 about three . . . afternoon A detail omitted in
F. Play performances began in the early afternoon: is
this a metatheatrical hint, that Falstaff is merely a
stage creation, born as he appears there?

148 something somewhat (adverbial); see Abbott
68.

149 hallooing . . . anthems hallooing to hunting
hounds or in the battle; Falstaff's hymn-singing is
mentioned also in *1H4* 2.4.133, possibly a survival of
the caricature of the original Oldcastle, a Lollard,
equated by the Elizabethans with the Puritans.

149 approve prove, demonstrate.

further, I will not: the truth is, I am only old in judgement and  150
understanding; and he that will caper with me for a thousand marks,
let him lend me the money and have at him. For the box of th'ear that
the prince gave you, he gave it like a rude prince, and you took it like a
sensible lord. I have checked him for it, and the young lion repents –
marry, not in ashes and sackcloth, but in new silk and old sack.  155
JUSTICE  Well, God send the prince a better companion.
FALSTAFF  God send the companion a better prince. I cannot rid my
hands of him.
JUSTICE  Well, the king hath severed you: I hear you are going with Lord
John of Lancaster against the Archbishop and the Earl of  160
Northumberland.
FALSTAFF  Yea, I thank your pretty sweet wit for it; but look you pray, all
you that kiss my Lady Peace at home, that our armies join not in a hot
day: for, by the Lord, I take but two shirts out with me, and I mean not
to sweat extraordinarily; if it be a hot day, and I brandish anything but  165
a bottle, I would I might never spit white again: there is not a
dangerous action can peep out his head, but I am thrust upon it. Well,
I cannot last ever, but it was alway yet the trick of our English nation, if
they have a good thing to make it too common. If ye will needs say I
am an old man, you should give me rest; I would to God my name  170
were not so terrible to the enemy as it is: I were better to be eaten to
death with a rust, than to be scoured to nothing with perpetual
motion.
JUSTICE  Well, be honest, be honest, and God bless your expedition.

150 further] Q; farther F    152 him. For] F; him for Q    152 th'ear] F; the yeere Q    156 SH JUSTICE] *Iust.* F; *Lord.* Q *(also at 159,
174, 177)*    156, 157 God] Q; heauen F *(Heauen at 157)*    159 severed you:] Q; seuer'd you and Prince *Harry*, F    162 Yea] Q; Yes
F    164 for, by the Lord, I] Q; for if I F    165 and I] & I Q; if I F    166 a bottle, I would I a bottle. I would I Q; my Bottle, would I
F    168–73 but it was ... motion] Q; *not in* F    174 God] Q; heauen F

151 **caper** compete in cutting capers (high jumps
with a scissor movement of the legs).

151 **marks** A mark was worth about two-thirds of a
pound sterling.

152 **have at him** An expression of defiance.

152–4 **For the ... lord** See 42–3 n.; 'checked'
= 'reproved'.

155 **marry** by the Virgin Mary; treated as a very
mild oath.

155 **sackcloth** penitent's garb.

155 **old sack** Canary wine, improved by age.

159 **severed you** F's addition of 'and Prince Harry'
sounds like an unnecessary 'improvement' by the
scribe.

159–61 **I hear ... Northumberland** See 49–51 n.

162 **I thank ... it** Implying that the separation was
promoted by the Lord Chief Justice.

162 **look you pray** be sure to pray.

165–6 **and I ... spit white again** may I never drink
again if, on a hot day, I use any weapon except the
bottle. In *1H4* 5.3.48–54 Falstaff wears a bottle
instead of a pistol; 'spitting white' was the result of
drinking, but can be taken as the opposite of the red
spit resulting from consumption or wounds, hence
'may I become consumptive (or be mortally wounded)
if...'

167 **his head** its head; referring to 'action'.

168–73 **but it ... motion** The longest omission in F,
possibly, as Chambers suggested, because 'anti-
patriotic'.

174 **be honest** behave yourself.

FALSTAFF  Will your lordship lend me a thousand pound to furnish me    175
forth?

JUSTICE  Not a penny, not a penny: you are too impatient to bear crosses.
Fare you well. Commend me to my cousin Westmoreland.

*[Exeunt Lord Chief Justice and Servant]*

FALSTAFF  If I do, fillip me with a three-man beetle. A man can no more
separate age and covetousness than a can part young limbs and    180
lechery; but the gout galls the one, and the pox pinches the other, and
so both the degrees prevent my curses. Boy!

PAGE  Sir.

FALSTAFF  What money is in my purse?

PAGE  Seven groats and two pence.    185

FALSTAFF  I can get no remedy against this consumption of the purse:
borrowing only lingers and lingers it out, but the disease is incurable.
Go bear this letter to my lord of Lancaster, this to the prince, this to
the Earl of Westmoreland, and this to old Mistress Ursula, whom I
have weekly sworn to marry since I perceived the first white hair of my    190
chin. About it, you know where to find me. A pox of this gout, or a
gout of this pox, for the one or the other plays the rogue with my great
toe. 'Tis no matter if I do halt: I have the wars for my colour, and my
pension shall seem the more reasonable. A good wit will make use of
anything: I will turn diseases to commodity.    195

*Exeunt*

---

178 SD] Capell subst.; not in Q, F; Exit. F2–4    179 fillip] Q; fillop F    180 a can] Q; he can F    182 curses. Boy!] curses. Boy? F; curses, boy. Q    190 of] Q; on F    191 find me.] Q subst., F; find me. Exit Page. Capell, et al.    193 toe. 'Tis] Q; toe: It is F    195 SD Exeunt] F; Exit. Capell, et al.; not in Q

---

175 **a thousand pound** The sum Falstaff manages later to borrow from Shallow (see 5.5.69–71), establishing a link between the two Justices.

175–6 **furnish me forth** equip me.

177 **to bear crosses** (1) endure adversities, (2) keep money (referring to silver coins marked with a cross). A frequent quibble; see *LLL* 1.2.32–4 and *AYLI* 2.4.12–14.

179 **fillip ... beetle** ram me down with a sledge-hammer; the 'beetle' was used to ram down paving stones, and the heaviest sort required three men to lift it.

179–80 **A man ... covetousness** Proverbial; see Tilley M568.

180 **a can** he (= a man) can.

181 **pox** venereal disease.

182 **both ... prevent** both age and youth (because of their diseases) anticipate.

185 **groats** A groat was worth fourpence (one-sixtieth of a pound sterling).

189 **Mistress Ursula** Not mentioned elsewhere in the play: either meant as the first name of Quickly, or the result of a confusion with Ursula, Hero's attendant in *Much Ado About Nothing*, a play probably written and certainly printed at the same time as *2H4*.

191–2 **A pox ... this pox** 'A pox' was a common form of curse; for the quibble see 181–2.

193 **colour** excuse, pretence.

195 **commodity** profit, expediency; see the Bastard's speech in *John* 2.1.567–98.

**1.3** *Enter th'*ARCHBISHOP [*of York*], THOMAS MOWBRAY (*Earl
Marshal*), *the* LORD HASTINGS, *and* LORD BARDOLPH

ARCHBISHOP  Thus have you heard our cause and known our means,
    And, my most noble friends, I pray you all
    Speak plainly your opinions of our hopes,
    And first, Lord Marshal, what say you to it?
MOWBRAY  I well allow the occasion of our arms,                          5
    But gladly would be better satisfied
    How in our means we should advance ourselves
    To look with forehead bold and big enough
    Upon the power and puissance of the king.
HASTINGS  Our present musters grow upon the file                        10
    To five-and-twenty thousand men of choice,
    And our supplies live largely in the hope
    Of great Northumberland, whose bosom burns
    With an incensèd fire of injuries.
LORD BARDOLPH  The question then, Lord Hastings, standeth thus:        15
    Whether our present five-and-twenty thousand
    May hold up head without Northumberland.
HASTINGS  With him we may.
LORD BARDOLPH                    Yea marry, there's the point;
    But if without him we be thought too feeble,
    My judgement is we should not step too far                    20
    Till we have his assistance by the hand;
    For in a theme so bloody-faced as this,
    Conjecture, expectation, and surmise

---

Act 1, Scene 3   1.3] *Scena Quarta.* F; *not in* Q   0 SD *Enter* ... HASTINGS,] Q; *Enter Archbishop, Hastings, Mowbray,* F   0 SD *and*
LORD BARDOLPH] F; *Fauconbridge, and Bardolfe.* Q   1 SH ARCHBISHOP] *Ar.* F (*or* / *Arch.* / *throughout scene); Bishop.* Q (*Bish.* /
*through rest of scene*)   1 cause] Q; *causes* F   1 known] Q; *kno* F; *know* F2–4   5 SH MOWBRAY] *Mow.* F; *Marsh.* Q   18 Yea] Q; I
F   21–4] F; *not in* Q

**Act 1, Scene 3**

**1.3** Based on two paragraphs in Holinshed, III,
529/1–2, which provide the location in York and the
conspirators' names: 'Richard Scroope archbishop of
Yorke Thomas Mowbraie earle marshall ... the lords
Hastings, Fauconbridge, Berdolfe'.

**0 SD** The Q version reproduces verbatim the list in
Holinshed, including the 'ghost character' Fauconbridge who has no role in the play.

**4 Lord Marshal** Master of Ceremonies, a courtesy
title for Thomas Mowbray, the son of Thomas Mowbray, first Duke of Norfolk, the rival of Bullingbrook
banished by Richard II (see *R2* 1.1–3).

**5 allow ... arms** grant that we have good cause for
taking arms.

**7 in our means** with the means at our disposal.

**10 upon the file** according to our records.

**11 men of choice** picked troops.

**12 our supplies live** we count for reinforcements.

**21–4, 36–55** The only reason for the omission of
these lines from Q seems to be the reduction of Lord
Bardolph's role, to give the actor an opportunity of
doubling longer parts in the later part of the play,
where Lord Bardolph disappears; compare
1.1.166–79 n.

**23 Conjecture ... surmise** Rumour's words in
Induction 16 (see n.); Lord Bardolph – the incarna-
tion of Rumour in 1.1 – is now warning against
Rumour's deceptions.

Of aids incertain, should not be admitted.

ARCHBISHOP 'Tis very true, Lord Bardolph, for indeed                    25
  It was young Hotspur's cause at Shrewsbury.

LORD BARDOLPH It was, my lord; who lined himself with hope,
  Eating the air, and promise of supply,
  Flatt'ring himself in project of a power
  Much smaller than the smallest of his thoughts,                       30
  And so with great imagination,
  Proper to madmen, led his powers to death,
  And, winking, leaped into destruction.

HASTINGS But, by your leave, it never yet did hurt
  To lay down likelihoods and forms of hope.                            35

LORD BARDOLPH Yes, if this present quality of war –
  Indeed the instant action, a cause on foot –
  Lives so in hope, as in an early spring
  We see th'appearing buds, which to prove fruit
  Hope gives not so much warrant as despair                             40
  That frosts will bite them. When we mean to build,
  We first survey the plot, then draw the model,
  And when we see the figure of the house,
  Then must we rate the cost of the erection,
  Which if we find outweighs ability,                                   45
  What do we then, but draw anew the model
  In fewer offices, or at least desist
  To build at all? Much more in this great work

---

24 incertain] F; uncertain F3–4, *Rowe*  26 cause] Q; case F  27 was, my lord; who] *Capell;* was my Lord, who Q; was (my Lord) who F  28 and] Q; on F  29 in] Q; with F  36–55] F; *not in* Q  36–7 Yes, if... war – / Indeed ... action, a ... foot – ] Yes, if ... warre, / Indeed ... action: a ... foot, F; Yes, in ... war, / Indeed ... action (a ... foot) *Malone;* Yes, if ... war / Impede ... act; a ... foot *Pope*  38 hope,] *Rowe;* hope: F; hope – *Davison*  47 offices, or] *Collier²;* offices? Or F  47 at least] F; at last *Capell*

26 **cause** reason (of Hotspur's death); see 1; F's 'case' is an 'improvement' in the direction of the obvious.

27 **lined** fortified.

28 **Eating the air** Proverbial (Tilley M226) for 'feeding on false hopes', i.e. promise of reinforcements (supply); compare *Ham.* 3.2.94: 'I eat the air, promise-crammed.'

29 **project** expectation, anticipation.

31–2 **imagination ... madmen** Compare *MND* 5.1.7–8: 'The lunatic, the lover, and the poet / Are of imagination all compact.'

33 **winking** with his eyes shut.

36–7 The corruption of these lines is due to damage to the original when 36–55 were marked for omission in the copy for Q. Dozens of emendations have been suggested, the most significant of which are recorded in the collation, but here only punctuation has been retouched, to underline Lord Bardolph's further *caveat:* 'Yes, there is no harm in nursing hopes, provided we keep in mind that, at this stage, the hopes for the sort of action we are undertaking are like those we entertain when we see early spring buds, well aware that they may be withered by frost.'

37 **instant** (1) imminent (= 'on foot'), (2) quick, urgent.

41–62 **When we ... tyranny** An expansion of the parable in Luke 14.28–30, possibly connected with Shakespeare's own preoccupation with the rebuilding of New Place in Stratford, acquired in 1597.

45 **ability** available resources.

47 **offices** rooms, especially service-rooms.

47 **at least** at worst (the least favourable case).

(Which is almost to pluck a kingdom down
And set another up) should we survey                          50
The plot of situation and the model,
Consent upon a sure foundation,
Question surveyors, know our own estate,
How able such a work to undergo,
To weigh against his opposite; or else                       55
We fortify in paper, and in figures,
Using the names of men instead of men,
Like one that draws the model of an house
Beyond his power to build it; who, half through,
Gives o'er, and leaves his part created cost                 60
A naked subject to the weeping clouds,
And waste for churlish winter's tyranny.

HASTINGS  Grant that our hopes, yet likely of fair birth,
Should be still-born, and that we now possessed
The utmost man of expectation:                               65
I think we are a body strong enough,
Even as we are, to equal with the king.

LORD BARDOLPH  What, is the king but five-and-twenty thousand?

HASTINGS  To us no more, nay not so much, Lord Bardolph,
For his divisions, as the times do brawl,                    70
Are in three heads: one power against the French,
And one against Glendower; perforce a third
Must take up us. So is the infirm king
In three divided, and his coffers sound
With hollow poverty and emptiness.                           75

ARCHBISHOP  That he should draw his several strengths together
And come against us in full puissance

54 undergo,] F; undergo. / A careful leader sums what force he brings *Collier²*   55 To] F; How *Capell;* And *Hudson*   55 opposite;] *Theobald;* Opposite? F   56 We] F; *Bard.* We Q   58 an] Q; a F   58 house] F; house, Q   60 part created] Q; part-created   66 are a body] F; are so, body Q; are so a body *conj. Collier*   71 Are] F; And Q; Stand *Vaughan*

**51 plot** (1) site (as at 42), (2) plan of action.

**52 Consent upon** Agree in finding.

**55 his opposite** (1) adverse factors, (2) the resources ('estate') of our enemies. Collier's inability to account for this expression made him suspect that a line had been dropped; see collation 54.

**56 figures** (1) arithmetical figures, (2) plans, design as at 43).

**60 part created cost** costly building erected only in part. A metonymy; see Sonnet 64.1–2: 'defaced / The rich proud cost'.

**64–5 we now … expectation** we already had all the men we could expect, i.e. we could not count on any reinforcements.

**70 as … brawl** in view of the present disturbances.

**71 against the French** Referring to the expedition in the summer of 1405, led by the Earl of Kent and 'lord Thomas of Lancaster' (the Duke of Clarence, born in Lancaster, like John); see Holinshed, III, 528/2–529/1.

**74–5 his coffers … emptiness** Holinshed repeatedly refers to Henry's requests for funds both from the clergy and the laity; see III, 525, 530, etc.

Need not to be dreaded.

HASTINGS                              If he should do so,
He leaves his back unarmed, the French and Welsh
Baying him at the heels: never fear that.                              8c
LORD BARDOLPH  Who is it like should lead his forces hither?
HASTINGS  The Duke of Lancaster and Westmoreland;
Against the Welsh, himself and Harry Monmouth;
But who is substituted against the French
I have no certain notice.

ARCHBISHOP                           Let us on,                        85
And publish the occasion of our arms.
The commonwealth is sick of their own choice,
Their over-greedy love hath surfeited:
An habitation giddy and unsure
Hath he that buildeth on the vulgar heart.                            90
O thou fond Many, with what loud applause
Didst thou beat heaven with blessing Bullingbrook,
Before he was what thou wouldst have him be!
And being now trimmèd in thine own desires,
Thou, beastly feeder, art so full of him                              95
That thou provok'st thyself to cast him up.
So, so, thou common dog, didst thou disgorge
Thy glutton bosom of the royal Richard,
And now thou wouldst eat thy dead vomit up,
And howl'st to find it. What trust is in these times?                 100
They, that when Richard lived would have him die,
Are now become enamoured on his grave;

---

78 not to be] Q; not be F   78–80 If ... that.] *As verse*, F; *as prose*, Q   79–80 He ... heels:] F; French and Welch he leaues his back vnarmde, they baying him at the heeles Q   84 against] Q; 'gainst F   85–108 Let us ... worst.] F; *not in* Q   91 Many] F; meyny Douce   94 trimmèd] *conj. Malone;* trimm'd F; trimm'd up F2–4, *Rowe*

79–80 the French ... heels The printer of Q (see collation) misinterpreted a correction in the MS., where 'French and Welsh' was added in the margin to replace 'they' before 'baying'.

81 Lord Bardolph asks for information he had already learned from Morton at 1.1.132–5.

82 Duke of Lancaster An improper designation: though born at Lancaster, John was Duke of Bedford.

84 substituted deputed, delegated.

85–108 Let us ... worst The Archbishop's speech was omitted from Q for obvious political reasons.

89–90 Proverbial, from Luke 6.49, on the house built without foundations.

90 vulgar heart support of the populace.

91 fond Many foolish multitude; a collective personification; there is no need to emend to 'meyny', from French *mesnie*, communalty.

94 trimmèd ... desires dressed up with the garment you wanted; with a possible reference to the 'dressing' of food for the table; see 95–6 n.

95–6 Clothing and feeding are constantly associated in the Elizabethan mind, hence the brusque transition from one metaphor to the other, resuming the imagery initiated at 87–8.

97–100 common dog ... find it The 'dog returning to his vomit' is proverbial, from Prov. 26.11 and 2 Pet. 2.22.

Thou that threw'st dust upon his goodly head
When through proud London he came sighing on
After th'admired heels of Bullingbrook,                                  105
Criest now: 'O earth, yield us that king again
And take thou this!' O thoughts of men accursed!
Past and to come seems best; things present, worst.
MOWBRAY  Shall we go draw our numbers, and set on?
HASTINGS  We are Time's subjects, and Time bids be gone.            110

*Exeunt*


**2.1**  *Enter* HOSTESS *of the tavern, and an officer*[, FANG, *followed by
yeoman* SNARE]


HOSTESS  Master Fang, have you entered the action?
FANG  It is entered.
HOSTESS  Where's your yeoman? Is't a lusty yeoman? Will a stand to't?
FANG  Sirrah – Where's Snare?
HOSTESS  O Lord, ay, good Master Snare.                                   5
SNARE  Here, here.
FANG  Snare, we must arrest Sir John Falstaff.
HOSTESS  Yea, good Master Snare, I have entered him and all.
SNARE  It may chance cost some of us our lives, for he will stab.
HOSTESS  Alas the day, take heed of him: he stabbed me in mine own      10

---

108 Past ... worst.] *Italicised in* F   109 SH MOWBRAY] F; *Bish.* Q   110 bids be] Q; bids, be F   110 SD] *ex.* Q; *not in* F   Act 2,
Scene 1   2.1] *Actus Secundus. Scæna Prima.* F; *not in* Q   0 SD *Enter ... an officer,*] Q; *Enter Hostesse, with two Officers,* F; *Enter ...
Fang an officer.* / *conj. Berger–Williams after Wilson*   0 SD FANG, ... SNARE] *This edn; or two.* Q; *Fang, and Snare.* F; Phang, *and his
boy with her; and* Snare *following.* / *Capell;* FANG *and* SNARE, Snare *lagging behind.* / *Riverside*   1 Fang] F; Phang Q (*throughout, also
in* SHs)   3 Is't] Q; Is it F   3 a stand] Q; he stand F   3 to't] Q; to it F   4 Sirrah – Where's] Sirra, wheres Q, F; [*to the Boy.*] Sirrah,
*where's Capell;* Sirrah! Where's *Wilson*   5 O Lord, ay,] O Lord I, Q; I, I, F   5 Snare.] Q, F; Snare. / *Enter* SNARE. *conj. Berger–
Williams after Wilson*   8 Yea] Q; I F   9 lives, for he] Q; liues: he F

---

103–8 Modelled on York's report in *R2* 5.2.1–40.

108 seems A singular form for the plural; see
1.1.33. The whole line is italicised in F to underline its
gnomic quality.

109 draw our numbers collect our people.

**Act 2, Scene 1**

2.1. The presence of Hostess Quickly establishes
Eastcheap as the location, Elizabethan staging making
no distinction between indoor (the tavern) and outdoor (the street) settings.

0 SD The permissive SD of Q ('an officer or two')
leaves uncertain the entrance of Snare, Sergeant
Fang's yeoman; the fact that he is missed at 4 –
'Sirrah' is addressed to him and not to an unrecorded
'Boy', as Capell imagined – suggests his lagging
behind.

1 Master An exaggerated form of address for
Fang, as well as for Snare at 5 and 8.

1 entered the action recorded the lawsuit.

3 Will a For 'a' = 'he' see 1.2.32–3; so at 16, 19,
etc.

4 See 0 SD n.; but Davison suggests that Fang does
not see Snare because he is right behind him, and the
comic business would be enhanced if Snare were the
exceptionally thin actor Sincklo (see 5.4.0 SD n.);
according to J. D. Wilson Sincklo doubled Snare and
Feeble in 3.2 as well as the Beadle in 5.4, while
another actor doubled Fang and Bullcalf in 3.2.

10 stabbed A sexual quibble typical of the
Hostess's language; see 'weapon' (12), 'foin' ('make a
thrust at'), and her reaction to Fang's mention of
'thrust' (14–15).

house, most beastly, in good faith. A cares not what mischief he does:
if his weapon be out, he will foin like any devil, he will spare neither
man, woman, nor child.

FANG  If I can close with him, I care not for his thrust.

HOSTESS  No, nor I neither, I'll be at your elbow.                              15

FANG  And I but fist him once, and a come but within my view –

HOSTESS  I am undone by his going. I warrant you, he's an infinitive thing
upon my score. Good Master Fang, hold him sure; good Master
Snare, let him not 'scape. A comes continuantly to Pie Corner –
saving your manhoods – to buy a saddle, and he is indited to dinner to    20
the Lubber's Head in Lumbert Street to Master Smooth's the
silkman. I pray you since my exion is entered, and my case so openly
known to the world, let him be brought in to his answer. A hundred
mark is a long one for a poor lone woman to bear, and I have borne,
and borne, and borne, and have been fubbed off, and fubbed off, and    25
fubbed off, from this day to that day, that it is a shame to be thought
on. There is no honesty in such dealing, unless a woman should be
made an ass, and a beast, to bear every knave's wrong. – Yonder he
comes, and that arrant malmsey-nose knave Bardolph with him. Do

11 house, most ... A cares] Q; house, and that most beastly: he cares F   11–12 does: if] Q; doth, if F   12 out, he] Q; out. Hee
F   16 And ... and a] Q; If ... if he F   16 view –] view. Q; Vice. F; vice – *Capell*   17 by ... you, he's] Q; with his going, I warrant he
F   19 'scape. A] scape, a Q; 'scape, he F   19 continuantly] F; continually Q   20 indited] Q, F; invited F3–4, *Rowe*   21 Lubber's
... Lumbert] Q; lubbars ... Lombard, F, *Rowe*   22 pray you] Q; pra'ye F   22 exion] Q, F; Action F3–4, *Rowe*   24 one] Q, F; loan]
*Theobald, Hanmer (meaning 'loan'); score Capell; ow'n White (meaning 'owing'); own Cowl*   25–6 off, and fubbed off, from] Q; off,
from F   28 wrong. – Yonder] wrong: yonder Q; wrong. / *Enter Falstaffe and Bardolfe.* / Yonder F   28 knave] Q; *not in* F

12 **if ... out** F punctuation (see collation) misses
out the sexual quibble.

14 **close** grapple (*OED* sv *v* 13).

16 **And I but fist** If I just grab. For 'and' = 'if' see
1.1.13.

16 **view** Many editors prefer F's 'vice' = 'firm grip'.

17 **undone ... going** If he goes to the wars he will
never pay his debts.

17 **infinitive** The Hostess means 'infinite', referring to Falstaff's numberless debts entered in her
accounts ('score').

19 **continuantly** Meaning 'incontinently', an
ambiguous refinement on 'at once, suddenly'.

19 **Pie Corner** The corner of Giltspur Street and
Cock Lane in Smithfield, the centre of horse-trading
(see 1.2.38–41), with many saddlers' shops.

20 **saving your manhoods** The Hostess's
improvement on 'saving your reverence', said apolo-
getically when mentioning something unpleasant: Pie
Corner, according to Davison, was a resort of prostitutes, which would give 'saddle' a sexual innuendo.

20 **indited** A refinement on 'invited', but 'to
indite' = 'to summon for trial'.

21 **Lubber's ... Street** A tavern, the Libbard's or
Leopard's Head ('lubber' means 'big clumsy fellow')
in Lombard Street, so named after the Italian (Lombard) merchants and bankers who settled there in the
thirteenth century.

22 **exion** Affected pronunciation of 'action'; see 1.

22 **case** A quibble on the popular designation of the
female genitals.

23 **brought ... answer** put on trial.

24 **one** score, reckoning.

24 **lone** unmarried or widowed; but in *1H4*, where
she is called Mistress Quickly only once (3.3.92), the
Hostess describes herself as 'an honest man's wife'
(3.3.119).

25 **fubbed off** put off with pretexts.

29 **arrant** unmitigated, notorious; mostly associated with 'knave' – see 5.1.34 and 5.4.1.

29 **malmsey-nose** Malmsey was a red wine, therefore 'red-nosed'; see 1.2.36 n.

your offices, do your offices, Master Fang and Master Snare, do me,    30
do me, do me your offices.

*Enter Sir John* [FALSTAFF] *and* BARDOLPH *and the* [PAGE-]BOY

FALSTAFF How now, whose mare's dead? What's the matter?

FANG I arrest you at the suit of Mistress Quickly.

FALSTAFF Away, varlets! Draw, Bardolph, cut me off the villain's head,
throw the quean in the channel.                                       35

HOSTESS Throw me in the channel? I'll throw thee in the channel. Wilt
thou, wilt thou, thou bastardly rogue? Murder, murder! Ah, thou
honeysuckle villain, wilt thou kill God's officers, and the king's? Ah,
thou honeyseed rogue, thou art a honeyseed, a man-queller, and a
woman-queller.                                                        40

FALSTAFF Keep them off, Bardolph.

OFFICERS A rescue, a rescue!

HOSTESS Good people, bring a rescue or two. Thou wot, wot thou, thou
wot, wot ta? Do, do, thou rogue! Do, thou hempseed!

PAGE Away, you scullian, you rampallian, you fustilarian! I'll tickle your   45
catastrophe!

*Enter* LORD CHIEF JUSTICE *and his Men*

JUSTICE What is the matter? Keep the peace here, ho!

31 SD] Q; *after 31, Pope; not in* F    31 SD PAGE-BOY] *Boy* Q; Page *Capell; not in* F    33 I] Q; *Sir Iohn*, I F    33 Mistress Quickly] Q
*corr.*, F; mistris, quickly Q *uncorr.*    36 thee in the channel] Q; thee there F    37, 38 Ah,] a Q; O F    42 SH OFFICERS] *Offic.* Q; *Fang* F
43 or two] Q; *not in* F; or two. / *The Page attacks her* / Wilson    43–4 Thou ... ta] Q; thou wilt not? thou wilt not? F    45 SH PAGE] F;
*Boy* Q; *Fal.* F    3–4    45 scullian] Q; Scullion F    45 fustilarian] Q; Fustillirian F    45 tickle] Q; tucke F    46 SD] Q; *Enter Ch. Iustice.*
F    47 SH JUSTICE] *Iust.* F *(also at 85, 93, 102; Ch. Iust. / in all other cases); Lord* Q *(or / Lo. / throughout scene)*    47 What is] Q;
what's F

**30 do me** An ethic dative to reinforce her request,
but with a possible sexual pun.

**32 whose ... dead?** Proverbial (Tilley M657) for
'What's all the fuss?'

**34 varlets** knaves (originally 'under-servants').

**35 quean** hussy, harlot.

**35 channel** gutter, open sewer running along the
street; this suggests an outdoor location.

**37 bastardly** the Hostess's coinage: 'bastard' plus
'dastardly'.

**38 honeysuckle** murderous; the Hostess means
'homicide' or 'homicidal'; she makes another try at the
same word with 'honeyseed' (39).

**42–3 A rescue** The officers are alarmed by the
attempt to 'rescue' the prisoner from their hands (a
common occurrence in London streets at the time),
but the Hostess takes 'rescue' to mean 'reinforcements' for the officers.

**43–4 wot ... ta** The Hostess falls into broad
dialect: 'wot' = 'wilt', 'ta' = 'thou'. The words are
addressed to the Page.

**44 hempseed** Both 'homicidal' (see 38–9) and
'gallows-bird' (the hanging rope was made of hemp).

**45–6** F3, F4 and many editors transfer this speech
to Falstaff, but it is more appropriate to the minuscule
Page, who is trying to rescue his monumental master
from the grip of the Hostess rather than from the
officers.

**45 scullian** Q's spelling denotes the Page's intention to give a feminine ending to 'scullion', the lowest
male kitchen servant.

**45 rampallian** Later uses of the word suggest 'a
ramping strumpet'.

**45 fustilarian** An original coinage based on
'fustilugs' = 'fat, frowzy woman' (*OED* sv).

**45–6 tickle ... catastrophe** 'tickle' meant
'chastise, whip', and is found in jocular threats mainly
connected with the victim's posterior, as seems the
case here; see *More* Add.II (Hand B) I: 'wele tickle
ther turnips'.

HOSTESS  Good my lord, be good to me. I beseech you stand to me.

JUSTICE  How now, Sir John? What are you brawling here?
                Doth this become your place, your time, and business?            50
                You should have been well on your way to York.
                Stand from him, fellow, wherefore hang'st thou upon him?

HOSTESS  O my most worshipful lord, and't please your grace, I am a poor
                widow of Eastcheap, and he is arrested at my suit.

JUSTICE  For what sum?                                                           55

HOSTESS  It is more than for some, my lord, it is for all – all I have; he hath
                eaten me out of house and home, he hath put all my substance into
                that fat belly of his; but I will have some of it out again, or I will ride
                thee a-nights like the mare.

FALSTAFF  I think I am as like to ride the mare, if I have any vantage of       60
                ground to get up.

JUSTICE  How comes this, Sir John? What man of good temper would
                endure this tempest of exclamation? Are you not ashamed to enforce
                a poor widow to so rough a course to come by her own?

FALSTAFF  What is the gross sum that I owe thee?                                65

HOSTESS  Marry, if thou wert an honest man, thyself and the money too:
                thou didst swear to me upon a parcel-gilt goblet, sitting in my
                Dolphin chamber at the round table by a sea-coal fire, upon
                Wednesday in Wheeson week, when the prince broke thy head for
                liking his father to a singing man of Windsor – thou didst swear to me   70
                then, as I was washing thy wound, to marry me, and make me my lady

---

49 What] Q; What, *Pope;* What! *Knight*   52 thou upon] Q; upon F; thou on *Pope;* on *Collier*   56 all – all] all: all F, *Capell;* al Q
59 a-nights] a nights Q; o'Nights F   62 What] Q; Fie, what a F; Fie! what *Capell*   68 upon] Q; on F   69 Wheeson] Q; Whitson
F   70 liking his father] Q; lik'ning him F

---

48 **stand** to support, stand up for.

49 **What** Why; see 1.2.90.

53 **and't please** See 1.2.46.

54 **Eastcheap** The street running eastward from
Cheapside; Stow (*Survey of London*, 1598, p. 170)
reports a turmoil raised in a tavern there in 1410 by
Thomas and John, the king's sons, requiring the
intervention of the mayor and sheriffs; in *FV* sig. B1
the 'bloody fray' in Eastcheap is attributed to Prince
Hal and his companions, and is the occasion of his
first arrest.

58–9 **ride . . . the mare** The Hostess means 'night-
mare', but Falstaff in the next line gives a sexual turn
to the expression 'ride the mare', which was used also
of a boys' game (see 2.4.202) and in jocular references
to hanging: the 'three-legged mare' was a name for
the gallows.

60–1 **vantage of ground** favourable opportunity.

64 **so . . . course** The Justice is unconsciously
affected by the 'riding' imagery.

67 **parcel-gilt** partly gilded; the precision of detail
in the Hostess's speech is prompted by her notion of
what a witness's deposition in a trial should be.

68 **Dolphin chamber** Inn rooms were distinguished by names; see *1H4* 2.4.27, 38.

68 **sea-coal** Mineral coal, transported by sea, as
distinct from charcoal.

69 **Wheeson** Dialectal for Whitsun.

70 **liking** likening.

70 **singing man of Windsor** The professional
musicians of the royal chapel enjoyed a mixed reputation (they 'roare deep in the Quire, deeper in the
Tauerne', Earle, *Microcosmographie*, 1628, no. 69),
and there may be an allusion to John Magdalen, of the
king's chapel, who passed himself off as Richard II in
a plot aimed at deposing Henry IV (Stow, *Annales*, pp.
515–16).

thy wife. Canst thou deny it? Did not goodwife Keech the butcher's
wife come in then and call me gossip Quickly, coming in to borrow a
mess of vinegar, telling us she had a good dish of prawns, whereby
thou didst desire to eat some, whereby I told thee they were ill for a      75
green wound? And didst thou not, when she was gone downstairs,
desire me to be no more so familiarity with such poor people, saying
that ere long they should call me madam? And didst thou not kiss me,
and bid me fetch thee thirty shillings? I put thee now to thy book-oath,
deny it if thou canst.                                                      80

FALSTAFF  My lord, this is a poor mad soul, and she says up and down the
town that her eldest son is like you. She hath been in good case, and
the truth is poverty hath distracted her. But for these foolish officers, I
beseech you I may have redress against them.

JUSTICE  Sir John, Sir John, I am well acquainted with your manner of      85
wrenching the true cause the false way. It is not a confident brow, nor
the throng of words that come with such more than impudent
sauciness from you, can thrust me from a level consideration: you
have, as it appears to me, practised upon the easy-yielding spirit of
this woman, and made her serve your uses both in purse and in          90
person.

HOSTESS  Yea, in truth, my lord.

JUSTICE  Pray thee, peace. Pay her the debt you owe her, and unpay the
villainy you have done with her: the one you may do with sterling
money, and the other with current repentance.                             95

FALSTAFF  My lord, I will not undergo this sneap without reply. You call
honourable boldness impudent sauciness: if a man will make curtsy
and say nothing, he is virtuous. No, my lord (my humble duty
remembered), I will not be your suitor. I say to you I do desire
deliverance from these officers, being upon hasty employment in the      100
king's affairs.

76 thou not] Q; not thou F    77 so familiarity] Q; familiar F    81 mad] F; made Q    88–9 consideration: you ... practised] Q;
consideration, I know you ha' practis'd F    90–1 and ... person.] Q; *not in* F    92 Yea, in truth] Q; Yes in troth F    93 Pray thee] Q;
Prethee F    94 with her] Q; her F    97 make] Q; *not in* F    98 lord (my] lord my Q; Lord (your F    99 do desire] Q; desire F

72 **Keech** Lump of suet; in *H8* 1.1.55 Wolsey is
called 'a keech', an allusion to his being a butcher's
son.
  73 **gossip** neighbour.
  74 **mess** small quantity (*OED* sv *sb* 1c).
  76 **green** fresh, unhealed (*OED* sv *a* 10).
  77 **familiarity** familiar; see Munday, *John a Kent*
(*c.* 1590) 348.
  79 **book-oath** oath taken on the Bible.
  81–2 **she says ... you** Implying she had had an
affair with the Justice.

82 **in good case** well-off.
  88 **level** balanced, just.
  90–1 **and ... person** Omitted by F, possibly to
avoid the sexual allusion in 'person'; compare the
omission of 'with' in 'done with her' at 94.
  95 **current** (1) present, (2) genuine (of coins;
compare 'sterling money').
  96 **sneap** snub.
  99 **I ... suitor** I will not beg for favour.

JUSTICE  You speak as having power to do wrong; but answer in th'effect
of your reputation, and satisfy the poor woman.

FALSTAFF  Come hither, hostess.

*[Takes her aside]*

*Enter [Master* GOWER *as] messenger*

JUSTICE  Now, Master Gower, what news?                                       105

GOWER  The king, my lord, and Harry Prince of Wales
Are near at hand; the rest the paper tells.

*[Gives a letter]*

FALSTAFF  As I am a gentleman!

HOSTESS  Faith, you said so before.

FALSTAFF  As I am a gentleman. Come, no more words of it.                   110

HOSTESS  By this heavenly ground I tread on, I must be fain to pawn both
my plate and the tapestry of my dining chambers.

FALSTAFF  Glasses, glasses, is the only drinking, and for thy walls a pretty
slight drollery, or the story of the prodigal, or the German hunting in
waterwork, is worth a thousand of these bed-hangers, and these fly-        115
bitten tapestries. Let it be ten pounds, if thou canst. Come, and 'twere
not for thy humours, there's not a better wench in England. Go wash
thy face, and draw the action. Come, thou must not be in this humour
with me, dost not know me? Come, come, I know thou wast set on to
this.                                                                       120

HOSTESS  Pray thee, Sir John, let it be but twenty nobles, i'faith I am loath
to pawn my plate, so God save me, la.

FALSTAFF  Let it alone, I'll make other shift. You'll be a fool still.

HOSTESS  Well, you shall have it, though I pawn my gown. I hope you'll

104 SD.1] Capell subst.; not in Q, F    104 SD.2] This edn; enter a messenger. Q (at 105); Enter M. Gower F    106 Harry] Q; Henrie
F    107 SD] Dyce; not in Q, F; They draw aside. / Holland    109 Faith] Q; Nay F    114 slight] F; sleight Q    115 bed-hangers] bed
hangers Q; bed-hangings F    116 tapestries.] F; tapestrie, Q    116 and 'twere] Q; if it were F    118 the action] Q; thy action F
119 me, dost ... Come, come,] me, dost not know me, come, come Q; me, come, F    121 Pray thee] Q; Prethee F    121 nobles,
i'faith I am loath] Q; Nobles, I loath F    122 so God save me] Q; in good earnest F    124 though] Q; although F

102 **having ... wrong** being authorised to
misbehave.

102–3 **in ... reputation** in accordance with the
status you claim.

104 SD.2 GOWER The name of the messenger
seems chosen at random, probably suggested by the
paragraph devoted to the poet John Gower as the
father, with Chaucer, of modern English in Holinshed's life of Henry IV (III, 541/2/64 ff.). In the
comedy of languages in *H5* 3.2, Captain Gower
represents English.

111 **By ... ground** Mixing such oaths as 'by this
heavenly light', 'by the ground I tread on'.

111 **fain** content.

113 **Glasses ... drinking** Glass began to replace
metal in drinking-vessels in the late sixteenth century.

114 **drollery** Dutch comic genre painting.

114–15 **German ... waterwork** Boar-hunting
scenes painted in distemper on imitation tapestry.

115 **bed-hangers** cheap bed-curtains.

116 **and** if.

118 **draw the action** withdraw the suit; see 1.

119 **set on** instigated.

121 **nobles** gold coins worth about a third of a
pound sterling.

123 **still** always.

come to supper. You'll pay me all together?                                    125

FALSTAFF  Will I live? [*To Bardolph*] Go with her, with her, hook on, hook
on.

HOSTESS  Will you have Doll Tearsheet meet you at supper?

FALSTAFF  No more words, let's have her.

                    [*Exeunt Hostess, Officers, Bardolph and Page*]

JUSTICE  I have heard better news.                                             130

FALSTAFF  What's the news, my lord?

JUSTICE  Where lay the king tonight?

GOWER  At Basingstoke, my lord.

FALSTAFF  I hope, my lord, all's well. What is the news, my lord?

JUSTICE  Come all his forces back?                                            135

GOWER  No, fifteen hundred foot, five hundred horse
      Are marched up to my lord of Lancaster
      Against Northumberland, and the Archbishop.

FALSTAFF  Comes the king back from Wales, my noble lord?

JUSTICE  You shall have letters of me presently.                              140
      Come, go along with me, good master Gower.

FALSTAFF  My lord.

JUSTICE  What's the matter?

FALSTAFF  Master Gower, shall I entreat you with me at dinner?

GOWER  I must wait upon my good lord here, I thank you, good Sir John.         145

JUSTICE  Sir John, you loiter here too long, being you are to take soldiers
      up in counties as you go.

FALSTAFF  Will you sup with me, Master Gower?

JUSTICE  What foolish master taught you these manners, Sir John?

FALSTAFF  Master Gower, if they become me not, he was a fool that             150
      taught them me. This is the right fencing grace, my lord, tap for tap,
      and so part fair.

125 all together?] al together. Q; altogether? F   126 SD] *Capell subst.; not in* Q, F   129 SD] *Capell subst.; exit hostesse and sergeant.* Q
*(after 127); not in* F   130 better] Q; bitter F   131 my lord?] Q; (my good Lord?) F   132 tonight?] Q; last night? F   133, 136 SH
GOWER] *Rowe; Mess.* Q; *Mes.* F   133 Basingstoke] F; Billingsgate Q   145 SH GOWER] Q (*Gow.*), F   146] *As prose,* Q; *as two lines
divided after* heere. F   147–8] *As prose,* F; *as three lines divided at* ...long, / ...vp / ...go. Q   147 counties] Q; Countries F

126 **Will I live?** As sure as I live.

126–7 **hook on** stick to her; Bardolph must make
sure that the Hostess is fetching the money.

133 **Basingstoke** A market town west of London;
not mentioned in the sources, it looks like the F
scribe's attempt at emending Q's 'Billingsgate' (the
London fish market), which in turn was probably the
result not of misreading but of the Q compositor's
absent-mindedness.

134 A line of verse (like 139) including a
hypermetrical vocative.

146–7 Falstaff is to recruit his soldiers on his way to
York; that leaves unexplained his detour to Gloucestershire for that purpose in 3.2, and suggests that
the recruiting scene belonged to an earlier part of the
original play, when Falstaff was on his way to
Shrewsbury via Coventry, through which he was
ashamed to march his 'charge of foot' (*1H4* 4.2.1–48).

151 **grace** style.

151 **tap for tap** tit for tat; see Marston, *Malcontent*
(1603) 3.2.71: 'these fencing tip-tap courtiers'.

152 **fair** on good terms.

JUSTICE  Now the Lord lighten thee, thou art a great fool.

*Exeunt*

2.2  *Enter* PRINCE HENRY *and* POINS

PRINCE  Before God, I am exceeding weary.

POINS  Is't come to that? I had thought weariness durst not have attached
one of so high a blood.

PRINCE  Faith, it does me, though it discolours the complexion of my
greatness to acknowledge it: doth it not show vildly in me to desire      5
small beer?

POINS  Why, a prince should not be so loosely studied as to remember so
weak a composition.

PRINCE  Belike then my appetite was not princely got, for by my troth, I do
now remember the poor creature small beer. But indeed these          10
humble considerations make me out of love with my greatness. What
a disgrace is it to me to remember thy name – or to know thy face
tomorrow – or to take note how many pairs of silk stockings thou hast
with these, and those that were the peach-coloured once – or to bear
the inventory of thy shirts, as: one for superfluity, and another for use.   15

153 SD] F; *not in* Q  Act 2, Scene 2  2.2] *Scena Secunda.* F; *not in* Q  0 SD PRINCE HENRY *and* POINS] *Rowe; Prince, Poynes, sir
Iohn Russel, with other.* Q; *Prince Henry, Pointz, Bardolfe, and Page.* F  1 Before God,] Q; Trust me F  2 SH] *Poynes* Q *(throughout
scene except / Poyne / at 49 and / Poine / at 71); Poin.* F *(throughout)*  2 Is't] Q; Is it F  4 Faith, it does] Q; It doth F  5 vildly] Q; vildely
F; vilely F4  9 by my troth,] Q; (in troth) F  12 name–] *This edn;* name? Q, F; name! *Hanmer*  13 tomorrow–] *This edn;* to-
morow? Q, F; tomorrow! *Hanmer*  13–14 hast with] Q; hast? (Viz. F, *Rowe*  14 were the] Q; were thy F  14 once–] once, Q; ones?]
F, *Rowe*  15 another] Q; one other F

153 **lighten thee** (1) enlighten you, (2) reduce your
weight.

**Act 2, Scene 2**
2.2 Probably meant to continue in the same location
as 2.1. The survival in Q entrance SD of the words 'Sir
John Russell with other' (i.e. the prince's companions,
called 'knights' in *FV*) suggests that this was set from a
sheet of an earlier version of the play in which
Bardolph's name was Russell or Rossil (see pp. 5 and 9–
15 above). The reutilised sheet must have contained a
tavern scene preparatory to the prince's reformation,
roughly corresponding to scene vi in *FV* (sigs. C1–C3),
immediately preceding *1H4* 3.2 in the final version.

0 SD For the Q version see above; F's version is an
anticipatory rather than a 'massed' entry.

2 **attached** Literally, 'taken into custody', possibly
prompted by Oldcastle's surprise in *FV* at not finding
the prince in prison, to which he had been committed
by the Lord Chief Justice, and by the prince's reply:
'Didst thou not know that I am a Princes son, why tis
inough for me to looke into a prison.'

4–5 **discolours … greatness** makes my high rank
blush for shame.

5 **vildly** vilely, unseemly.

6 **small** watered down, weak.

7 **so loosely studied** (1) educated so badly, (2)
versed in immoral (loose) matters; see *MV* 2.2.196:
'Like one well studied in a sad ostent'.

8 **composition** (1) brew, mixture, (2) invention
(alluding to his poor jokes).

10 **creature** Compare *Oth.* 2.3.309–10: 'good wine
is a good familiar creature'.

11–13 **What … tomorrow** It is degrading for
noblemen to take notice of the name or appearance of
the commoners they come into touch with; see *John*
1.1.187: 'new-made honour doth forget men's
names'.

14 **with these** Most editors prefer the F reading
'Viz. these', implying that Poins owns only two pairs of
stockings, but Q makes good sense: 'apart from these'
he has only one other pair.

14 **peach-coloured** flesh-coloured; fashionable
amongst court gallants.

15 **for superfluity** as a spare.

But that the tennis-court-keeper knows better than I, for it is a low
ebb of linen with thee when thou keepest not racket there, as thou
hast not done a great while, because the rest of the low countries have
made a shift to eat up thy holland; and God knows whether those that
bawl out the ruins of thy linen shall inherit His kingdom: but the      20
midwives say the children are not in the fault; whereupon the world
increases, and kindreds are mightily strengthened.

POINS  How ill it follows, after you have laboured so hard, you should talk
    so idly! Tell me, how many good young princes would do so, their
    fathers being so sick as yours at this time is.                    25

PRINCE  Shall I tell thee one thing, Poins?

POINS  Yes faith, and let it be an excellent good thing.

PRINCE  It shall serve among wits of no higher breeding than thine.

POINS  Go to, I stand the push of your one thing that you will tell.

PRINCE  Marry, I tell thee it is not meet that I should be sad now my father  30
    is sick, albeit I could tell to thee, as to one it pleases me for fault of a
    better to call my friend, I could be sad, and sad indeed too.

POINS  Very hardly, upon such a subject.

PRINCE  By this hand, thou thinkest me as far in the devil's book as thou
    and Falstaff, for obduracy and persistency. Let the end try the man,  35
    but I tell thee my heart bleeds inwardly that my father is so sick; and
    keeping such vile company as thou art hath in reason taken from me
    all ostentation of sorrow.

POINS  The reason?

PRINCE  What wouldst thou think of me if I should weep?                40

POINS  I would think thee a most princely hypocrite.

---

17 keepest] Q; kept'st F   18 of the] Q; of thy F   19 made a shift to] F; *not in* Q   19–22 and God ... strengthened.] Q; *not in* F
20 bawl] *Pope;* bal Q   20 out] Q; out of *Pope;* out from *Capell*   25 being] Q; lying F   25 at this time] Q; *not in* F   27 faith,] Q; *not in*
F   29 you will] Q; you'l F   30 Marry] Mary Q; Why F   34 By this hand] Q; *not in* F   37 vile] Q; vild F

---

16–17 it is ... racket there He does not attend
daily ('keep') the tennis court only when he has no
spare shirt to change into while playing.

18–19 the rest ... holland He has sold or pawned
his best shirt to pay for his sexual indulgence; punning
on: 'low countries' = (1) the Netherlands, (2) the
sexual organ; 'holland' = (1) the country, (2) fine
linen made in Holland for high quality shirts. There
are further puns on 'rest' = (1) repose, (2) remainder;
'made a shift' = (1) managed, contrived, (2) changed
clothes.

19–22 and God ... strengthened Omitted by F as
much because of indecent innuendoes (see 2.1.90–
1 n.) as of profanity. The bastards of Poins bawl out of
his ruined linen because (1) they are swaddled in his
discarded shirts, (2) they are the consequences of the

money got from the sale of his best shirts; see 18–19 n.

20 inherit His kingdom go to Heaven (Matt.
25.34).

21 not in the fault Being a bastard is not the child's
fault.

29 stand the push am prepared to take the thrust
(*1H4* 3.2.66).

33 Very hardly Not likely; the prince should rather
rejoice at his father's death because he is going to
inherit *his* kingdom.

35 Let ... man Proverbial; see Dent E116.1.

38 ostentation outward manifestation; see 'ostent'
in *MV* 2.2.196 quoted at 7 n.

41–5 Alluding to the current saying 'The weeping
of an heir is laughter under a visor' (Dent W248.1),
which dates back to the Latin author Aulus Gellius.

PRINCE  It would be every man's thought, and thou art a blessed fellow to
think as every man thinks: never a man's thought in the world keeps
the roadway better than thine: every man would think me an hypocrite
indeed; and what accites your most worshipful thought to think so?    45

POINS  Why, because you have been so lewd and so much engraffed to
Falstaff.

PRINCE  And to thee.

POINS  By this light, I am well spoke on, I can hear it with mine own ears:
the worst that they can say of me is that I am a second brother, and    50
that I am a proper fellow of my hands, and those two things I confess I
cannot help. By the Mass, here comes Bardolph.

### Enter BARDOLPH *and* [PAGE-]BOY

PRINCE  And the boy that I gave Falstaff: a had him from me Christian,
and look if the fat villain have not transformed him ape.

BARDOLPH  God save your grace.                                          55

PRINCE  And yours, most noble Bardolph.

POINS  Come, you virtuous ass, you bashful fool, must you be blushing?
Wherefore blush you now? What a maidenly man at arms are you
become? Is't such a matter to get a pottle-pot's maidenhead?

PAGE  A calls me e'en now, my lord, through a red lattice, and I could    60
discern no part of his face from the window; at last I spied his eyes,
and methought he had made two holes in the ale-wife's petticoat and
so peeped through.

---

49 By this light] Q; Nay F    49 spoke on] Q; spoken of F    52 By the Mass] Q; Looke, looke F    52 SD] Q; *Enter Bardolfe.* F *(after
54)*    53 a] Q; he F    54 look] Q; see F    55 God] Q; *not in* F    57 SH POINS] Q, F; *Bardolph [to Page] / Theobald subst.*    57 virtuous]
Q; pernitious F    59 Is't] Q; is it F    60 SH PAGE] F; *Boy* Q *(throughout scene)*    60 A calls] Q; He call'd F    60 e'en now] enow Q; euen
now F    62 petticoat] Q; new Petticoat F; red peticote *Oxford*    63 so] Q; *not in* F

45 **accites** (1) induces, (2) summons (see 5.2.140);
compare *More* Add.III (Hand C) 17: 'which might
accite thee to embrace and hugg them'.

46 **lewd** loose.

46 **engraffed** closely attached; a coinage from
'grafting' in gardening; see 5.3.2.

50 **second brother** Only the first-born inherited
the estate, so that younger sons were left to their own
devices for a living.

51 **a proper ... hands** good in a fight; proverbial
(Tilley M163).

53–4 **a had ... ape** Performing apes were tricked
up in fantastic dress, and so apparently is the Page,
whom Falstaff ('a' = 'he') had received from the
prince as a normal boy ('Christian').

56 **And yours** Playing on 'grace' as (1) the form of
address for royalty, (2) the grace of God, of which
Bardolph is in need.

57–9 The speech is obviously addressed to
Bardolph, playing on the scarlet hue of his face (see
1.2.36 n.), and not, as many editors have thought,
spoken by Bardolph to the Page.

57 **virtuous** Preferable to F's 'pernitious', since
blushing is a sign of virtuous feeling as well as of
bashfulness.

59 **to get ... maidenhead** to open and drain a pot
of ale.

60 **A calls** He called; using the historic present for
dramatic effect.

60 **red lattice** Alehouses had red latticed windows,
the same colour as Bardolph's face.

62 **ale-wife's petticoat** A red petticoat was the
badge of prostitutes.

PRINCE  Has not the boy profited?

BARDOLPH  Away, you whoreson upright rabbit, away!  65

PAGE  Away, you rascally Althaea's dream, away!

PRINCE  Instruct us, boy: what dream, boy?

PAGE  Marry, my lord, Althaea dreamt she was delivered of a firebrand, and therefore I call him her dream.

PRINCE  A crown's-worth of good interpretation: there 'tis, boy.  70

POINS  O that this blossom could be kept from cankers! Well, there is sixpence to preserve thee.

BARDOLPH  And you do not make him hanged among you, the gallows shall have wrong.

PRINCE  And how doth thy master, Bardolph?  75

BARDOLPH  Well, my lord; he heard of your grace's coming to town: there's a letter for you.

POINS  Delivered with good respect. And how doth the martlemas your master?

BARDOLPH  In bodily health, sir.  80

POINS  Marry, the immortal part needs a physician, but that moves not him: though that be sick, it dies not.

PRINCE  I do allow this wen to be as familiar with me as my dog, and he holds his place, for look you how he writes.

*[Hands a letter to Poins]*

POINS  *[Reads]* 'John Falstaff, knight' – Every man must know that as oft as  85
he has occasion to name himself: even like those that are kin to the
king, for they never prick their finger but they say: 'There's some of

---

64 Has] Q; Hath F  65 rabbit] Rabbet F; rabble Q  68 Althaea] F; Althear Q  70 'tis] Q; it is F  71 blossom] Q; good Blossome
F  73 And] Q; If F  73 hanged] Q; be hang'd F  74 have wrong] Q; be wrong'd F  76 my lord] Q; my good Lord F  84 how] Q;
not in F  84 SD] *This edn, after Hanmer; not in* Q, F  85 SH] Q, F; *speech continued to Prince, Sisson*  85 SD *Reads*] *Rowe;* Letter. F; *not
in* Q  85 Every] Q, F; *Poins. Every Sisson*  86 has] Q; hath F

---

64 **profited** i.e. from Falstaff's teaching.

66 **Althaea's dream** A perhaps deliberate confusion between Hecuba who, when pregnant with Paris, had the prophetic dream that she was delivered of a firebrand that burned down Troy (see *Tro.* 2.2.110), and Althaea who, at the birth of her son Meleager, was told by the Fates that he would live as long as a brand then in the fire was not consumed; Althaea took the brand out of the fire, but when the adult Meleager killed her brothers, she threw the brand back (see *2H6* 1.1.234).

71 **cankers** caterpillars and other plant pests; see *1H4* 1.3.137: 'This ingrate and cankered Bullingbrook.'

72 **sixpence to preserve thee** Alluding to the cross on Elizabethan sixpenny coins.

73 **And . . . among you** If you don't all manage to get him hanged.

78 **with good respect** ceremoniously (ironical for its opposite). This is one of the letters handed to the Page (not to Bardolph) at 1.2.188–9.

78 **martlemas** The feast of St Martin (11 November), associated with the slaughter of pigs and cattle to ensure provisions for the winter.

83 **wen** wart, fatty excrescence.

83 **dog** See Falstaff's remark to the Chief Justice at 1.2.115–16.

84 SD There is some confusion in the original text as to who is reading the letter (see collation to 85–104), but it seems likely that Poins begins and the prince takes it back at 92, objecting to Poins's lengthy comment.

the king's blood spilt.' 'How comes that', says he that takes upon him not to conceive. The answer is as ready as a borrower's cap: 'I am the king's poor cousin, sir.'

PRINCE Nay, they will be kin to us, or they will fetch it from Japhet. But the letter [*Taking it back*]: 'Sir John Falstaff, knight, to the son of the king nearest his father, Harry Prince of Wales, greeting.'

POINS Why, this is a certificate.

PRINCE Peace. 'I will imitate the honourable Romans in brevity–'

POINS He sure means brevity in breath, short-winded.

[PRINCE] 'I commend me to thee, I commend thee, and I leave thee. Be not too familiar with Poins, for he misuses thy favours so much that he swears thou art to marry his sister Nell. Repent at idle times as thou mayst, and so farewell.

Thine by yea and no, which is as much as to say, as thou usest him: Jack Falstaff with my familiars; John with my brothers and sisters; and Sir John with all Europe.'

POINS My lord, I'll steep this letter in sack and make him eat it.

PRINCE That's to make him eat twenty of his words. But do you use me thus, Ned? Must I marry your sister?

POINS God send the wench no worse fortune, but I never said so.

PRINCE Well, thus we play the fools with the time, and the spirits of the wise sit in the clouds and mock us. Is your master here in London?

BARDOLPH Yea, my lord.

88 that', says he that] *Rowe, after* F4; that (saies he) that Q, F **89** conceive. The] *Rowe, after* F4; conceiue? the F; conceiue the Q **89** borrower's] *Theobald;* borowed Q, F **91** or] Q; but F **91–2** But the] Q; But to the F **92** letter [*Taking it back*]: 'Sir] *This edn;* letter, Sir Q, F; letter. / *Poins.* Sir *Hanmer* **94** POINS Why] Q, F; Why *Hanmer* **95** Romans] Romanes Q, F; Roman *Warburton;* Roman's *Cam.* **95** brevity–'] *This edn;* breuitie. Q, F **96** He sure] Q; Sure he F **97** SH] *Theobald; not in* Q, F **102** familiars] F; family Q **103** sisters] Q; *Sister* F **104** SH] Q; *not in* F **104** I'll] Q; I will F **107** God ... no] Q; May the Wench haue no F **110** Yea] Q; Yes F

**88–9 takes ... conceive** pretends not to understand.

**89 borrower's** 'borrowed' in Q and F makes no sense, while it is natural to think of the would-be borrower with cap in hand.

**91 Japhet** Noah's third son from whom all Gentiles (Europeans) were thought to have descended (Gen. 10.2–5), as the Asians from Shem and the Africans from Ham.

**94 certificate** A patent issued by a sovereign to a subject; in letters the addressee's name should come before that of the writer.

**97 I commend me ... leave thee** I present my regards, I approve of you, and say goodbye; the tripartite *veni, vidi, vici* pattern emblematic of Roman brevity (see 1.1.21 and 4.1.390–2).

**99 at idle times** (1) at your leisure, (2) for your idleness and dissipation.

**101 by yea and no** A mild Puritan oath (from Matt. 5.34), see 3.2.8; taken as a survival of the satire on 'Oldcastle', a Lollard.

**101–2 as thou usest him** A formula in challenges; see Aguecheek's message to Cesario, *TN* 3.4.169.

**103 brothers and sisters** Another possible survival of Oldcastle's Puritanical Lollard affiliation, though in *FV* Oldcastle's name with his familiars was not Jack but 'Jockey'.

**104 sack** See 1.2.155; compare the Summoner in *1 Oldcastle* 550–619, forced to eat up the summons he was to serve on Sir John.

**105 twenty** quite a number; playing on 'words' as 'oaths'.

**108 play ... time** Compare Sonnet 124.13–14: 'To this I witness call the fools of time, / Which die for goodness, who have lived for crime.'

PRINCE  Where sups he? Doth the old boar feed in the old frank?

BARDOLPH  At the old place, my lord, in Eastcheap.

PRINCE  What company?

PAGE  Ephesians, my lord, of the old church.

PRINCE  Sup any women with him?                                            115

PAGE  None, my lord, but old Mistress Quickly and Mistress Doll
Tearsheet.

PRINCE  What Pagan may that be?

PAGE  A proper gentlewoman, sir, and a kinswoman of my master's.

PRINCE  Even such kin as the parish heifers are to the town bull. Shall we   120
steal upon them, Ned, at supper?

POINS  I am your shadow, my lord, I'll follow you.

PRINCE  Sirrah, you boy and Bardolph, no word to your master that I am
yet come to town; there's for your silence.

BARDOLPH  I have no tongue, sir.                                           125

PAGE  And for mine, sir, I will govern it.

PRINCE  Fare you well: go.

                                          *[Exeunt Page and Bardolph]*
This Doll Tearsheet should be some road.

POINS  I warrant you, as common as the way between St Albans and
London.                                                                   130

PRINCE  How might we see Falstaff bestow himself tonight in his true
colours, and not ourselves be seen?

POINS  Put on two leathern jerkins and aprons, and wait upon him at his
table as drawers.

PRINCE  From a god to a bull: a heavy descension! It was Jove's case.      135

---

120–1 Shall … supper?] *As separate line,* F    124 come to town;] Q; in Towne. F    124 there's … silence] *As separate line,* F
127 you] Q; ye F    127 SD] *Capell subst.; not in* Q, F    133 leathern] Q; Leather F    134 as] Q; like F    135 descension!] descension,
Q; declension: F

111 **frank** pig-pen; recalling the proverbial expression 'He feeds like a boar in a frank' (Tilley B483),
with a possible allusion to the Boar's Head tavern in
Eastcheap.

114 **Ephesians … church** boon companions,
topers (see *Wiv.* 4.5.18); with reference to Paul's
description of them before conversion (Eph. 5.3–8),
but see *1 Oldcastle* 1928–30: 'I am neither heretike nor
puritane, but of the old church; ile sweare, drinke ale,
kisse a wench…'

118 **Pagan** Heathen, not a Christian, or 'normal'
person (see 53, 'a had him from me Christian'); the
meaning 'prostitute' (*OED*) is later.

120 **town bull** The bull kept at the parish or town

expense to serve in turn the different cattle breeders.

128 **some road** common whore; from the proverbial 'as common as the highway' (Tilley H457), with a
specific reference to the Great North Road going
through St Albans (129–30).

131 **bestow himself** acquit himself, behave (*OED*
sv *v* 5c).

131–2 **in his true colours** according to his real
nature; proverbial, Dent C520.1.

134 **drawers** drawers of ale (tavern waiters), normally apprentices of a publican; see 136.

135 **heavy descension** serious degradation; alluding to the rape of Europa, when Jove transformed
himself into a bull.

From a prince to a prentice: a low transformation, that shall be mine;
for in everything the purpose must weigh with the folly. Follow me,
Ned.

*Exeunt*


**2.3** *Enter* NORTHUMBERLAND, *his* LADY, *and* LADY PERCY, *wife to*
*Harry Percy*

NORTHUMBERLAND  I pray thee, loving wife, and gentle daughter,
      Give even way unto my rough affairs:
      Put not you on the visage of the times
      And be like them to Percy troublesome.
LADY NORTHUMBERLAND  I have given over, I will speak no more,          5
      Do what you will, your wisdom be your guide.
NORTHUMBERLAND  Alas, sweet wife, my honour is at pawn,
      And, but my going, nothing can redeem it.
LADY PERCY  O, yet for God's sake go not to these wars;
      The time was, father, that you broke your word,                     10
      When you were more endeared to it than now,
      When your own Percy, when my heart's dear Harry
      Threw many a northward look to see his father
      Bring up his powers, but he did long in vain.
      Who then persuaded you to stay at home?                              15
      There were two honours lost: yours and your son's.
      For yours, the God of heaven brighten it;
      For his, it stuck upon him as the sun

---

Act 2, Scene 3   2.3] *Scena Tertia.* F; *not in* Q   0 SD *his* LADY] F; *and his wife* Q   0 SD *and . . . Percy*] *and the wife to Harry Percie.* Q; *and Harrie Percies Ladie.* F   1 pray thee] Q; prethee F   2 even] Q; an euen F   5, 50 SH LADY NORTHUMBERLAND] *Rowe;* Wife. Q, F   9, 53 SH LADY PERCY] *La.* F; *Kate.* Q   9 God's] Q; heauens F   10 that] Q; when F   11 endeared] endeer'd F; endeere Q   12 heart's dear Harry] Q; heart-deere-*Harry* F   17 the God of heaven] Q; may heauenly glory F

---

**137 weigh with** counterbalance.

**Act 2, Scene 3**
**2.3** According to Holinshed, Northumberland's
absence from Gaultree was due to the rebels' haste,
not to his decision. The scene is the last in which
Northumberland appears and the only one in *Part*
*Two* with Lady Percy, an important character in *Part*
*One*.
  **2 even** (1) free, open, (2) smooth, in contrast with
'rough'.

**3 visage** (1) aspect, (2) visor, mask.
  **10–14** On Northumberland's failure to intervene at
Shrewsbury see Induction 37 and *1H4* 4.1.13–85.
  **11 endeared** attached to, bound by (honour).
  **17 brighten it** give it new lustre.
  **18 stuck** Used of the lustre of fixed heavenly
bodies; see *Ant.* 5.2.79–80: 'His face was like the
heavens, and therein stuck / A sun and moon.'

In the grey vault of heaven, and by his light
Did all the chivalry of England move                              20
To do brave acts. He was indeed the glass
Wherein the noble youth did dress themselves.
He had no legs that practised not his gait;
And speaking thick, which Nature made his blemish,
Became the accents of the valiant,                                25
For those that could speak low and tardily
Would turn their own perfection to abuse
To seem like him. So that in speech, in gait,
In diet, in affections of delight,
In military rules, humours of blood,                              30
He was the mark and glass, copy and book,
That fashioned others. And him – O wondrous! – him –
O miracle of men! – him did you leave,
Second to none, unseconded by you,
To look upon the hideous god of war                               35
In disadvantage, to abide a field
Where nothing but the sound of Hotspur's name
Did seem defensible: so you left him.
Never, O never do his ghost the wrong
To hold your honour more precise and nice                         40
With others than with him. Let them alone:
The marshal and the archbishop are strong.

23–45 He … grave.] F; *not in* Q   32 him – O wondrous! – him] him, O wondrous! him, F; him, O wondrous him! *Rowe*

19 **grey** The morning sky is described as 'grey and bright' in *Tit.* 2.2.1.

**21–2 the glass … themselves** See *More* *752–3: 'Ile be thy glasse, dress thy behauiour according to my cariage.'

**23–45** The omission of this long passage in Q might have been due to the fact that in 1600 the rebel Hotspur so favourably described might have been identified with the Earl of Essex; more likely it was intended to lighten the part of Lady Percy, as the boy who played it had in the next scene to create the exacting new role of Doll Tearsheet (compare the case of Lord Bardolph in 1.3).

**24 thick** fast and loud; see Cotgrave *French Dictionary* (1632): 'Bretonner. To speake thick and short'.

27 **turn … abuse** renounce their correct (quiet and slow) enunciation.

29 **affections of delight** choice of pleasures.

30 **humours of blood** moods.

31 **mark** point of reference.

32 **wondrous! – him** F's punctuation is at least as dramatically effective as (and rhetorically more correct than) that suggested by Rowe.

34 **unseconded** not supported.

36 **abide a field** face a battle.

38 **defensible** to provide defence.

40 **precise and nice** punctiliously upheld; synonyms used for emphasis.

       Had my sweet Harry had but half their numbers,
       Today might I, hanging on Hotspur's neck,
       Have talked of Monmouth's grave.

NORTHUMBERLAND                Beshrew your heart,    45
       Fair daughter, you do draw my spirits from me
       With new lamenting ancient oversights.
       But I must go and meet with danger there,
       Or it will seek me in another place
       And find me worse provided.

LADY NORTHUMBERLAND         O fly to Scotland,    50
       Till that the nobles and the armèd commons
       Have of their puissance made a little taste.

LADY PERCY If they get ground and vantage of the king,
       Then join you with them like a rib of steel
       To make strength stronger; but, for all our loves,    55
       First let them try themselves: so did your son,
       He was so suffered, so came I a widow,
       And never shall have length of life enough
       To rain upon remembrance with mine eyes,
       That it may grow and sprout as high as heaven    60
       For recordation to my noble husband.

NORTHUMBERLAND Come, come, go in with me: 'tis with my mind
       As with the tide swelled up unto his height
       That makes a still stand, running neither way.
       Fain would I go to meet the archbishop,    65
       But many thousand reasons hold me back.
       I will resolve for Scotland: there am I
       Till time and vantage crave my company.

                                  *Exeunt*

---

**43 numbers** See 1.3.109 n.

**45 Beshrew** A mild, affectionate or jocular form of curse.

**46 spirits** the vital spirits that, like the humours (30), conditioned man's vitality.

**52** Have put to trial their strength.

**53 get ... of** gain superiority over ('ground' and 'vantage' are synonymous).

**54 rib of steel** A favourite metaphor in Shakespeare, from the metal hoops of barrels.

**57 was so suffered** was allowed to try his strength alone.

**57 came** became (*OED* come *v* 2a).

**59 rain ... eyes** water with tears the plant of remembrance (rosemary).

**61 For recordation to** In memory of.

**64 a still stand** a moment or point of stillness.

**2.4** *Enter* FRANCIS *and another* DRAWER

FRANCIS  What the devil hast thou brought there: apple-johns? Thou knowest Sir John cannot endure an apple-john.

DRAWER  Mass, thou sayst true: the prince once set a dish of apple-johns before him and told him there were five more Sir Johns, and putting off his hat said 'I will now take my leave of these six dry, round, old, withered knights.' It angered him to the heart, but he hath forgot that.    5

FRANCIS  Why then, cover and set them down, and see if thou canst find out Sneak's noise: Mistress Tearsheet would fain hear some music. Dispatch: the room where they supped is too hot, they'll come in straight.    10

*Enter* WILL

WILL  Sirrah, here will be the prince and Master Poins anon, and they will put on two of our jerkins and aprons, and Sir John must not know of it: Bardolph hath brought word.

FRANCIS  By the Mass, here will be old utis: it will be an excellent stratagem.    15

DRAWER  I'll see if I can find out Sneak.

*Exit [with Francis]*

Act 2, Scene 4   2.4] *Scœna Quarta.* F; *not in* Q   0 SD] *This edn, after Ridley; Enter a Drawer or two* Q; *Enter two Drawers.* F   1, 7 SH FRANCIS] Q; 1.*Drawer* F   1 the devil] Q; *not in* F   3 SH DRAWER] *Draw.* Q; 2.*Draw.* F   3 Mass,] Q; *not in* F   8 hear] Q; haue F   8–9 music. Dispatch] *Pope; musique. / Dra. Dispatch* Q; *Musique.* F   9–10 Dispatch ... straight.] Q; *not in* F   10 SD] Q *(after 13); in this position, Davison; not in* F; *Enter Third Drawer / Alexander (after music at 8)*   11 SH WILL] *Davison; Francis* Q; 2.*Draw.* F   14 SH FRANCIS] *Davison; Dra.* Q; 1.*Drawer* F; 3 *Drawer / Alexander*   14 By the Mass] Q; *Then* F   16 SH DRAWER] *Davison; Francis* Q; 2.*Draw.* F   16 SD.1 *with Francis*] *This edn, after Davison; not in* Q, F; *with third drawer / Alexander*

**Act 2, Scene 4**
**2.4** The location commonly given is the Boar's Head tavern in Eastcheap, but the name is never mentioned in either part of *Henry IV*: such a tavern existed in Elizabethan times and an allusion to it was seen in 2.2.111. Significantly, this is the only scene in *2H4* where the prince and Falstaff meet before the final rejection, while two completely new characters are introduced with emblematic names, Pistol and Doll Tearsheet (see pp. 15–18 above).

**1–16** The confusion in the directions and the distribution of speeches (see collation) is possibly due to the fact that the speakers don't matter: the drawers are marking time to allow for the impersonator of Lady Northumberland to change back into the Hostess and for the boy who played Lady Percy to dress as Doll. It is clear that, after an exchange between two drawers, a third brings the news of the arrival of the prince and Poins, and though 'Will' in

the misplaced Q SD is probably the book-keeper's designation of the actor doubling this small part (like 'Sincklo' in 5.4), it may be accepted as a character's name to avoid cumbersome SHs such as 'First, Second, Third Drawer'.

**1 apple-johns** A type of apple maturing near St John's day (27 December), but eaten when shrivelled; see *1H4* 3.3.4: 'and withered like an old apple-john'.

**7 cover** lay the cloth on the table.

**8 noise** concert of musicians; a collective noun. See *FV* sig. B3ᵛ, where the prince, after boxing the Lord Chief Justice on the ear, orders Ned to 'prouide a noyse of Musitians'.

**9 Dispatch** The expression is normally used at the end of a speech (see 5.5.4); Q must be mistaken in assigning it to a new speaker and F solved the problem by omitting the whole sentence.

**14 old utis** a fine to-do; 'old' is merely an intensive, while 'utis' is obsolete for 'outcry'.

*Enter* HOSTESS *and* DOLL TEARSHEET

HOSTESS  I'faith, sweetheart, methinks now you are in an excellent good
temperality. Your pulsidge beats as extraordinarily as heart would
desire, and your colour, I warrant you, is as red as any rose, in good
truth, la; but i'faith, you have drunk too much canaries, and that's a        20
marvellous searching wine, and it perfumes the blood ere one can say
'What's this.' How do you now?

DOLL  Better than I was – hem.

HOSTESS  Why, that's well said: a good heart's worth gold. – Lo, here
comes Sir John.                                                               25

*Enter* FALSTAFF [*, singing*]

FALSTAFF  When Arthur first in court –
Empty the jordan –

                                                          [*Exit Will*]

And was a worthy king –
How now, Mistress Doll?

HOSTESS  Sick of a calm, yea, good faith.                                     30

FALSTAFF  So is all her sect: and they be once in a calm they are sick.

DOLL  A pox damn you, you muddy rascal, is that all the comfort you give
me?

FALSTAFF  You make fat rascals, Mistress Doll.

DOLL  I make them? Gluttony and diseases make them, I make them not.          35

16 SD.2 HOSTESS] F; *mistris Quickly* Q   17 SH HOSTESS] *Host.* F; *Quickly* Q   17, 20 I'faith] Q; *not in* F   19–20 in good truth, la] Q;
*not in* F   21 one] Q; *wee* F   23, 32, 35 SH DOLL] F; *Tere.* Q   24 SH HOSTESS] *Host.* F; *Qui.* Q   24 that's] Q; that was F   24 Lo,] Q;
looke F   25 SD] F; *enter sir Iohn.* Q   25 SD *singing*] Capell; *not in* Q, F   26 SH FALSTAFF] *Falst.* F; *sir Iohn* Q   26–9] *So arranged,
Rowe subst.; prose,* Q, F   27 SD] *Davison, after Capell (Exit Drawer.); Exit Francis / Alexander; not in* Q, F   30 good faith] Q; *good-
sooth* F   31 and] Q; if F   32 A pox damn you] Q; *not in* F   35 them, I] F; I Q

18 **temperality ... pulsidge** Quicklyisms for
'temper' and 'pulse'.

18 **extraordinarily** The Hostess means
'ordinarily', regularly.

20 **canaries** She means Canary wine.

21 **searching** penetrating.

21 **perfumes** The Hostess intends 'perfuses'
(meaning 'suffuses' or 'permeates').

23 **hem** A conventional notation for a hiccough;
but see 3.2.179 n.

26, 28 From the popular ballad, 'Sir Launcelot du
Lake': 'When Arthur first in Court began / And was
approved king'.

27 **jordan** chamber-pot.

30 **calm** The Hostess means 'qualm' (fainting fit),
but Falstaff pretends to take her literally.

31 **sect** (1) sex (women in general), (2) profession
(prostitutes), (3) the religious sect, the Family of
Love, who were accused of practising free love.

31 **and ... sick** 'and' = 'if'; playing on (1) the
proverbial fickleness of women, (2) the idea that
prostitutes are out of work only when sick.

32 **muddy rascal** Originally 'rascal' was the name
for young deer, defined as 'muddy' when sluggish and
out of season; see *Ham.* 2.2.594: 'a dull and muddy-
mettled rascal'; and compare 'muddy conger' at 44.

34 **make fat rascals** A contradiction in terms since
young deer are lean.

FALSTAFF  If the cook help to make the gluttony, you help to make the
diseases, Doll; we catch of you, Doll, we catch of you. Grant that, my
poor virtue, grant that.

DOLL  Yea, joy, our chains and our jewels.

FALSTAFF  Your brooches, pearls and ouches – for to serve bravely is    40
to come halting off, you know; to come off the breach with his pike
bent bravely; and to surgery bravely; to venture upon the charged
chambers bravely –

DOLL  Hang yourself, you muddy conger, hang yourself.

HOSTESS  By my troth, this is the old fashion: you two never meet but you    45
fall to some discord; you are both, i'good truth, as rheumatic as two
dry toasts, you cannot one bear with another's confirmities. What the
good-year! One must bear, and that must be you, you are the weaker
vessel, as they say, the emptier vessel.

DOLL  Can a weak empty vessel bear such a huge full hogshead? There's a    50
whole merchant's venture of Bordeaux stuff in him: you have not seen
a hulk better stuffed in the hold. Come, I'll be friends with thee, Jack:
thou art going to the wars, and whether I shall ever see thee again or
no, there is nobody cares. ‹

36 help to] Q; *not in* F    39 Yea, joy] Q; I marry, F; Yea, Mary's joys *Davison*    41 off, you know;] *Rowe*; off, you know Q; off: you know, F    43 bravely – ] *Rowe*; brauely. Q, F    44] Q; *not in* F    45 By my troth] Q; Why F    50 SH DOLL] *Dol.* F; *Dorothy* Q *(catchword / Doll.)*

**39 Yea, joy** In F 'I [= Ay] marry', a mild expletive which suggests the existence of a stronger oath in the original; Humphreys thinks that 'joy' in Q is a misreading of 'Jesu' (see 237); but 'joy' may be an ironical term of endearment for 'gem', connected with what follows.

**39 our chains ... jewels** Doll plays on 'catch of you' at 37 (= be infected), taking it to mean 'steal from you'.

**40 brooches ... ouches** Possibly an adaptation of the popular ballad 'The Boy and the Mantle', but all three words are also euphemisms for scabs, carbuncles and skin sores caused by venereal disease; the original meaning of 'ouch' is a gold brooch set with diamonds.

**40–3 for to ... chambers bravely** A sequence of quibbles on military metaphors turned into sexual innuendoes connected with venereal disease.

**44** Omitted by F, not, as frequently suggested, by mistake for 40–3, but because it brings out the obscene double-meaning in Falstaff's speech; 'conger' is the sea-eel, haunting muddy shallows, with a sexual implication that accounts for its being an abusive epithet; compare Dekker, *Shoemakers'*

*Holiday* 4.128–9: 'you soused conger', and *1 Oldcastle* 545–6: 'I could eate this conger.'

**46–7 rheumatic ... dry toasts** choleric; the Hostess makes the same mistake in *H5* 2.4.38; the choleric humour being hot and dry, Doll and Falstaff grate upon each other.

**47 confirmities** Quicklyism for 'infirmities', with biblical reference to Rom. 15.1.

**47–8 What the good-year** The favourite exclamation of impatience of Sir Thomas More's second wife; see Appendix 2, p. 224 below, for the influence of Harpsfield's account of Lady More on the Hostess's language.

**48 bear** Playing on the proverbial 'Women are made to bear'; see *Shr.* 2.1.200.

**48–9 weaker vessel** Proverbial (Tilley w655), from 1 Pet. 3.7, with a quibble at 50 on 'vessel' = (1) container, (2) merchant ship.

**50 hogshead** (1) wine-barrel, (2) swinish person.

**51 merchant's ... stuff** shipload of Bordeaux wine; for 'merchant's venture' (literally 'a merchant-man's contents at risk in a sea voyage'), see 1.1.180–6 n.

**52 hulk** See 1.1.19 n.

*Enter* DRAWER

DRAWER  Sir, Ancient Pistol's below, and would speak with you.  55

DOLL  Hang him, swaggering rascal, let him not come hither. It is the foul-mouthedst rogue in England.

HOSTESS  If he swagger, let him not come here. No, by my faith, I must live among my neighbours, I'll no swaggerers, I am in good name and fame with the very best. Shut the door, there comes no swaggerers  60 here: I have not lived all this while to have swaggering now. Shut the door I pray you.

FALSTAFF  Dost thou hear, hostess?

HOSTESS  Pray ye pacify yourself, Sir John, there comes no swaggerers here.  65

FALSTAFF  Dost thou hear? It is mine ancient.

HOSTESS  Tilly-vally, Sir John, ne'er tell me. And your ancient swagger, a comes not in my doors. I was before Master Tisick the debuty t'other day, and as he said to me – 'twas no longer ago than Wedsday last, ay, good faith – 'Neighbour Quickly', says he – Master Dumb our  70 minister was by then – 'Neighbour Quickly', says he, 'receive those that are civil, for', said he, 'you are in an ill name.' Now a said so, I can tell whereupon. 'For', says he, 'you are an honest woman, and well thought on, therefore take heed what guests you receive; receive', says he, 'no swaggering companions.' There comes none here. You  75 would bless you to hear what he said! No, I'll no swaggerers.

FALSTAFF  He's no swaggerer, hostess, a tame cheater, i'faith, you may

55 Pistol's] Q; *Pistoll* is F   58 No, by my faith] Q; *not in* F   59 among] Q; amongst F   64 ye] Q; you F   67–8 And your … swagger, a comes] *Conj. Maxwell;* & your .. swaggrer comes Q; your … Swaggerer comes F   68 debuty t'other] Q; Deputie, the other F   69 'twas] Q; it was F   69 Wedsday] Q; Wednesday F   69–70 ay, good faith – ] I good faith Q; *not in* F; i'good faith, *Cam.*   70 Dumb] Dumbe Q; Dombe F   72 said] Q; sayth F   72 a] Q; hee F   77 i'faith] Q; hee F

55 **Ancient** Ensign, standard-bearer; a military rank.

56 **swaggering** boastful, hectoring; Pistol is characterised as the type of the *miles gloriosus* even before his first appearance on stage.

59 **I'll** 'have' is understood.

60 **comes** A singular form for the plural.

64 **pacify** A mixture of 'satisfy' and 'peace, keep quiet'.

67 **Tilly-vally** Another exclamation of impatience characteristic of Lady More; see 47–8 n.

67–8 **And … a comes** If your ancient swagger, he comes; the use of the ampersand (&) and of 'swaggrer' for 'swagger a' in Q obscured the conditional structure of the sentence.

68 **I was … debuty** Tisick (= 'consumptive, racked by cough') is an appropriate name for a petty magistrate deputising for an alderman in a City ward, before whom the Hostess was summoned for keeping a disorderly house; see *1H4* 3.3.114–15.

70 **Master Dumb** Non-preaching parsons were called 'dumb dogs'.

72–3 **a said … whereupon** I know his reasons for saying so.

75 **companions** fellows; see 1.2.156–7.

75–6 **You … bless you** You would be surprised; from the exclamation 'Bless me!'

77 **tame cheater** innocuous sharper at games.

stroke him as gently as a puppy greyhound; he'll not swagger with a
Barbary hen if her feathers turn back in any show of resistance. Call
him up, drawer.                                                         80

HOSTESS  Cheater call you him? I will bar no honest man my house, nor
no cheater, but I do not love swaggering; by my troth, I am the worse
when one says 'swagger'. Feel, masters, how I shake, look you, I
warrant you.

DOLL  So you do, hostess.                                               85

HOSTESS  Do I? Yea in very truth do I, and 'twere an aspen leaf. I cannot
abide swaggerers.

*Enter Ancient* PISTOL, BARDOLPH *and* PAGE

PISTOL  God save you, Sir John.

FALSTAFF  Welcome, Ancient Pistol. Here, Pistol, I charge you with a
cup of sack: do you discharge upon mine hostess.                       90

PISTOL  I will discharge upon her, Sir John, with two bullets.

FALSTAFF  She is pistol-proof, sir: you shall not hardly offend her.

HOSTESS  Come, I'll drink no proofs, nor no bullets; I'll drink no more
than will do me good for no man's pleasure, I.

PISTOL  Then to you, Mistress Dorothy: I will charge you.               95

DOLL  Charge me? I scorn you, scurvy companion. What, you poor, base,
rascally, cheating, lack-linen mate! Away, you mouldy rogue, away, I
am meat for your master.

PISTOL  I know you, Mistress Dorothy.

DOLL  Away, you cutpurse rascal, you filthy bung, away. By this wine, I'll   100
thrust my knife in your mouldy chaps, and you play the saucy cuttle

---

78 he'll] Q; hee will F   82 by my troth] Q; *not in* F   85 SH DOLL] *Dol.* F; *Teresh.* Q   86 and 'twere] Q; if it were F   87 SD
BARDOLPH *and* PAGE] *Rowe; and Bardolfes boy.* Q; *and Bardolph and his Boy.* F   88 God] Q; *not in* F   92 not] Q; *not in* F   96, 100,
109 SH DOLL] *Dol.* F; *Doro.* Q   101 and] Q; if F

79 **Barbary hen** (1) Guinea hen whose feathers are
easily ruffled, (2) prostitute.

82 **I am the worse** I feel ill.

86 **and 'twere ... leaf** as if I were an aspen leaf;
proverbial (Tilley L140).

87 SD Both Q and F treat the Page as being
Bardolph's and not Falstaff's 'boy', and F repeats the
mistake at 3.2.44 SD; but see 2.2.53–4.

89–92 **I charge ... offend her** Another sequence
of military/sexual quibbles (see 40–3 n.) based on
the name of Pistol: charge = (1) order (to drink), (2)
load (a pistol); discharge = (1) empty the cup (by
toasting the Hostess), (2) fire (a pistol), (3) get sexual
satisfaction; pistol-proof = (1) proof against pistol
fire, (2) past the age of childbearing, (3) able to cope
with Pistol; offend = (1) wound, (2) give offence.

96 **scurvy companion** See 75; 'scurvy', literally
'covered with scabs', is a common term of abuse.

97 **lack-linen mate** fellow that cannot afford to
wear a shirt; see the inventory of Poins's linen at
2.2.13–20.

98 **meat for your master** Punning on 'mate' –
proverbial (Tilley M837) in the sense 'too good for
you', with sexual overtones ('I am game for').

100 **filthy bung** Cant term for pickpocket; 'bung'
= 'purse', and the original expression was probably
'filch-bung'. But with a possible sexual implication,
'bung' being the plug of a barrel.

101 **and you ... cuttle** if you try your dirty tricks;
'cuttle-bung' was a cant term for the knife used by
pickpockets to cut the purse strings.

with me. Away, you bottle-ale rascal, you basket-hilt stale juggler,
you. Since when, I pray you, sir? God's light, with two points on your
shoulder? Much!

PISTOL   God let me not live, but I will murther your ruff for this.                    105

FALSTAFF   No more, Pistol, I would not have you go off here: discharge
   yourself of our company, Pistol.

HOSTESS   No, good Captain Pistol, not here, sweet captain.

DOLL   Captain? Thou abominable damned cheater, art thou not ashamed
   to be called captain? And captains were of my mind, they would                  110
   truncheon you out for taking their names upon you before you have
   earned them. You a captain? You slave, for what? For tearing a poor
   whore's ruff in a bawdy-house? He a captain? Hang him, rogue, he
   lives upon mouldy stewed prunes and dried cakes. A captain? God's
   light, these villains will make the word as odious as the word 'occupy',         115
   which was an excellent good word before it was ill-sorted, therefore
   captains had need look to't.

BARDOLPH   Pray thee go down, good ancient.

FALSTAFF   Hark thee hither, Mistress Doll.

---

103 God's light] Q; what F   105 God … but] Q; *not in* F   106 SH FALSTAFF] *Sir Iohn* Q; *not in* F   106–7] Q; *not in* F   110 And]
Q; If F   114–15 God's light] Q; *not in* F   115–16 word as … sorted,] Q; word Captaine odious: F

102 **basket-hilt stale juggler** Referring to the
practice of fencing with cudgels which were provided
with basketwork hilts, extremely popular among
lower-class Londoners; Pistol is compared to the
unfashionable ('stale') entertainers at country fairs
who exhibited their prowess at cudgel-fencing.

103–4 **with … shoulder** Generally taken to refer
to the laces (see 1.1.53) securing the armour to the
chest, but more likely Doll is placing the finishing
touches to her picture of the 'lack-linen mate' (97),
replacing the shirt with two napkins secured by two
points across the shoulders; see *1H4* 4.2.42–5:
'There's not a shirt and a half in all my company, and
the half shirt is two napkins tacked together and
thrown over the shoulders like a herald's coat without
sleeves.'

104 **Much** Ironical for 'You have much to show!'

105 **murther your ruff** Prostitutes wore large
ruffs round their necks and the tearing of the ruff
became synonymous with sexual assault; see 112–13.

106–7 Falstaff's speech is omitted in F, probably
because of the obvious obscene innuendoes ('go off',
'discharge'; see 89–92 n.).

108 **Captain** As with Fang and Snare (2.1.1 n.) the
Hostess ingratiatingly exaggerates Pistol's rank.

110 **And … mind** If captains thought like me.

111 **truncheon … out** throw you out by cudgel-
ling; a nonce use of truncheon as a verb.

114 **lives … cakes** feeds on left-overs from
bawdy-houses and pastry-cook shops; stewed prunes
are always associated with bawdy-houses (= stews) in
Elizabethan plays (see e.g. *MM* 2.1.89–114), possibly
because they were thought to prevent venereal
diseases; compare Falstaff to the Hostess in *1H4*
3.3.112–13: 'There's no more faith in thee than in a
stewed prune.'

115–16 **as odious … ill-sorted** Omitted by F as
part of the bowdlerising process. Doll's remark on the
bad company ('ill-sorted') into which 'occupy' had
fallen is supported by *OED* (Occupy *v* 8), which notes
that the verb fell out of use during the seventeenth
century and most of the eighteenth; the dictionary
collected 194 quotations covering the sixteenth century and only eight for the next hundred years. See
*More* 341: 'dooth ask him interest for the occupation',
said of a lover who asks his mistress's husband to pay
for her keep; and compare Jonson (VIII, 610, from
*Discoveries*): 'Many, out of their owne obscene Appre-
hensions, refuse proper and fit words, as *occupie*,
*nature*, and the like.'

PISTOL  Not I. I tell thee what, Corporal Bardolph: I could tear her, I'll be   120
    revenged of her.

PAGE  Pray thee go down.

PISTOL  I'll see her damned first. To Pluto's damnèd lake – by this hand!
    To th'infernal deep,
        With Erebus and tortures vile also.                           125
    Hold hook and line, say I, down, down, dogs, down faitors:
        Have we not Hiren here?

HOSTESS  Good Captain Peesel, be quiet, 'tis very late, i'faith. I beseek
    you now, aggravate your choler.

PISTOL  These be good humours indeed! Shall pack-horses               130
    And hollow pampered jades of Asia,
    Which cannot go but thirty mile a day,
    Compare with Caesars, and with Cannibals,
    And Troyant Greeks?
    Nay, rather damn them with King Cerberus,                      135
    And let the welkin roar. – Shall we fall foul for toys?

HOSTESS  By my troth, captain, these are very bitter words.

---

121 of] Q; on F   122 SH PAGE] F; *Boy.* Q *(also at 184)*   123 damnèd] *Rowe;* damnd Q; damn'd F   123 by this hand] Q; *not in* F   124 th'infernal] Q; the Infernall F   125, 127] *As verse, this edn; as prose,* Q, F   125 With] Q; where F   125 vile] Q; vilde F   126 faitors:] *Capell;* faters Q; Fates F   128 'tis] Q; it is F   128 i'faith] Q; *not in* F   130–3] *As verse, Pope; as prose,* Q, F   132 mile] Q; miles F   133 Caesars] Q; *Caesar* F   133 Cannibals] Q, F; Canniball F3–4   134–6] *As verse, Capell; as prose,* Q, F; *as three lines ending ... with / ... roar / ... toys. Pope*   134 Troyant] troiant Q; Troian F

**120 Corporal Bardolph** Another title freely bestowed by the Hostess: in *1H4* and *Wiv.* Bardolph has no military rank, though in *H5* 2.1.2 he is addressed as 'Lieutenant Bardolph' by Nym, whose rank seems actually to be that of corporal.

**123–7** From this point on Pistol adopts his characteristic language modelled on that of the Braggart in John Eliot's *Ortho-epia Gallica* (1593); see J. W. Lever, 'Shakespeare's French fruits', *S.Sur.* 6 (1953), 79–90. Though printed as prose by Q and F, Pistol's speeches are in irregular verse borrowed or adapted from sensational Elizabethan plays.

**123–5 To Pluto's ... also** Reminiscent of Peele's *Battle of Alcazar* (1594, MSR 1907, 1230–54) and Greene's *Alphonsus* (*c.* 1594, MSR 1926, 946). 'Pluto's ... lake' must be the River Styx; Erebus, the son of Chaos and Night, personified the classical hell.

**126 Hold ... line** From an early ballad on angling; see *Lear* 3.6.6–7: 'Nero is an angler in the lake of darkness.'

**126 faitors** Archaic for 'traitors, rogues'; F reading 'Fates' looks forward to the reference at 160.

**127** Possibly referring to Peele's lost play *The Turkish Mahomet and Hiren the Fair Greek*; Pistol, romance-fashion, has named his sword 'Hiren' ('Peace'), playing on the near homophony with 'iron'.

**128 Peesel** The Hostess's pronunciation of 'Pistol' emphasises the pun on 'pizzle', already implicit in the exchanges at 89–92.

**128 beseek** Conflating 'seek' and 'beseech'.

**129 aggravate** The Hostess means the exact opposite: 'assuage', 'placate'.

**130 good humours** See 2.3.30; in *H5* and *Wiv.* this use of 'humours' becomes the main feature of Corporal Nym's language.

**131–2** From *Tamburlaine Part 2* 4.3.1–2: 'Holla, you pampered jades of Asia, / What, can ye draw but twenty miles a day?'

**133–4** The names are picked from the ranting speeches in *Ortho-epia Gallica*, with a fine confusion in the use of 'Cannibals' (implying 'Hannibals', paired off with 'Caesars') and of 'Troyant' as a definition of 'Greeks' – but 'Troyant Greeks' could mean 'the Greeks besieging Troy'.

**135 Cerberus** Not a king, but the three-headed watch-dog of Hades.

**136 let ... roar** A recurrent tag in drinking songs, recalled also in *Tamburlaine Part 1* 4.2.45.

**136 fall ... toys** quarrel over trifles.

BARDOLPH  Be gone, good ancient; this will grow to a brawl anon.

PISTOL  Die men like dogs, give crowns like pins!
    Have we not Hiren here?                                          140

HOSTESS  A'my word, captain, there's none such here. What the good-
    year, do you think I would deny her? For God's sake, be quiet.

PISTOL  Then feed and be fat, my fair Calipolis –
    Come, give's some sack.

    [*Sings*] *Se fortuna mi tormenta, ben sperato mi contenta* –          145
    Fear we broadsides? No, let the fiend give fire –
    Give me some sack! [*To his sword*] And sweetheart, lie thou there.
    Come we to full points here? and are etceteras no things?

FALSTAFF  Pistol, I would be quiet.

PISTOL  Sweet knight, I kiss thy neaf. What, we have seen the seven stars.   150

DOLL  For God's sake, thrust him downstairs, I cannot endure such a
    fustian rascal.

PISTOL  Thrust him downstairs? Know we not Galloway nags?

---

139–40] *As verse*, F; *as prose*, Q    139 Die] F; *not in* Q    141 A'] Q; On F; O' *Theobald*    142 For God's sake] Q; I pray F    143–6] *As verse, Capell; as prose*, Q, F    144 give's] giues Q; giue me F    145 [*Sings*] Se ... contenta – ] *This edn, conj. Keightley; si fortune me tormente sperato me contento*, Q, F (contente.)    147–8] *As prose*, Q, F; *as two lines ending* ... there / ... nothing. *Pope, Capell*    147 SD] *Capell subst.; not in* Q, F    148 here?] Q; here; [*seizing upon a bottle.*] / *Capell;* here, F    148 no things?] Q; nothing. F    151 For God's sake] Q; *not in* F

139 Die ... dogs Proverbial (Tilley D509).

139 give ... pins In *Tamburlaine* the hero gives away conquered kingdoms to his followers as if they were trifles; see e.g. *Part 1* 4.4.116–17.

141 there's ... here The Hostess takes 'Hiren' to be the name of a whore that Pistol believes to be in the house.

143 In *Battle of Alcazar*, 596, 617–18, Muly Mahomet enters offering to his starving wife a piece of lion's flesh on the point of his sword, saying 'Feede then and faint not faire Calypolis / ... Feede and be fat that we may meete the foe / With strength and terror to reuenge the wrong.' Wilson surmises that Pistol is offering the Hostess an apple-john picked at sword-point from the dish on the table (see 1–6).

145 'If Fortune tortures me, the hoped-for good makes me happy.' In spite of Douce's statement that an old rapier in his possession bore this inscription in French, it is unlikely that Pistol is reading the words on his sword; rather, after calling for wine, he breaks into song with a snatch from an Italian madrigal, as at 5.5.89. There is no reason to believe that the mis-spellings in Q and F reproduce Pistol's mispro-nunciations.

146 give fire shoot.

147 sweetheart ... there Weapons are frequently

addressed as if they were persons; see Juliet in *Rom.* 4.3.23: 'Lie thou there' (to her dagger); and *Rom.* 5.3.169–70: 'O happy dagger, / This is thy sheath: there rust, and let me die.'

148 Come ... no things Is this all? Is there no further satisfaction? 'Full points' = (1) points of weapons, (2) full stops; both 'etcetera' and 'thing' refer to the female organ; see *Rom.* 2.1.37–8: 'O that she were / An open etcetera'; and *Rom.* 1.4.23–4: 'to sink in it, should you burthen love – / Too much oppression for a tender thing'. F's 'nothing' is another bowdlerisation.

150 neaf Dialectal for 'hand'; see *MND* 4.1.19: 'Give me your neaf.' Pistol is translating into vulgar English the affected Spanish salutation 'beso las manos' frequently satirised in plays.

150 we have ... stars we shared many night adventures; the 'seven stars' are the Pleiades; see 3.2.177: 'We have heard the chimes at midnight', but compare *1H4* 1.2.14: 'We that take purses go by the moon and the seven stars.'

152 fustian pretentious and worthless (*OED* sv *adj* 3); from a cheap cloth of cotton and flax simulating velvet.

153 Galloway nags (1) small horses bred in Gal-way used as hackneys, (2) prostitutes.

FALSTAFF Quoit him down, Bardolph, like a shove-groat shilling. Nay,
    and a do nothing but speak nothing, a shall be nothing here.                    155

BARDOLPH Come, get you downstairs.

PISTOL What, shall we have incision? Shall we imbrue?
    Then Death rock me asleep, abridge my doleful days!
    Why then, let grievous ghastly gaping wounds
    Untwind the sisters three; come, Atropos, I say!                              160

HOSTESS Here's goodly stuff toward.

FALSTAFF Give me my rapier, boy.

DOLL I pray thee, Jack, I pray thee, do not draw.

FALSTAFF Get you downstairs.

HOSTESS Here's a goodly tumult: I'll forswear keeping house afore I'll be     165
    in these tirrits and frights. So: murder I warrant, now. Alas, alas, put
    up your naked weapons, put up your naked weapons.
                        *[Exeunt Pistol and Bardolph]*

DOLL I pray thee, Jack, be quiet, the rascal's gone. Ah, you whoreson
    little valiant villain, you!

HOSTESS Are you not hurt i'th'groin? Methought a made a shrewd thrust     170
    at your belly.

                     *[Enter* BARDOLPH*]*

FALSTAFF Have you turned him out a'doors?

BARDOLPH Yea, sir; the rascal's drunk, you have hurt him, sir,
    i'th'shoulder.

FALSTAFF A rascal to brave me!                                               175

DOLL Ah, you sweet little rogue, you! Alas, poor ape, how thou sweatest!
    Come, let me wipe thy face: come on, you whoreson chops. Ah,

155 and a ... a] Q; if hee ... hee F   157–60] *As verse, Capell; as prose,* Q, F   157 imbrue?] Q, F; imbrue? [*Snatching up his sword.*] /
*Malone*   160 Untwind] vntwinde Q; vntwin'd F   161 goodly] Q; good F   163 pray thee ... pray thee] Q; prethee ... prethee
F   165 afore] Q; before F   167 SD] *Capell; not in* Q, F   168 pray thee] Q; prethee F   168 rascal's] Q; Rascall is F   170 a made] Q;
hee made F   171 SD] *Capell; not in* Q, F   172 a'doors] Q; of doors F   173 Yea] Q; Yes F   174 i'th'] Q; in the F   177–8 Ah, rogue,
i'faith] A rogue, yfaith Q; Ah Rogue, F

**154 Quoit him** Throw him like a quoit.

**154 shove-groat shilling** A coin used in the game
of shove-groat, which consists in making the coin
slide along a polished board into one of the compart-
ments at the end of it.

**155 and a ... here** if he speaks nonsense he must
leave.

**157 incision** blood-letting.

**157 imbrue** dye (with blood); see Thisbe in *MND*
5.1.344: 'Come, blade, my breast imbrue.'

**158 Death ... asleep** The first words of a song
attributed to Anne Boleyn while awaiting execution.
The context is in the vein of Thisbe's speech mentioned at 157, though echoing *Tamburlaine*.

**160 Untwind ... Atropos** Of the three Fates
('sisters three'), Clotho spun (untwined) the thread of
life, Lachesis drew (unwound) it, and Atropos cut it.

**161 toward** coming up.

**166 tirrits** The Hostess's coinage, conflating 'ter-
rors' and 'fits'.

**169, 176, 188 little** Affectionately playful like the
other epithets addressed by Doll to Falstaff, who is
still pretending to fight after Pistol is gone.

**170 shrewd** vicious.

**175 brave** defy.

**177 chops** fat cheeks; see *1H4* 1.2.136.

rogue, i'faith I love thee. Thou art as valorous as Hector of Troy,
worth five of Agamemnon, and ten times better than the nine
Worthies. Ah, villain!                                                              180

FALSTAFF  Ah, rascally slave! I will toss the rogue in a blanket.

DOLL  Do, and thou darest for thy heart; and thou dost, I'll canvas thee
between a pair of sheets.

PAGE  The music is come, sir.

*Enter* MUSIC

FALSTAFF  Let them play. – Play, sirs. Sit on my knee, Doll. A rascal       185
bragging slave! The rogue fled from me like quicksilver.

DOLL  I'faith, and thou followedst him like a church. Thou whoreson
little tidy Bartholomew boar-pig, when wilt thou leave fighting a-days
and foining a-nights, and begin to patch up thine old body for heaven?

*Enter the* PRINCE *and* POINS *disguised*

FALSTAFF  Peace, good Doll, do not speak like a death's-head, do not bid    190
me remember mine end.

DOLL  Sirrah, what humour's the prince of?

FALSTAFF  A good shallow young fellow, a would have made a good
pantler, a would ha'chipped bread well.

DOLL  They say Poins has a good wit.                                        195

FALSTAFF  He a good wit? Hang him, baboon: his wit's as thick as
Tewkesbury mustard, there's no more conceit in him than is in a
mallet.

DOLL  Why does the prince love him so, then?

180 Ah, villain!] a villaine! Q, ah Villaine. F    181 Ah, rascally] Q; A rascally F    182 and ... and] Q; if ... if F    184 SD] *Placed as in*
Q; *after 183* F    187 I'faith] Q; *not in* F    188–9 a-days ... a-nights] Q; on dayes ... on nights F    189 SD *disguised*] F; *not in* Q    192
humour's] Q; humor is F    193–4 a would ... a would] Q; hee would ... hee would F    194 ha'] a Q; haue F    195 has] Q; hath
F    196 wit's] Q; Wit is F    199 does] Q; doth F

178 **Hector** Leader of the Trojan army at the siege
of Troy; Agamemnon (179) was the leader of the
Greeks.

179–80 **nine Worthies** The outstanding heroes of
mankind celebrated in popular romances: three
Pagans, three Jews, and three Christians.

181 **toss ... blanket** The punishment of cowards.

182–3 **canvas ... sheets** Doll turns the punishment for Pistol into sexual reward for Falstaff.

187 **like a church** A puzzling choice of image in
contrast with 'quicksilver', possibly implying that Falstaff, though bulking large, had not moved from his
place while Bardolph was chasing Pistol away.

188 **tidy** bonny (*OED* sv *adj 2*).

188 **Bartholomew boar-pig** Roast pigs were the
staple food sold at Bartholomew Fair, the annual
carnival held in London on 24 August.

189 **foining** See 2.1.10 n.; again with a sexual
overtone.

190 **death's-head** Miniature skull carried as a
*memento mori*, sometimes with an appropriate motto.

194 **pantler ... chipped bread** A pantler was the
head servant in charge of keeping the bread for a large
family and chipping away the hard crusts without too
much waste.

196 **baboon** utterly stupid; in contrast with 'ape',
playfully said of Falstaff at 176.

197 **Tewkesbury mustard** The mustard made at
Tewkesbury (Gloucestershire) was appreciated for its
thickness.

198 **mallet** wooden hammer; compare the proverbial (Tilley B220) 'as dull as a beetle', the beetle being
a larger mallet; see 1.2.179 n.

FALSTAFF Because their legs are both of a bigness, and a plays at quoits    200
    well, and eats conger and fennel, and drinks off candles' ends for
    flap-dragons, and rides the wild mare with the boys, and jumps upon
    joint-stools, and swears with a good grace, and wears his boots very
    smooth like unto the sign of the Leg, and breeds no bate with telling
    of discreet stories, and such other gambol faculties a has that show a   205
    weak mind and an able body, for the which the prince admits him; for
    the prince himself is such another: the weight of a hair will turn scales
    between their avoirdupois.

PRINCE Would not this nave of a wheel have his ears cut off?

POINS Let's beat him before his whore.                                      210

PRINCE Look whe'er the withered elder hath not his poll clawed like a
    parrot.

POINS Is it not strange that desire should so many years outlive
    performance?

FALSTAFF Kiss me, Doll.                                                     215

PRINCE Saturn and Venus this year in conjunction? What says th'almanac
    to that?

POINS And look whether the fiery trigon his man be not lisping to his
    master's old tables, his notebook, his counsel-keeper!

FALSTAFF Thou dost give me flattering busses.                               220

200 a plays] Q; hee playes F   203 boots] Q; Boot F   205 a has] Q; hee hath F   207 a hair] Q; an hayre F   207 scales] Q; the Scales
F   210 Let's] Q; Let vs F   211 whe'er] where Q; if F   216 th'almanac] Q; the Almanack F   219 master's] master, Q; Masters F

201 **conger and fennel** conger-eel (see 44 n.)
seasoned with fennel to make it digestible.

201–2 **drinks ... flap-dragons** A tavern game
consisting in drinking liquor on which burning objects
(in this case candlewicks) are afloat.

202 **rides ... boys** 'Riding the wild mare' is a
variant of leap-frog.

204 **smooth** close-fitting.

204 **like ... Leg** The Leg was a shop sign
representing a close-fitting boot.

204 **breeds no bate** raises no quarrel (*OED* Bate
*sb¹*).

204–5 **with ... stories** by reporting gossip that
ought to remain private (discreet').

205 **gambol** playful.

208 **avoirdupois** weight.

209 **nave of a wheel** wheel-hub; punning on
'knave' and alluding to Falstaff's rotundity.

209 **ears cut off** The punishment for defaming
royalty.

211 **Look whe'er** Look whether (see 218); i.e. is it
(not) true that.

211 **elder** (1) elder-tree, sapless when withered,
(2) old man (withered = impotent).

211 **poll** top of the head (Doll is ruffling Falstaff's
sparse hair); playing on 'Poll' as the traditional name
for a parrot.

216 **conjunction** (1) in astrology, the apparent
overlapping of two heavenly bodies, as recorded in
almanacs, (2) sexual intercourse. The saturnine
temperament attributed to Falstaff was cold and
sluggish.

218 **fiery trigon** Continuing the astrological comparison: the signs of the Zodiac were divided into four
groups of three (trigons); Aries, Leo and Sagittarius
form the 'fiery trigon', being all of them hot and dry.
The allusion is once again to Bardolph's ('his man')
red face, see 1.2.36 n.

218–19 **his master's ... counsel-keeper** All
attributes of the Hostess, Falstaff's ex-mistress:
'tables' is the same as 'notebook' in the sense of
private diary, recording personal secrets; hence
'counsel-keeper' = 'confidant'. Apparently, while
Falstaff is busy with Doll, Bardolph in whispers
('lisping') courts the Hostess.

220 **busses** kisses.

DOLL  By my troth, I kiss thee with a most constant heart.

FALSTAFF  I am old, I am old.

DOLL  I love thee better than I love e'er a scurvy young boy of them all.

FALSTAFF  What stuff wilt have a kirtle of? I shall receive money a-
Thursday – shalt have a cap tomorrow. A merry song, come; a-grows    225
late, we'll to bed. Thou'lt forget me when I am gone.

DOLL  By my troth, thou'lt set me a-weeping and thou sayst so; prove that
ever I dress myself handsome till thy return! Well, hearken a'th'end.

FALSTAFF  Some sack, Francis!

PRINCE *and* POINS  Anon, anon, sir.    230

FALSTAFF  Ha? A bastard son of the king's? And art not thou Poins his
brother?

PRINCE  Why, thou globe of sinful continents, what a life dost thou lead?

FALSTAFF  A better than thou: I am a gentleman, thou art a drawer.

PRINCE  Very true, sir; and I come to draw you out by the ears.    235

HOSTESS  O, the Lord preserve thy grace! By my troth, welcome to
London. Now the Lord bless that sweet face of thine. O Jesu, are you
come from Wales?

FALSTAFF  Thou whoreson mad compound of majesty, by this light –
flesh and corrupt blood [*Placing his hand on Doll*], thou art welcome.    240

DOLL  How? You fat fool, I scorn you.

POINS  My lord, he will drive you out of your revenge, and turn all to a
merriment, if you take not the heat.

221 By my troth] Q; Nay truely F    224 wilt have] Q; wilt thou haue F    224–5 a-Thursday] Q; on Thursday F    225 shalt] Q; thou
shalt F    225–6 come; a-grows ... we'll] come a growes ... weel Q; come: it growes late wee will F    226 Thou'lt] thou't Q; Thou
wilt F    227 By my troth] Q; *not in* F    227 thou'lt] thou't Q; Thou wilt F    227 and] Q; if F    228 a'th'end] Q; the end F    236 grace]
Q; good Grace F    236 By my troth] Q; *not in* F    237 the Lord] Q; Heauen F    237 O Jesu] Q; what F    239–40 light – flesh] *Rowe*
*subst.*; light, flesh Q; light Flesh F    240 SD] *Rowe subst.*; *not in* Q, F

224 kirtle A garment (bodice and skirt) worn over
the petticoats and under the gown.

225 shalt The omission of the pronoun (restored in
F) is a common colloquialism when the verb ending
already indicates the person.

227 and if.

228 hearken a'th'end wait and see; proverbial
(Tilley E125).

230 Hal and Poins coming forward disguised as
drawers mimic Francis's invariable reply to a
customer's call; see *1H4* 2.4.37–97.

231 Poins his i.e. Poins's; a genitive. Not 'the
brother of the king's bastard son' but 'the brother
(= double) of Poins'.

233 globe ... continents (1) globe composed of
sinful parts, (2) conglobation of receptacles of sin, (3)
mass of sinful contents; with a further pun on the
virtue of 'continence'.

235 draw ... ears Punning on 'drawer'; and see
209 n.

238 from Wales See 1.2.82–3 and 2.1.106–7; but
at 1.3.79–83 the rebels speak as if the expedition to
Wales had hardly begun.

239 compound mass, lump; like 'globe' at 233.

239–40 by this ... blood Falstaff transforms the
current oath 'by this light' into a more concrete one by
turning 'light' into an adjective (= promiscuous, dis-
reputable) referring to 'flesh'; obviously he is not
referring to his own flesh and blood but to Doll's
sitting on his knees.

243 if ... heat if you don't act immediately; proverbial ('Strike while the iron is hot'), and see *Lear*
1.1.308: 'We must do something, and i'th'heat.'

PRINCE  You whoreson candle-mine, you, how vildly did you speak of me
now, before this honest, virtuous, civil gentlewoman?                        245

HOSTESS  God's blessing of your good heart, and so she is, by my troth.

FALSTAFF  Didst thou hear me?

PRINCE  Yea, and you knew me as you did when you ran away by Gad's
Hill – you knew I was at your back, and spoke it on purpose to try my
patience.                                                                     250

FALSTAFF  No, no, no, not so: I did not think thou wast within hearing.

PRINCE  I shall drive you then to confess the wilful abuse, and then I know
how to handle you.

FALSTAFF  No abuse, Hal, a'mine honour, no abuse.

PRINCE  Not – to dispraise me, and call me pantler and bread-chipper    255
and I know not what?

FALSTAFF  No abuse, Hal.

POINS  No abuse?

FALSTAFF  No abuse, Ned, i'th'world, honest Ned, none. I dispraised
him before the wicked, that the wicked might not fall in love with        260
thee; in which doing I have done the part of a careful friend and a true
subject, and thy father is to give me thanks for it. No abuse, Hal,
none, Ned, none; no, faith, boys, none.

PRINCE  See now whether pure fear and entire cowardice doth not make
thee wrong this virtuous gentlewoman, to close with us! Is she of the    265
wicked, is thine hostess here of the wicked, or is thy boy of the wicked,
or honest Bardolph, whose zeal burns in his nose, of the wicked?

POINS  Answer, thou dead elm, answer.

FALSTAFF  The fiend hath pricked down Bardolph irrecoverable, and his

244–5 me now] Q; me euen now F    246 God's] Q; *not in* F    246 of] Q; on F    248 Yea] Q; Yes F    254 a'] Q; on F    255 Not–]
*Dyce*; Not Q, F    255 bread-chipper] Q; Bread-chopper F    259 i'th'] Q; in the F    260–1 with thee] Q; with him F    263 faith] Q;
*not in* F    266 thy boy] Q; the Boy F

244 **candle-mine** Falstaff's fatness is a mine of
tallow to make candles with.

244 **vildly** An alternative spelling of 'vilely'.

248–9 **you knew ... Gad's Hill** Alluding to *1H4*
2.4.267 ff., when Falstaff, convicted of cowardice at
the Gad's Hill robbery, maintained that he had
recognised 'by instinct' that his assailant was Prince
Hal.

252 **wilful abuse** deliberate defamation of a royal
person; see 209 n.

260 **before the wicked** A parody of the typical
language of Puritans; see 2.2.101 n., and compare
*1H4* 1.2.94–5.

260–1 **with thee** After addressing Poins, Falstaff
now turns directly to Hal; in view of what follows, F's
'with him' is a mistaken 'regularisation'.

265 **to close with us** in order to pacify us (*OED*
Close *v* 14).

267 **zeal** 'burning zeal' was the supreme Puritan
virtue, but the reference is to the colour of Bardolph's
nose; see 1.2.36 n.

268 **dead elm** The elm-tree was the main support
for vines and was also used to make coffins. Poins may
mean (1) as a great consumer of wine Falstaff was the
support of vineyards, but is now too old, (2) he is too
old to serve women (see *Err.* 2.2.147: 'thou art an elm,
my husband, I a vine'), (3) he is already in the coffin.

269 **pricked down Bardolph** enlisted Bardolph
for his own; see the enrolment scene, 3.2.91–146.

face is Lucifer's privy kitchen, where he doth nothing but roast malt- 270
worms. For the boy, there is a good angel about him, but the devil
blinds him too.

PRINCE For the women?

FALSTAFF For one of them, she's in hell already, and burns poor souls;
for th'other, I owe her money, and whether she be damned for that I 275
know not.

HOSTESS No, I warrant you.

FALSTAFF No, I think thou art not, I think thou art quit for that. Marry,
there is another indictment upon thee, for suffering flesh to be eaten
in thy house, contrary to the law, for the which I think thou wilt howl. 280

HOSTESS All vict'lers do so; what's a joint of mutton or two in a whole
Lent?

PRINCE You, gentlewoman –

DOLL What says your grace?

FALSTAFF His grace says that which his flesh rebels against. 285

PETO *knocks at door*

HOSTESS Who knocks so loud at door? Look to th'door there, Francis.

*Enter* PETO

PRINCE Peto, how now, what news?

PETO The king your father is at Westminster,
And there are twenty weak and wearied posts

271–2 devil blinds] Q; Deuill outbids F; devil's behind *conj. Wilson;* devil attends *Humphreys;* devil binds *Davison;* devil brands *conj.*
*Berger–Williams* 272 too] Q, F; to't *Sisson* 274 she's] Q; shee is F 281 vict'lers] vitlars Q; Victuallers F 281 what's] Q; What is
F 285 SD] Q *(Peyto); not in* F 286 SD] F; *not in* Q 287 Peto] F; Peyto Q 288 SH PETO] F; *Peyto* Q

270 **Lucifer's ... kitchen** hell; with the usual
allusion to Bardolph's complexion.
270–1 **malt-worms** heavy drinkers; see *1H4*
2.1.75.
271–2 **the devil ... too** The Q reading, rejected or
emended by most editors (see collation), makes perfectly good sense: like everybody else ('too') also the
boy is blinded by the devil, so that he cannot see the
Good Angel constantly hovering about him – as
illustrated in Moralities and in Marlowe's *Doctor
Faustus*, where Mephistophilis prevents Faustus from
listening to the Good Angel's advice. Falstaff is described as the prince's 'ill angel' at 1.2.130.
274 **burns** Referring to the effects of venereal
disease, with which Doll infected her customers.
275 **damned for that** Puritans considered money-
lending (i.e. usury) a capital sin.
278 **quit for that** (1) absolved from the capital sin
of usury, (2) paid back, or rather 'closed the account'
without repayment.

279–80 **suffering ... house** (1) consenting to the
eating of meat in time of Lent, (2) using your house as
a brothel.
280 **howl** Always used in the Bible with reference
to the pains of the damned in hell.
281 **vict'lers** keepers of eating-houses. The
Hostess takes Falstaff's remark at 279–80 in its most
innocent meaning, but is betrayed by her use of
'mutton' which was current for 'prostitute'.
285 **grace** (1) the form of address to a prince, (2)
courtesy, forbearance; see 1.2.20 n., and *1H4*
1.2.17–18.
285 **his flesh ... against** (1) he feels revulsion for,
(2) he lusts after, is sexually roused; see *MM* 3.2.115:
'the rebellion of a cod-piece', and *MV* 3.1.34–6.
286 SD PETO This is the only appearance of Peto in
*Part Two* and he acts merely as a messenger; see 294–
9 n., and p. 19 above.
289 **posts** mounted messengers; see Induction 37.

Come from the North, and as I came along                              290
I met and overtook a dozen captains
Bare-headed, sweating, knocking at the taverns,
And asking everyone for Sir John Falstaff.

PRINCE  By heaven, Poins, I feel me much to blame
So idly to profane the precious time,                                 295
When tempest of commotion, like the south,
Borne with black vapour, doth begin to melt
And drop upon our bare unarmèd heads.
Give me my sword and cloak. Falstaff, good night.
                    *Exeunt Prince, Poins[, Bardolph and Peto]*

FALSTAFF  Now comes in the sweetest morsel of the night, and we must   300
hence and leave it unpicked.
                    *[Knocking at door]*
More knocking at the door? How now, what's the matter?

                    *[Enter* BARDOLPH]

BARDOLPH  You must away to court, sir, presently:
A dozen captains stay at door for you.

FALSTAFF  *[To Page]* Pay the musicians, sirrah. – Farewell, hostess,   305
farewell, Doll. You see, my good wenches, how men of merit are
sought after: the undeserver may sleep, when the man of action is
called on. Farewell, good wenches, if I be not sent away post, I will see
you again ere I go.

DOLL  I cannot speak. If my heart be not ready to burst – Well, sweet Jack,   310
have a care of thyself.

FALSTAFF  Farewell, farewell.
                    *Exit [with Bardolph, Page and Musicians]*

299] *As one line,* Q; *as two lines divided at* Cloake: F   299 SD] *Capell; Exeunt Prince and Poynes.* Q; *Exit* F   301 SD] *Capell subst.; not in* Q, F; *Knocking within. Exit Bardolph.* / *Humphreys*   302 SD] *Capell subst.; not in* Q, F; *after door? Humphreys*   305 SD] *Capell; not in* Q, F   312 SD *Exit*] Qb, F; *not in* Qa   312 SD *with . . . Musicians*] *Riverside subst.; not in* Q, F; *with Bardolph, Peto, Page and Musicians* / *Humphreys*

**292 Bare-headed** A sign of extreme haste: no self-respecting gentleman would go about without a hat.

**293 asking ... Falstaff** Wilson surmises he is summoned for neglect of duty.

**294–9** This speech would have suited better the conclusion of *1H4* 3.3, when Hal had wasted much more time with Falstaff, Bardolph and Peto, and in the original version it may have belonged there.

**296 commotion** rebellion (*OED* sv 4); see 4.1.36.

**296 south** The south wind, thought to bring stormy weather.

**297 Borne** Charged, pregnant; a meaning unrecorded in *OED*.

**299, 301, 302, 312 SD** The original directions are unhelpful for what concerns the action on a stage bustling with at least seven speaking characters plus the musicians and one or two drawers. This deliberate vagueness gives scope to the actors to arrange their 'business' as best suits the individual performance.

**300 the sweetest ... night** See 5.3.40.

**303 presently** immediately.

**305–20** This last section is a subtle exhibition of dramatic ambiguity. While the emptiness of Falstaff's boast is obvious, it is hard to say how far the Hostess's total reversal of her opinion of him is the result of his predicament (going to the wars) or of the new status implicit in his call to court.

HOSTESS Well, fare thee well. I have known thee these twenty-nine
years, come peascod time, but an honester and truer-hearted man –
Well, fare thee well.　　　　315

BARDOLPH [*At the door*] Mistress Tearsheet!

HOSTESS What's the matter?

BARDOLPH Bid Mistress Tearsheet come to my master.

HOSTESS O, run, Doll, run, run, good Doll! Come. – She comes
blubbered. – Yea, will you come Doll?　　　　320

　　　　　　　　　　　　　　　　　　　　　*Exeunt*


**3.1** *Enter the* KING *in his nightgown, alone with a Page*


KING　Go, call the Earls of Surrey and of Warwick;
　　　But ere they come, bid them o'er-read these letters
　　　And well consider of them. Make good speed.

　　　　　　　　　　　　　　　　　　　*Exit* [*Page*]

　　　How many thousand of my poorest subjects

---

316 SD] *Wilson; not in* Q, F; *within/Capell*　319–20 Come. – She . . . Doll] come, she . . . Doll? Q; *not in* F; *Bardolph.* Come!/
*Hostess.* She . . . blubbered. / *Bardolph.* Yea . . . Doll? *Vaughan, Wilson*　319–20 She comes blubbered. – ] she comes blubberd, Q;
*as* SD *Dyce*　320 Yea,] yea! Qb; yea? Qa　Act 3, Scene 1　3.1]*Actus Tertius. Scena Prima.* F; *not in* Q　0 SD *Enter . . . nightgown*] Qb;
*Enter the King* F; *not in* Qa　0 SD *alone with a Page*] alone. Qb; *with a Page.* F; *not in* Qa　1–106] Qb, F; *not in* Q　3 SD] *Exit.* F; *not in* Q

**314 peascod time** The time of the year when peas
form in their pods.

**319–20 Come. – She . . . Doll** Omitted in F
probably because the transcriber of the text could not
'regularise' it to his own content. 'Come' seems
contradictory, since Doll must instead 'go' out, and
Wilson accepted Vaughan's ingenious suggestion of
assigning the first 'Come' and the last sentence to
Bardolph waiting at the door, leaving the Hostess only
the remark 'She comes blubbered' (= 'tear-stained').
But also the Hostess must clear the stage at this point:
her first 'Come' is a friendly encouragement to the
tearful Doll while she is starting towards the door,
then she calls to Falstaff offstage 'She comes blubbered', and from the door repeats her appeal to Doll.

**Act 3, Scene 1**

**3.1** This scene, located in the royal palace and
marking the first appearance of the play's title character, was omitted from the first issue of Q (see discussion at pp. 3–5, 12 above, and in the Textual Analysis,
pp. 200–1 below). As it stands it is the pivotal scene of
*Part Two*, unnecessary for the development of the
action but central to the theme of the play.

**0 SD alone with a Page** The king may be said to be
alone since the three lines addressed to the mute Page

are merely functional to his long soliloquy; see 1.2.0
SD n. 'Nightgown' is not a nightshirt but a rich
dressing-gown.

**1 Surrey . . . Warwick** An odd choice of counsellors, unwarranted by the sources and not mentioned
in *1H4* (the *Duke* of Surrey in *R2* 4.1 is surely a
different person). From 65 it appears that
Shakespeare confuses Warwick with Richard Nevil
'the king-maker', who looms large in the *Henry VI*
plays, while in Henry IV's time the title belonged to
Richard Beauchamp, mentioned by Holinshed (III,
540/1) as the leader, with the Earl of Kent, of a
successful raid on the French coast in 1412. His
daughter Anne, by marrying Richard Nevil, transferred the Warwick title to the latter. Surrey, absent
from the rest of the play and a mute in this scene, is a
plausible name chosen at random, recalling the Surrey whose predominant role in *More* is paired off with
Shrewsbury – though not the battle but the earl of that
name. Holinshed (III, 536/2) records the death of
'Thomas Beauford earle of Surrie' in 1410.

**4–31** The uneasy sleep of the great is a poetical
commonplace, evidenced in Sonnet 39 in Sidney's
*Astrophil and Stella*, but see *H5* 4.1.259–84, and *Mac.*
2.2.32–40.

Are at this hour asleep? O Sleep! O gentle Sleep!                    5
Nature's soft nurse, how have I frighted thee,
That thou no more wilt weigh my eye-lids down
And steep my senses in forgetfulness?
Why rather Sleep liest thou in smoky cribs,
Upon uneasy pallets stretching thee                                 10
And hushed with buzzing night-flies to thy slumber,
Than in the perfumed chambers of the great,
Under the canopies of costly state
And lulled with sound of sweetest melody?
O thou dull god, why liest thou with the vile,                      15
In loathsome beds, and leavest the kingly couch
A watch-case, or a common 'larum bell?
Wilt thou upon the high and giddy mast
Seal up the ship-boy's eyes and rock his brains
In cradle of the rude imperious surge                               20
And in the visitation of the winds,
Who take the ruffian billows by the top,
Curling their monstrous heads and hanging them
With deafing clamour in the slippery clouds,
That, with the hurly, death itself awakes?                          25
Canst thou, O partial Sleep, give thy repose
To the wet sea-son in an hour so rude,
And, in the calmest and most stillest night
With all appliances and means to boot,

---

11 night-flies] Qb; Night, flies F; night, fly'st *Rowe*   14 sound] Qb; sounds F   15 vile] Qb; vilde F   18 mast] F; masse Qb
22 billows] F; pillowes Qb   24 deafing clamour] deaffing clamour Qb; deaf'ning Clamours F   26 thy] F; them Qb; then *Riverside*
27 sea-son] season Qb; Sea-Boy F

---

**9 cribs** cabins, hovels.

**10 uneasy pallets** uncomfortable straw-beds; playing on the contrast with the nearly homophonous 'palace'.

**13–14** If the speech is a late addition, this may have been suggested by 4.2.133–5, but see *MND* 4.1.81–3.

**17 watch-case ... bell** Either 'like a night-watchman in his sentry-box ready to sound the alarum bell', or comparing the king in his canopied bed with the mechanism of a watch in its precious case sounding alarms like a bell.

**18–25** The image of the sailor asleep on the topmast is from Prov. 23.34: 'Thou shalt be as thou layest in the middest of the sea, or sleepest vpon the top of the mast of a shyp', echoed also in *R3* 3.4.99–101. See

A. Davenport, '*2H4* and the *Homily Against Drunkenness*', *N&Q* 195 (1950), 160–2.

**19 Seal up** In falconry 'seel up' = sew up a hawk's eyes.

**21 visitation** A destructive agency falling upon a people, etc. (*OED sv* 8).

**24 deafing** drowning a sound with a louder one (*OED* Deaf *v* 3); see *John* 2.1.147.

**24 slippery** (1) quickly passing, (2) offering no hold.

**25 hurly** tumult, uproar; see *More* Add.II (Hand D) 236.

**27 sea-son** Unrecorded elsewhere, it is the only way to account for Q's 'season', which F changes into 'Sea-boy'.

Deny it to a king? Then happy low lie down,                    30
Uneasy lies the head that wears a crown.

*Enter* WARWICK *and* SURREY

WARWICK  Many good morrows to your majesty.
KING  Is it good morrow, lords?
WARWICK                              'Tis one o'clock, and past.
KING  Why then, good morrow to you all, my lords.
    Have you read o'er the letters that I sent you?                35
WARWICK  We have, my liege.
KING  Then you perceive the body of our kingdom
    How foul it is, what rank diseases grow,
    And with what danger near the heart of it.
WARWICK  It is but as a body yet distempered                      40
    Which to his former strength may be restored
    With good advice and little medicine.
    My Lord Northumberland will soon be cooled.
KING  O God, that one might read the book of fate
    And see the revolution of the times                           45
    Make mountains level, and the continent,
    Weary of solid firmness, melt itself
    Into the sea; and, other times, to see
    The beachy girdle of the ocean
    Too wide for Neptune's hips; how chance's mocks               50
    And changes fill the cup of alteration
    With divers liquors! O, if this were seen,

31 SD SURREY] F; *Surry, and sir Iohn Blunt.* Qb   35 letters] F; letter Qb   44 God] Qb; Heauen F   50 chance's mocks] chances
mockes Qb; Chances mocks F; chances mock *Rowe*   52–5 O, ... die.] Qb; *not in* F

31 Proverbial (Tilley c863).
  31 SD See 1 n.; Q adds to the mute Surrey the ghost
character of Sir John Blunt, a name out of a different
context in Holinshed; see 1.1.16 n.
  33 Alexandrines are used for lines divided between
two characters.
  37–42 The metaphor is based on the concept of the
'body politic', the state as one aspect of the person of
the ruler. The diseases of the country are reflected in
the 'body natural' of the king.
    42 little a little.
    45 revolution process of change.
    46 continent firm land.
    46–50 the continent ... hips The same imagery
as in Sonnet 64.5–8, from Ovid, *Metamorphoses* (trans.
Golding, 1567, fol. 190): 'Euen so haue places often

tymes exchaunged theyr estate. / For I haue seene it
sea which was sustanciall ground alate, / Againe
where sea was, I haue seene the same become dry
lond, / And shelles and scales of Seafish farre haue
lyen from any strond.' The seashore is seen as a girdle
round the waist of the sea god Neptune.
  50 chance's mocks the ironic tricks played by
chance; punning on 'changes' at 51, so that many have
taken 'chances' as a plural subject paralleling
'changes', and 'mocks' as a verb, either a singular
form for the plural or 'mock's' = 'mock us'.
  52–5 O, if ... die Omitted in F probably because
the passage was a marginal addition found only in the
MS. behind Q; in fact line 56 completes the first half
of 52 ('With divers liquors').

The happiest youth, viewing his progress through,
What perils past, what crosses to ensue,
Would shut the book and sit him down and die.                    55
'Tis not ten years gone
Since Richard and Northumberland, great friends,
Did feast together; and in two year after
Were they at wars. It is but eight years since
This Percy was the man nearest my soul,                          60
Who like a brother toiled in my affairs
And laid his love and life under my foot:
Yea, for my sake, even to the eyes of Richard
Gave him defiance. But which of you was by –
You, cousin Nevil, as I may remember –                           65
When Richard, with his eye brimful of tears,
Then checkèd and rated by Northumberland,
Did speak these words, now proved a prophecy:
'Northumberland, thou ladder by the which
My cousin Bullingbrook ascends my throne'? –                     70
Though then, God knows, I had no such intent
But that necessity so bowed the state
That I and greatness were compelled to kiss. –
'The time shall come', thus did he follow it,
'The time will come that foul sin, gathering head,               75
Shall break into corruption.' So went on,
Foretelling this same time's condition

58 year] Qb; yeeres F   68 prophecy:] Qb *subst.*, F; prophecy? *Capell*   70 Bullingbrook] Bullingbrooke F; Bolingbrooke Qb;
Bolingbroke *Pope, et al.*   70 throne'?–] *This edn;* throne, Qb; Throne: F; throne.' *Capell*   71 God] Qb; Heauen F

**59 eight years since** The reference is to the time of the deposition of Richard II, 1399, but the battle of Shrewsbury was in July 1403 and the Gaultree episode (4.1) in 1405, four and six years respectively after the deposition: Shakespeare is deliberately manipulating historical time.

**65 cousin Nevil** Addressed to Warwick; possibly another deliberate confusion, see 1 n. The reference is to *R2* 5.1.55–9, reported nearly verbatim at 69–70 and 74–6, but neither Warwick (or Nevil) nor Bullingbrook (Henry IV) was present in that scene.

**67 checked** See 1.2.154.

**67 rated** berated, reproved; see 5.2.69.

**70 Bullingbrook** The only mention of the name surviving in Q; see pp. 23–5 above.

**72 necessity ... state** The post-Machiavellian doctrine of 'reason of state', systematised by Giovanni Botero in *Ragione di Stato* (1589), had found great favour in European courts.

**73 greatness** eminence of rank, ruling power; turned to ironical account in *TN* 2.5.145–6: 'some achieve greatness, and some have greatness thrust upon 'em'.

**75 will** A change of auxiliary to emphasise repetition; *R2* 5.1.57 has 'shall' and Gurr notes that 'the metaphor is of a plague of boils, such as God imposed on the Egyptians and on Job'.

**77 time's condition** See 4.1.101 and 5.2.11. The 'condition of the time' is a recurrent preoccupation of this play as one aspect of the ruling 'Time theme'.

And the division of our amity.

WARWICK  There is a history in all men's lives
    Figuring the natures of the times deceased,                          80
    The which observed, a man may prophesy,
    With a near aim, of the main chance of things
    As yet not come to life, who in their seeds
    And weak beginning lie intreasurèd.
    Such things become the hatch and brood of time,                      85
    And by the necessary form of this
    King Richard might create a perfect guess
    That great Northumberland, then false to him,
    Would of that seed grow to a greater falseness,
    Which should not find a ground to root upon                          90
    Unless on you.

KING               Are these things then necessities?
    Then let us meet them like necessities,
    And that same word even now cries out on us.
    They say the bishop and Northumberland
    Are fifty thousand strong.

WARWICK            It cannot be, my lord:                95
    Rumour doth double, like the voice and echo,
    The numbers of the feared. Please it your grace
    To go to bed. Upon my soul, my lord,
    The powers that you already have sent forth
    Shall bring this prize in very easily.                               100
    To comfort you the more, I have received
    A certain instance that Glendower is dead.

---

80 natures] Qb; nature F    83 who] Qb; which F    84 beginning] Qb; beginnings F    96 voice and] voice, and Qb, F; voice an *Ridley,*
*conj. Vaughan*    98 soul] Qb; Life F

79–84 There is a history ... intreasurèd Time as
history: Warwick restates the classical concept of
*Historia magistra vitae,* History as life's teacher (79),
since by bodying forth ('figuring') past events ('times
deceased') it allows us to guess what is in store
('intreasurèd') for the future.

83 who which; frequent with personifications, as at
21–2 'winds, Who'.

83 in their seeds See *Mac.* 1.3.58: 'if you can look
into the seeds of time'.

85 hatch ... time See *Ham.* 3.1.164–7: 'There's
something in his soul / O'er which his melancholy sits
on brood / And I do doubt the hatch and the disclose /
Will be some danger.'

86 by the ... this thanks to the pattern established
by such a precedent.

89 of that seed out of that beginning.

91, 92 necessities (1) inescapable, established
facts (see 86), (2) reasons of state (see 72), (3) urgent
practical needs.

102 instance evidence, proof.

102 Glendower is dead The only new piece of
information contained in this scene, disregarding
historical fact: Holinshed (III, 536) gives 1409 as the
date of Glendower's death, but he seems actually to
have survived Henry IV.

Your majesty has been this fortnight ill,
And these unseasoned hours perforce must add
Unto your sickness.

KING                              I will take your counsel,          105
And were these inward wars once out of hand,
We would, dear lords, unto the Holy Land.

*Exeunt*

**3.2** *Enter Justice* SHALLOW *and Justice* SILENCE

SHALLOW  Come on, come on, come on, sir, give me your hand, sir, give
    me your hand, sir. An early stirrer, by the Rood! And how doth my
    good cousin Silence?

SILENCE  Good morrow, good cousin Shallow.

SHALLOW  And how doth my cousin your bedfellow? And your fairest          5
    daughter and mine, my god-daughter Ellen?

SILENCE  Alas, a black ousel, cousin Shallow.

107 SD] F; not in Qb  Act 3, Scene 2   3.2] *Scena Secunda.* F; *not in* Q   0 SD] Qa *(Silens),* Qb; *Enter Shallow and Silence: with Mouldie, Shadow, Wart, Feeble, Bull-calfe.* F   1 on, sir,] Qb; *on* Qa, F   3 Silence] Qa, F; Silens Qb   4 SH SILENCE] Qb; *Sil.* F *(throughout scene);* Si. Qa *(to 44)*   7 SH SILENCE] Silens Qb *(so to 74)*

**103 this fortnight ill** The king's illness (unhistorical) was referred to at 1.2.82–90 and 2.2.30–43.

**104 unseasoned** unseasonable, unsuitable.

**106 inward** intestine, civil (of a war).

**107 unto the Holy Land** The purpose announced by Henry at the end of *R2* (5.6.49–50) and at the beginning of *1H4* (1.1.19–27), but lost sight of since, is recalled here in preparation for his last speech at 4.2.363–7.

**Act 3, Scene 2**

**3.2** The enrolment scene was suggested by *FV* scene x (sigs. D4–E1). The location is generally given as Gloucestershire because of Falstaff's statements at 4.1.430–2 and 475, reinforced by *Wiv.* 1.1.5–6; but they sound like survivals of an earlier version of *Henry IV* as a single play, in which the equivalent of this scene must have occurred when Falstaff was enrolling his 'charge of foot' (see *1H4* 3.3.186) on his way to Coventry and Shrewsbury, before what now is *1H4* 4.2. Now Falstaff's destination is 'the North' (2.4.290) and a long detour through Gloucestershire is unthinkable: nothing in this scene points in that direction; indeed, the mention of Stamford at 31 suggests that Shallow lives in Lincolnshire.

**0 SD** F includes also the entrance of the five recruits, but modern editors prefer to have them enter one by one as they are called, after 81. The omission of any direction for them in Q was probably meant to leave the entrances to the actors' discretion, and, to avoid having them standing idle for the first part of the scene, it seems reasonable to have them all come in when Mouldy is called at 80–1, remaining in the background to watch the proceedings and coming forward in turn for the individual interviews.

**1 Come on ... come on** The trick of repetition as the main feature of Shallow's language is anticipated in the character of Justice Suresby in *More* ii (see Schücking, 'Shakespeare and *Sir Thomas More*', *RES* 1 (1925), 54). 'Come on' echoes the Hostess's repeated 'come' at the end of 2.4, suggesting (as noted by J. Jowett and G. Taylor in private communication) that the two scenes were consecutive and 3.1 was added as a belated afterthought.

**2 by the Rood** by the Cross; a mild oath already old-fashioned in Shakespeare's time.

**5 bedfellow** wife; in Shallow's opinion a tactful periphrasis.

**7 black ousel** blackbird; Queen Elizabeth being fair, dark hair and complexion were a disadvantage in the marriage market; see *LLL* 4.3.243–65.

SHALLOW By yea and no, sir. I dare say my cousin William is become a
good scholar – he is at Oxford still, is he not?

SILENCE Indeed, sir, to my cost. 10

SHALLOW A must then to the Inns a'Court shortly. I was once at
Clement's Inn where I think they will talk of mad Shallow yet.

SILENCE You were called Lusty Shallow then, cousin.

SHALLOW By the Mass, I was called anything, and I would have done
anything indeed too, and roundly too. There was I, and little John 15
Doit of Staffordshire, and black George Barnes, and Francis Pickbone, and Will Squele, a Cotswold man – you had not four such
swinge-bucklers in all the Inns a'Court again. And I may say to you
we knew where the bona robas were and had the best of them all at
commandment. Then was Jack Falstaff, now Sir John, a boy, and 20
page to Thomas Mowbray, Duke of Norfolk.

SILENCE This Sir John, cousin, that comes hither anon about soldiers?

SHALLOW The same Sir John, the very same. I see him break Scoggin's
head at the Court gate, when a was a crack not thus high; and the very
same day did I fight with one Samson Stockfish, a fruiterer, behind 25
Gray's Inn. Jesu, Jesu, the mad days that I have spent! And to see how
many of my old acquaintance are dead.

SILENCE We shall all follow, cousin.

SHALLOW Certain, 'tis certain, very sure, very sure. Death, as the

8 no] Qa, Qb; nay F   11 A] Qa, Qb; Hee F   11 a'Court] Qa, Qb; of Court F   14 By the Mass] Qa, Qb; *not in* F   16 Barnes] Qa, Qb; *Bare* F   17 Cotswold] Cotsole Qa, Qb; Cot-sal- F   18 a'Court] Qa, Qb; of Court F   22 This ... cousin] Qa, Qb; Coosin, this sir Iohn Qb   23 I see] Qa, Qb; I saw F   23 Scoggin's] Skoggins Qa, Qb; *Scoggan's* F   24 a was] Qa, Qb; hee was F   26 Jesu, Jesu] Qa, Qb; Oh F   27 my] Qa, Qb; mine F   29–30 as ... saith] Qa, Qb; *not in* F

8 **By yea and no** Shallow also has more than a
touch of the Puritan; see 2.2.101 n.

12 **Clement's Inn** An Inn of Chancery, attended
by students who did not manage to enter the Inns of
Court; near the church of St Clement Danes, north of
the Strand.

13 **Lusty** (1) lively, merry, (2) lustful.

15 **roundly** thoroughly.

15–17 **little John ... Cotswold man** Some names
are allusive: 'Doit' = a trifle (a coin worth half a
farthing), 'Pickbone' refers to avarice, 'Squele' to
'squealing' or telling on people; the Midlands origin
of two of his companions may support Shallow's
Gloucestershire connection.

18 **swinge-bucklers** swashbucklers.

19 **bona robas** jolly wenches; from Italian *buona
roba*, good stuff.

21 **page ... Norfolk** It has been stated that Sir
John Oldcastle, or the historical Sir John Fastolf

(appearing in *1H6*), was connected with the Duke of
Norfolk, Bullingbrook's rival banished in *R2* 1.3, but
the only evidence for such a connection is this passage
which refers only to the fictional Falstaff.

23 **Scoggin** The name of Edward VI's court fool,
whose apocryphal *Jests* were published in 1566,
passed into common use to designate a buffoon (*OED*
sv). The incidents here reported must refer to the
sport of fencing with cudgels or backswords; see 52
and 2.4.102.

24 **crack** lively lad (*OED* sv *sb* 11).

25 **Samson Stockfish** The irony is in the contrast
between name and surname, 'stockfish' meaning
'coward'; see *1H4* 2.4.245.

25–6 **behind Gray's Inn** In Gray's Inn Fields,
north of Holborn.

29–30 **the psalmist** Ps. 89.47: 'What man is hee
that liueth, and shall not see death?'

psalmist saith, is certain to all, all shall die. How a good yoke of      30
bullocks at Stamford Fair?

SILENCE  By my troth, I was not there.

SHALLOW  Death is certain. Is old Dooble of your town living yet?

SILENCE  Dead, sir.

SHALLOW  Jesu, Jesu, dead! A drew a good bow, and dead! A shot a fine      35
shoot. John a'Gaunt loved him well and betted much money on his
head. Dead! A would have clapped i'th'clout at twelve score, and
carried you a forehand shaft a fourteen and fourteen and a half, that it
would have done a man's heart good to see. How a score of ewes,
now?      40

SILENCE  Thereafter as they be: a score of good ewes may be worth ten
pounds.

SHALLOW  And is old Dooble dead?

SILENCE  Here come two of Sir John Falstaff's men, as I think.

*Enter* BARDOLPH *and one with him*

Good morrow, honest gentlemen.      45

BARDOLPH  I beseech you, which is Justice Shallow?

---

31 Stamford] F; Samforth Qa, Qb   32 By my troth] Qa, Qb; Truly Cousin F   33, 43 Dooble] Qa, Qb; *Double* F   35 Jesu, Jesu, dead! A] Qa, Qb; Dead? See, see: hee F   35 A shot] Qa, Qb; hee shot F   35 fine] Qb, F; fiue Qa   36 a'] Qa, Qb; of F   37 A would] Qa, Qb; he would F   37 i'th'] Qa, Qb; in the F   38 a fourteen] Qa, Qb; at foureteene F   44 SD] Qa, Qb; *Enter Bardolph and his Boy.* F *(after 43)*   45 Good] Qa *corr.,* Qb; *Bardolfe* Good Qa *uncorr.; Shal.* Good F

---

30–1 **How ... Fair** A mental association between the Psalms and Ecclesiastes 38.24–5: 'How can he get wisedome that holdeth the plough ... and his talke is but of the breeding of bullocks?' Stamford was an important market town in Lincolnshire on the Great North Road to York.

33 **old Dooble** Suggesting by its cavernous sound a person doubled up by old age.

35 **A drew ... bow** He was a good archer.

36 **John a'Gaunt** Henry IV's father, Duke of Lancaster, fourth son of Edward III; see *R2 passim,* and Falstaff's comment at 259–63.

37 **A ... score** He could hit the centre of the target ('clout' = a piece of cloth marking the centre) with an arrow at a distance of 240 (twelve score) yards.

38 **carried ... half** i.e. he would shoot straight over a distance of 280 or 290 yards. A special feat: 'a forehand shaft' is an arrow shot directly on the target without the curved trajectory necessary for long distances; 'you' is an ethical dative emphasising 'carried' = 'covered a distance'.

41 **Thereafter ... be** it depends on their quality; 'good' should be emphasised.

44 **SD** It is hard to see why Bardolph should be escorted by an unnamed mute companion whose presence is never mentioned in the rest of the scene; as with the 'ghost characters' in the SDs at 1.3.0, 2.2.0, 3.1.31 and 4.2.0, the author must have changed his mind after writing the direction but did not correct it. F was misled by the faulty SD at 2.4.87 into assuming that the 'one with' Bardolph must be his non-existent 'boy' (personal attendant).

45 In the first printing of Q this line was assigned to Bardolph, but, when it was noticed that the next line had the same SH, the former was removed in the course of press-correction, turning the line into a continuation of Silence's speech, and the arrangement was maintained when the sheet was reset to accommodate 3.1 (see Textual Analysis, pp. 200–1 below); but F moved Bardolph's entrance back to 43 and took this to be a separate speech by Shallow. The condescending form of address ('honest gentlemen') is more appropriate to either judge than to the menial Bardolph, but considering the latter's general tone it could be a piece of impertinence on his part, perhaps added in the margin for insertion at the beginning of his speech, and its uncertain placing in the MS. may have originated the confusion.

SHALLOW I am Robert Shallow, sir, a poor esquire of this county, and
one of the king's justices of the peace. What is your good pleasure
with me?

BARDOLPH My captain, sir, commends him to you, my captain Sir John    50
Falstaff, a tall gentleman, by heaven, and a most gallant leader.

SHALLOW He greets me well, sir; I knew him a good backsword man.
How doth the good knight? May I ask how my lady his wife doth?

BARDOLPH Sir, pardon, a soldier is better accommodated than with a
wife.                                                                  55

SHALLOW It is well said, in faith, sir, and it is well said indeed too: 'better
accommodated'! It is good, yea indeed is it. Good phrases are surely,
and ever were, very commendable. 'Accommodated': it comes of
*accommodo*. Very good, a good phrase.

BARDOLPH Pardon, sir, I have heard the word – phrase call you it? By this    60
day, I know not the phrase, but I will maintain the word with my sword
to be a soldierlike word, and a word of exceeding good command, by
heaven. Accommodated, that is when a man is, as they say, accommodated, or when a man is being whereby a may be thought to be
accommodated, which is an excellent thing.                            65

*Enter Sir John* FALSTAFF

SHALLOW It is very just. – Look, here comes good Sir John. Give me your
good hand, give me your worship's good hand. By my troth, you like
well and bear your years very well. Welcome, good Sir John.

48 good] Qa, F; *not in* Qb   51 by heaven] Qa, Qb; *not in* F   54 accommodated] F; accommodate Qa, Qb   56 in faith] Qa, Qb; *not in*
F   58 ever were] Qa, Qb; euery where F   60 Pardon, sir] Qa, F; Pardon me sir Qb   60–1 By this day] Qa, F; by this good day
Qb   62–3 by heaven] Qa, Qb; *not in* F   64 a may be thought] Qa, Qb; he thought F   65 SD] Qb; *Enter Falstaffe* Qa, F   66 SH
SHALLOW] *Shal.* F; *Iust.* Qa, Qb   67 good hand . . . good hand] Qa, Qb; hand . . . good hand F   67 By my troth, you like] Qa, Qb;
Trust me, you looke F

50 commends ... you See 2.2.97; 'him'
= 'himself'.

51 tall valiant (*OED* sv *adj* 3).

52 backsword man A fencer using a cudgel with a
wicker hilt; see 2.4.102, and *More* 461: 'hees the best
back sworde man in England'.

54, 57, 58, 63–5 accommodated The affected use
of this word became fashionable at the end of the
sixteenth century, so that it was still incomprehensible
to the Hostess in Jonson's *Every Man in his Humour*
(1599) 1.4.125–8, and Jonson commented in *Discoveries* (cxlii, 2): 'You are not to cast a Ring for the
perfumed termes of the time, as *Accommodation,
Complement, Spirit*, etc.: But use them properly in
their place.'

59 *accommodo* First-person present tense of the

Latin verb *accommodare* = (1) to fit, (2) to make
comfortable, (3) to mend.

60–1 phrase call ... the phrase The term 'phrase'
for 'expression' is as new to Bardolph as 'accommodated' to Shallow.

62 of ... good command (1) useful upon many
occasions, (2) 'soldierlike'. Bardolph's first use of the
word is comically apt but he doesn't understand it;
here he supposes it part of the military mystique, like
the orders used in drill (see 227–32).

64 a may be thought F's simplified form 'he
thought' detracts from the humour of Bardolph's
tautological definition.

67–8 like well are in good condition, do well (*OED*
sv *v*[1] 4); 'look' in F is an oversimplification.

FALSTAFF I am glad to see you well, good Master Robert Shallow. Master Soccard, as I think.                                                        70

SHALLOW No, Sir John, it is my cousin Silence, in commission with me.

FALSTAFF Good Master Silence, it well befits you should be of the peace.

SILENCE Your good worship is welcome.

FALSTAFF Fie, this is hot weather, gentlemen. Have you provided me      75
here half a dozen sufficient men?

SHALLOW Marry have we, sir. Will you sit?

FALSTAFF Let me see them, I beseech you.

SHALLOW Where's the roll, where's the roll, where's the roll? Let me see,
let me see, let me see. So, so, so, so, so. So, so, yea marry, sir. – Rafe   80
Mouldy! – Let them appear as I call, let them do so, let them do so.

[*Enter* MOULDY, SHADOW, WART, FEEBLE, BULLCALF]

Let me see, where is Mouldy?

MOULDY Here, and't please you.

SHALLOW What think you, Sir John, a good-limbed fellow, young,
strong, and of good friends.                                                85

FALSTAFF Is thy name Mouldy?

MOULDY Yea, and't please you.

FALSTAFF 'Tis the more time thou wert used.

SHALLOW Ha, ha, ha, most excellent, i'faith. Things that are mouldy lack
use, very singular good, in faith. Well said, Sir John, very well said.    90

FALSTAFF Prick him.

---

70 Soccard] Qa, Qb; *Surecard* F    71, 72 Silence] F; *Scilens* Qa; Silens Qb    74 SH SILENCE] F; *Scil.* Qa; *Silens* Qb    76 sufficient] Qa, Qb; of sufficient F    79–80 Let me see ... see.] Qa, F; *only twice in* Qb    80 so, ... so. So, so,] so, ... so (so, so) Qa, Qb; so, so, so, so: F    81 SD] *This edn; not in* Qa, Qb, F    83 and't] Qa; and it Qb; if it F    87 and't] Q; if it F    89 i'faith] Q; *not in* F    90 in faith] Q; *not in* F    91 FALSTAFF Prick him.] F; *Iohn prickes him.* Q (*as* SD)

---

70 **Soccard** Most editors prefer F's 'Surecard', ironical for a cocksure person, but Soccard may evoke a corpse in a shroud, from the obsolete verb 'to sock' = 'to sew up in a shroud' (*OED* sv *v¹*) plus the pejorative ending *-ard*, as in 'drunkard', 'laggard', etc.

71 **Silence** Q spells 'Scilens' here and for most of the rest of the scene, a spelling found only in the manuscript pages of *More* thought to be in Shakespeare's handwriting.

71 **in commission** sharing the functions (of justices of the peace).

72–3 **of the peace** Playing on (1) justice of the peace, (2) to keep peace = to be silent.

76 **half a dozen** The basic inconsistency in this scene is the constant talk of choosing *four* men out of

*six* offered (see 156–7 and 198–205), while in fact no more than five are offered of whom three are chosen.

76 **sufficient** able, fit.

80 **So ... So, so** Q's punctuation suggests that the last two 'so's have a stronger emphasis: brackets designated vocatives.

81 SD For the placing and contents of this see 0 SD n.

83, 87 **and't** if it.

85 **of good friends** well-connected, from a respectable family.

91 **Prick him** Mark him down on the list; see 2.4.269. Misunderstanding the MS., Q printed this as a SD.

MOULDY  I was pricked well enough before, and you could have let me alone. My old dame will be undone now for one to do her husbandry and her drudgery. You need not to have pricked me: there are other men fitter to go out than I.                                                      95

FALSTAFF  Go to; peace, Mouldy, you shall go, Mouldy, it is time you were spent.

MOULDY  Spent?

SHALLOW  Peace, fellow, peace, stand aside: know you where you are? – For th'other, Sir John. Let me see – Simon Shadow!                            100

FALSTAFF  Yea marry, let me have him to sit under: he's like to be a cold soldier.

SHALLOW  Where's Shadow?

SHADOW  Here, sir.

FALSTAFF  Shadow, whose son art thou?                                        105

SHADOW  My mother's son, sir.

FALSTAFF  Thy mother's son! Like enough, and thy father's shadow: so the son of the female is the shadow of the male. It is often so indeed – but much of the father's substance!

SHALLOW  Do you like him, Sir John?                                          110

FALSTAFF  Shadow will serve for summer: prick him, for we have a number of shadows fill up the muster-book.

SHALLOW  Thomas Wart!

FALSTAFF  Where's he?

WART  Here, sir.                                                             115

FALSTAFF  Is thy name Wart?

WART  Yea, sir.

FALSTAFF  Thou art a very ragged Wart.

---

**92 and]** Q; if F   **100 see – ]** see: F; see Q   **101 Yea marry]** Q; I mary F   **109 but much]** Q; but not F; but not much *Capell*; not much *Dyce²*   **112 fill]** Q; to fill F

---

**92 pricked** Punning on (1) be marked, (2) be vexed, (3) turn sore (or mouldy), with a further sexual innuendo connected with 'do her husbandry and her drudgery' at 93–4; see Sonnet 20.13: 'she pricked thee out for women's pleasure'.

**93 dame** 'wife' rather than 'mother'; see 92 n., and compare 'my dame' in *FV* scene x (sig. D4ᵛ).

**97 spent** (1) used (see 89–90: 'things that are mouldy lack use'), (2) consumed; with a sexual innuendo.

**100 th'other** the others; a collective plural; see 1.1.86 n.

**101 cold** (1) cool (like the shadow cast by a tree), (2) cowardly.

**105, 106, 107, 108 son** Playing on the homophony with 'sun'.

**107 thy\father's\shadow** (1) the image (shadow = portrait) of your father, (2) the unsubstantial projection of your reputed father.

**109 but much ... substance** Playing on the contrast shadow/substance; 'much' is used ironically as at 2.4.104, implying that he is a bastard, having got nothing (a mere shadow) from his 'father'.

**111 serve** (1) be useful, (2) do military service.

**111–12 a number ... muster-book** Many of the names listed in the military rolls are mere shadows, since captains used to draw the pay for dead or imaginary men that figured as members of their companies.

**118 ragged** (1) tattered (of dress), (2) rough, sore (of a wart); but see Induction 35, and 1.1.151 n.

SHALLOW  Shall I prick him, Sir John?

FALSTAFF  It were superfluous, for his apparel is built upon his back, and    120
the whole frame stands upon pins. Prick him no more.

SHALLOW  Ha, ha, ha, you can do it, sir, you can do it, I commend you
well. – Francis Feeble!

FEEBLE  Here, sir.

SHALLOW  What trade art thou, Feeble?    125

FEEBLE  A woman's tailor, sir.

SHALLOW  Shall I prick him, sir?

FALSTAFF  You may, but if he had been a man's tailor, he'd ha'pricked
you. Wilt thou make as many holes in an enemy's battle as thou hast
done in a woman's petticoat?    130

FEEBLE  I will do my good will, sir, you can have no more.

FALSTAFF  Well said, good woman's tailor, well said, courageous Feeble.
Thou wilt be as valiant as the wrathful dove or most magnanimous
mouse. Prick the woman's tailor well, Master Shallow, deep, Master
Shallow.    135

FEEBLE  I would Wart might have gone, sir.

FALSTAFF  I would thou wert a man's tailor, that thou mightst mend him
and make him fit to go. I cannot put him to a private soldier, that is the
leader of so many thousands. Let that suffice, most forcible Feeble.

FEEBLE  It shall suffice, sir.    140

FALSTAFF  I am bound to thee, reverend Feeble. – Who is next?

SHALLOW  Peter Bullcalf o'th'Green.

FALSTAFF  Yea marry, let's see Bullcalf.

BULLCALF  Here, sir.

FALSTAFF  'Fore God, a likely fellow. Come, prick Bullcalf till he roar    145
again.

---

119 him, Sir] Q; him downe, / sir F   120 for his] F; for Q   128 he'd ha'] heed a Q; he would have F   140 sir] Q; *not in* F   141 next]
Q; the next F   142 o'th'] Q; of the F   143 let's] Q; let vs F   145 'Fore God] Q; Trust me F   145 prick] Q; pricke me F

---

121 **the whole ... pins** i.e. his body structure is like
(1) torn clothes held together by pins, (2) the frame of
an Elizabethan house joined together by wooden pegs
(= pins); also (3) his body is supported by weak legs
(= pins).

126 **woman's tailor** Tailors had a reputation for
cowardice and effeminacy; see the proverb 'It takes
nine tailors to make a man'; but as an equivalent of
'tail' the word was used with a sexual innuendo
developed in 'man's tailor' at 128, especially taken in
connection with 'prick' = (1) mark (see 91), (2) fit,
decorate.

128–9 **he'd ... you** he would have fitted you with a
suit; but see 92 n. and 126 n.

129 **battle** army; see 4.1.154, 179.

131 **do my good will** do my best; with a possible
sexual innuendo.

134 **deep** Playing on the contrast with 'shallow'.

138 **put him to** enlist him as.

139 **thousands** Referring to the lice in Wart's
clothes.

145 **likely** able-bodied.

145–6 **prick Bullcalf ... roar again** See *1H4*
2.4.260 where Falstaff 'roared as ever I heard bullcalf'; 'again' = 'in response' (to the pricking).

BULLCALF  O Lord, good my lord captain.

FALSTAFF  What, dost thou roar before thou art pricked?

BULLCALF  O Lord, sir, I am a diseased man.

FALSTAFF  What disease hast thou?                                            150

BULLCALF  A whoreson cold, sir, a cough, sir, which I caught with ringing
in the king's affairs upon his coronation day, sir.

FALSTAFF  Come, thou shalt go to the wars in a gown; we will have away
thy cold and I will take such order that thy friends shall ring for thee. –
Is here all?                                                                 155

SHALLOW  Here is two more called than your number: you must have but
four here, sir, and so I pray you go in with me to dinner.

FALSTAFF  Come, I will go drink with you, but I cannot tarry dinner. I am
glad to see you, by my troth, Master Shallow.

SHALLOW  O Sir John, do you remember since we lay all night in the         160
Windmill in Saint George's Field?

FALSTAFF  No more of that, Master Shallow.

SHALLOW  Ha, 'twas a merry night. And is Jane Nightwork alive?

FALSTAFF  She lives, Master Shallow.

SHALLOW  She never could away with me.                                      165

FALSTAFF  Never never, she would always say she could not abide Master
Shallow.

SHALLOW  By the Mass, I could anger her to th'heart. She was then a
bona roba; doth she hold her own well?

FALSTAFF  Old, old, Master Shallow.                                         170

SHALLOW  Nay, she must be old, she cannot choose but be old; certain
she's old, and had Robin Nightwork by old Nightwork, before I came
to Clement's Inn.

SILENCE  That's fifty-five year ago.

147, 149 O Lord] Q; Oh F   148 thou art] Q; th'art F   156 Here] Q; There F   159 by my troth] Q; in good troth F   162 Master
Shallow.] Q; good Master *Shallow:* No more of that. F   163 'twas] Q; it was F   168 By the Mass] Q; *not in* F   174 SH SILENCE]
*Sil.* F; *Scilens* Q   174 year] Q; yeeres F

152 in the king's affairs on business connected
with the king; church bells were rung to celebrate
each anniversary of the coronation, which marked the
beginning of the new administrative year.

153 gown dressing-gown worn by sick people.

154 ring for thee (1) ring the bells in your place,
(2) ring the bells for your funeral.

156–7 two more ... but four It is assumed that
Falstaff has already interviewed six men; see 76 n.

158 tarry dinner spare the time for dinner.

160–1 the Windmill ... Field There was actually
in 1600 a windmill in St George's Field, near the

notorious district of Southwark, and the allusion may
be to a tavern which had taken its name from it, or to
the fact that the disused windmill had been turned
into a brothel. The name of Jane Nightwork (163)
leaves no doubt about her profession.

165 could away could get along, could put up
(*OED* Away *adv* 16).

169 bona roba jolly wench; see 19 n.

174 Silence acts as chronicler of Shallow's life: it
appears from the context that Shallow must now be in
his early seventies and Falstaff (a page when Shallow
was at Clement's Inn) in his late sixties.

SHALLOW  Ha, cousin Silence, that thou hadst seen that that this knight    175
and I have seen! Ha, Sir John, said I well?

FALSTAFF  We have heard the chimes at midnight, Master Shallow.

SHALLOW  That we have, that we have, that we have in faith, Sir John, we
have. Our watchword was 'Hem, boys.' Come let's to dinner, come
let's to dinner. Jesus, the days that we have seen! Come, come.    180

*Exeunt [Falstaff, Shallow and Silence]*

BULLCALF  Good Master Corporate Bardolph, stand my friend, and
here's four Harry ten shillings in French crowns for you. In very
truth, sir, I had as lief be hanged, sir, as go; and yet for mine own part,
sir, I do not care, but rather because I am unwilling, and for mine own
part have a desire to stay with my friends; else, sir, I did not care for    185
mine own part so much.

BARDOLPH  Go, to, stand aside.

MOULDY  And good master corporal captain, for my old dame's sake,
stand my friend: she has nobody to do anything about her when I am
gone, and she is old and cannot help herself. You shall have forty, sir.    190

BARDOLPH  Go to, stand aside.

FEEBLE  By my troth, I care not, a man can die but once: we owe God a
death. I'll ne'er bear a base mind; and't be my destiny, so; and't be
not, so. No man's too good to serve's prince, and let it go which way it
will, he that dies this year is quit for the next.    195

BARDOLPH  Well said, th'art a good fellow.

---

175 Silence] F; Scilens Q    178 That we have, . . . have] Q; *only twice in* F    179 'Hem, boys.'] *Theobald;* Hemboies Q; Hem-Boyes F
180 Jesus] Q; Oh F    180 SD] *exeunt.* Q; *not in* F    188 old dame's] Q *corr.,* F; dames Q *uncorr.*    189 has] Q; hath F    192 By my troth]
Q; *not in* F    192 God] Q; *not in* F    193 and't . . . and't] Q; if it . . . . if it F    194 man's] Q; man is F    194 serve's] Q; serue his F    196
th'art] Q; thou art F

---

177 **We . . . midnight** On the nostalgia for night
adventures see 2.4.150 n.

179 **Hem, boys** A drinking-cry, that may also have
been used as a password by students of the Inns of
Court and Chancery to be let into the City gates late at
night; see D.S. Bland, *N&Q* ns 25 (1978), 132.
Compare *1H4* 2.4.17: 'they cry hem!'

181 **Corporate** An obvious blunder, but see
2.4.120 n. for Bardolph's rank.

182 **four . . . French crowns** An elaborate way of
saying one pound, giving the impression that they are
two. Bullcalf is offering to pay in French crowns (*écus*,
worth four shillings each) the equivalent of four ten-
shilling pieces minted in Henry VII's reign; forty
shillings are two pounds, but the 'Harry ten shillings'
had been devalued and were worth only five shillings
each, so that four of them were worth one pound, or
five French crowns.

187, 191, 202 **Go to** Get along with you; denoting
condescension.

188–9 **my old dame . . . do anything** Equivocat-
ing on 'dame' as 'wife' or 'mother'; see 93 n., and the
sexual innuendoes at 93–7.

190 **forty** forty shillings, i.e. two pounds.

192–3 **a man . . . once, we . . . death** Two proverbial expressions (Tilley M219 and G237); for the
second see *1H4* 5.1.126, *Jack Straw* sig. B1, and *More*
vii, 670: 'I doo owe God a death.'

193–4 **I'll . . . prince** Tags from *FV* scene x (sigs.
D4, E1): 'he is not too good to serue y$^e$ king?'; 'doest
thinke we are so base minded to die among French
men?'

195 **he that . . . next** A proverb condemned as
'heathen' and 'too common among Christians' by
Thomas White in a sermon at St Paul's Cross in 1577;
see *ODEP* 186 and Dent D326.1.

FEEBLE  Faith, I'll bear no base mind.

*Enter* FALSTAFF *and the* JUSTICES

FALSTAFF  Come, sir, which men shall I have?

SHALLOW  Four of which you please.

BARDOLPH  Sir, a word with you: I have three pound to free Mouldy and      200
Bullcalf.

FALSTAFF  Go to, well.

SHALLOW  Come, Sir John, which four will you have?

FALSTAFF  Do you choose for me.

SHALLOW  Marry then, Mouldy, Bullcalf, Feeble and Shadow.                  205

FALSTAFF  Mouldy and Bullcalf: for you, Mouldy, stay at home till you
are past service; and for your part, Bullcalf, grow till you come unto it.
I will none of you.

SHALLOW  Sir John, Sir John, do not yourself wrong: they are your
likeliest men, and I would have you served with the best.                 210

FALSTAFF  Will you tell me, Master Shallow, how to choose a man? Care I
for the limb, the thews, the stature, bulk, and big assemblance of a
man? Give me the spirit, Master Shallow. Here's Wart: you see what
a ragged appearance it is. A shall charge you and discharge you with
the motion of a pewterer's hammer: come off and on swifter than he        215
that gibbets on the brewer's bucket. And this same half-faced fellow,
Shadow: give me this man. He presents no mark to the enemy, the
foeman may with as great aim level at the edge of a penknife. And for a
retreat, how swiftly will this Feeble, the woman's tailor, run off! O,

---

197 Faith, I'll] Q; Nay, I will F   197 SD] Q; *not in* F   213 Here's Wart:] Q; Where's *Wart?* F   214 A shall] Q; hee shall F

199 **Four** See 76 n.

200 **three pound** One from Bullcalf and two from
Mouldy, but if Bullcalf's bribe is reckoned at pre-
Elizabethan value (see 182 n.), Bardolph is quietly
pocketing one pound. On the misuse of the king's
press to extort money see *1H4* 4.2.11–35.

206–7 **for you … unto it** Punning on
'service' = (1) military service, (2) sexual potency:
Mouldy is nearly too old for it (editors suggest reading: 'stay at home *still*: you are past service'), the other,
being merely a 'calf', is too young to be a 'town bull'
(see 2.2.120 n.).

210 **likeliest** ablest; as at 145.

211–13 **Care I … spirit** Compare 1 Sam. 16.7:
'Looke not on his fashion, or on the height of his
stature … For man looketh on the outwarde
appearance, but the Lorde beholdeth the hart.'
Another survival of the satire on Oldcastle's
Puritanism?

212 **assemblance** (1) appearance, (2) build, frame.

214 **charge … discharge** you load and fire ('you'
is an ethic dative).

215 **motion … hammer** Pewter was worked by
very rapid strokes of a small hammer.

215 **come off and on** Interpreted as either 'retire
and advance' or 'lower and raise the gun', but more
likely indicating a passage from complete stillness to
full action; see *More* ii, 221: 'Come off or on', meaning
'Stay still or act.'

216 **gibbets … bucket** Possibly 'gibbets
on' = puts on the 'gibbet', a wooden bar across the
shoulders to carry buckets hanging from each end of
it.

216 **half-faced** so thin that his face can be seen
only in profile.

218 **as great aim** as great a chance of hitting.

218 **level at** aim at, fire against.

give me the spare men, and spare me the great ones. – Put me a caliver        220
into Wart's hand, Bardolph.

BARDOLPH  Hold, Wart! Traverse! Thas, thas, thas!

FALSTAFF  Come, manage me your caliver: so, very well, go to, very good,
exceeding good. O, give me always a little, lean, old, chopped, bald
shot. Well said, i'faith, Wart. Th'art a good scab. Hold, there's a        225
tester for you.

SHALLOW  He is not his craft's master, he doth not do it right. I remember
at Mile End Green, when I lay at Clement's Inn – I was then Sir
Dagonet in Arthur's show – there was a little quiver fellow and a
would manage you his piece thus, and a would about and about, and        230
come you in, and come you in. 'Rah, tah, tah!' would a say; 'Bounce'
would a say, and away again would a go, and again would a come. I
shall ne'er see such a fellow.

FALSTAFF  These fellows will do well, Master Shallow. God keep you,
Master Silence, I will not use many words with you. Fare you well,        235
gentlemen both, I thank you. I must a dozen mile tonight. Bardolph,
give the soldiers coats.

SHALLOW  Sir John, the Lord bless you, God prosper your affairs, God

---

222 Thas, . . . thas] Q; thus, thus, thus F   225 i'faith] Q; *not in* F   225 Th'art] Q; thou art F   229–32 and a . . . a . . . a . . . a . . . a . . .
a] Q; and hee . . . hee . . . hee . . . hee . . . hee . . . he F   234 will] F; wooll Q   234 God . . . you] Q; Farewell F   235 Silence] F; Scilens
Q   238 the Lord] Q; Heauen F   238 God . . . . God] Q; and . . . . and F

---

220 **spare men . . . spare me** Playing on 'spare' as
adjective = 'lean, thin', and as verb = 'don't give'.

220, 223 **me** Ethic dative.

220 **caliver** A light musket. A manuscript list of
able-bodied men of Gloucestershire compiled in
1608 includes the name of the carpenter Thomas
Warter, aged between 50 and 60, described as 'fitt to
serue with a Calyuer' (E. R. Wood in Humphreys).
Had Shakespeare in his early Stratford days met
young Warter from Chipping Camden, boasting of his
ability with a caliver? Note the coincidence of first
name (113) and the humorous metaphor from car-
pentry at 121.

222 **Traverse** As a command, either 'March up
and down' or 'Take aim' (*OED* sv *v* 5 and 8, though
the earliest example for the latter is 1628).

222 **Thas** 'Thus' pronounced as a word of
command.

224–5 **a little . . . shot** In the list mentioned at
220 n. Warter is described as 'of lower stature';
'chopped' = dried up; 'shot' = (1) marksman, (2) an
animal left over after the best of the herd have been
picked.

225 **Well said** Well done; the current meaning at
the time, see 5.3.6.

225 **scab** (1) wart, (2) scurvy fellow, rascal.

226 **tester** sixpence.

228 **Mile End Green** Now Stepney Green, used at
the time as a drilling-ground for the citizen militia.

228–9 **I was . . . show** Shallow appeared as
Dagonet, King Arthur's fool, in an archery display
performed yearly at Mile End Green by the Society of
Arthur's Knights, each member of which took the
name of a knight of the Round Table.

229 **quiver fellow** nimble.

229–32 **a would manage . . . would a come** i.e. he
would execute single-handed the drill of a whole
company of musketeers: the first rank after firing went
round ('about and about') to the rear to reload, then
the second rank fired and went to the rear, and so on
through the other ranks till the first fired again ('come
you in'). 'Rah, tah, tah' is the noise of reloading the
caliver and 'Bounce' = 'boom'; see Peele, *Old Wives
Tale* (MSR edn, 80): 'bounce quoth the guns'. Dod-
dering old Shallow is trying to enact all this while
speaking.

237 **coats** Recruits were given 'coat money' with
which to buy white smocks bearing a red cross.

send us peace. At your return visit our house, let our old acquaintance
be renewed. Peradventure I will with ye to the court.                    240

FALSTAFF 'Fore God, would you would.

SHALLOW Go to, I have spoke at a word. God keep you.

FALSTAFF Fare you well, gentlemen.

*Exeunt [Shallow and Silence]*

On, Bardolph, lead the men away.

*[Exeunt Bardolph and the rest]*

As I return, I will fetch off these justices. I do see the bottom of Justice    245
Shallow. Lord, Lord, how subject we old men are to this vice of lying!
This same starved justice hath done nothing but prate to me of the
wildness of his youth and the feats he hath done about Turnbull
Street, and every third word a lie, duer paid to the hearer than the
Turk's tribute. I do remember him at Clement's Inn, like a man made    250
after supper of a cheese-paring. When a was naked, he was, for all the
world, like a forked radish, with a head fantastically carved upon it
with a knife. A was so forlorn that his dimensions to any thick sight
were invincible. A was the very genius of famine, yet lecherous as a
monkey and the whores called him mandrake. A came ever in the    255
rearward of the fashion, and sung those tunes to the overscutched
housewives that he heard the carmen whistle, and swear they were his
fancies or his good-nights. And now is this Vice's dagger become a

**239** peace. At your] *Collier subst.;* peace at your Q; Peace. As you F    **239** our] Q; my F    **240** ye] Q; you F **241** 'Fore God] Q; I
F    **241** would.] Q; would, Master *Shallow.* F    **242** God keep you.] Q; Fare you well. *Exit.* F    **243** SD] *Dyce; exit* Q; *not in* F    **244**
On] F; *Shal.* On Q    **244** SD] *Capell subst.; not in* F    **246** Lord, Lord] Q; *not in* F    **251** a was] Q; hee was F    **253, 254** A was] Q;
Hee was F    **254** invincible] Q, F; invisible *Rowe*    **254–5** yet ... mandrake] Q; *not in* F    **255** A came] Q; hee came F    **255** ever] F;
ouer Q    **256–8** and sung ... good-nights.] Q; *not in* F

**242 spoke at a word** meant what I said; see *Wiv.*
1.3.13–14: 'I have spoke ... I am at a word.'

**244–68** Taking as Falstaff's the exit at 243, Q gives
the whole of this speech to Shallow.

**245 fetch off** cheat.

**246 Lord ... lying** See *1H4* 5.4.145–6: 'Lord,
Lord, how this world is given to lying!'

**248–9 Turnbull Street** In Smithfield, a haunt of
thieves and whores.

**249 duer paid** paid more punctually.

**250 Turk's tribute** Delays by his subjects in
paying tribute due to the Sultan were punished with
death.

**250–3 a man ... knife** Banbury cheese had so
thick a rind that it could be carved like soft wood.

**252 forked radish** A reference to the mandrake
root; see **255**.

**253–4 A was ... invincible** He was so thin (*OED*
Forlorn *adj* 5b) that his outlines ('dimensions') could
not be made out by dim-sighted people. 'Invincible'
then means 'could not be mastered', but it may be a

compositor's misreading of 'invisible', a commonly
accepted emendation.

**254 genius** embodiment.

**254–8 yet ... good-nights** F bowdlerises this
passage, reducing it to a nine-word sentence; see
collation.

**255 mandrake** For the reputation of this plant see
1.2.10 n.

**256–7 overscutched housewives** worn-out
whores (in contrast with the bona robas he boasted
of); 'overscutched' = well-whipped; 'housewives'
= hussies.

**258 fancies ... good-nights** impromptu love
songs and serenades.

**258 Vice's dagger** Shallow is compared to the
dagger of lath (thin wood) traditionally flourished by
the Vice in popular Moralities; see *1H4* 2.4.137 and
compare *TN* 4.2.124–8: 'Like to the old Vice /
... Who with dagger of lath / In his rage and his wrath
/ Cries, ah, ha! to the devil'.

squire, and talks as familiarly of John a'Gaunt as if he had been sworn
brother to him, and I'll be sworn a ne'er saw him but once in the tilt-          260
yard, and then he burst his head for crowding among the marshal's
men. I saw it and told John a'Gaunt he beat his own name, for you
might have thrust him and all his apparel into an eel-skin: the case of a
treble hautboy was a mansion for him, a court; and now has he land
and beefs. Well, I'll be acquainted with him if I return, and't shall go          265
hard but I'll make him a philosopher's two stones to me. If the young
dace be a bait for the old pike, I see no reason in the law of nature but I
may snap at him. Let time shape, and there an end.                          *Exit*

**4.1** *Enter the* ARCHBISHOP [*of York*], MOWBRAY, HASTINGS, *within
the forest of Gaultree*

ARCHBISHOP  What is this forest called?
HASTINGS  'Tis Gaultree forest, and't shall please your grace.
ARCHBISHOP  Here stand, my lords, and send discoverers forth

259, 262 a'Gaunt] Q; of Gaunt F    260 a ne'er] Q; hee neuer F    263 thrust] Q; truss'd F    264 has] Q; hath F    268 him. Let] him:
let Q *uncorr.*, F; him, till Q *corr.*    268 SD] *Exeunt.* F; *not in* Q    Act 4, Scene 1    4.1] *Actus Quartus. Scena Prima.* F; *not in* Q    0 SD
MOWBRAY,] F; *Mowbray, Bardolfe,* Q    0 SD HASTINGS . . . *Gaultree*] Q; *Hastings, Westmerland, Coleuile.* F    1 SH ARCHBISHOP]
*Bish.* Q (*or / Bishop*), F (*throughout scene*)

259 talks . . . John a'Gaunt See 36 n., but Falstaff
had not yet arrived when Shallow mentioned him, and
a few lines later (262–3) Falstaff himself boasts of his
familiarity with John of Gaunt.

261–2 burst . . . men had his head broken by the
guards for trying to get to the officials presiding over
the tournament (for the Marshal's function see
1.3.4 n.).

262 his own name Playing on 'gaunt' = thin,
slender, as in *R2* 2.1.73–83.

263 eel-skin Used as a close-fitting sheath for
small objects.

264 treble hautboy oboe, requiring a long thin
case; 'treble' (high-pitched) may refer to Shallow's
voice.

265–6 shall . . . but I'll it is very hard luck if I don't.

266 philosopher's two stones The philosopher's
stone was supposed to turn base metal into gold; the
duplication plays on 'stone' = testicle.

266–7 If . . . pike The dace is a small fish used as
bait; the reference is to the proverb 'The great fish eat
the small', which is the 'law of nature' mentioned
immediately after.

**Act 4, Scene 1**
4.1 The whole scene conflates details contained in

the two contrasting accounts of the episode in Holinshed, III, 529–30. The location in the entrance SD (a
rare occurrence in Shakespeare's plays) echoes
Holinshed's 'a plaine within the forrest of Galtree'
(just north of York), and is not necessarily a call for
property trees in the discovery place.

0 SD Q includes Lord Bardolph among the characters entering here, but the author must soon have
realised that Lord Bardolph had no part in the
Gaultree episode, having fled to Scotland with Northumberland (Holinshed, III, 530/2/40–3), and as
usual (see 1.3.0 SD or 3.1.31 SD) Shakespeare did not
bother to cross his name out. The inclusion of Westmerland and Colevile in the F SD is due to scribal
misunderstandings: the scribe preparing the copy
must have noticed the appearance of Westmoreland
speech headings on the MS. page from 27 onwards,
but missed Westmoreland's entrance, which was
unconspicuously noted in the right-hand margin;
reading on, he found at 351 only Falstaff's entrance
and not Colevile's, who speaks shortly after, so he
assumed that both Westmoreland and Colevile were
present from the beginning of the scene.

2 and't if it.
3 discoverers scouts.

To know the numbers of our enemies.
HASTINGS We have sent forth already.
ARCHBISHOP                                              'Tis well done.
    My friends and brethren in these great affairs,
    I must acquaint you that I have received
    New-dated letters from Northumberland;
    Their cold intent, tenor and substance thus:
    Here doth he wish his person, with such powers
    As might hold sortance with his quality,
    The which he could not levy, whereupon
    He is retired to ripe his growing fortunes
    To Scotland; and concludes in hearty prayers
    That your attempts may overlive the hazard
    And fearful meeting of their opposites.
MOWBRAY Thus do the hopes we have in him touch ground
    And dash themselves to pieces.

*Enter a* MESSENGER

HASTINGS                                              Now, what news?
MESSENGER West of this forest, scarcely off a mile,
    In goodly form comes on the enemy,
    And, by the ground they hide, I judge their number
    Upon or near the rate of thirty thousand.
MOWBRAY The just proportion that we gave them out.
    Let us sway on and face them in the field.

*Enter* WESTMORELAND

ARCHBISHOP What well-appointed leader fronts us here?
MOWBRAY I think it is my Lord of Westmoreland.
WESTMORELAND Health and fair greeting from our general,
    The prince Lord John and Duke of Lancaster.
ARCHBISHOP Say on, my Lord of Westmoreland, in peace,
    What doth concern your coming.

---

12 could] Q *corr.*, F; would Q *uncorr.*    18 SD *a* MESSENGER] F; *messenger* Q    24 SD] Q *(after 25),* F

7–16 Northumberland's letter is the author's invention.
    11 **hold sortance** sort with, be in accordance with (unrecorded elsewhere).
    16 **their opposites** See 1.3.55 n.
    17 **touch ground** touch bottom; a metaphor from shipwrecks.

20 **form** formation.
23 **just proportion** correct estimate.
24 **sway on** move on (*OED* Sway *v* 4b).
25 **well-appointed** in full military regalia; compare 1.1.190.
28 **Duke of Lancaster** See 1.3.82 n.

WESTMORELAND                    Then, my lord,                30
    Unto your grace do I in chief address
    The substance of my speech. If that rebellion
    Came like itself in base and abject routs
    Led on by bloody youth, guarded with rage,
    And countenanced by boys and beggary –            35
    I say, if damned commotion so appear
    In his true, native and most proper shape,
    You, reverend father, and these noble lords
    Had not been here to dress the ugly form
    Of base and bloody insurrection                   40
    With your fair honours. You, Lord Archbishop,
    Whose see is by a civil peace maintained,
    Whose beard the silver hand of peace hath touched,
    Whose learning and good letters peace hath tutored,
    Whose white investments figure innocence,         45
    The dove and very blessed spirit of peace,
    Wherefore do you so ill translate yourself
    Out of the speech of peace, that bears such grace,
    Into the harsh and boist'rous tongue of war –
    Turning your books to graves, your ink to blood,  50
    Your pens to lances and your tongue divine
    To a loud trumpet and a point of war?
ARCHBISHOP Wherefore do I this? So the question stands.
    Briefly, to this end: we are all diseased,
    And with our surfeiting and wanton hours          55
    Have brought ourselves into a burning fever

---

30 Then, my lord] Q *corr.*, F; *not in* Q *uncorr.*   34 rage] Q, F; rags *Singer²*, *Dyce*   36 appear] Q, F; appear'd *Pope*   45 figure] Q *corr.*,
F; figures Q *uncorr.*   55–79] F; *not in* Q

**34 guarded with rage** escorted by Rage; another
personification, like Rebellion ('like itself' = in its
proper figure), Youth and Beggary; but many read
'guarded with rags', where 'guarded' means
'trimmed, faced' in the sartorial sense; see *1H4*
5.1.74–5: 'to face the garment of rebellion / With
some fine colour'.

**35 countenanced** approved.

**36 so appear** A conditional form (= 'were so to
appear'); there is no need for Pope's emendation to
'appeared'.

**44 good letters** scholarship.

**45 investments** robes.

**47 translate** (1) translate from one language into
another, (2) transform, (3) transfer (from the See of
peace to that of war).

**52 point** short phrase sounded as a signal (*OED* sv
sb 9); a musical term.

**55–79** This speech, omitted in Q possibly as too
authoritative a justification for rebellion, adds to the
Archbishop's reasons listed in Holinshed a typically
Shakespearean argument found also, with reference
to the individual instead of the state, in Sonnet 118:
'to prevent our maladies unseen, / We sicken to shun
sickness when we purge', bringing 'to medicine a
healthful state / Which, rank of goodness, would by
ills be cured' – see 63–6.

And we must bleed for it; of which disease
Our late King Richard being infected died.
But, my most noble Lord of Westmoreland,
I take not on me here as a physician,                                      60
Nor do I, as an enemy to peace,
Troop in the throngs of military men,
But rather show a while like fearful war
To diet rank minds, sick of happiness,
And purge th'obstructions which begin to stop                             65
Our very veins of life. Hear me more plainly:
I have in equal balance justly weighed
What wrongs our arms may do, what wrongs we suffer,
And find our griefs heavier than our offences.
We see which way the stream of time doth run                              70
And are enforced from our most quiet there
By the rough torrent of occasion,
And have the summary of all our griefs,
When time shall serve, to show in articles
Which long ere this we offered to the king                                75
And might by no suit gain our audience.
When we are wronged and would unfold our griefs
We are denied access unto his person
Even by those men that most have done us wrong.
The dangers of the days but newly gone,                                   80
Whose memory is written on the earth
With yet-appearing blood, and the examples
Of every minute's instance, present now,
Hath put us in these ill-beseeming arms,

71 our most] F; careless *conj. Humphreys*   71 there] F; sphere *Hanmer;* shore *Wilson, conj. Vaughan;* flow *Sisson*   80 days] F; daie's Q

57 **must bleed for it** Playing on the practice of blood-letting as a cure; see *More* x, 1179–80: 'we the Phisitians that effect this good, / now by choise diett, annon, by letting blood'.

57–8 **of which … died** This justification of the killing of Richard II contrasts with the rebels' attitude towards Bullingbrook's usurpation.

63 **show … war** put on for the time being the frightening appearance of war.

64 **rank** surfeited; see Sonnet 118, quoted at 55–79 n.

71 Most editors emend this line, but sense can be made out of it by taking 'quiet' as a noun and 'there' as referring to 'the stream of time' (70): the 'torrent of occasion' (i.e. pressure of circumstances) forces us away from utter peace ('most quiet') into the stream of time.

73 **summary … griefs** list of all our grievances: the 'articles' (74) handed to Westmoreland for submission to the king; see Holinshed, III, 529.

83 **Of every … instance** (1) of which there is evidence every minute, (2) urged every minute upon us.

84 **Hath** A singular form used for the plural.

Not to break peace or any branch of it,                                      85
But to establish here a peace indeed
Concurring both in name and quality.
WESTMORELAND  Whenever yet was your appeal denied?
Wherein have you been gallèd by the king?
What peer hath been suborned to grate on you,                                90
That you should seal this lawless bloody book
Of forged rebellion with a seal divine,
And consecrate commotion's bitter edge?
ARCHBISHOP  My brother general: the commonwealth.
To brother born unhouseled cruelty                                           95
I make my quarrel in particular.
WESTMORELAND  There is no need of any such redress,
Or, if there were, it not belongs to you.
MOWBRAY  Why not to him in part, and to us all
That feel the bruises of the days before,                                    100
And suffer the condition of these times
To lay a heavy and unequal hand

83] Q *uncorr.; not in* Q *corr.,* F   93 bitter edge?] Q; *civil page? Theobald;* title-page. *Herford*   94] Q, F (generall,); My brother, general! the commonwealth! *Knight*   95] Q *uncorr.; not in* Q *corr.,* F   95 unhouseled] *Bulloch;* an houshold Q   102–3 To ... honours] *Divided as in* Q; *one line in* F

90 **suborned to grate** induced with bribes to harass.

91–2 **seal ... divine** The metaphor is from the censorship exercised by religious authorities on the publication of books.

93 And sanctify the cruel sword ('edge', see 1.1.170 n.) of rebellion ('commotion', see 36 and 2.4.296 n.). It is hard to see why this line – a perfect parallel to 91–2 – should have been eliminated in the corrected version of Q and in F. Possibly the omission is a misinterpretation of the placing of deletion marks added to the foul papers in a page of the manuscript heavily interfered with in view of the major omissions at 55–79 and 103–39.

94–6 The passage is irrecoverably corrupt. The omission of 95 in the corrected state of Q and in F does not improve the meaning, which requires amplification rather than compression. As it stands the speech is elliptically constructed on a double antithesis: (1) brother general / brother born, (2) general / particular. The Archbishop's 'quarrel' has two motivations, one general – the wrongs inflicted on the commonwealth – the other personal – the execution by Bullingbrook of William Scroop, Earl of Wiltshire (see *R2* 3.2.141), who is described by Holinshed and

in *1H4* 1.3.271 as the Archbishop's brother. Scroop is his brother by birth ('born'), while the commonwealth represents the brotherhood of men ('brother general').

95 **unhouseled** without being allowed to receive the last sacrament; an additional cruelty to people suffering violent death – see *Ham.* 1.5.76–7: 'Cut off even in the blossoms of my sin, / Unhouseled, disappointed, unanealed'. The emendation of Q's 'an household', palaeographically sound, was suggested by J. Bulloch (1878) and supported by G. West ('Scroop's quarrel', *ELN* 18 (1981), 174–5), quoting Holinshed on the end of Scroop, Bushy and Green (III, 498/2/71–4): 'On the morow next insuing they were arraigned ... and found giltie of treason, ... and foorthwith had their heads smit off.' This is immediately followed by the mention of Sir John Russell; see 2.2 n. and p. 15 above, n. 1.

99 **to him ... all** Redress belongs in some measure to the Archbishop for the killing of his brother and to us for all the rest, i.e. the wrongs suffered by the commonwealth.

101 **condition ... times** See 3.1.77 n.

102 **unequal** unfair, unjust.

Upon our honours.

WESTMORELAND          O my good Lord Mowbray,
Construe the times to their necessities,
And you shall say indeed it is the time          10
And not the king that doth you injuries.
Yet for your part it not appears to me
Either from the king or in the present time
That you should have an inch of any ground
To build a grief on. Were you not restored          11
To all the Duke of Norfolk's signories,
Your noble and right well-remembered father's?

MOWBRAY What thing, in honour, had my father lost
That need to be revived and breathed in me?
The king that loved him, as the state stood then,          11
Was force perforce compelled to banish him,
And then that Henry Bullingbrook and he
Being mounted and both rousèd in their seats,
Their neighing coursers daring of the spur,
Their armèd staves in charge, their beavers down,          12
Their eyes of fire sparkling through sights of steel,
And the loud trumpet blowing them together,
Then, then, when there was nothing could have stayed
My father from the breast of Bullingbrook,
O, when the king did throw his warder down,          12
His own life hung upon the staff he threw.
Then threw he down himself and all their lives

---

103–39 O my ... king.] F; *not in* Q    116 force] *Theobald;* forc'd, F

103–39 O my ... king Omitted by Q, so that the surviving part of Westmoreland's speech at 140 ff. becomes meaningless; there is no doubt of the political motivation for the cut: apart from the usual reasons, Mowbray's position in 107–14 found a close parallel in Elizabethan times in that of the son of the last Duke of Norfolk, restored to the properties but not to the title of his father, who had been executed in 1572 for plotting against the queen.
104 **Construe** Judge, Interpret.
104 **necessities** See 3.1.91, 92 n.
110–11 **restored ... signories** In *R2* 4.1.87–9 Bullingbrook had undertaken to repeal Thomas Mowbray, Duke of Norfolk's banishment and restore him to 'all his lands and signories' (estates), but when informed of Norfolk's death he made no provisions for his son Thomas Mowbray, for whose title see 1.3.4 n.

116 **force perforce** A common adverbial expression; see 4.2.46; F's reading 'forc'd perforce', though acceptable, is probably due to the usual e/d confusion in Elizabethan handwriting.
117 **then** that just at the time when.
117–29 **Henry Bullingbrook ... Bullingbrook** A rendering in epic form of the stage action implied in *R2* 1.3.99–122.
118 **rousèd** raised.
119 **daring ... spur** defying the riders to spur them into action.
120 **armèd ... charge** lances at rest, ready to charge.
120 **their beavers** visors of their helmets.
121 **sights** slits in the visors.
125 **warder** staff of command; see *R2* 1.3.118.
127 **all their lives** the lives of all those; see Abbott 218.

That by indictment and by dint of sword
Have since miscarried under Bullingbrook.

WESTMORELAND You speak, Lord Mowbray, now you know not
    what.                                                                     130
    The Earl of Hereford was reputed then
    In England the most valiant gentleman.
    Who knows on whom fortune would then have smiled?
    But if your father had been victor there,
    He ne'er had borne it out at Coventry,                                  135
    For all the country, in a general voice,
    Cried hate upon him, and all their prayers and love
    Were set on Hereford, whom they doted on,
    And blessed and graced indeed more than the king.
    But this is mere digression from my purpose.                           140
    Here come I from our princely general
    To know your griefs, to tell you from his grace
    That he will give you audience; and wherein
    It shall appear that your demands are just,
    You shall enjoy them, everything set off                               145
    That might so much as think you enemies.

MOWBRAY But he hath forced us to compel this offer,
    And it proceeds from policy, not love.

WESTMORELAND Mowbray, you overween to take it so:
    This offer comes from mercy, not from fear,                            150
    For lo, within a ken our army lies,
    Upon mine honour, all too confident
    To give admittance to a thought of fear.
    Our battle is more full of names than yours,
    Our men more perfect in the use of arms,                               155
    Our armour all as strong, our cause the best;
    Then reason will our hearts should be as good.

---

139 indeed] *Theobald;* and did F    140 But] F; *West.* But Q

128 **by indictment ... sword** either through the miscarriage of justice or by brute force.

131 **Earl of Hereford** In fact, Bullingbrook's title in *R2* is *Duke* of Hereford.

135 **ne'er ... out** would never have won the day.

139 **indeed** Theobald's emendation of F's 'and did' is generally accepted, though palaeographically the early Cambridge editors' 'and eyed' ('eid') is sounder.

145 **set off** (1) offset, forgotten, (2) weighed against.

148 **policy** 'cunning' rather than 'expediency'.

151 **a ken** sight.

154 **battle** army deployed; see 3.2.129.

154 **names** (1) titled people, (2) numbers.

157 **reason will** it stands to reason that.

Say you not then our offer is compelled.

MOWBRAY Well, by my will we shall admit no parley.

WESTMORELAND That argues but the shame of your offence:  160
A rotten case abides no handling.

HASTINGS Hath the Prince John a full commission,
In very ample virtue of his father,
To hear and absolutely to determine
Of what conditions we shall stand upon?  165

WESTMORELAND That is intended in the general's name.
I muse you make so slight a question.

ARCHBISHOP Then take, my Lord of Westmoreland, this sched-
ule,
For this contains our general grievances.
Each several article herein redressed,  170
All members of our cause, both here and hence,
That are ensinewed to this action,
Acquitted by a true substantial form
And present execution of our wills,
To us and our purposes confined  175
We come within our aweful banks again
And knit our powers to the arm of peace.

WESTMORELAND This will I show the general. Please you, lords,
In sight of both our battles we may meet
At either end in peace – which God so frame –  180
Or to the place of difference call the swords

---

175 our] Q; to our F  175 confined] confinde, Q, F; confirmed *Hanmer;* consign'd *Malone*  180 At] Q, F; And *Theobald*
180 God] Q; Heauen F

---

**161** Proverbial (Tilley s6): 'It is a bad case that will abide no clouting'; 'case' = box, container, with an obvious quibble.

**163** As a plenipotentiary for his father.

**166 intended** understood, implicit.

**168 schedule** list (of grievances); see 73 n.; closer in diction to Stow's report (*Annales*, p. 529) than to Holinshed's.

**172 ensinewed** (1) joined by strong sinews, (2) ready with all their strength.

**173 by a ... form** through valid legal proceedings.

**175** This clause does not refer to 'wills' but to 'We' in the next line: without going beyond the aims we set ourselves – anticipating the metaphor of the overflowing stream.

**176 our aweful banks** the boundaries imposed by our reverence ('awe') for the king; the old spelling is retained for the sake of the authentic meaning (compare 5.2.85). For the metaphor compare *More* Add.II (Hand D) 162: 'whiles they ar ore the banck of their obedyenc'.

**179 battles** armies in battle formation; as at 154.

**180 At either end** Normally emended to '*And* either end', taking 'end' as verb; but 'end' as noun allows a double construction: 'we meet peacefully on both sides (or call for battle)'; 'we meet either on the side of peace (or, on the opposite side, we call for battle)'.

                    Which must decide it.
ARCHBISHOP                    My lord, we will do so.
                                        *Exit Westmoreland*
MOWBRAY  There is a thing within my bosom tells me
          That no conditions of our peace can stand.
HASTINGS  Fear you not, that if we can make our peace          185
          Upon such large terms, and so absolute,
          As our conditions shall consist upon,
          Our peace shall stand as firm as rocky mountains.
MOWBRAY  Yea, but our valuation shall be such
          That every slight and false-derivèd cause,          190
          Yea, every idle, nice and wanton reason,
          Shall to the king taste of this action,
          That, were our royal faiths martyrs in love,
          We shall be winnowed with so rough a wind
          That even our corn shall seem as light as chaff,     195
          And good from bad find no partition.
ARCHBISHOP  No, no, my lord, note this: the king is weary
          Of dainty and such picking grievances,
          For he hath found to end one doubt by death
          Revives two greater in the heirs of life,            200
          And therefore will he wipe his tables clean
          And keep no telltale to his memory
          That may repeat and history his loss
          To new remembrance; for full well he knows
          He cannot so precisely weed this land                205
          As his misdoubts present occasion:
          His foes are so enrooted with his friends
          That, plucking to unfix the enemy,
          He doth unfasten so and shake a friend.

182 SD] Q *(after* it)*; not in* F    185 not, that if] Q, F; not that, if F2, *Pope*    189 Yea] Q; I F    198 Of dainty . . . picking] Q, F; Of picking
out such dainty *Johnson*

187 **consist upon** (1) stand upon (see 165), (2) insist on securing.
189 **our valuation** the king's opinion of us.
190 **false-derivèd** wrongly attributed.
191 **nice and wanton** petty and frivolous.
193 **were . . . love** even if we suffered martyrdom for our loyalty to the king.
194–5 **winnowed . . . chaff** The agricultural image implies that the king will enquire too curiously; see Luke 22.31: 'Satan hath desired you, to winow you, as wheate.'
198 **Of dainty . . . picking** Of fastidiousness and

such trifling; possibly the line is corrupt and 'picking' is a verbal noun qualified by 'dainty'.
199 **doubt** risk, fear.
200 **heirs of life** survivors.
201 **tables** records, slates.
203 **history** recount, record (the only use of 'history' as a verb in Shakespeare).
205 **precisely** completely.
206 **misdoubts** suspicions.
207–9 **foes . . . friend** See Matt. 13.29: 'lest whyle ye geather vp the tares, ye roote vp also the wheate with them', and compare 194–6.

So that this land, like an offensive wife                                    210
That hath enraged him on to offer strokes,
As he is striking, holds his infant up
And hangs resolved correction in the arm
That was upreared to execution.

HASTINGS  Besides, the king hath wasted all his rods                        215
On late offenders, that he now doth lack
The very instruments of chastisement,
So that his power, like a fangless lion,
May offer, but not hold.

ARCHBISHOP                                  'Tis very true;
And therefore be assured, my good lord marshal,                            220
If we do now make our atonement well,
Our peace will, like a broken limb reunited,
Grow stronger for the breaking.

MOWBRAY                                     Be it so.
Here is returned my Lord of Westmoreland.

*Enter* WESTMORELAND

WESTMORELAND  The prince is here at hand. Pleaseth your lordship                                                                        225
To meet his grace just distance 'tween our armies.

MOWBRAY  Your grace of York, in God's name then set forward.

ARCHBISHOP  [*To Mowbray*] Before, and greet his grace. – My lord, we
come.

*Enter Prince* JOHN [*of Lancaster*] *and his army*                       (4.2.0)

JOHN  You are well encountered here, my cousin Mowbray;
Good day to you, gentle Lord Archbishop,                                    230

223–4 Be . . . Westmoreland.] *Divided as in* F; *one line in* Q   227 God's] Q; heauen's F   227 set] Q; *not in* F   228 SD.1 *To Mowbray*]
*Conj. Berger–Williams; not in* F   228 we come.] Q, F; we come. *Exeunt. / Scene II / Capell, et al.*   228 SD.2] Q *(after 226); Enter Prince*
*Iohn.* F; *Enter from one side Mowbray, the Archbishop, Hastings and others, from the other side Prince John of Lancaster, Westmoreland . . .*
*and others. / Capell subst.*

213 hangs . . . correction suspends, interrupts the
blow already determined upon.
215 wasted . . . rods spent all his punishments.
219 offer threaten; see 211.
221 atonement reconciliation.
222–3 a broken . . . breaking Proverbial: 'A
broken bone is the stronger when it is well set' (Tilley
B515).
226 just distance midway.
227–8 Some sort of movement is implied in these

speeches, but certainly not a general exit as indicated
by Capell and most modern editors, who begin a new
scene with the entrance of Prince John. As noted by
Berger–Williams, pp. 251–2, Mowbray is sent
forward to greet the prince upon his entrance at one
side of the stage and then the two parties meet at the
centre.
229 cousin A common form of address between
noblemen, not involving family ties; see 306.
230 gentle of noble blood; see 306 and 1.1.189 n.

And so to you, Lord Hastings, and to all.
My Lord of York, it better showed with you
When that your flock, assembled by the bell,                    (5)
Encircled you to hear with reverence
Your exposition on the holy text,                              235
Than now to see you here an iron man talking,
Cheering a rout of rebels with your drum,
Turning the word to sword, and life to death.                  (10)
That man that sits within a monarch's heart
And ripens in the sunshine of his favour,                      240
Would he abuse the countenance of the king?
Alack, what mischiefs might he set abroach
In shadow of such greatness! With you, Lord Bishop,            (15)
It is even so. Who hath not heard it spoken
How deep you were within the books of God?                     245
To us the speaker in His parliament,
To us th'imagined voice of God himself,
The very opener and intelligencer                              (20)
Between the grace, the sanctities of heaven
And our dull workings. O, who shall believe                    250
But you misuse the reverence of your place,
Imply the countenance and grace of heaven
As a false favourite doth his prince's name                    (25)
In deeds dishonourable? You have ta'en up,
Under the counterfeited zeal of God,                           255
The subjects of His substitute, my father,

---

232 Than] F; That Q   236 talking,] Q; *not in* F   245 God?] Q; Heauen? F   247 th'imagined] *Rowe;* th'imagine Q, F   247 God
himself] Q; Heauen it selfe F   252 Imply] Q; Employ F   253–4 name / ... dishonourable? You] F *subst.;* name: / ...
dishonourable you Q   254 ta'en] tane Q; taken F   255 God] Q; Heauen F   256 His] his Q; Heauens F

---

232–8 Compare 41–52.

236 **iron** (1) in armour (see 84), (2) merciless.

236 **talking** Omitted in F, possibly because considered pleonastic.

238 **word to sword** Another punning antithesis as at 50–2, playing on 'word' as 'Scripture'; see *Wiv.* 3.1.44–5: 'What, the sword and the word? Do you study them both, master parson?'

239–40 **man ... favour** Compare Nashe, *Pierce Penilesse* (1592, sig. E2ᵛ): 'which of them [famous men] sat in the sunne-shine of his soueraignes grace'.

241, 252 **countenance** patronage, favourable aspect.

242 **set abroach** broach, start.

245 **deep ... God** (1) learned you were in theology, (2) much in favour you were with God; see 2.2.34–5 and the proverbial 'to be in one's books' (Tilley B534).

248 **intelligencer** informer, go-between. .

251 **But you** That you don't.

252 **Imply** Implicate, Involve; more appropriate than F's 'Employ' (use).

255 **zeal** Punning on 'seal' = (1) you profess a false zeal for God (see 2.4.267), (2) you pretend to act with God's approval ('seal').

256 **substitute** The king, according to the Tudor doctrine, was God's deputy in the state or body politic; see *R2* 1.2.37–8: 'God's is the quarrel, for God's substitute, / His deputy anointed in His sight'.

And both against the peace of heaven and him
Have here upswarmed them.

ARCHBISHOP                              Good my Lord of Lancaster,              (30)
I am not here against your father's peace,
But, as I told my Lord of Westmoreland,                              260
The time misordered doth, in common sense,
Crowd us and crush us to this monstrous form
To hold our safety up. I sent your grace                             (35)
The parcels and particulars of our grief,
The which hath been with scorn shoved from the court,       265
Whereon this Hydra son of war is born,
Whose dangerous eyes may well be charmed asleep
With grant of our most just and right desires,                       (40)
And true obedience, of this madness cured,
Stoop tamely to the foot of majesty.                                 270

MOWBRAY  If not, we ready are to try our fortunes
To the last man.

HASTINGS                 And though we here fall down,
We have supplies to second our attempt;                              (45)
If they miscarry, theirs shall second them,
And so success of mischief shall be born,                            275
And heir from heir shall hold his quarrel up
Whiles England shall have generation.

JOHN  You are too shallow, Hastings, much too shallow             (50)
To sound the bottom of the after-times.

WESTMORELAND  Pleaseth your grace to answer them
                  directly                                            280
How far forth you do like their articles.

266 Hydra son] Hidra, son Q; Hydra-Sonne F   276 his] Q; this F   278, 282 SH JOHN] F; *Prince.* Q   278] *As one line*, Q; *as two lines divided at* / (Hastings) F

258 **upswarmed them** raised them up in swarms like angry bees; a Shakespearean coinage.
261 **in common sense** according to the general feeling.
262 **monstrous form** abnormal, fearful course of action; but see the imagery of 266–7.
264 **parcels** details.
265 **shoved** kept out; compare 77–9.
266 **Hydra** The many-headed monster (see Induction 18–19) proverbially compared with the unruly populace (Tilley H278).
267 **dangerous eyes** The metaphor moves from

Hydra to another mythological monster, hundred-eyed Argus, Juno's watchman, who was charmed asleep by Mercury's music.
273 **supplies to second** reinforcements (see 1.3.12) that will renew.
274–7 A prophecy of the Wars of the Roses, suggested by the myth of Hydra, whose heads grew again as soon as they were cut off.
275 **success … born** (1) a sequence of misfortunes will take place, (2) the bloody events will generate descendants.
277 **generation** progeny, ability to generate.

JOHN  I like them all, and do allow them well,

    And swear here by the honour of my blood,          (55)

    My father's purposes have been mistook,

    And some about him have too lavishly          285

    Wrested his meaning and authority.

    My lord, these griefs shall be with speed redressed,

    Upon my soul they shall. If this may please you,         (60)

    Discharge your powers unto their several counties

    As we will ours; and here, between the armies,         290

    Let's drink together, friendly, and embrace,

    That all their eyes may bear those tokens home

    Of our restorèd love and amity.         (65)

ARCHBISHOP  I take your princely word for these redresses.

JOHN  I give it you and will maintain my word,         295

    And thereupon I drink unto your grace.

HASTINGS  Go, captain, and deliver to the army

    This news of peace. Let them have pay, and part,        (70)

    I know it will well please them. Hie thee, captain.

                           *Exit [Captain]*

ARCHBISHOP  To you, my noble Lord of Westmoreland.         300

WESTMORELAND  I pledge your grace; and if you knew what

       pains

    I have bestowed to breed this present peace

    You would drink freely. But my love to ye         (75)

    Shall show itself more openly hereafter.

ARCHBISHOP  I do not doubt you.

WESTMORELAND               I am glad of it.         305

    Health to my lord and gentle cousin Mowbray.

MOWBRAY  You wish me health in very happy season,

    For I am on the sudden something ill.         (80)

ARCHBISHOP  Against ill chances men are ever merry,

---

288 soul] Q; Life F  295 SH JOHN] F; *not in* Q  297 SH HASTINGS] F; *Prince* Q  299] *As one line,* Q; *as two lines divided at* them.
F  299 SD] *Exit.* F; *not in* Q  301–2] *Divided as in* Q; *as three lines ending* ...Grace: / ...bestow'd / ...Peace, F

282 **allow** approve.

285 **lavishly** freely, arbitrarily.

288–93 **If this ... amity** Shakespeare transfers to
Prince John the deception attributed by Holinshed to
Westmoreland.

295–9 The wrong attribution of these speeches in Q
(see collation) must originate in the habit of adding
speech headings in foul papers only after writing out
the speeches.

301–4 **if you ... hereafter** ironical double-speak.

307 **happy** opportune, timely.

308 **something** somewhat; a typical premonitory
feeling.

309 **Against** In anticipation of; with reference to
the proverbial 'lightening before death' (Tilley L277)
as e.g. in *Rom.* 5.3.88–90: 'How oft when men are at
the point of death / Have they been merry, which their
keepers call / A lightening before death.'

But heaviness foreruns the good event.                          310
WESTMORELAND  Therefore be merry, coz, since sudden
  sorrow
  Serves to say thus: some good thing comes tomorrow.
ARCHBISHOP  Believe me, I am passing light in spirit.          (85
MOWBRAY  So much the worse, if your own rule be true.
     *Shout [within]*
JOHN  The word of peace is rendered. Hark how they shout!       315
MOWBRAY  This had been cheerful after victory.
ARCHBISHOP  A peace is of the nature of a conquest,
  For then both parties nobly are subdued               (90
  And neither party loser.
JOHN                                     Go, my lord,
  And let our army be dischargèd too.                    320
       *Exit [Westmoreland]*
  And, good my lord, so please you, let our trains
  March by us, that we may peruse the men
  We should have coped withal.
ARCHBISHOP                              Go, good Lord Hastings,  (95
  And, ere they be dismissed, let them march by.
        *Exit [Hastings]*
JOHN  I trust, lords, we shall lie tonight together.            325

    *Enter* WESTMORELAND

  Now, cousin, wherefore stands our army still?
WESTMORELAND  The leaders, having charge from you
  to stand,
  Will not go off until they hear you speak.                (100
JOHN  They know their duties.

    *Enter* HASTINGS

HASTINGS  My lord, our army is dispersed already.              330
  Like youthful steers unyoked they take their courses

---

314 SD] Q; *not in* F   314 SD *within*] Capell; *not in* Q, F   315 SH JOHN] F; *Prince.* Q *(and for the rest of the scene except 375, 393,*
320 SD] *Exit.* F *(at 322); not in* Q   324 SD] *Exit.* F; *not in* Q   325 SD] Q *(at 324),* F   330 My lord ... already] Q; *Our Army is*
*dispers'd* F   331 take their courses] Q; *tooke their course* F

310 **heaviness** sadness.
311 **coz** cousin; see 229 n.
313 **light** cheerful; in contrast with 'heaviness' at
310.
314 See 309 n.

321 **trains** retinues; the personal following of a
commander in chief was the highest in rank in the
army.
322 **peruse** survey.
331 **steers** calves.

East, West, North, South, or like a school broke up,
Each hurries toward his home and sporting-place.                    (105)

WESTMORELAND Good tidings, my Lord Hastings, for
      the which
      I do arrest thee, traitor, of high treason –                 335
      And you, Lord Archbishop, and you, Lord Mowbray,
      Of capital treason I attach you both.

MOWBRAY Is this proceeding just and honourable?                    (110)

WESTMORELAND Is your assembly so?

ARCHBISHOP Will you thus break your faith?

JOHN                             I pawned thee none.               340
      I promised you redress of these same grievances
      Whereof you did complain, which by mine honour
      I will perform with a most Christian care.                   (115)
      But for you rebels, look to taste the due
      Meet for rebellion.                                          345
      Most shallowly did you these arms commence,
      Fondly brought here, and foolishly sent hence.
      Strike up our drums, pursue the scattered stray:             (120)
      God, and not we, hath safely fought today.
      Some guard these traitors to the block of death,            350
      Treason's true bed and yielder up of breath.

                                        *Exeunt*

*Alarum. Excursions. Enter* FALSTAFF [*and Sir John*              (4.3.0)
                COLEVILE]

333 toward] Q; towards F   345 rebellion.] Q; Rebellion, and such Acts as yours. F   349 God] Q; Heauen F   349 hath] Q; haue
F   350 these traitors] F; this traitour Q   351 SD.1 *Exeunt*] F; *not in* Q; *Exeunt. / Scene III / Capell, et al.*   351 SD.2 *Alarum.* . . .
COLEVILE]*Alarum   Enter Falstaffe   excursions* Q, *Enter Falstaffe and Colleuile.* F; 4.2 *Alarum. Excursions. Enter Sir John Falstaff and
Coleville* / Oxford

332–3 **like ... place** Another domestic comparison, as at 210–14; and see *Rom.* 2.2.156–7.
  333 **sporting-place** playground.
  337 **attach** incriminate (implying instant arrest).
  339 **assembly** Referring to legislation against
unlawful assembly.
  340 **pawned** pledged.
  345 F completes the line with 'and such Acts as
yours', a scribal addition to regularise the metre. The
pause after 'rebellion' suggested by the incomplete
line is dramatically more effective.
  346 **shallowly** inconsiderately, stupidly; like
'fondly' and 'foolishly' at 347; compare 'shallow' at
278, and of course the name of the Justice.
  348 **stray** stragglers; soon to appear on stage in the
person of Colevile.

349 The standard formula in victory celebrations
(see e.g. *H5* 4.8.106–12) sounds as hollow in the
circumstances as the tortuous final couplet at 350–1.
  350 **these traitors** Surely better than the singular
found in Q.
  351 SD.2 All editors since Capell begin a new scene
(4.3) here; in fact the stage is cleared for a moment,
but the location is the same, the rounding up of
stragglers had been anticipated at 348, and there is
continuity in the action; besides, in F Colevile is
present from the beginning of 4.1 (see 0 SD n.). This
section of the scene is the obvious counterpart to *1H4*
5.4.111–65, and there is reason to believe that some
lines or speeches were actually transferred here from
that context (see 430–2).

FALSTAFF What's your name, sir, of what condition are
you, and of what place?

COLEVILE I am a knight, sir, and my name is Colevile of the
Dale.                                                                                  355

FALSTAFF Well then, Colevile is your name, a knight is                    (5
your degree, and your place the dale. Colevile shall be
still your name, a traitor your degree, and the dungeon
your place, a place deep enough; so shall you be still
Colevile of the Dale.                                                              360

COLEVILE Are not you Sir John Falstaff?                                      (10)

FALSTAFF As good a man as he, sir, whoe'er I am. Do ye
yield, sir, or shall I sweat for you? If I do sweat, they are
the drops of thy lovers, and they weep for thy death;
therefore rouse up fear and trembling, and do                            365
observance to my mercy.                                                         (15)

COLEVILE I think you are Sir John Falstaff, and in that
thought yield me.

FALSTAFF I have a whole school of tongues in this belly of
mine, and not a tongue of them all speaks any other                     370
word but my name. And I had but a belly of any                           (20
indifferency, I were simply the most active fellow in
Europe. My womb, my womb, my womb undoes me. –
Here comes our general.

*Retreat. Enter Prince* JOHN, WESTMORELAND *and the rest*

353 place?] Q; place, I pray? F   354–5] *As prose,* Q; *as two lines divided at* Sir: F   357–8 shall be still] shalbe still Q; shall still be
F   374 SD] *Enter Iohn Westmerland, and the rest. Retraite* Q; *Enter Prince Iohn, and Westmerland.* F

**354–5 Colevile of the Dale** The name is out of
Holinshed (III, 530/2/31–5) who lists him with 'the
lord Hastings, the lord Fauconbridge [see 1.3.0
SD n.], and sir Iohn Griffith' as captured and
beheaded at Durham by the royal army 'marching
northwards against the earle of Northumberland'.
The Archbishop and Mowbray had been executed
earlier, 'the morrow after Whitsuntide in a place
without the citie [of York]'.

**358–9 the dungeon ... deep enough** 'Dale'
means also 'pit', which is another name for 'dungeon'
(underground prison), with reference to hell. See
P. G. Phialas, 'Colevile of the Dale', *SQ* 9 (1958),
86–8.

**363–4 they are ... lovers** The drops of sweat shed
by Falstaff in his action against Colevile become the
tears of Colevile's friends weeping over his fate.

**365 fear and trembling** A biblical tag (see Eph
6.5), hinting at Falstaff's Puritanism; see 2.2.101
103 n.

**365–6 do observance** pay homage by kneeling
down.

**369–71 I have ... name** The size of my bell-
proclaims my name, i.e. makes me recognised by
everybody in every country.

**369 school** large number.

**371 And I ... indifferency** If my belly were only of
normal size.

**373 womb** abdomen; an obsolete meaning, but
with a jocular reference here to the belly of a pregnant
woman.

JOHN The heat is past, follow no further now,　　　　　　375
　　　Call in the powers, good cousin Westmoreland.　　　　(25)

　　　　　　　　　　[*Exit Westmoreland*]

　　　Now, Falstaff, where have you been all this while?
　　　When everything is ended, then you come:
　　　These tardy tricks of yours will, on my life,
　　　One time or other break some gallows' back.　　　　380

FALSTAFF I would be sorry, my lord, but it should be thus. I　　(30)
　　never knew yet but rebuke and check was the reward of
　　valour. Do you think me a swallow, an arrow, or a bullet?
　　Have I, in my poor and old motion, the expedition of
　　thought? I have speeded hither with the very extremest　　385
　　inch of possibility, I have foundered nine score and odd　　(35)
　　posts; and here, travel-tainted as I am, have in my pure
　　and immaculate valour taken Sir John Colevile of the
　　Dale, a most furious knight and valorous enemy. But
　　what of that? He saw me and yielded, that I may justly　　390
　　say, with the hook-nosed fellow of Rome, 'There,　　(40)
　　cousin, I came, saw, and overcame.'

JOHN It was more of his courtesy than your deserving.

FALSTAFF I know not: here he is, and here I yield him, and I
　　beseech your grace let it be booked with the rest of this　　395
　　day's deeds, or, by the Lord, I will have it in a particular　　(45)
　　ballad else, with mine own picture on the top on't,
　　Colevile kissing my foot. To the which course if I be

---

375 further] Q; farther F　376 SD] Rowe; not in Q, F; Exit Westmerland. Retrait. / Riverside　391–2 There, cousin,] there cosin Q
catchword: their ); not in F; there, Caesar, Theobald; your cousin Capell; thrasonic Ridley; three words Humphreys　396 by the
Lord] Q; I swear F　397 else] Q; not in F　397 on't] Q; of it F

---

375 **heat** urgency of action.

380 **break ... back** get you hanged; his weight
would break down the gallows like a horse's back,
alluding to the familiar name 'wooden horse' for the
gallows; see *More* xvii, † 1924.

381 **but ... thus** if it were otherwise.

384 **expedition** speed.

386–7 **foundered ... posts** broken down no fewer
than one-hundred-and-eighty post-horses. In *1H4*
2.4.242–3 Falstaff is called 'horse-back-breaker'; and
see 380 n.

391 **hook-nosed ... Rome** The hook nose was the
main feature of Julius Caesar's medallion portrait in

North's Plutarch, which was certainly known to
Shakespeare. See illustration 6, p. 31 above.

391–2 **There, cousin** These words, omitted by F,
have perplexed commentators, and Humphreys suggests emending them to 'three words'; but Falstaff,
jocularly impersonating Caesar, may well be addressing the prince in this familiar way.

392 **came ... overcame** *veni, vidi, vici* in North's
translation of Plutarch; see 1.1.21 and 2.2.97.

393 Proverbial (Tilley G337).

395 **booked** recorded.

396–7 **particular ballad** ballad specially written
about me.

enforced, if you do not all show like gilt twopences to me
and I in the clear sky of Fame o'ershine you as much as                    400
the full moon doth the cinders of the element (which                       (50)
show like pins' heads to her), believe not the word of the
noble. Therefore let me have right, and let desert
mount.

JOHN  Thine's too heavy to mount.                                          405

FALSTAFF  Let it shine then.                                               (55)

JOHN  Thine's too thick to shine.

FALSTAFF  Let it do something, my good lord, that may do
me good, and call it what you will.

JOHN  Is thy name Colevile?                                                410

COLEVILE  It is, my lord.                                                  (60)

JOHN  A famous rebel art thou, Colevile.

FALSTAFF  And a famous true subject took him.

COLEVILE  I am, my lord, but as my betters are
That led me hither. Had they been ruled by me,                             415
You should have won them dearer than you have.                             (65)

FALSTAFF  I know not how they sold themselves, but thou
like a kind fellow gavest thyself away gratis, and I thank
thee for thee.

*Enter* WESTMORELAND

JOHN  Now, have you left pursuit?                                          420

WESTMORELAND  Retreat is made, and execution stayed.                       (70)

JOHN  Send Colevile with his confederates
To York, to present execution.
Blunt, lead him hence and see you guard him sure.

*Exit [Blunt] with Colevile*

418 gratis] Q; *not in* F   420 Now] Q; *not in* F   424 SD] F *subst.; not in* Q

399 **show … to me** appear like counterfeit coins,
in comparison with me. Counterfeiters gilded over
twopenny pieces to pass them for gold half-crowns,
worth thirty pence each.

401 **cinders of the element** The stars, fragments
of the element of fire, no larger than pin-heads in
comparison with the moon.

404 **mount** ascend.

405 **heavy** (1) weighty, (2) heinous.

407 **thick** (1) opaque, (2) thick-set.

410, 412, 422 **Colevile** Pronounced as a trisyllable,
so that perhaps 410 and 411 are a single line.

417–19 Perhaps this is meant as verse (lines ending
at 'thou' and 'away'), but 413 and all Falstaff's other
speeches are in prose.

423 **To York** See 354–5 n.

423 **present execution** immediate beheading; at
421 'execution' meant the elimination of stragglers.

424 **Blunt** The only mention of this person by a
character in the play; he is obviously one of 'the rest' at
374 SD, but he is included as a mute in the Q entrance
stage directions at 3.1.31 and 5.2.41, and see 1.1.16 n.

And now dispatch we toward the court, my lords,                    425
I hear the king my father is sore sick.                            (75)
Our news shall go before us to his majesty,
Which, cousin, you shall bear to comfort him,
And we with sober speed will follow you.
FALSTAFF  My lord, I beseech you give me leave to go              430
  through Gloucestershire, and when you come to court,            (80)
  stand my good lord in your good report.
JOHN  Fare you well, Falstaff. I, in my condition,
  Shall better speak of you than you deserve.

                                         *Exeunt [all but Falstaff]*

FALSTAFF  I would you had the wit: 'twere better than your        435
  dukedom. Good faith, this same young sober-blooded              (85)
  boy doth not ḷove me, nor a man cannot make him laugh.
  But that's no marvel, he drinks no wine. There's never
  none of these demure boys come to any proof, for thin
  drink doth so overcool their blood, and making many             440
  fish meals, that they fạll into a kind of male green-           (90)
  sickness, and then when they marry they get wenches.
  They are generally fools and cowards – which some of
  us should be too, but for inflammation. A good sherris-
  sack hath a twofold operation in it: it ascends me into the     445
  brain, dries me there all the foolish and dull and crudy        (95)
  vapours which environ it, makes it apprehensive, quick,

432 lord in] Q; Lord, 'pray, in F   433–4]*As verse,* F; *as prose* Q   434 SD] *Exit.* F; *not in* Q   435 had the] Q; had but the F   439 none]
Q; any F

426 In fact after the Gaultree action the king personally supervised the executions and led an army northward against Northumberland.

428 cousin Addressed to Westmoreland; see 4.2.80–90.

429 sober unhurried.

430–2 This speech too has been read as verse (lines ending at 'go' and 'court'), and seen as a survival of an earlier version. The mention of Gloucestershire suggests that it belonged to the original version of what is now *1H4* 5.4.130–65; see 351 SD.2 n. and p. 12 above.

433–4 Compare *1H4* 5.4.157–8, where Prince Hal says much the same thing.

433 in my condition (1) out of my natural disposition, (2) in my capacity as commander.

438–9 never none A current colloquialism, 'improved' in F to 'never any'.

439 come to any proof that has proved any good.

441–2 male green-sickness Green-sickness was

the common name for chlorosis, a form of anaemia characteristic of girls at puberty.

442 get wenches beget only female children; i.e. the weaker sex.

444 but for inflammation were it not that strong drink inflames our spirit; a recognition that cowardice in people like him is counteracted not by valour but by imagination; see the narrative of the Gad's Hill encounter in *1H4* 2.4.

444–5 sherris-sack Spanish wine from Xeres (Jerez); sherry. The passage on the effects of wine echoes Timothy Bright's *Treatise of Melancholy* (1586), amply used by Shakespeare in *Hamlet*.

445–6 me … me Ethic datives; see 2.1.30 n.

446 crudy curdled.

447 vapours Exhalations supposed to develop in the body and ascend to the brain, obstructing it.

447 apprehensive quick in understanding.

447 quick lively.

forgetive, full of nimble, fiery and delectable shapes,
which delivered o'er to the voice, the tongue, which is
the birth, becomes excellent wit. The second property      450
of your excellent sherris is the warming of the blood,    (100)
which before, cold and settled, left the liver white and
pale, which is the badge of pusillanimity and cowardice;
but the sherris warms it and makes it course from the
inwards to the parts' extremes: it illumineth the face     455
which, as a beacon, gives warning to all the rest of this  (105)
little kingdom – man – to arm; and then the vital
commoners and inland petty spirits muster me all to
their captain, the heart, who, great and puffed up with
this retinue, doth any deed of courage: and this valour    460
comes of sherris. So that skill in the weapon is nothing  (110)
without sack, for that sets it a-work; and learning a mere
hoard of gold kept by a devil, till sack commences it and
sets it in act and use. Hereof comes it that Prince Harry
is valiant, for the cold blood he did naturally inherit of  465
his father he hath, like lean, sterile and bare land,     (115)
manured, husbanded and tilled, with excellent
endeavour of drinking good and good store of fertile
sherris, that he is become very hot and valiant. If I had a
thousand sons, the first human principle I would teach     470

---

455 illumineth] Q; illuminateth F   459–60 with this] Q; with his F   470 human] Q; *not in* F

**448 forgetive** imaginative; from 'forge'. The stress is on the first syllable.

**450 becomes** Either a singular form for the plural, referring to 'shapes', or depending on 'sherris-sack'.

**451 warming of the blood** Proverbial: 'Good wine makes good blood' (Tilley w461).

**452–3 liver ... cowardice** 'white-livered' is a frequent definition of 'coward' in Shakespeare; see *R3* 4.4.464: 'white-livered runagate', and *H5* 3.2.32: 'for Bardolph, he is white-livered and red-faced'.

**455 parts' extremes** extremities of the various parts of the body.

**457 little kingdom – man** Referring to the current notion of man as microcosm, establishing a correspondence between body natural and body politic (see 256), as in *JC* 2.1.67–8: 'the state of man / Like to a little kingdom'.

**457–60 vital ... retinue** According to the microcosm metaphor, the heart is seen as the leader of troops gathered in town and country ('inland'), which

are represented by those highly refined fluids known as 'spirits' (see 2.3.46 n.) natural, animal and vital, that were supposed to be carried by the blood to the different parts of the body, determining both physical and mental characteristics.

**462–4 learning ... use** Wine is seen as the promoter not only of military but also of intellectual valour. Learning is a secret hoard, like those believed to be guarded by evil spirits, till it is tapped by wine, which has the same effect as the taking of degrees by scholars, formerly called 'Commencement' in Cambridge and 'Act' (discussion of a thesis) in Oxford (*OED* Act *sb* 8).

**467 husbanded** cultivated.

**468 good and good store** of good quality and a lot; see *FV* scene ii (sig. B1): 'the young Prince, and three or foure more of his companions, ... called for wine good store'.

**470 human** (1) mundane (opposed to 'divine'), (2) virile.

them should be to forswear thin potations, and to addict            (120)
themselves to sack.

> *Enter* BARDOLPH

How now, Bardolph?
BARDOLPH  The army is dischargèd all and gone.
FALSTAFF  Let them go. I'll through Gloucestershire, and          475
there will I visit Master Robert Shallow, esquire. I have           (125)
him already tempering between my finger and my
thumb, and shortly will I seal with him. Come away.

> *Exeunt*

**4.2**  *Enter the* KING[, *carried in a chair*], WARWICK, *Thomas*            (4.4.0)
Duke of CLARENCE, *Humphrey* [*Duke*] *of* GLOUCESTER
[, *Attendants*]

KING  Now lords, if God doth give successful end
      To this debate that bleedeth at our doors,
      We will our youth lead on to higher fields,
      And draw no swords but what are sanctified:
      Our navy is addressed, our power collected,                  5    (5)
      Our substitutes in absence well invested,
      And everything lies level to our wish;
      Only we want a little personal strength,

---

472 SD] *Placed as in* F; *at* 473 Q    478 SD] F; *not in* Q    Act 4, Scene 2    4.2] *Scene Secunda.* F; *not in* Q; *Scene IV.* / *Capell, et al.*; 4.3
*Oxford*    0 SD *carried in a chair*] *Sisson; not in* Q, F    0 SD WARWICK,] F; *Warwike, Kent,* Q    0 SD *Attendants*] *This edn, after Capell; not
in* Q, F    1 God] Q; *Heauen* F    2 bleedeth] Q, F; *breedeth conj. Cam.*

**475 Gloucestershire** See 430–2 n. and pp. 5 and
12 above.

**477–8 tempering … seal with him** Sealing-wax
was softened before use by warming it with the
fingers; Falstaff proposes to manipulate Shallow so as
to conclude with him ('seal') an advantageous
agreement.

**Act 4, Scene 2**

**4.2** Most editors, having divided Scene 1 into three,
begin 4.4 here. The location, as made clear at 359–61,
is the Jerusalem chamber mentioned by Holinshed
(III, 541) as in Westminster Abbey, but transferred
here to the royal palace. The announcements at 81–
101 transpose to 20 March 1413 (the date of Henry
IV's death) events that had taken place in 1405 (the
Gaultree episode) and in 1408 (the defeat of Northumberland and Lord Bardolph at Bramham Moor).

**0 SD** Q includes in the entrance direction also
'Kent', another available but unemployed character,
like Fauconbridge at 1.3.0 SD and Blunt at 3.1.31 SD.
As in 3.1, the manipulation of historical facts in this
scene requires new interlocutors for the king: with the
exception of Warwick, the other characters entering
here have never appeared before. The name of Kent
is from Holinshed, where Edmund, Earl of Kent, is
the partner and rescuer of Thomas, Duke of
Clarence, in an action against the French in May 1405
(III, 528/2–529/1), and his son is the leader with
Warwick of a raid in France in 1412; see 3.1.1 n.

**3–7** Referring to the projected Crusade; see
3.1.107 n., and Holinshed, III, 541/1/5–13.

**5 addressed** prepared.

**6 substitutes … invested** deputies have already
been appointed.

**7 level** in accordance with.

And pause us till these rebels now afoot
Come underneath the yoke of government.                    10    (10)

WARWICK  Both which we doubt not but your majesty
    Shall soon enjoy.
KING                    Humphrey my son of Gloucester,
    Where is the prince your brother?
GLOUCESTER  I think he's gone to hunt, my lord, at
    Windsor.
KING  And how accompanied?
GLOUCESTER                    I do not know, my lord.        15    (15)
KING  Is not his brother Thomas of Clarence with him?
GLOUCESTER  No, my good lord, he is in presence here.
CLARENCE  What would my lord and father?
KING  Nothing but well to thee, Thomas of Clarence.
    How chance thou art not with the prince thy brother?  20    (20)
    He loves thee, and thou dost neglect him, Thomas.
    Thou hast a better place in his affection
    Than all thy brothers; cherish it, my boy,
    And noble offices thou mayst effect
    Of mediation, after I am dead,                          25    (25)
    Between his greatness and thy other brethren.
    Therefore omit him not, blunt not his love,
    Nor lose the good advantage of his grace
    By seeming cold or careless of his will,
    For he is gracious if he be observed,                  30    (30)
    He hath a tear for pity, and a hand
    Open as day for meting charity;
    Yet notwithstanding, being incensed, he is flint,
    As humorous as winter, and as sudden

---

12–13 Humphrey ... brother?] *As verse, Pope; as prose,* Q, F    12 Gloucester] F; Gloster Q    32 meting] meeting Q, *Riverside;* melting F    33 notwithstanding,] F; notwithstanding Q    33 he is] Q; hee's F

9–10 See 3.1.106–7; the same reason for postponing the Crusade given in *1H4* 1.1.47–8.

19–48 Based on Stow, *Annales,* p. 545, where the king 'lieng greeuously diseased' addresses Prince Hal, expressing his fear that Clarence may oppose the succession; Hal's sober reply prompts the praise of his character at 30–41.

27 omit neglect; see *2H6* 3.2.382.

30 gracious ready to grant favours; see 'grace' at 28.

30, 36 observed humoured, shown respect; see 'observe' at 49.

32 meting meting out, apportioning (see 'mete', 77 n.); most editors accept F's 'melting' as an attribute of 'charity' ('tearful' or 'feeling pity'), while Furnivall takes Q's 'meeting' as 'meeting the needs of charity, giving alms'.

34 humorous (1) changeable under the action of the different humours which were supposed to govern man's character, (2) moist, humid, as the winter season.

As flaws congealèd in the spring of day.      35  (35)
His temper therefore must be well observed;
Chide him for faults, and do it reverently,
When you perceive his blood inclined to mirth;
But, being moody, give him time and scope,
Till that his passions, like a whale on ground,      40  (40)
Confound themselves with working. Learn this, Thomas,
And thou shalt prove a shelter to thy friends,
A hoop of gold to bind thy brothers in,
That the united vessel of their blood,
Mingled with venom of suggestion,      45  (45)
As force perforce the age will pour it in,
Shall never leak, though it do work as strong
As aconitum, or rash gunpowder.

CLARENCE  I shall observe him with all care and love.

KING  Why art thou not at Windsor with him, Thomas?      50  (50)

CLARENCE  He is not there today, he dines in London.

KING  And how accompanied?

CLARENCE  With Poins and other his continual followers.

KING  Most subject is the fattest soil to weeds,
    And he, the noble image of my youth,      55  (55)
    Is overspread with them, therefore my grief

---

39 time] Q; Line F    51, 53 SH CLARENCE] *Clar.* F; *Tho.* Q    52 accompanied?] Q; accompanyed? Canst thou tell that? F
53 Poins] *Poines* Q, F3–4, *Pointz* F, F2

35 **flaws congealèd** (1) snowflakes turned to ice (*OED* Flaw *sb*¹ 1), (2) sharp bursts of passion (*OED* Flaw *sb*² 2).

35 **spring of day** (1) daybreak, dawn, (2) early youth.

36 **temper** mood.

39 **time** The Q reading makes sense; F replaces with 'Line', thinking of the phrase 'to give line' = 'to allow full play'.

40 **whale on ground** A not uncommon occurrence, but most editors refer to Holinshed's report (III, 1259) of the stranding of a whale near Ramsgate in 1574.

41 **Confound** Consume, ruin.

41 **working** exertion.

43 **hoop of gold** The usual metaphor of the barrel-hoop of steel for strength and cohesion (see 'rib of steel' at 2.3.54 and *Ham.* 1.3.63) is turned into that of a precious ring, emblem of union, and then of a gold chalice ('vessel', 44) used in pledging 'love and amity', but into which poison may be poured: see the Gaultree episode at 4.1.291–304.

44 **vessel** chalice (see 43 n.); but also 'blood vessel', that may burst under the effect of poison.

45 **suggestion** suspicion.

46 **force perforce** See 4.1.116.

48 **aconitum** wolf's bane, a herb considered the most violent of poisons.

48 **rash gunpowder** Compare *Rom.* 5.1.60–5: 'A dram of poison, such soon-spreading gear / ... that the trunk may be discharged of breath / As violently as hasty powder fired / Doth hurry from the fatal cannon's womb'.

52 F completes the line with 'Canst thou tell that?', an unnecessary addition probably devised by the 'regulariser', who seems to have been particularly active in this scene; see 120, 132, 179, 204–5.

53 **continual** constant.

54 Proverbial (Tilley W241); see Lyly, *Euphues*, I, 251: 'The fattest grounde bringeth foorth nothing but weedes if it be not well tilled.' Is the choice of proverb suggested by Falstaff ('the fattest soil')?

Stretches itself beyond the hour of death.
The blood weeps from my heart when I do shape
In forms imaginary th'unguided days
And rotten times that you shall look upon          60     (60)
When I am sleeping with my ancestors.
For when his headstrong riot hath no curb,
When rage and hot blood are his counsellors,
When means and lavish manners meet together,
O, with what wings shall his affections fly          65     (65)
Towards fronting peril and opposed decay!
WARWICK   My gracious lord, you look beyond him quite:
The prince but studies his companions
Like a strange tongue, wherein, to gain the language,
'Tis needful that the most immodest word          70     (70)
Be looked upon and learnt; which once attained,
Your highness knows comes to no further use
But to be known and hated. So, like gross terms,
The prince will in the perfectness of time
Cast off his followers, and their memory          75     (75)
Shall as a pattern or a measure live
By which his grace must mete the lives of other,
Turning past-evils to advantages.
KING   'Tis seldom when the bee doth leave her comb
In the dead carrion.

*Enter* WESTMORELAND

72 further] Q; farther F   77 other] Q; others F   78 past-evils] Q, F; past euils *Dering MS.*   80 SD] *Placed as in* F; *after Westmerland?*
Q

58 **blood … heart** Each sigh drained a drop of blood from the heart.

59 **unguided** with no proper ruler.

63 **rage** raging passions.

64 **lavish** unrestrained, licentious.

65 **affections** inclinations, natural propensities.

66 **fronting … decay** the dangers facing and the ruin destroying him.

67 **look … quite** completely misunderstand him as if you were looking at somebody who had done much more evil than he has.

68–71 **The prince … learnt** Compare Hal on his proficiency in learning the drawers' language, in *1H4* 2.4.6–20.

73–8 **So, like … advantages** Exactly the line of reasoning of the prince in *1H4* 1.2.195–217.

76 **pattern** model; like cast-off clothes (see 75) the

rejected companions will serve as tailors' patterns to measure the people he shall meet.

76–7 **measure … other** See Mark 4.24: 'With what measure you meate, with the same shal it be measured to you agayne.'

77 **mete** apportion, adjudge; see 32 n.

77 **other** A collective plural; see 1.1.86 n.

78 **past-evils** Hyphenated for emphasis: 'great evils' rather than 'evils of the past'.

79–80 **'Tis … carrion** Recalling Judges 14.8: '[Samson] turned out of the way to see the carkeise of the Lion: and beholde, there was a swarme of Bees and hony in the carkeise of the Lion', implying that as the bee will not be deterred from making its honeycomb by the surrounding corruption, so the prince will not renounce taking pleasure in a corrupt company.

Who's here, Westmoreland?                                    80   (80)

WESTMORELAND Health to my sovereign, and new hap-
    piness
    Added to that that I am to deliver.
    Prince John your son doth kiss your grace's hand:
    Mowbray, the Bishop Scroop, Hastings and all
    Are brought to the correction of your law.                85   (85)
    There is not now a rebel's sword unsheathed,
    But Peace puts forth her olive everywhere.
    The manner how this action hath been borne
    Here at more leisure may your highness read,
    With every course in his particular.                      90   (90)

KING  O Westmoreland, thou art a summer bird,
    Which ever in the haunch of winter sings
    The lifting up of day.

*Enter* HARCOURT

Look, here's more news.

HARCOURT  From enemies heavens keep your majesty,
    And when they stand against you, may they fall           95   (95)
    As those that I am come to tell you of.
    The Earl Northumberland, and the Lord Bardolph,
    With a great power of English, and of Scots,
    Are by the shrieve of Yorkshire overthrown.
    The manner and true order of the fight                   100  (100)
    This packet, please it you, contains at large.

KING  And wherefore should these good news make me
    'sick?

---

84 Bishop Scroop,] *Theobald;* Bishop, Scroope, Q, F   90 course in his] Q; course, in his F; course, in this *conj. Johnson*   93 SD]
*Placed as in* F; *after* newes. Q   94 heavens] Q; Heauen F   99 shrieve] Q; Sherife F   102] *As one line*, Q; *as two lines divided at* newes F

90 **course** stage of the proceedings; possibly from
bear-baiting, in which it designated each attack
against the bear; see *OED* sv *sb* 26b, and *Lear* 3.7.54: 'I
am tied to th'stake and I must stand the course.'

90 **his particular** its every detail.

92 **haunch** backside, end; Wilson takes 'haunch of
winter' to mean 'backwinter', a sudden return of
winter conditions in spring; the reference is to the
king's failing health, but see 123.

93 **lifting ... day** sunrise; see 'spring of day' at 35.

93 SD HARCOURT Unhistorical; another name for a
messenger picked at random out of the Chronicles;
see Gower at 2.1.104 SD.2.

97–9 The reference is to the battle of Bramham
Moor in 1408; see 4.2 n.

99 **shrieve** The monosyllabic form of 'sheriff'; see
*More* Add.II (Hand D) 168.

101 **at large** in full; see *More* 413.

102 According to Holinshed (III, 541/1/12–16) the
king's last illness was 'a sore sicknesse, which was not
a leprosie, striken by the hand of God ... as foolish
friers imagined; but a verie apoplexie, of which he
languished till his appointed houre'; 'apoplexy' is
mentioned earlier, see 1.2.86.

Will Fortune never come with both hands full,
But whet her fair words still in foulest terms?
She either gives a stomach and no food –                    105   (105)
Such are the poor, in health – or else a feast
And takes away the stomach – such are the rich
That have abundance and enjoy it not.
I should rejoice now at this happy news,
And now my sight fails, and my brain is giddy.              110   (110)
O me, come near me, now I am much ill.

GLOUCESTER  Comfort your majesty.

CLARENCE                              O my royal father!

WESTMORELAND  My sovereign lord, cheer up yourself,
    look up.

WARWICK  Be patient, princes, you do know these fits
Are with his highness very ordinary.                        115   (115)
Stand from him, give him air: he'll straight be well.

CLARENCE  No, no, he cannot long hold out these pangs;
Th'incessant care and labour of his mind
Hath wrought the mure that should confine it in
So thin that life looks through.                            120   (120)

GLOUCESTER  The people fear me, for they do observe
Unfathered heirs and loathly births of nature.
The seasons change their manners, as the year
Had found some months asleep and leaped them over.

CLARENCE  The river hath thrice flowed, no ebb between,     125   (125)

---

104 whet] *This edn*, wet Q; write F    104 terms] termes Q; Letters F    112, 121, 130 SH GLOUCESTER] *Glo.* F; *Hum.* Q    116] *As one line*, Q; *as two lines divided at* ayre: F    117 out ... pangs;] Q *subst.*; out: ... pangs, F    120 through.] Q; through, and will breake out. F

---

104 whet ... terms always set a bitter edge (whet = sharpen) on good things, turning them into bad. Most editors prefer F's simplified reading (see collation), but Q's 'wet' was an accepted alternative form of 'whet', see *OED* Whet *v*, which under 1c quotes the figurative use from Guazzo (trans. Pettie), *Civile Conversation*, 1581: 'they ... had not yet whetted their tongues'. H. Hulme (*Explorations in Shakespeare's Language*, 1962, p. 295) takes 'wet' as a variant of 'wit' in the sense of 'bequeath'.

105–8 Proverbial (Tilley M366); see W. Warner, *Albion's England*, 1586, V, 27: 'The rich for meate seeke stomackes, and the poore for stomackes meate.'

118–20 care ... through Compare Daniel, *Civil Wars*, III, st. 116: 'paine, and griefe, / ... Besieged the hold that could not long defend, / ... Wearing the wall so thin that now the mind / Might well looke thorough, and his frailty find'.

119 wrought the mure worn the wall.

120 F completes the line (see collation) – probably an addition by a regulariser; see 52.

121 fear me frighten me.

121–2 observe ... nature record portents such as children born from virgins and monstrous productions of Nature. Prodigies announced the death of rulers; see *JC* 1.3.9–32, *Ham.* 1.1.113–25, and Daniel, *Civil Wars*, I, sts. 114–16, relating portents at the deposition of Richard II.

123 seasons ... manners See *MND* 2.1.106–14.

123 as as if.

125–8 Closely echoing Holinshed, III, 540/2/47–9, who dates the event ('Three floods without ebbing between') 12 October 1412, with no reference to the death of Edward III in 1377.

And the old folks – Time's doting chronicles –
Say it did so a little time before
That our great-grandsire Edward sicked and died.

WARWICK  Speak lower, princes, for the king recovers.

GLOUCESTER  This apoplexy will certain be his end.                    130  (130)

KING  I pray you take me up and bear me hence
     Into some other chamber.

          [*The King is laid on a bed*]                                    (4.5.0)

Let there be no noise made, my gentle friends,
Unless some dull and favourable hand
Will whisper music to my weary spirit.                                  135

WARWICK  Call for the music in the other room.

KING  Set me the crown upon my pillow here.                                 (5)

CLARENCE  His eye is hollow, and he changes much.

WARWICK  Less noise, less noise.

          *Enter* PRINCE HENRY

PRINCE                          Who saw the Duke of Clarence?

CLARENCE  I am here, brother, full of heaviness.                       140

PRINCE  How now, rain within doors, and none abroad?
     How doth the king?

GLOUCESTER                    Exceeding ill.                              (10)

PRINCE  Heard he the good news yet? Tell it him.

GLOUCESTER  He altered much upon the hearing it.

PRINCE  If he be sick with joy, he'll recover without physic.          145

132 chamber.] Q; Chamber: softly 'pray. F; chamber. Softly, pray. / *Scene V.* / *Another chamber.* / *Cam.*; chamber. Softly, pray. *Exeunt.* / *Scene V.* / *Globe*   132 SD] *This edn, after Capell; not in* Q, F   139 SD] F; *Enter Harry.* Q   141–2] *As verse*, Q; *as prose*, F   143] *As one line*, Q; *as two lines divided at* yet? F   144 altered] Q *corr.*, F; vttred Q *uncorr.*   145] *As prose*, Q; *as two lines divided at* Ioy F

130 **apoplexy** See 102 n.

132 F adds 'Softly, pray' to complete the line, a regularisation like those noted at 52 and 120.

132 **SD** The direction is not in Q or F, but most editors since 1864 introduce exit and entrance directions and begin here a new scene, though the continuity is obvious in spite of the change of locale; see p. 36 above, and illustration 7, showing alternative proposals by Walter Hodges for the staging of this scene.

134–5 See *FV* scene viii (sig. C3'): 'Draw the Curtaines and depart my chamber a while, / And cause some Musicke to rocke me a sleepe.'

134 **dull** that lulls the spirit, inducing sleep.

134 **favourable** kindly.

136 **the other room** Neither the 'other chamber' of 132, where the king has now been transferred, nor the Jerusalem room where he was taken ill, but probably the music gallery or upper stage.

137–351 Most of the rest of the scene is an amplification of *FV* scene viii (sigs. C3ᵛ–D1), based on Hall; compare Holinshed, III, 541/1/22–47.

139 **SD** The prince's entrance must take place through the same door as the king's at 4.2.0 SD, but his exit at 177 and re-entrance at 217 are through another door, to indicate that he moves to a different room from the one where the others withdraw at 150.

140 **heaviness** sadness; see 4.1.310.

141–7 In spite of the presence of obvious verse rhymes, line divisions in these speeches cannot be established with any assurance.

145 **physic** See 1.1.137.

WARWICK  Not so much noise, my lords; sweet prince,
    speak low,
    The king your father is disposed to sleep.                    (15)
CLARENCE  Let us withdraw into the other room.
WARWICK  Will't please your grace to go along with us?
PRINCE  No, I will sit and watch here by the king.                150
                    [*Exeunt all but the Prince*]
    Why doth the crown lie there upon his pillow
    Being so troublesome a bedfellow?                             (20)
    O polished perturbation! Golden care!
    That keep'st the ports of slumber open wide
    To many a watchful night – sleep with it now!                155
    Yet not so sound, and half so deeply sweet
    As he whose brow, with homely biggen bound,                   (25)
    Snores out the watch of night. O majesty!
    When thou dost pinch thy bearer, thou dost sit
    Like a rich armour worn in heat of day,                       160
    That scald'st with safety; by his gates of breath
    There lies a downy feather which stirs not:                   (30)
    Did he suspire, that light and weightless down
    Perforce must move. My gracious lord, my father!
    This sleep is sound indeed, this is a sleep                   165
    That from this golden rigol hath divorced
    So many English kings. Thy due from me                        (35)
    Is tears and heavy sorrows of the blood,
    Which nature, love, and filial tenderness
    Shall, O dear father, pay thee plenteously.                   170
    My due from thee is this imperial crown
    Which, as immediate from thy place and blood,                 (40)

146–7] *Divided as in Pope; as prose, Q; as three lines ending* … (My Lords) / … lowe, / … sleepe. F    **149** Will't] F; Wilt Q    **150** SD]
*Rowe³ subst.; not in* Q, F    **157** he whose] Q, F; he who, his *Keightley;* he who, 's *Vaughan*    **161** safety; by … breath] F (breath,),
*Rowe³;* safty (by … breath) Q    **162** downy] F4; dowlny Q; dowlney F    **163** down] F4; dowlne Q, F    **164** move. … lord, … father!]
F (Father,), *Rowe;* moue … lord … father: Q

**148 the other room** See 136 n.
**153–8 O polished … night** Compare 3.1.4–31 n.
**154 ports** gates (the eyes).
**155 sleep … now** Either 'may you sleep in spite of
it', or 'how can you sleep with it beside you?'
**157 biggen** nightcap.
**158 the watch of night** the length of the night;
'watches' were the subdivisions of the night for sentry
duty.

**161 gates of breath** mouth and nose.
**162–3 downy … down** The spellings 'dowlny' and
'dowlne' (see collation) are considered peculiar to
Shakespeare.
**166 rigol** circle, ring (= the crown).
**172 immediate** direct heir, first in line of succession; as in *Ham.* 1.2.109.

Derives itself to me. Lo where it sits,
        [*Putting it on his head*]
Which God shall guard; and, put the world's whole strength
Into one giant arm, it shall not force                    175
This lineal honour from me: this from thee
Will I to mine leave, as 'tis left to me.            *Exit*     (45)
KING Warwick, Gloucester, Clarence!

    *Enter* WARWICK, GLOUCESTER, CLARENCE

CLARENCE Doth the king call?
WARWICK                          What would your majesty?
KING Why did you leave me here alone, my lords?           180
CLARENCE We left the prince my brother here, my liege,
        Who undertook to sit and watch by you.                (50)
KING The Prince of Wales? Where is he? Let me see him.
        He is not here.
WARWICK This door is open: he is gone this way.           185
GLOUCESTER He came not through the chamber where we
        stayed.                                               (55)
KING Where is the crown? Who took it from my pillow?
WARWICK When we withdrew, my liege, we left it there.
KING The prince hath ta'en it hence. Go seek him out.
        Is he so hasty, that he doth suppose               190
        My sleep my death?
        Find him, my Lord of Warwick, chide him hither.      (60)
                                [*Exit Warwick*]
        This part of his conjoins with my disease
        And helps to end me. See, sons, what things you are,
        How quickly Nature falls into revolt               195

---

173 where] Q; heere F   173 SD] *Johnson subst.; not in* Q, F   174–7] *Divided as in* Q; *as five lines ending* …guard: / …Arme, / …from me: / …leaue, / …to me. F   174 God] Q; Heauen F   179 majesty?] Q; Maiestie? how fares your Grace? F   181–2] *As verse,* F; *as prose,* Q   183–4] *As verse, Capell; as prose,* Q   184] Q; *not in* F   186 SH GLOUCESTER] *Glo.* F; *Hum.* Q   189] *As one line,* Q; *as two lines divided at* hence: F   190–1] *Divided as in Capell (after* F); *as one line,* Q   191–6] *Divided as in* Q; *as six lines ending* …Warwick) / …conioynes / …end me. / …are: / …reuolt, / …Obiect? F   192 SD] *Capell; not in* Q, F

173 **Derives itself** Descends.
173 **where** F's 'heere' puts an unnecessary stress on the implicit action of the prince.
179 Clarence's and Warwick's speeches form a single pentameter, so that the addition in F of 'How fares your Grace?' to complete Warwick's line is obviously mistaken; see 52 n.
184 This half-line is omitted by F in order to regularise the metre.

190–6 Q's line division, including several shorter lines for dramatic effect, is preferable to F's redistribution in an unsuccessful attempt to give the passage a more regular appearance.
193 **part** piece of conduct, action; like an actor's 'part'.
194 **sons** A hypermetrical vocative.

When gold becomes her object!
For this the foolish over-careful fathers                                    (65)
Have broke their sleep with thoughts,
Their brains with care, their bones with industry;
For this they have engrossèd and pilled up                         200
The cankered heaps of strange-achievèd gold;
For this they have been thoughtful to invest                          (70)
Their sons with arts and martial exercises,
When like the bee tolling from every flower,
Our thighs packed with wax, our mouths with honey,        205
We bring it to the hive; and like the bees
Are murdered for our pains. This bitter taste                           (75)
Yields his engrossments to the ending father.

*Enter* WARWICK

Now where is he that will not stay so long
Till his friend Sickness' hands determined me?                       210
WARWICK  My lord, I found the prince in the next room,
Washing with kindly tears his gentle cheeks,                          (80)
With such a deep demeanour in great sorrow
That tyranny, which never quaffed but blood,
Would, by beholding him, have washed his knife                   215
With gentle eye-drops. He is coming hither.

198–9] *Divided as in* Q, F; *divided at* care *Capell*   198 sleep] Q; sleepes F   200 pilled] pilld Q; pyl'd F   204 tolling] Q; culling
F   204–5 flower, / Our] Q; flower / The vertuous Sweetes, our F   205–8] *Divided as in* Q; *as five lines ending* ... Wax, / ... Hiue; /
... paines. / ... engrossements, / ... Father. F   205 thighs] thigh, Q; Thighes F; thighs are *Pope;* thighs all *Hanmer*   208 SD]
*Placed as in* F; *at* 210 Q   210 Sickness' hands] *This edn;* sickness hands Q, *Collier;* Sicknesse hath F; sickness have *Ridley*   215–16
knife / ... -drops.] F; knife, / ... -drops, Q

**200 engrossèd** collected.
**200 pilled up** plundered; more effective than F's
'pyl'd' = piled, accumulated.
**201 cankered** (1) rusty, tarnished, (2) morally
corrupt; see 'cankers' at 2.2.71.
**201 strange-achievèd** acquired (1) by venturing
in foreign parts (see 1.1.180–6 n.), (2) by crooked
means, (3) not for themselves but for others.
**202 invest** endow, instruct in; see 'invested' at 6.
**204–8** F's substantial variants seem to be due to the
transcriber's wish to clarify the meaning of 'tolling'
(= exacting a toll or tribute), which is replaced with
'culling ... the virtuous sweets' ('virtuous' = having
beneficent properties), a misleading amplification
since 200–1 make it clear that neither the means of
acquisition nor the wealth itself accumulated for one's
heirs is necessarily 'virtuous'.

**205 thighs** F's reading, but probably the compositor of Q took the *s* in the manuscript for a comma;
see collation.
**207–8 This ... father** His acquisitions yield this
bitter taste to the father at the point of death; a reverse
construction. For 'engrossments' (= acquisitions) see
'engrossèd' at 200; 'yields' is a singular form instead
of a plural – see 1.1.33 n.
**210 his ... me** Sickness is personified as the
prince's friend who puts an end ('determined') to the
king his father. Modern editors prefer F's reading (see
collation), though replacing 'hath' with the subjunc-
tive 'have' and considering 'hands' as a misreading of
'haue'.
**212 kindly** filial; not from 'kind' = 'gentle', but
from 'kin' = 'family tie'.
**214 tyranny** cruelty.

KING  But wherefore did he take away the crown?                    (85)

          *Enter* PRINCE HENRY

    Lo where he comes. Come hither to me, Harry.
    Depart the chamber, leave us here alone.
          *Exeunt* [*Gloucester, Clarence, Warwick*]
PRINCE  I never thought to hear you speak again.                    220
KING  Thy wish was father, Harry, to that thought.
    I stay too long by thee, I weary thee.                          (90)
    Dost thou so hunger for mine empty chair
    That thou wilt needs invest thee with my honours
    Before the hour be ripe? O foolish youth,                       225
    Thou seek'st the greatness that will overwhelm thee.
    Stay but a little, for my cloud of dignity                      (95)
    Is held from falling with so weak a wind
    That it will quickly drop: my day is dim.
    Thou hast stol'n that which after some few hours                230
    Were thine without offence, and at my death
    Thou hast sealed up my expectation.                             (100)
    Thy life did manifest thou lovedst me not,
    And thou wilt have me die assured of it.
    Thou hidst a thousand daggers in thy thoughts,                  235
    Whom thou hast whetted on thy stony heart
    To stab at half an hour of my life.                             (105)
    What, canst thou not forbear me half an hour?
    Then get thee gone, and dig my grave thyself,
    And bid the merry bells ring to thine ear                       240
    That thou art crownèd, not that I am dead.
    Let all the tears that should bedew my hearse                   (110)

---

217 SD] *Placed as in* F; *Enter Harry.* Q *(at 216)*   219 SD] *exeunt.* Q; *Exit.* F   220 SH PRINCE] *P.Hen.* F; *Harry* Q   223 mine] Q; my
F   224 my] Q; mine F   235 hidst] Q; hid'st F; hidest *Cam.*   236 Whom] Q; Which F   237 life] Q, F; frail life F3–4, *Rowe*
240 thine] Q; thy F

219 **Depart the chamber** See *FV*, quoted at
134–5 n.
  221 **Proverbial** (Tilley B239).
  223 **chair** throne.
  224 **invest** endow; as at 202.
  227 **cloud of dignity** earthly greatness, insubstantial as a cloud.
  228 **wind** (1) the wind supporting the clouds, (2) the breath keeping the king alive.
  229 **dim** (1) weak, (2) getting dark.

232 **sealed ... expectation** confirmed my worst
surmises; for the negative value of 'expectation' see
5.2.31 and 125.
  235 **a thousand daggers** Possibly reminiscent of
the episode in *FV* scene vi (sigs. c2ᵛ–c3) (see Holinshed, III, 539/1/1–2/27), when Hal offered his father
a dagger, asking to be killed rather than suspected of
disloyalty.
  238 **forbear ... hour** (1) grant me half an hour
more, (2) put up with me, let me be for half an hour.

Be drops of balm to sanctify thy head:
Only compound me with forgotten dust.
Give that which gave thee life unto the worms,                    245
Pluck down my officers, break my decrees,
For now a time is come to mock at Form:                          (115)
Harry the fifth is crowned, up, Vanity,
Down, royal state, all you sage counsellors, hence!
And to the English court assemble now                            250
From every region, apes of idleness!
Now, neighbour confines, purge you of your scum.                 (120)
Have you a ruffian that will swear, drink, dance,
Revel the night, rob, murder, and commit
The oldest sins the newest kind of ways?                         255
Be happy, he will trouble you no more:
England shall double gild his treble guilt,                      (125)
England shall give him office, honour, might;
For the fifth Harry from curbed licence plucks
The muzzle of restraint, and the wild dog                        260
Shall flesh his tooth on every innocent.
O my poor kingdom! Sick with civil blows,                        (130)
When that my care could not withhold thy riots
What wilt thou do when riot is thy care?
O, thou wilt be a wilderness again,                              265
Peopled with wolves, thy old inhabitants.
PRINCE O, pardon me, my liege. But for my tears,                 (135)
The moist impediments unto my speech,

---

248 Harry] Q; Henry F    253 will] Q; swill F    257 gild] Q; gill'd F; guil'd F4    257 guilt] F; gilt Q    261 on] Q; in F    262 kingdom!
Sick ... blows,] kingdome! sicke ... blowes: Q; kingdome (sicke ... blowes) F; kingdom sick ... blows! *Theobald*    267] *Divided as
in* Q; *as two lines divided at* (my Liege) F    268 moist] Q; most F

243 **balm** consecrated oil (for anointing the king at
his coronation); capitalised in Q.

244 **compound** mix; see *Ham.* 4.2.5–6: 'What have
you done ... with the dead body? – Compounded it
with dust, whereto 'tis kin.'

247 **Form** The rule of the state, i.e. law and order;
see *More* Add.II (Hand D) 269: 'gyue vp yo^r sealf to
forme'.

251 **apes of idleness** fools, tainted with all vices of
which idleness was proverbially the begetter, and as
such presented as a Vice in Moralities; for 'apes' see
2.2.53–4 n.

252 **confines** states, countries.

257 **gild** cover up, paint over; the quibble with

'guilt' is very common, see *H5* 2 Chorus 26 and *Mac.*
2.2.56–7.

261 **flesh** plunge into the flesh (*OED* sv *v* 3); see
1.1.149 n.

262 **civil blows** intestine conflicts.

263–4 **my care ... thy care** Developing the
rhetorical figure of epanalepsis, with a play on
'care' = (1) statesmanship, (2) interest, inclination;
and on 'riot' = (1) debauchery, (2) tumult, civil dis-
order. The king is addressing his 'poor kingdom'
(262) personified in Prince Hal, its future ruler.

267–305 The prince's speech closely echoes *FV*
scene viii (sigs. C4–C4^v).

267 **But** Had it not been for.

I had forestalled this dear and deep rebuke
Ere you with grief had spoke, and I had heard                270
The course of it so far. There is your crown;
And He that wears the crown immortally                      (140)
Long guard it yours. If I affect it more
Than as your honour and as your renown,
Let me no more from this obedience rise,                    275
Which my most inward true and duteous spirit
Teacheth this prostrate and exterior bending,              (145)
God witness with me. When I here came in
And found no course of breath within your majesty,
How cold it struck my heart! If I do feign,                280
O, let me in my present wildness die,
And never live to show th'incredulous world               (150)
The noble change that I have purposèd.
Coming to look on you, thinking you dead,
And dead almost, my liege, to think you were,             285
I spake unto this crown as having sense,
And thus upbraided it: 'The care on thee depending        (155)
Hath fed upon the body of my father;
Therefore thou best of gold art worse than gold,
Other, less fine, in carat more precious,                 290
Preserving life in med'cine potable;
But thou, most fine, most honoured, most renowned,        (160)
Hast eat thy bearer up.' Thus, my most royal liege,
Accusing it, I put it on my head,

---

276 inward . . . duteous] Q; true, and inward duteous F; inward-true and duteous *Hudson*    277 Teacheth this] Q, F; Teacheth, this
*Capell*    277–8 bending, . . . me.] Q; bending. . . . me, F    278 God] Q; Heauen F    286 this] Q; the F    289 worse than] Q; worst of
F    290 Other, . . . fine, in carat] Q *subst.*; Other, . . . fine in Charract, is F    293] *As one line,* Q; *as two lines divided at* vp. F    293 thy]
Q; the F    293 most] Q; *not in* F

269 **dear and deep** grievous and heartfelt.
273 **affect** long for.
275 **obedience** obeisance, kneeling down; see
4.1.365–6.
276–8 **Which . . . me** God is my witness that my
kneeling down ('prostrate . . . bending') is not mere
form ('exterior'), but reflects the depth ('inward') and
sincerity ('true') of my feeling of respect and
obedience ('duteous spirit'); an awkward construction. Most editors accept F's punctuation, considering
'God witness with me' as linked with the next sentence, as in *FV*.

279 **course** current; but see the different uses of
the word at 90 and 271.
282–3 See 73–8 n.
289–91 **thou . . . potable** Most editors adopt the
simplified reading of F (see collation), but Q makes
sense: 'You (= crown), though made of pure gold, are
not real gold, since the other sort of gold (i.e. "aurum
potabile", a liquid medicine supposed to contain the
properties of gold), though much less refined, is more
precious, the measure of its purity ("carat") being its
healing property.'
293 **eat** eaten (Abbott 343).

To try with it, as with an enemy                                     295
That had before my face murdered my father,
The quarrel of a true inheritor.                                    (165)
But if it did infect my blood with joy,
Or swell my thoughts to any strain of pride,
If any rebel or vain spirit of mine                                 300
Did with the least affection of a welcome
Give entertainment to the might of it,                             (170)
Let God for ever keep it from my head,
And make me as the poorest vassal is
That doth with awe and terror kneel to it.                          305
KING  God put in thy mind to take it hence,
That thou mightst win the more thy father's love,                  (175)
Pleading so wisely in excuse of it.
Come hither, Harry, sit thou by my bed,
And hear, I think, the very latest counsel                          310
That ever I shall breathe. God knows, my son,
By what by-paths and indirect crooked ways                         (180)
I met this crown, and I myself know well
How troublesome it sat upon my head.
To thee it shall descend with better quiet,                         315
Better opinion, better confirmation,
For all the soil of the achievement goes                           (185)
With me into the earth. It seemed in me
But as an honour snatched with boisterous hand,
And I had many living to upbraid                                    320

303 God] Q; heauen F   306 KING God put in] Q; *King.* O my Sonne! / Heauen put it in F   307 win] Q; ioyne F   311 God] Q; Heauen F   314 sat] *Capell;* sate Q, F

**295 try** put to the test (in a dispute (= 'quarrel', as at 297)); see *OED* Try *v* 5c.

**297 true inheritor** i.e. the rights of the legitimate heir.

**298 infect** (1) affect, (2) corrupt, taint.

**299 strain** (1) excess, (2) musical pitch.

**301 affection of** inclination towards (suggesting also 'infection'; see 298).

**302 Give entertainment** Show appreciation.

**306** F's 'O my Sonne' and 'My gracious Liege' at 348 are hypermetrical vocatives probably interpolated for emphasis in performance.

**309–47** The lengthy deathbed 'counsel' of the king is not in Holinshed but in Stow's *Annales*, pp. 545–6;

lines 309–14 are closely modelled on *FV* scene viii (sig. C4ᵛ), suggesting that they may reproduce verbatim the lost full text of that play, which has reached us in a badly corrupted form.

**311 God knows** The expression is both in *FV* and in Holinshed, III, 541/1/41–2.

**313 met** Suggesting that Henry came by the crown not by his will but by chance or necessity; see 3.1.72 n.

**317 soil** (1) stain, reproach, (2) ground, foundation, (3) earth (see 318).

**320 living** Referring either to 'I', i.e. during my life, or to 'many', i.e. there lived many who took advantage of the assistance they claim to have given me.

My gain of it by their assistances,
Which daily grew to quarrel and to bloodshed, (190)
Wounding supposèd peace. All these bold fears
Thou seest with peril I have answerèd,
For all my reign hath been but as a scene 325
Acting that argument; and now my death
Changes the mood, for what in me was purchased (195)
Falls upon thee in a more fairer sort.
So thou the garland wear'st successively,
Yet though thou stand'st more sure than I could do, 330
Thou art not firm enough since griefs are green,
And all my friends, which thou must make thy friends, (200)
Have but their stings and teeth newly ta'en out,
By whose fell working I was first advanced,
And by whose power I well might lodge a fear 335
To be again displaced; which to avoid
I cut them off, and had a purpose now (205)
To lead out many to the Holy Land,
Lest rest and lying still might make them look
Too near unto my state. Therefore, my Harry, 340
Be it thy course to busy giddy minds
With foreign quarrels, that action hence borne out (210)
May waste the memory of the former days.
More would I, but my lungs are wasted so

---

323] *As one line*, Q; *as two lines divided at* Peace. F　324 answerèd] F, *Dering MS.*; answerd Q　327 mood] Q, F *(*Moode*)*; Mode F3–4
332 my friends] *Rann, conj. Thyrwhitt*; thy friends Q, F; the foes *Keightley*　340] *As one line*, Q; *as two lines divided at* State, F

323 **fears** fearful acts; as at 1.1.95.

325–6 **a scene ... argument** A stage metaphor; see 1.1.151–9 n.; 'argument' is the technical term for the summary prefixed to the text of a play.

327 **mood** (1) mode, tone (in music), (2) frame of mind.

327 **purchased** acquired, as opposed to inherited; 'purchase' was current for 'booty'; see *More* 5, and Add.II (Hand B) 53.

329 **garland** A description of the crown found in Holinshed.

329 **successively** by right of succession.

331 **since ... green** as long as their grievances (see 4.1.73 n.) are still fresh.

332 **my friends** Q and F have 'thy friends', justifiable only if the word 'friends' is spoken with heavy irony.

334 The king attributes the 'indirect crooked way' (312) by which he came by the crown rather to the pernicious actions ('fell working') of his early supporters (see 320–1) than to his own doing.

337–40 **had a purpose ... state** The Machiavellian reason for undertaking the Crusade, never stated before (see 3.1.107 n.), was suggested by Daniel, *Civil Wars*, III, st. 127.

339–40 **look Too near** survey too closely; i.e. in order to see how he got hold of it.

341 **giddy** unstable, restless.

342 **action hence borne out** undertakings in foreign parts ('hence' = away).

343 **waste** rub out, disintegrate; see 'wasted' at 344.

That strength of speech is utterly denied me.                    345
How I came by the crown, O God forgive,
And grant it may with thee in true peace live.                   (215)
PRINCE You won it, wore it, kept it, gave it me:
Then plain and right must my possession be,
Which I with more than with a common pain                        350
'Gainst all the world will rightfully maintain.

*Enter Lord* JOHN *of Lancaster*

KING Look, look, here comes my John of Lancaster.                (220)
JOHN Health, peace and happiness to my royal father.
KING Thou bring'st me happiness and peace, son John,
But health, alack, with youthful wings is flown                  355
From this bare withered trunk. Upon thy sight
My worldly business makes a period.                              (225)
Where is my Lord of Warwick?
PRINCE                                    My Lord of Warwick!

[*Enter* WARWICK]

KING Doth any name particular belong
Unto the lodging where I first did swoon?                         360
WARWICK 'Tis called Jerusalem, my noble lord.
KING Laud be to God, even there my life must end.                (230)
It hath been prophesied to me, many years,
I should not die but in Jerusalem,
Which vainly I supposed the Holy Land.                           365
But bear me to that chamber, there I'll lie:
In that Jerusalem shall Harry die.                               (235)
                                              *Exeunt*

---

346 God] Q; heauen F   348 PRINCE You won] Q; *Prince. My gracious Liege: / You wonne* F   351 SD] *Enter Lancaster.* Q; *Enter Lord Iohn of Lancaster, and Warwicke.* F   352] *As one line,* Q; *as two lines divided at* looke, F   353 SH JOHN] F; *Lanc.* Q   353] *As one line,* Q; *as two lines divided at* Happinesse, F   358 SD] *Cam.; not in* Q; *at 351* F   360 swoon] F4; swound Q; swoon'd F   362 God] Q; heauen F   362] *As one line,* Q; *as two lines divided at* heauen: F   367 SD] F; *not in* Q

346–51 The three stilted rhymed couplets closely echoing in content the speeches of the two Henrys in *FV* suggest a direct borrowing from the earlier play; see 309–47 n.
348 For the additional vocative in F see 306 n.

356 **trunk** (1) body, (2) tree-trunk – bare and withered.
357 **period** stop, conclusion.
361–7 Following closely Holinshed, III, 541/1/63–2/7, which is derived in its turn from Fabian.

**5.1** *Enter* SHALLOW, FALSTAFF, BARDOLPH *and* PAGE

SHALLOW  By cock and pie, sir, you shall not away tonight. – What, Davy I
say!

FALSTAFF  You must excuse me, Master Robert Shallow.

SHALLOW  I will not excuse you, you shall not be excused, excuses shall
not be admitted, there is no excuse shall serve, you shall not be          5
excused. – Why, Davy!

*[Enter* DAVY]

DAVY  Here, sir.

SHALLOW  Davy, Davy, Davy, Davy, let me see, Davy, let me see, Davy,
let me see – Yea marry, William cook, bid him come hither. – Sir
John, you shall not be excused.                                            10

DAVY  Marry, sir, thus: those precepts cannot be served; and again, sir:
shall we sow the hade land with wheat?

SHALLOW  With red wheat, Davy. But for William cook – are there no
young pigeons?

DAVY  Yes, sir. Here is now the smith's note for shoeing and              15
plough-irons.

SHALLOW  Let it be cast and paid. – Sir John, you shall not be excused.

DAVY  Now, sir, a new link to the bucket must needs be had. And, sir, do
you mean to stop any of William's wages about the sack he lost at
Hinckley Fair?                                                             20

---

Act 5, Scene 1  5.1] *Actus Quintus. Scæna Prima.* F; *not in* Q  0 SD SHALLOW,] Q *(at 4.2.366); Shallow, Silence,* F  0 SD
BARDOLPH *and* PAGE] *Bardolfe, Page, and Dauie.* F; *Bardolfe* Q *(at 4.2.367)*  1 sir] Q; *not in* F  6 SD] *Theobald; not in* Q, F  8 Davy,
Davy, let] Q; *Dauy,* let F  8–9 see, Davy, … marry, William] Q; see: *William* F  12 hade land] Q; head-land F  18 Now] Q; *not in*
F  19 lost at] Q; lost the other day at F  20 Hinckley] F; Hunkly Q

**Act 5, Scene 1**
5.1 The mention of Hinckley Fair at 20 and
Woncot at 31 brings the location closer to Gloucestershire, but creates problems with the time:
Hinckley is a market town near Coventry and the fair
was held on 26 August, while the Gaultree episode
occurred in May. Woncot is either Wilmcote, one
mile from Stratford-upon-Avon, or Woodmancote, a
suburb of Dursley in Gloucestershire. *Shrew* Induction 2.20 mentions Wincot, at the border between
Gloucestershire and Warwickshire.
1 By cock and pie A mild oath; 'cock' is a
euphemism for God, while 'pie' was the idiomatic
designation of the rule book of the Roman Catholic
church services.
1 Davy Another new character introduced to
enliven the last part of the play; for F he is present

from the beginning of the scene – another confusion
like Worcester at 4.1.0 SD.
11 precepts Writs (in law) connected with Shallow's position as a justice.
11 again besides.
12 hade land In F 'head-land', the strip of land left
unploughed at the side of a field to allow for the
turning of the plough.
13 red wheat A variety sown later, and deeper in
colour, than the ordinary grain.
15 note bill.
17 cast added up and checked.
18 link … bucket Either 'rope or chain for the
pail', or 'chain for the yoke'.
20 Hinckley Fair See 5.1 n.; Q has 'Hunkly', a
misreading of the minims in the manuscript.

SHALLOW  A shall answer it. – Some pigeons, Davy, a couple of short-legged hens, a joint of mutton, and any pretty little tiny kickshaws, tell William cook.

DAVY  Doth the man of war stay all night, sir?

SHALLOW  Yea, Davy. I will use him well, a friend i'th'court is better than  25
a penny in purse. Use his men well, Davy, for they are arrant knaves and will backbite.

DAVY  No worse than they are back-bitten, sir, for they have marvellous foul linen.

SHALLOW  Well conceited, Davy. About your business, Davy.  30

DAVY  I beseech you, sir, to countenance William Visor of Woncot against Clement Perkes a'th'Hill.

SHALLOW  There is many complaints, Davy, against that Visor – that Visor is an arrant knave, on my knowledge.

DAVY  I grant your worship that he is a knave, sir; but yet God forbid, sir,  35
but a knave should have some countenance at his friend's request. An honest man, sir, is able to speak for himself, when a knave is not. I have served your worship truly, sir, this eight years and if I cannot once or twice in a quarter bear out a knave against an honest man, I have little credit with your worship. The knave is mine honest friend,  40
sir, therefore I beseech you let him be countenanced.

SHALLOW  Go to, I say, he shall have no wrong. Look about, Davy.

*[Exit Davy]*

– Where are you, Sir John? Come, come, come, off with your boots. Give me your hand, Master Bardolph.

---

21 A] Q; He F  25 Yea] Q; Yes F  28 back-bitten] Q; bitten F  28 marvellous] F; maruailes Q  32 a'th'] Q; of the F  33 There is] Q; There are F  35 God] Q; these F  38 this] Q; these F  38 if] F; *not in* Q  40 have little] Q; haue but a very litle F  41 beseech you] Q; beseech your Worship F  42–4] *As prose*, Q; *as four lines ending* . . . too, / . . . *Dauy.* / . . . *Boots.* / . . . *Bardolfe.* F  42 I say, he] Q; I say he F  42 SD] *Capell; not in* Q, F  43 Come, . . . come,] Q; Come, F

---

**21 A . . . it** He shall be fined for it.

**21–2 short-legged hens** More meaty than long-legged ones.

**22 kickshaws** trifles, dainties; a phonetic rendering of French *quelque chose*.

**24 man of war** Ironical for 'soldier', playing on Falstaff's size: warships were large 'hulks', see 1.1.19n.

**25–6 a friend . . . purse** Proverbial (Tilley F687).

**28 back-bitten** Playing on 'backbite' (= react) at 27: their backs are bitten by lice.

**28 marvellous** Frequently used adverbially; Wilson considers Q's 'maruailes' a typical Shakespearean spelling; see 'meruiles' in Q2 *Ham*. 2.1.3 and 'maruailes' in Q1 (1600) of *MND* 3.1.2 and 4.1.24.

**30 Well conceited** Very witty; see 'conceit' at 2.4.197.

**31 countenance** support, back up.

**31–2 William . . . Hill** For 'Woncot' see 5.1 n.; R. W. Huntley (*Glossary of the Cotswold Dialect*, 1868, p. 20) notes that a family called Visor or Vizard lived in Woodmancote and another named Purchase or Perkis lived on nearby Stinchcombe Hill.

**39 bear out** back up; like 'countenance' at 31.

**40 honest friend** good, true friend; playing on 'honest man' at 37.

**42 Look about** Get busy.

BARDOLPH I am glad to see your worship.                                    45

SHALLOW I thank thee with my heart, kind Master Bardolph; [*To the
Page*] and welcome, my tall fellow. – Come, Sir John.

FALSTAFF I'll follow you, good Master Shallow.

[*Exit Shallow*]

Bardolph, look to our horses.

[*Exit Bardolph with Page*]

If I were sawed into quantities, I should make four dozen of such     50
bearded hermits' staves as Master Shallow. It is a wonderful thing to
see the semblable coherence of his men's spirits and his: they by
observing him do bear themselves like foolish justices; he by conversing with them is turned into a justice-like servingman. Their spirits
are so married in conjunction, with the participation of society, that    55
they flock together in consent like so many wild geese. If I had a suit to
Master Shallow, I would humour his men with the imputation of
being near their master; if to his men, I would curry with Master
Shallow, that no man could better command his servants. It is certain
that either wise bearing or ignorant carriage is caught, as men take     60
diseases, one of another. Therefore let men take heed of their
company. I will devise matter enough out of this Shallow to keep
Prince Harry in continual laughter the wearing out of six fashions –
which is four terms – or two actions, and a shall laugh without
intervallums. O, it is much that a lie with a slight oath and a jest with a    65
sad brow will do with a fellow that never had the ache in his shoulders!

46 with my] Q; with all my F    46 SD] *Rowe; not in* Q, F    48 SD] *Capell; not in* Q, F    49 SD] *Capell; not in* Q, F    53 him] Q; of him F
64 a shall] Q; he shall F    64 without] Q; with F

47 **tall fellow** valiant man; as at 3.2.51; some
believe this to be addressed to Bardolph, but it has
more point if said to the little Page; see 'giant' at 1.2.1
and 1.2.7–14.

50 **quantities** bits, small pieces.

51 **hermits' staves** i.e. long and thin; see the
comparison of Shallow to the Vice's dagger and to an
oboe-case at 3.2.258–64.

52 **semblable coherence** close correspondence.

53–4 **conversing** associating.

55 **married in conjunction** rendered identical
with each other.

55 **with ... society** by their close partnership.

56 **flock ... geese** Proverbial: 'Birds of a feather
flock together' and 'As wise as a goose' (ironical); see
*1H4* 2.4.137–8: 'drive all the subjects afore thee like a
flock of wild geese'.

57–8 **with ... near** by claiming to be intimate with.

58 **curry** curry favour.

60 **carriage** behaviour.

61–2 **let ... company** Proverbial, *ODEP* 138: 'As a
man is, so is his company': a bit of dramatic irony in
view of Falstaff's opinion of his relationship with the
prince.

63–5 **the wearing ... intervallums** i.e. he shall
laugh continually for a whole year. The language is
that of the Inns of Court: the judicial year was divided
into four terms in each of which a court session was
held, with long recesses ('intervallum' in legal Latin)
in between. The implication is that fashions wear out
quickly (six different ones in twelve months) while
court actions drag out at least two terms each.

66 **sad brow** serious countenance, straight face.

66 **a fellow ... shoulders** a young man not yet
prevented from laughing by the back-ache.

O, you shall see him laugh till his face be like a wet cloak ill laid up.
SHALLOW [*Within*] Sir John!
FALSTAFF I come, Master Shallow, I come, Master Shallow.          *Exit*


**5.2** *Enter the Earl of* WARWICK *and the* LORD CHIEF JUSTICE

WARWICK How now, my Lord Chief Justice, whither away?
JUSTICE How doth the king?
WARWICK Exceeding well: his cares are now all ended.
JUSTICE I hope, not dead.
WARWICK                     He's walked the way of nature,
          And to our purposes he lives no more.
JUSTICE I would his majesty had called me with him:                              5
          The service that I truly did his life
          Hath left me open to all injuries.
WARWICK Indeed I think the young king loves you not.
JUSTICE I know he doth not, and do arm myself                                    1(
          To welcome the condition of the time,
          Which cannot look more hideously upon me
          Than I have drawn it in my fantasy.

*Enter* [*Prince*] JOHN *of Lancaster*, GLOUCESTER *and* CLARENCE

WARWICK Here come the heavy issue of dead Harry.

68 SD] *Theobald; not in* Q, F   69 SD] *Exeunt* F; *not in* Q   Act 5, Scene 2   5.2] *Scene Secunda.* F; *not in* Q   0 SD] F; *Enter Warwike,*
*duke Humphrey, L. chiefe Iustice, Thomas Clarence, Prince Iohn, Westmerland.* Q *corr.; Enter . . . Prince, Iohn Westmerland.* Q *uncorr.*   3]
*As one line,* Q; *as two lines divided at* Cares F   13 SD] F *subst.; Enter Iohn, Thomas, and Humphrey.* Q

67 **a wet . . . up** A cloak not properly spread out to
dry gets creased and wrinkled.

**Act 5, Scene 2**
5.2 The confirmation of the Lord Chief Justice is
unhistorical, Holinshed (III, 543/2/41–2) remarking
that Henry V 'elected the best learned men in the
lawes of the realme, to the offices of justice'. The
scene is modelled on *FV* sig. D4, where the king
appoints the Lord Chief Justice 'Protector ouer my
Realme' during the French expedition, at the end of a
long scene including Hal's companions' rejoicing at
the succession (see 5.3.96–116), their dismissal (see
5.5), the bishops' encouragement and the decision to
wage war in France after the episode of the tennis
balls (*H5* 1.2).
   0 SD The massed entrance direction in Q and the

curious misplacing of a comma in the uncorrected
version (see collation) suggest that the author's initial
intention had been to have all those affected by the
succession on stage at once (including Westmoreland
who had appeared in 4.2); after his change of mind the
printer misinterpreted an attempt at crossing out
superfluous names.
   1–2 A single line if 'my Lord Chief Justice' is an
interpolated hypermetrical vocative.
   3 **well . . . ended** Proverbial (Tilley H347), and see
*Rom.* 5.1.17: 'she is well and nothing can be ill'.
   7–8 **service . . . injuries** The Justice's forebodings
are prompted by the episode of the prince's arrest; see
67–70 and 1.2.42–3.
   11 **condition of the time** See 3.1.77 n.
   14, 24, 25 **heavy** sad; see 1.1.121.
   14 **issue** descendants.

O, that the living Harry had the temper                    15
Of he, the worst of these three gentlemen!
How many nobles then should hold their places,
That must strike sail to spirits of vile sort!

USTICE  O God, I fear all will be overturned.

OHN  Good morrow, cousin Warwick, good morrow.          20

GLOUCESTER *and* CLARENCE  Good morrow, cousin.

OHN  We meet like men that had forgot to speak.

WARWICK  We do remember, but our argument
Is all too heavy to admit much talk.

OHN  Well, peace be with him that hath made us heavy.    25

USTICE  Peace be with us, lest we be heavier.

GLOUCESTER  O good my lord, you have lost a friend indeed,
And I dare swear you borrow not that face
Of seeming sorrow: it is sure your own.

OHN  Though no man be assured what grace to find,        30
You stand in coldest expectation.
I am the sorrier, would 'twere otherwise.

CLARENCE  Well, you must now speak Sir John Falstaff fair,
Which swims against your stream of quality.

USTICE  Sweet princes, what I did, I did in honour,      35
Led by th'impartial conduct of my soul.
And never shall you see that I will beg
A ragged and forestalled remission.
If truth and upright innocency fail me,
I'll to the king my master that is dead                   40

16 Of he] Q; Of him F   18 vile] Q; vilde F   19 O God] Q; Alas F   21 SH GLOUCESTER *and* CLARENCE] *Glou. Cla.* F; *Prin. ambo* Q   27 SH GLOUCESTER] *Glou.* F; *Humph.* Q   36 th'impartial] Q; th'Imperiall F   38 forestalled] forestald Q; fore-stall'd F; forestaled *Wilson*   38–9 remission. ... me,] F; remission, ... me. Q

18 **strike ... sort** lower their sails (i.e. submit) to vulgar people.

**20, 21 cousin** See 4.1.229 n.

**23 our argument** the subject of our speeches; see 4.2.325–6 n.

**31 coldest expectation** the most unfavourable anticipation; see 4.2.232 n.

**33** If the line is read with the name 'Oldcastle' in place of 'Falstaff', it needs only the removal of 'Well' to make it scan perfectly, suggesting that this scene belonged at least in part to the earlier one-play *Henry IV*.

**34 swims ... quality** The proverbial 'swimming against the stream' (Dent S930.1) is modified to mean 'oppose successfully the honours belonging to you'.

**38 ragged** beggarly, base.

**38 forestalled remission** Either (1) pardon secured in advance by some cowardly gesture of submission (in *FV* the Justice, upon hearing of the death of Henry IV, releases – 'For feare of my Lord the yong Prince' – the thief Cutbert Cutter – Gadshill – whose arrest had caused the box on the ear episode); or (2) a pardon that would be refused before being begged for. A. K. McIlwraith (*TLS* 19 January 1933) reads 'forestaled' = rendered stale or distasteful before it is received, by the ignominy of begging it.

And tell him who hath sent me after him.

*Enter* PRINCE HENRY *and* BLUNT

WARWICK  Here comes the prince.

JUSTICE  Good morrow, and God save your majesty.

PRINCE  This new and gorgeous garment, majesty,
Sits not so easy on me as you think.                                    45
Brothers, you mix your sadness with some fear.
This is the English, not the Turkish court:
Not Amurath an Amurath succeeds,
But Harry Harry. Yet be sad, good brothers,
For, by my faith, it very well becomes you.                             50
Sorrow so royally in you appears
That I will deeply put the fashion on
And wear it in my heart. Why then, be sad,
But entertain no more of it, good brothers,
Than a joint burden laid upon us all.                                   55
For me, by Heaven, I bid you be assured
I'll be your father and your brother too.
Let me but bear your love, I'll bear your cares.
Yet weep that Harry's dead, and so will I;
But Harry lives that shall convert those tears                          60
By number into hours of happiness.

BROTHERS  We hope no otherwise from your majesty.

PRINCE  You all look strangely on me. – And you most:
You are, I think, assured I love you not.

JUSTICE  I am assured, if I be measured rightly,                        65
Your majesty hath no just cause to hate me.

PRINCE  No? How might a prince of my great hopes forget

41 SD] *Enter the Prince and Blunt* Q *(at 41–2); Enter Prince Henrie.* F *(after 42)*   43 God] Q; heauen F   46 Brothers, you mix] F; Prothers, you mixt Q   50 by my faith] Q; to speake truth F   59 Yet] Q; But F   62 SH BROTHERS] *Bro.* Q; *Iohn, &c.* F   62 otherwise] Q; other F

41 SD BLUNT Though a mute, this elusive character, on whom see notes to 1.1.16, 3.1.31 SD and 4.1.424, is acceptable here to avoid having the new king enter unattended.

48 Amurath ... succeeds When Murad III succeeded his father Selim II as emperor of the Turks in 1574, he had all his brothers killed, and the same was done by his successor Mahomet III in 1596. Actually no Amurath (Murad) ever succeeded another Amurath, but the name became synonymous with tyranny in Elizabethan plays.

52 deeply in deadly earnest. Compare Hamlet's comment on his mourning attire, *Ham.* 1.2.76–86.

61 By number One (hour of happiness) for one (tear).

63 strangely coldly, as if I were a stranger.

67–110 The episode of the Lord Chief Justice committing the prince to prison is reported briefly by Holinshed (III, 543/2/12–16), and at great length by Stow (*Annales*, pp. 547–8), at the beginning of their respective treatments of the reign of Henry V, but Shakespeare is closer to Stow's source, Sir Thomas Elyot's *Governour*, 1531, sigs. P7–P8ᵛ.

So great indignities you laid upon me?
What! Rate, rebuke, and roughly send to prison
Th'immediate heir of England? Was this easy?                    70
May this be washed in Lethe and forgotten?
JUSTICE  I then did use the person of your father:
The image of his power lay then in me;
And in th'administration of his law,
Whiles I was busy for the commonwealth,                          75
Your highness pleasèd to forget my place,
The majesty and power of law and justice,
The image of the king whom I presented,
And struck me in the very seat of judgement;
Whereon, as an offender to your father,                          80
I gave bold way to my authority
And did commit you. If the deed were ill,
Be you contented, wearing now the garland,
To have a son set your decrees at nought?
To pluck down justice from your aweful bench?                    85
To trip the course of law, and blunt the sword
That guards the peace and safety of your person?
Nay, more, to spurn at your most royal image,
And mock your workings in a second body?
Question your royal thoughts, make the case yours,               90
Be now the father and propose a son,
Hear your own dignity so much profaned,
See your most dreadful laws so loosely slighted,
Behold yourself so by a son disdained;
And then imagine me taking your part,                            95

95 your] Q; you F

71 **washed in Lethe** According to classical
mythology, oblivion came by drinking and not by
bathing in the water of Lethe, the river of Hades; that
Shakespeare thought otherwise is shown by *R3*
4.4.251–2, where remembrance is drowned in Lethe,
and *TN* 4.1.62: 'Let fancy still my sense in Lethe
steep.' In Dante, *Purgatorio*, 31, 101, Beatrice immer-
ses Dante in Lethe up to his chin to force him to drink
the water.

72 **did use the person of** impersonated, represented; see the Justice committing the prince to prison in
*FV* sig. B3ᵛ: 'your father whose liuely person here in
this place I doo represent'.

73, 78, 88 **image** emblematic counterpart.

79 **struck me** In Elyot and Stow the prince
threatens but does not strike the Justice. In *FV* and in
Holinshed, however, 'he had with his fist stroke the
cheefe iustice'.

83 **garland** crown; see 4.2.329 n.

85 **aweful** reverend; see 4.1.176 n.

85 **bench** The Lord Chief Justice presided over
the Court of King's Bench.

89 **mock ... body** ridicule your decrees as applied
by your representative.

91 **propose** imagine (*OED* sv *v* 2d).

92 **profaned** blasphemed; the king's person was
holy and any offence against him was sacrilege.

And in your power soft silencing your son.
After this cold considerance, sentence me,
And, as you are a king, speak in your state
What I have done that misbecame my place,
My person, or my liege's sovereignty.                              100
PRINCE   You are right Justice, and you weigh this well.
Therefore still bear the balance and the sword,
And I do wish your honours may increase
Till you do live to see a son of mine
Offend you and obey you as I did.                                  105
So shall I live to speak my father's words:
'Happy am I that have a man so bold
That dares do justice on my proper son;
And not less happy, having such a son
That would deliver up his greatness so.'                           110
Into the hands of Justice you did commit me –
For which I do commit into your hands
Th'unstainèd sword that you have used to bear,
With this remembrance: that you use the same
With the like bold, just, and impartial spirit                     115
As you have done 'gainst me. There is my hand:
You shall be as a father to my youth,
My voice shall sound as you do prompt mine ear,
And I will stoop and humble my intents
To your well-practised wise directions.                            120
And, princes all, believe me, I beseech you,
My father is gone wild into his grave,
For in his tomb lie my affections.
And with his spirits sadly I survive

109 not] Q; no F   110–11 so.' ... Justice you] so, ... Iustice you Q; so, ... Iustice. You F

96 **soft** gently; adverbial.

97 **considerance** reflection, consideration.

101 **right Justice** Justice personified. By placing a comma after 'right', many editors turn 'justice' into an ordinary vocative.

102 **still ... sword** For the confirmation of the Justice in his office see 5.2 n. The scales ('balance') are the emblem of the judiciary power, while the Sword of Spiritual Justice, referred to also at 86 and 113, was given the king with the words 'with this sword do justice' during the coronation ceremony.

106–10 The king's words are close to those reported by Elyot and Stow, but closer still to the

Latin version in John Case's *Sphaera Civitatis* (1588, p. 179); see D. T. Starne, 'More about the Prince Hal legend', *PQ* 15 (1936), 358–66.

110 **greatness** high position; see 3.1.73 n.

114 **remembrance** note entered in the records; a law term.

122–3 My wildness is now in my father's tomb, because I have buried my passions ('affections') at his death.

124 **spirits** character (determined by the vital spirits; see 4.1.457–60 n.).

124 **sadly** soberly, gravely.

To mock the expectation of the world,           125
To frustrate prophecies, and to raze out
Rotten opinion, who hath writ me down
After my seeming. The tide of blood in me
Hath proudly flowed in vanity till now;
Now doth it turn, and ebb back to the sea,        130
Where it shall mingle with the state of floods,
And flow henceforth in formal majesty.
Now call we our high court of parliament,
And let us choose such limbs of noble counsel
That the great body of our state may go         135
In equal rank with the best-governed nation;
That war, or peace, or both at once, may be
As things acquainted and familiar to us;
In which you, father, shall have foremost hand.
Our coronation done, we will accite,            140
As I before remembered, all our state,
And, God consigning to my good intents,
No prince nor peer shall have just cause to say:
God shorten Harry's happy life one day.

                                       *Exeunt*

**5.3** *Enter* FALSTAFF, SHALLOW, SILENCE, DAVY, BARDOLPH, PAGE

SHALLOW   Nay, you shall see my orchard, where, in an arbour, we will eat

126 raze] *Theobald*, race Q, F   139 you,] Q *corr.*, F; your Q *uncorr.*   142, 144, God] Q; heauen F   Act 5, Scene 3   5.3] *Scena Tertia.* F; *not in* Q   o SD FALSTAFF, ... SILENCE,] F, *sir Iohn*, ... *Scilens*, Q   o SD DAVY, ... PAGE] Q; *Bardolfe, Page, and Pistoll.* F   1 my] Q; mine F

**125 expectation** anticipations; as at 31.

**125–8 To mock ... seeming** Anticipated in Hal's speech on 'redeeming time' in *1H4* 1.2.197–217; if this scene was substantially part of the one-play version of *Henry IV*, then the speech in *1H4* may have been added when the play was revised.

**128 After my seeming** As I appeared.

**129 proudly** overbearingly.

**131 state of floods** majesty of the ocean.

**133 we** The king adopts from this moment the *pluralis majestatis*.

**134 limbs ... counsel** The usual metaphor of the human body for the state or 'body politic'; see 135 and 3.1.37–42 n. The good counsellors are its limbs. Compare Holinshed: 'he chose men of grauitie, wit and high policie, by whose wise counsell he might at all times rule to his honour and dignitie'.

**135–6 go ... rank** march side by side.

**140 accite** summon; see 2.2.45 n.

**141 remembered** mentioned.

**141 state** people of high rank.

**142 consigning** Literally 'subscribing together' (with me), i.e. endorsing.

**Act 5, Scene 3**

**5.3** From Shallow's first speech it appears that properties have been arranged in the discovery space to represent an arbour.

**o SD** The omission of Davy's entrance in F is mere inadvertence, while the inclusion of Pistol (who enters only at 67) is the usual scribal anticipation, as at 2.2 and 4.1. In this scene, as in 3.2, Q uses in most cases the spelling 'Scilens' for 'Silence'; see 3.2.71 n.

a last year's pippin of mine own graffing, with a dish of caraways, and
so forth – come, cousin Silence – and then to bed.

FALSTAFF 'Fore God, you have here goodly dwelling, and rich.

SHALLOW Barren, barren, barren; beggars all, beggars all, Sir John. 5
Marry, good air. – Spread, Davy, spread, Davy, well said, Davy.

FALSTAFF This Davy serves you for good uses: he is your servingman
and your husband.

SHALLOW A good varlet, a good varlet, a good varlet, Sir John. By the
Mass, I have drunk too much sack at supper. A good varlet. Now sit 10
down, now sit down. – Come, cousin.

SILENCE Ah, sirrah, quoth a, we shall

[*Sings*]   Do nothing but eat and make good cheer,
And praise God for the merry year,
When flesh is cheap and females dear, 15
And lusty lads roam here and there,
So merrily,
And ever among so merrily.

FALSTAFF There's a merry heart, good Master Silence! I'll give you a
health for that anon. 20

SHALLOW Give Master Bardolph some wine, Davy.

DAVY Sweet sir, sit – I'll be with you anon. Most sweet sir, sit. Master
page, good master page, sit. Proface! What you want in meat, we'll
have in drink, but you must bear. The heart's all.          [*Exit*]

SHALLOW Be merry, Master Bardolph, and my little soldier there, be 25
merry.

2 mine own] Q; my owne F   3 Silence] F; Scilens Q (*also at 31, 39, 41, 106*)   4 'Fore God] Q; *not in* F   4 goodly ... rich] Q; a
goodly ... a rich F   9–10 By the Mass] Q; *not in* F   12 SH SILENCE] *Sil.* F; *Scilens* Q (*also at 27, 32, 36, 40, 42, 84*)   12–18] *As
verse, Malone, conj. Capell; as prose,* Q, F   13, 27, 36, 59 SD *Sings*] *Rowe subst.; not in* Q, F   14 God] Q; heauen F   19 SH FALSTAFF]
*Fal.* F; *sir Iohn* Q   19 Silence] F; Silens Q   21] Q; Good M. *Bardolfe:* some wine, *Dauie.* F   24 must] Q; *not in* F   24 SD] *Theobald;
not in* Q, F

2 **pippin** A variety of apple kept for a year before
eating.

2 **graffing** grafting; see 'engraffed', 2.2.46 n.

2 **caraways** sweets made with caraway seeds; supposed to counteract the ventosity engendered by
eating apples.

2–3 **and so forth** This phrase is used repetitiously
to mock the speech-habits of a minor character in
Thomas Heywood's *1 Edward IV* (before 1599).

6 **Spread** Lay the cloth on the table.

6 **well said** well done; see 3.2.225.

8 **husband** husbandman, general handyman.

9 **varlet** Playing on the literal meaning (= personal
attendant) and the derogatory meaning (see
2.1.34 n.).

12 **sirrah** An expletive not directed to anybody in
particular.

12 **quoth a** he said; generally prefacing proverbial
sayings.

13–18, 27–30, 36–8, 59–61 The original editions
print these snatches of song as prose.

18 **ever among** all the while.

23 **Proface** From Italian 'buon pro vi fac-
cia' = 'may it do you good', said instead of grace when
sitting at table.

23–4 **What ... drink** Proverbial (Tilley M845).

24 **bear** put up with it.

24 **heart** good intentions, welcoming spirit.

SILENCE  [*Sings*] Be merry, be merry, my wife has all
     For women are shrews, both short and tall.
     'Tis merry in hall when beards wags all
     And welcome merry Shrovetide, be merry, be merry.        30

FALSTAFF  I did not think Master Silence had been a man of this mettle.

SILENCE  Who, I? I have been merry twice and once ere now.

*Enter* DAVY

DAVY  There's a dish of leather-coats for you.

SHALLOW  Davy!

DAVY  Your worship, I'll be with you straight. – A cup of wine, sir.        35

SILENCE  [*Sings*] A cup of wine, that's brisk and fine,
     And drink unto thee, leman mine,
     And a merry heart lives long-a.

FALSTAFF  Well said, Master Silence.

SILENCE  And we shall be merry, now comes in the sweet a'th'night.        40

FALSTAFF  Health and long life to you, Master Silence.

SILENCE  [*Sings*] Fill the cup, and let it come,
     I'll pledge you a mile to th'bottom.

SHALLOW  Honest Bardolph, welcome. If thou wantest anything and wilt
     not call, beshrew thy heart. – Welcome my little tiny thief, and        45
     welcome indeed too. I'll drink to Master Bardolph, and to all the
     cabilleros about London.

DAVY  I hope to see London once ere I die.

BARDOLPH  And I might see you there, Davy!

27–30] *As verse*, F; *as prose*, Q    29 wags] Q; wagge F    32 SD] Q; *not in* F    36–8] *As verse, Capell; as prose*, Q, F    37 thee,] *Wilson; the
, F    40 And] Q; If F    40 a'th'] Q; of the F    42 SD] *Capell subst.; not in* Q, F    42–3] *As verse, Capell; as prose*, Q, F    47 cabilleros] Q;
Cauileroes F    49 And] Q; If F

27–30 The song is untraced but J.H. Long, *Shakespeare's Use of Music*, 1971, pp. 86–9, suggests that this and 13–18 are parts of the same Shrovetide wassail song, to the tune of the carol 'Be merry, be merry'; 29 is a traditional old saw, see Tilley H55.

30 Shrovetide The three days before Ash Wednesday, traditionally devoted to Carnival celebration preceding the beginning of Lent.

32 merry (1) witty, (2) tipsy.

32 twice and once now and again; jocular.

33 leather-coats russet apples; their rough skin resembled leather.

37 thee, leman The original reads 'the leman' (= the lover); much less effective than the vocative typical of drinking-songs.

38 Proverbial (Tilley H320a); and compare *LLL* 5.2.18: 'a light heart lives long'.

39 Well said This does not mean that Silence has been speaking rather than singing; for 'well said' = 'well done' see 6 n.

40 And F replaces with 'If', an obvious miscorrection, possibly influenced by 'And' = 'If' at 49.

40 now … a'th'night Compare 2.4.300.

42 let it come pass it round; a drinking-cry; see *2H6* 2.3.66.

43 a mile to th'bottom the whole cupful, were it a mile deep; proverbial (Tilley A207).

45 beshrew A playful form of curse; see 2.3.45 n.

45 tiny thief Another affectionate use of an insult addressed to the Page; see Lady Percy calling Hotspur 'thief' in *1H4* 3.1.234.

47 cabilleros gallants; from Spanish 'caballeros'.

SHALLOW  By the Mass, you'll crack a quart together, ha, will you not,     50
  Master Bardolph?
BARDOLPH  Yea, sir, in a pottle pot.
SHALLOW  By God's liggens I thank thee: the knave will stick by thee, I
  can assure thee that. A will not out, a; 'tis true bred.
BARDOLPH  And I'll stick by him, sir.                                      55
SHALLOW  Why, there spoke a king: lack nothing, be merry.
                        *One knocks at door*
  Look who's at door there, ho; who knocks?
FALSTAFF  Why, now you have done me right.
SILENCE  [*Sings*] Do me right,
              And dub me knight,                                          60
              Samingo.
  Is't not so?
FALSTAFF  'Tis so.
SILENCE  Is't so? Why, then say an old man can do somewhat.
DAVY  And't please your worship, there's one Pistol come from the court   65
  with news.
FALSTAFF  From the court? Let him come in.

                        *Enter* PISTOL

  How now, Pistol?
PISTOL  Sir John, God save you.
FALSTAFF  What wind blew you hither, Pistol?                              70
PISTOL  Not the ill wind which blows no man to good; sweet knight, thou

---

50 By the Mass] Q; *not in* F    52 Yea] Q; Yes F    53 By God's liggens] Q; *not in* F    54 that. A] that a Q, that. He F    54 a; 'tis] Q; he is
F    56 SD] Q (*at 57*); *not in* F    57 Look who's] Q; Looke, who's F    59, 64, 73 SH SILENCE] *Sil.* F; *Silens* Q    59–62] *As verse,
Malone; as prose,* Q, F    65 And't] Q; If it F    67 SD] *Placed as in* F; *at 66* Q    69 God] Q; *not in* F    69 you.] Q; you sir. F    71 no man]
Q; none F    71 good; sweet knight,] Q; good, sweet Knight: F

---

50 **crack … together** Not 'split between you', but
'empty together' a quart pot of ale (two pints).

52 **pottle pot** A two-quart (i.e. four-pint) tankard;
see 2.2.59.

53 **By God's liggens** An oath found nowhere else;
possibly 'liggens' is a diminutive of 'lid' ('lid-kins',
compare 'bodikins'); 'by God's lid' was a current oath,
see *Tro.* 1.2.211.

54 **A … a** He won't leave you (like a dog sticking to
the scent); compare the cockfighting proverb 'A good
cock will never out' (Dent C486.1) and *Ant.* 2.7.30–1:
'I am not so well as I should be, but I'll ne'er out', with
reference to drinking.

58 **done me right** done the right thing by me (i.e.
got drunk); 'do me right' (see next line) was a drink-
ing-challenge.

59–61 A quotation from the French drinking-song
'Monsieur Mingo' set to the music of Orlando di
Lasso (see F. Sternfeld, 'Lasso's music for
Shakespeare's "Samingo"', *SQ* 9 (1958), 105–16,
which provides the score). It is quoted in Nashe,
*Summer's Last Will and Testament.* 'Samingo' (in
Nashe 'Domingo') is a corruption of 'Sir Mingo', the
titular knight of the song, with reference to the effect
of drink ('mingo' is Latin for 'micturate'); 'dub me
knight' refers to the habit of drinking kneeling down,
as in the ceremony of knighting.

70 **What … hither** Proverbial (Tilley W441).

71 **ill wind … good** Proverbial (Tilley W421).

art now one of the greatest men in this realm.

SILENCE  By'r Lady, I think a be, but goodman Puff of Barson.

PISTOL  Puff? – Puff i'thy teeth, most recreant coward base!
    Sir John, I am thy Pistol and thy friend,       75
    And helter-skelter have I rode to thee,
    And tidings do I bring, and lucky joys,
    And golden times, and happy news of price.

FALSTAFF  I pray thee now, deliver them like a man of this world.

PISTOL  A foutre for the world and worldlings base!       80
    I speak of Africa and golden joys.

FALSTAFF  O base Assyrian knight, what is thy news?
    Let King Cophetua know the truth thereof.

SILENCE  [*Sings*] And Robin Hood, Scarlet, and John.

PISTOL  Shall dunghill curs confront the Helicons?       85
    And shall good news be baffled?
    Then Pistol lay thy head in Furies' lap.

SHALLOW  Honest gentleman, I know not your breeding.

PISTOL  Why then, lament therefor.

SHALLOW  Give me pardon, sir. If, sir, you come with news from the   90
court, I take it there's but two ways, either to utter them, or conceal
them. I am, sir, under the king in some authority.

PISTOL  Under which king, besonian? Speak or die.

---

72 this] Q; the F   73 By'r lady] Q; Indeed F   73 a] Q; he F   74–8] *As verse, Pope; as prose,* Q, F   74 i'thy] ith thy Q, in thy F   76 And] Q; *not in* F   79, 82 SH FALSTAFF] *Fal.* F; *Iohn* Q   79 pray thee] Q; prethee F   80–3] *As verse,* F; *as prose,* Q   83 Cophetua] *Pope;* Couetua Q; Couitha F   84 SD] *Knight subst., Johnson; not in* Q, F   85–7] *As verse,* F; *as prose,* Q   88] *As prose,* Q; *as two lines divided at* Gentleman, F   93] *As one line,* Q; *as two lines divided at* King? F

---

73 **a be, but** he is, except for; Silence takes 'greatest' as referring to Falstaff's size rather than to his new importance.

73 **goodman** The title of people below the rank of gentleman.

73 **Barson** There is a Barston some fifteen miles north-east of Stratford and a Barcheston twelve miles south-east.

74 **Puff** Boast, swagger.

74 **recreant** forsworn.

79 **a man … world** an ordinary person, using plain language.

80, 95 **a foutre for** a fig for; the French 'foutre' is stronger, referring to sexual assault.

81 Pistol reverts to his typical braggart language, based on sensational Elizabethan plays (see 2.4.123–5 n.); 'Afric' is constantly associated with gold in Marlowe's *Tamburlaine*.

82 **Assyrian** Chosen at random by Falstaff in imitation of Pistol's bombastic style.

83 **King Cophetua** The legend of the African King Cophetua who married a beggar girl was the subject of popular ballads, referred to by Shakespeare in *LLL* 4.1.65, *Rom.* 2.1.14, *R2* 5.3.80.

84 From the ballad 'Robin Hood and the Pinder of Wakefield'; for the tune see Long, *Shakespeare's Use of Music*, p. 92.

85 **Helicons** Mount Helicon was the seat of the Muses, but Pistol takes Helicon as an alternative name for Muse, and considers himself one of them.

87 **lay … lap** give thyself up to the goddesses of revenge.

88 **breeding** social status.

93 **besonian** From Italian 'bisogno' or 'bisognoso' = beggarly person lacking all essentials, physically and mentally – used of recruits with no qualifications or training.

SHALLOW  Under King Harry.

PISTOL                              Harry the Fourth, or Fifth?

SHALLOW  Harry the Fourth.

PISTOL                              A foutre for thine office!                95
    Sir John, thy tender lambkin now is king:
    Harry the Fifth's the man, I speak the truth.
    When Pistol lies, do this and fig me, like
    The bragging Spaniard.

FALSTAFF                            What, is the old king dead?

PISTOL  As nail in door. The things I speak are just.             100

FALSTAFF  Away, Bardolph, saddle my horse! – Master Robert Shallow,
choose what office thou wilt in the land: 'tis thine. – Pistol, I will
double-charge thee with dignities.

BARDOLPH  O joyful day! I would not take a knighthood for my fortune!

PISTOL  What? I do bring good news.                               105

FALSTAFF  Carry Master Silence to bed. Master Shallow, my Lord
Shallow, be what thou wilt: I am fortune's steward. Get on thy boots,
we'll ride all night. O sweet Pistol! Away, Bardolph.

                                  *[Exit Bardolph]*

    Come, Pistol, utter more to me, and withal devise something to do
thyself good. – Boot, boot, Master Shallow! I know the young king is   110
sick for me. Let us take any man's horses, the laws of England are at
my commandment. Blessed are they that have been my friends, and
woe to my Lord Chief Justice!

PISTOL  Let vultures vile seize on his lungs also!

---

95–9 A foutre . . . Spaniard.] *As verse*, F; *as prose*, Q   100] *As one line*, Q; *as two lines divided at* doore. F   101–3] *As prose*, Q; *as four lines ending* . . . Horse, / . . . wilt / . . . thee / . . . Dignities. F   104 knighthood] F; Knight Q   108 SD] *Capell; not in* Q, F   112 Blessed] Q; Happie F   112 that] Q; which F   113 to] Q; vnto F   114–16] *As verse*, F; *as prose*, Q   114 vile] Q; vil'de F

---

95 A foutre . . . office The implication is that the new king is going to dismiss all people in office, replacing them with his followers; see *FV* sig. D1.

98 do . . . fig me 'do this' is an action pointer to the indecent gesture Pistol is making with his thumb between two fingers, known as 'the fig of Spain' (hence 'Spaniard' at 99); the same gesture is implicit in 'a foutre' at 80 and 95.

100 As nail in door Proverbial (Tilley D567).

103 double-charge (1) load with honours, (2) load as a firearm (see 2.4.89–92 n.). Quibbling on Pistol's name.

110 Boot Used as a verb: put on your riding-boots.

111 sick longing; with an unconscious pun on 'sick of me'.

113 woe . . . Justice In *FV* sig. D1 Ned boasts at the news of the king's death: 'I shall be Lord chief Iustice.'

114 vultures . . . lungs An allusion either to the myth of Tityus, a giant who tried to rape the mother of Apollo and Artemis, for which he was bound in Hades with two vultures tearing at his liver, or to that of Prometheus who was bound to a rock for having stolen fire from heaven, with an eagle gnawing at his vitals – echoed by Pistol also in *Wiv.* 1.3.85: 'Let vultures gripe thy guts.'

'Where is the life that late I led?' say they;                    115
Why, here it is: welcome these pleasant days!

*Exeunt*

5.4  *Enter* HOSTESS QUICKLY, DOLL TEARSHEET *and* BEADLES

HOSTESS  No, thou arrant knave, I would to God that I might die, that I
    might have thee hanged. Thou hast drawn my shoulder out of joint.
BEADLE  The constables have delivered her over to me, and she shall have
    whipping-cheer, I warrant her. There hath been a man or two killed
    about her.                                                         5
DOLL  Nut-hook, nut-hook, you lie. Come on, I'll tell thee what, thou
    damned tripe-visaged rascal: and the child I go with do miscarry,
    thou wert better thou hadst struck thy mother, thou paper-faced
    villain.
HOSTESS  O the Lord, that Sir John were come! I would make this a    10
    bloody day to somebody. But I pray God the fruit of her womb
    miscarry.
BEADLE  If it do, you shall have a dozen of cushions again: you have but

116 these] Q; those F   Act 5, Scene 4   5.4] *Scene Quarta*. F; *not in* Q   0 SD] F; *Enter Sincklo and three or foure officers.* Q   1 to God
that] Q; *not in* F   3, 13, 19, 27 SH BEADLE] *Sincklo* Q; *Off. / or / Officer* F   4 -cheer] Q; cheere enough F   4 two killed] Q; two
(lately) kill'd F   6, 16, 22, 24, 26 SH DOLL] *Dol.* F; *Whoore.* Q   7 and ... I go] Q; if ... I now go F   8 wert] Q; had'st F   10 O the
Lord] Q; O F   10 I] Q; hee F   11 I pray God] Q; I would F   12 miscarry] Q; might miscarry F

115 **Where ... led** A line from a lost poem or ballad
quoted also in *Shr.* 4.1.140.

### Act 5, Scene 4

0 SD Q omits from the entrance the Hostess and
Doll, and instead of *Beadles* has *Sincklo and three or
foure officers*; the name Sincklo replaces 'Beadle' in all
speech headings. John Sincklo or Sinclair was a
member of the Chamberlain's Men who had acted
also in other companies so that his name appears in
*3H6* 3.1, *Shr.* Induction 1.88 and in the 'plot' of
*2 Seven Deadly Sins* (*c.* 1590–1), as well as in the
Induction to Marston's *The Malcontent*, a play
acquired by the King's Men in 1604. Actors' names
appear in authorial stage directions when the roles
they are supposed to double are last-minute additions
to the playscript, so that the author takes over the
casting task from the book-keeper; see Will Kemp in
*Rom.* 4.5.101 SD.

3 **delivered ... me** The constable delivered minor
criminals to the beadles – parish officers in charge of
punishing petty offences.

4 **whipping-cheer** plenty of whipping; the punishment of whores ('cheer' = 'a meal').

6 **Nut-hook** A hooked pole used to pull down the
branches of nut-trees; the epithets and allusions in
the women's speeches confirm that the actor Sincklo
must have been particularly thin and tall, probably
doubling for Shadow (not Feeble, as suggested by
Wilson) in 3.2, and possibly for Snare; see 2.1.4 n.

7 **tripe-visaged** sallow, pock-marked; see 'paper-
faced' at 8.

7 **and ... go with** if the child I am pregnant with –
implying that it is Falstaff's.

10 **I would** F reads 'he would', referring to Falstaff;
both readings are tenable.

12 **miscarry** A blunder; she means 'may not miscarry', but it could be taken literally as a threat of the
revenge Falstaff would take in the event.

13–14 **you shall ... now** One of the cushions is
being used as padding to pretend pregnancy.

eleven now. Come, I charge you both go with me, for the man is dead
that you and Pistol beat amongst you. 15

DOLL I'll tell you what, you thin man in a censer: I will have you as
soundly swinged for this, you bluebottle rogue, you filthy famished
correctioner: if you be not swinged, I'll forswear half-kirtles.

BEADLE Come, come, you she-knight-errant, come.

HOSTESS O God, that right should thus overcome might! Well, of 20
sufferance comes ease.

DOLL Come, you rogue, come, bring me to a justice.

HOSTESS Ay, come, you starved bloodhound.

DOLL Goodman death, goodman bones.

HOSTESS Thou atomy, thou. 25

DOLL Come, you thin thing, come, you rascal.

BEADLE Very well.

*Exeunt*

**5.5** *Enter three* GROOMS *strewing rushes*

FIRST GROOM More rushes, more rushes!

SECOND GROOM The trumpets have sounded twice.

THIRD GROOM 'Twill be two a'clock ere they come from the coronation.

15 amongst] Q; among F   16 you what, you] Q; thee what, thou F   20 O God] Q; O F   22] *As prose,* Q; *as two lines divided at* come:
F   23 Ay] I Q; Yes F   25 atomy] Q; Anatomy F   26] Q; *as two lines divided at* Thing: F   27 SD] F; *not in* Q   Act 5, Scene 5   5.5]
*Scena Quinta.* F; *not in* Q   0 SD] *Dyce, after Capell; Enter strewers of rushes.* Q; *Enter two Groomes.* F   3 SH THIRD GROOM] 3 Q;
1.*Groo.* F   3 'Twill] Q; It will F   3 a'clock] Q; of the Clocke F

14–15 **the man ... amongst you** An unexpected
hint at Pistol's continued attendance at Mistress
Quickly's premises, in spite of his reception in 2.4,
probably added in preparation for their being a married couple in *H5*.

16 **thin ... censer** Perfume pans were embossed
with figures in low relief.

17 **bluebottle** Beadles wore blue coats.

18 **correctioner** Officer in charge of whipping
whores in Bridewell, the 'house of correction'.

18 **half-kirtles** A kirtle included skirt and bodice:
the half-kirtle was the lower part, i.e. the skirt.

19 **she-knight-errant** (1) female heroine of
romance, (2) street-walker at night, i.e. professional
prostitute.

20 **right ... might** The Hostess means the
opposite, referring to the proverb 'Might overcomes
right' (Tilley M922).

20–1 **of ... ease** Another proverb (Tilley S955).

24 For 'Goodman' see 5.3.73 n.; 'death' and
'bones' imply that the beadle is as thin as a skeleton.

25 **atomy** The Hostess's blunder for 'anatomy'
(corrected in F), meaning 'skeleton', but somehow
appropriate since 'atomy' or 'atom' indicated an invisible particle.

**Act 5, Scene 5**

5.5 Based on *FV* sigs. D1ᵛ–D2, but see the headnote
to 5.2. Holinshed (III, 543/2/4–11) reports briefly the
banning ('ten miles') of the prince's companions.
Probably the versified parts of the scene are taken
from an earlier version, while the prose speeches were
added or adapted at the time of rewriting: this would
explain the confusions in the allotment of prose
speeches.

0 SD The F version is intended to save one extra
actor, and the same preoccupation with economy in
production may have prompted the omission of the

Dispatch, dispatch!

*Exeunt*

*Trumpets sound and the* KING *and his train pass over the stage. After them
enter* FALSTAFF, SHALLOW, PISTOL, BARDOLPH *and the* [PAGE-]BOY

FALSTAFF Stand here by me, Master Shallow; I will make the king do          5
you grace. I will leer upon him as a comes by, and do but mark the
countenance that he will give me.

PISTOL God bless thy lungs, good knight.

FALSTAFF Come here, Pistol, stand behind me. – O, if I had had time to
have made new liveries, I would have bestowed the thousand pound I          10
borrowed of you; but 'tis no matter: this poor show doth better, this
doth infer the zeal I had to see him.

SHALLOW It doth so.

FALSTAFF It shows my earnestness of affection –

PISTOL It doth so.                                                          15

FALSTAFF My devotion –

PISTOL It doth, it doth, it doth.

FALSTAFF As it were, to ride day and night, and not to deliberate, not to
remember, not to have patience to shift me –

SHALLOW It is best, certain.                                                20

FALSTAFF But to stand stained with travel, and sweating with desire to
see him, thinking of nothing else, putting all affairs else in oblivion, as
if there were nothing else to be done but to see him.

---

4 Dispatch, dispatch!] Q; *not in* F   4 SD.1 *Exeunt*] *Exit Groo.* F; *not in* Q   4 SD.2–3] Q; *Enter Falstaffe, Shallow, Pistoll, Bardolfe, and
Page.* F   5 Master Shallow] Q; *M. Robert Shallow* F   6 a comes] Q; he comes F   8 God] Q; *not in* F   11 'tis] Q; it is F   13 SH
SHALLOW] *Shal.* F; *Pist.* Q   14 of] Q; *in* F   15, 17 SH PISTOL] Q, F; *Shallow.* Hanmer   18–19] *As prose,* Q; *as three lines ending
…night, / …remember, / …me.* F   20 best,] Q; most F   21 SH FALSTAFF] F; *not in* Q   22 else in] Q; *in* F

---

procession at 4 SD.2–3. Rushes were strewn in the
roadway on the route of royal processions.

4 **Dispatch** See 2.4.9 n.; F omits, there being no
procession *going* to the coronation: the one returning
from it is not expected for a while.

4 SD.2 'Passing over the stage' was a form of dumb
show, when a group of actors entered at one side and
exited at the other.

6 **grace** favour.

6 **leer** look smilingly; without the modern implication of idiocy or malignancy.

7 **countenance** reception, as shown by the facial
expression; see 4.1.241, 252 n.

10 **new liveries** Presumably with the king's arms
on them.

10–11 **thousand … borrowed** An unexpected

piece of information, but see 4.1.475–9 and Falstaff
asking the same sum of the Lord Chief Justice at
1.2.175–6.

12 **doth infer** shows, demonstrates implicitly.

13, 15, 17 SH Q gives all three speeches to Pistol and
F transfers only the first to Shallow, while modern
editors give all three to the latter. It seems logical that
Shallow should reply to a speech partly addressed to
him, but the next two interruptions may well be
Pistol's parodying Shallow's trick of repetition.

19 **shift me** change my clothes.

20 **best, certain** Q's reading is dramatically
stronger than F's 'most certain'.

21–3 The attribution of this speech to Shallow in Q
is due to the accidental omission of the new speech
heading.

PISTOL  'Tis *semper idem*, for *obsque hoc nihil est*; 'tis all in every part.

SHALLOW  'Tis so, indeed.                                                    25

PISTOL  My knight, I will inflame thy noble liver,

And make thee rage.

Thy Doll, and Helen of thy noble thoughts,

Is in base durance and contagious prison,

Haled thither                                                               30

By most mechanical and dirty hands.

Rouse up Revenge from ebon den with fell Alecto's snake,

For Doll is in. Pistol speaks nought but truth.

FALSTAFF  I will deliver her.

*The trumpets sound*

PISTOL  There roared the sea, and trumpet clangour sounds.                   35

*Enter the* KING *and his train*

FALSTAFF  God save thy grace, King Hal, my royal Hal.

PISTOL  The heavens thee guard and keep,

Most royal imp of fame.

FALSTAFF  God save thee, my sweet boy.

KING  My Lord Chief Justice, speak to that vain man.                         40

JUSTICE  Have you your wits? Know you what 'tis you speak?

FALSTAFF  My king, my Jove, I speak to thee, my heart.

KING  I know thee not, old man. Fall to thy prayers.

How ill white hairs becomes a fool and jester!

---

24 'tis all] F; tis Q   26–33] *As verse, Capell subst.; as prose*, Q, F   34 SD] F *(at 35); not in* Q   35 SD] Q; *Enter King Henrie the Fift, Brothers, Lord Chiefe Iustice.* F   36,39 God] Q; *not in* F   37–8] *As verse, this edn; as prose*, Q, F   41]*As one line*, Q; *as two lines divided at* wits? F   44 becomes] Q; become F

---

24 **semper ... est** The Latin mottoes mean 'ever the same' (a favourite of Queen Elizabeth's) and 'apart from this there is nothing' (*obsque* is a mistake for *absque*).

24 **'tis ... part** Pistol translates the mottoes into the current proverb 'All in all and all in every part' (Tilley A133), describing the nature of the soul and therefore a condition of absolute perfection.

26 **liver** The seat of passion and courage; see 1.2.138–9 n.

26–33 If the whole of 5.4 is a late addition to the play (see 5.4.0 SD n.) this speech too must have been introduced at the last moment.

30 **Haled** Dragged; see *More* 4: 'whether wilt thou hale me?'

31 **mechanical** base, vulgar; as belonging to a manual worker ('mechanic').

32 **Rouse up Revenge** Echoing Kyd's *Spanish*

*Tragedy*, where Revenge, a character in the play, is repeatedly invoked with 'Awake, Revenge!'

32 **ebon den** dark cave, black as ebony, i.e. hell.

32 **Alecto's snake** Alecto, one of the three Furies, was described in Virgil's *Aeneid* VII as crowned with snakes. See 5.3.87.

33 **Pistol ... truth** See 5.3.100.

35 **trumpet ... sounds** See *E3* 5.1.149: 'There sound the Trumpets clangor.'

37–8 Though printed as prose, the rhythm ('heavens' was pronounced as a monosyllable) suggests Pistol's typical versification.

38 **imp** descendant of a noble house; archaic. See *Battle of Alcazar* 2.1.46: 'the imp of royal race'.

43 **I ... not** The words of the bridegroom (a figure of Christ) to the foolish virgins in Matt. 25.10–12.

44 **becomes** A singular form for the plural.

I have long dreamt of such a kind of man,                    45
So surfeit-swelled, so old and so profane,
But being awaked, I do despise my dream.
Make less thy body hence, and more thy grace,
Leave gormandising, know the grave doth gape
For thee thrice wider than for other men.                    50
Reply not to me with a fool-born jest,
Presume not that I am the thing I was,
For God doth know – so shall the world perceive –
That I have turned away my former self;
So will I those that kept me company.                         55
When thou dost hear I am as I have been,
Approach me, and thou shalt be as thou wast,
The tutor and the feeder of my riots;
Till then I banish thee, on pain of death,
As I have done the rest of my misleaders,                    60
Not to come near our person by ten mile.
For competence of life I will allow you,
That lack of means enforce you not to evils;
And as we hear you do reform yourselves,
We will, according to your strengths and qualities,          65
Give you advancement. – Be it your charge, my lord,
To see performed the tenor of my word.
Set on.

                                        *Exit King [and train]*

FALSTAFF  Master Shallow, I owe you a thousand pound.

SHALLOW  Yea, marry, Sir John, which I beseech you to let me have home   70
with me.

FALSTAFF  That can hardly be, Master Shallow. Do not you grieve at this.
I shall be sent for in private to him. Look you, he must seem thus to
the world. Fear not your advancements: I will be the man yet that shall
make you great.                                              75

47 awaked] awakt Q; awake F   53 God] Q; heauen F   63 evils] Q; euill F   65 strengths] Q; strength F   67–8] *Divided as in Pope;
as one line*, Q, F   67 my word] Q; our word F   68 SD] *Exit King*. F; *not in* Q   69, 72, 79, 82 SH FALSTAFF] *Fal*. F; *Iohn* Q   70 Yea]
Q; I F   74 advancements] Q; aduancement F

46 **surfeit-swelled** swollen by overfeeding; see        58 **riots** The term with which Henry IV describes
'gormandising' at 49.                                      Prince Hal's behaviour at 4.2.62 and 264.
48 **hence** henceforward.                                    61 **ten mile** The ten-mile limit is specified in *FV*
48 **grace** virtue.                                       and Holinshed, but not in Stow.
51 **fool-born** (1) a born fool, (2) fool-borne, put up      62 **competence of life** sufficient allowance; men-
with only by fools.                                       tioned by Holinshed and Stow, but not in *FV*.
52–5 See 5.2.125–8 n.

SHALLOW  I cannot perceive how, unless you give me your doublet and
stuff me out with straw. I beseech you, good Sir John, let me have five
hundred of my thousand.

FALSTAFF  Sir, I will be as good as my word. This that you heard was but a
colour.                                                                         80

SHALLOW  A colour that I fear you will die in, Sir John.

FALSTAFF  Fear no colours, go with me to dinner. Come, Lieutenant
Pistol, come, Bardolph. I shall be sent for soon at night.

*Enter the* LORD CHIEF JUSTICE *and Prince* JOHN, [*with Officers*]

JUSTICE  Go, carry Sir John Falstaff to the Fleet,
Take all his company along with him.                                            85

FALSTAFF  My lord, my lord –

JUSTICE  I cannot now speak, I will hear you soon.
Take them away.

PISTOL  *Se fortuna mi tormenta, ben sperato mi contenta –*
*Exeunt [all but Prince John and Lord Chief Justice]*

JOHN  I like this fair proceeding of the king's:                                90
He hath intent his wonted followers
Shall all be very well provided for,
But all are banished till their conversations
Appear more wise and modest to the world.

JUSTICE  And so they are.                                                       95

JOHN  The king hath called his parliament, my lord.

JUSTICE  He hath.

---

76 cannot] Q; cannot well F   76 you give] Q; you should giue F   81 that I fear you] Q; I feare, that you F   82–3] *As prose, Pope; as three lines ending* ... *dinner: /* ... *Bardolfe, /* ... *night.* Q, F   83 SD] *Enter Iustice and prince Iohn* Q (*at 82–3); not in* F   89] *This edn (see 2.4.145 above); Si fortuna me tormenta spero contenta.* Q; *Si fortuna me tormento, spera me contento.* F   89 SD] *Exit. Manet Lancaster and Chiefe Iustice.* F; *exeunt.* Q (*at 88*)

76–7 I cannot ... straw The unexpected melancholy witticisms of Shallow here and at 81 are the final
master touches to his character, in contrast with
Falstaff's serenely impudent reminder of the
thousand pounds cheated out of him.

80 colour pretence.

81 A colour ... die in A double pun: 'colour' = (1)
pretence, (2) collar (with a reference to the hanging
noose), (3) dye; 'die in' = (1) end your life (by hanging), (2) be dyed with.

82 Fear no colours Have no fear; proverbial
(Tilley C520); 'colours' = 'enemy standards'.

82–3 Lieutenant Pistol Falstaff promotes Pistol
from 'Ancient' (2.4.55) to lieutenant, in the same way
as the Hostess, to ingratiate herself with him, had
made him 'Captain' (2.4.108), but Pistol is still an
ancient in *H5*.

83 soon at night early in the evening; Dent S639.1
quotes Munday, *Fidele and Fortunio* 114, 126, 274.

84 Fleet A prison in the City, though it is hard to
see what offence Falstaff has committed. This line
may have been adapted from the earlier version of the
play: if one eliminates 'Go' and replaces 'Falstaff'
with 'Oldcastle' it again scans perfectly; see 5.2.33 n.

89 See 2.4.145 n. The repetition of a song about ill-
fortune and hope at this juncture is a master touch of
dramatic irony.

91–4 This point, amplifying 62–6, is particularly
stressed by Stow (*Annales*, p. 549).

93 conversations behaviours.

96 parliament From Holinshed.

JOHN  I will lay odds that, ere this year expire,
        We bear our civil swords and native fire
        As far as France. I heard a bird so sing,                    100
        Whose music, to my thinking, pleased the king.
        Come, will you hence?

                                                        *Exeunt*


## EPILOGUE


First my fear, then my curtsy, last my speech.
    My fear is your displeasure, my curtsy my duty, and my speech to
beg your pardons. If you look for a good speech now, you undo me,
for what I have to say is of mine own making; and what indeed I
should say will, I doubt, prove mine own marring. But to the purpose,    5
and so to the venture. Be it known to you, as it is very well, I was lately
here in the end of a displeasing play, to pray your patience for it and to
promise you a better. I meant indeed to pay you with this, which, if

100 heard] Q; heare F    102 SD] *Exeunt* / FINIS. F; *not in* Q   **Epilogue**   EPILOGUE] Q, F; *Epilogue / Spoken by a Dancer. / Pope,*
*Capell, et al.*    8 meant] Q; *did meane* F

**98–101 I will . . . France** Preparatory to the events
in *H5* and suggested by *FV*, where the dismissal of
Hal's companions, the confirmation of the Lord Chief
Justice and the declaration of war against France are
all part of one scene.

**99 civil swords** Either 'the swords of the citizens'
or 'the swords used till now in civil wars'; see 'civil
blows' at 4.2.262.

**100 I . . . sing** Proverbial (Tilley B374).

**102** The addition of a short prose sentence after the
formal rhymed couplets closing the action of a play is a
frequent Shakespearean device to allow the actors to
clear the stage before the Epilogue or the traditional
jig at the end of the evening's entertainment.

**Epilogue**
The unusual prose epilogue (but see that spoken by
Rosalind in *As You Like It*) is divided into three
sections written at different times and serving different purposes; Pope's specification 'spoken by a
dancer' could apply only to the second section and
possibly the third. The first section (1–13) is an
apology for an unfortunate previous performance (see
7 n.) and the mention of the queen at 12–13 suggests
the political nature of the trouble and the fact that the
audience addressed was in the know. The second
section (14–19) could be alternative to the first,
replacing it from the words 'If you look' (3) to the end;
it appears to have been written when the episode
referred to in the first section was forgotten, and to
have been entrusted to a popular actor introducing the

final jig. The third section (20–6) is an afterthought
added when it seemed necessary to apologise for the
misguided use of the name Oldcastle in an earlier but
not yet forgotten version of the play. The transfer in F
of the prayer for the queen from 12–13 to the end is an
attempt at unifying what are in fact three alternative
epilogues.

**1 curtsy** bow, obeisance.

**4 what . . . making** Suggesting that the author
himself is speaking this part of the Epilogue.

**4–5 making . . . marring** A current quibble ('make
or mar', Tilley M48) used in many plays of
Shakespeare.

**5 doubt** fear.

**6 to the venture** I will run the risk, like the
merchant venturers in their undertakings; see
1.1.180–6 n. and 2.4.51 n.; 'ill venture' at 9 is an
unsuccessful voyage.

**7 a displeasing play** Not necessarily by the same
author, though acted by the same company. We have
no precise record of the Chamberlain's Men's plays
for 1597–8, so there is no saying which one was
withdrawn after a few performances and why. If the
'displeasure' refers to offence taken by people in
authority, we could guess at a case like that of *The Isle
of Dogs*, withdrawn by Pembroke's Men in 1597, or
even the 'Oldcastle' version of *Henry IV* (see p. 10
above for its possible performance in 1596), but the
reference may be to an ordinary 'flop' in the previous
theatre season.

like an ill venture it come unluckily home, I break, and you, my gentle
creditors, lose. Here I promised you I would be, and here I commit       10
my body to your mercies: bate me some, and I will pay you some, and,
as most debtors do, promise infinitely. And so I kneel down before
you, but, indeed, to pray for the queen.

If my tongue cannot entreat you to acquit me, will you command
me to use my legs? And yet that were but light payment, to dance out      15
of your debt. But a good conscience will make any possible satisfaction, and so would I. All the gentlewomen here have forgiven me; if
the gentlemen will not, then the gentlemen do not agree with the
gentlewomen, which was never seen in such an assembly.

One word more, I beseech you: if you be not too much cloyed with       20
fat meat, our humble author will continue the story with Sir John in it,
and make you merry with fair Katherine of France, where, for
anything I know, Falstaff shall die of a sweat, unless already a be killed
with your hard opinions; for Oldcastle died martyr, and this is not the
man. My tongue is weary; when my legs are too, I will bid you good       25
night.

12–13 And so ... queen.] Q; *not in* F    17 would] Q; *will* F    19 seen] Q; *seene before* F    23 a be] Q; *he be* F    24 martyr] Q; *a Martyr* F
26 night.] Q; *night; and so kneele downe before you: But (indeed) to pray for the Queene.* F

9 **break** (1) break the promise, (2) go bankrupt.

11 **bate me some** grant me a discount.

15 **use my legs** Introducing the jig that concluded
all performances in public theatres.

17–19 **All ... assembly** The appeal to the women
in the audience to prevail with their menfolk in favour
of the play resembles that in the epilogue of *AYLI* 11–
23, spoken by the boy impersonating Rosalind; here,
though, the speaker is sure of his popularity (17) and
appreciated as a jig-dancer (14–15), which suggests
not, as Wilson surmises, the child acting Falstaff's
page, but the clown Will Kemp, a sharer of the
Chamberlain's Men till 1599 and highly celebrated
for his jigs.

20 **One word more** Suggesting that this paragraph
is an afterthought; see headnote.

22 **make you ... France** The promise is kept in *H5*
3.4 and 5.2, but the suggestion of the humorous
exploitation of Katherine comes from *FV* scene xviii
(sigs. F3ᵛ–F4) and scene xx (sigs. G2–G2ᵛ).

23 **Falstaff ... sweat** Falstaff is again going to
exhibit his cowardice; see *1H4* 2.2.80: 'Falstaff sweats
to death' (= is in a blue funk). The unfulfilled promise
to show Falstaff in France in *H5* suggests that this was
written when the next history (late 1599) was as yet
uncompleted. The retention of this sentence in the
Epilogue after the decision to leave Falstaff out of *H5*
counts on its being taken in the literal sense, in line
with the Hostess's description of Falstaff's terminal

illness (*H5* 2.1.118–19) as 'a burning quotidian
tertian', which would make him sweat considerably.
The debate in commentaries whether 'sweat' means
'sweating sickness' (a name for the plague) or
'venereal disease' and its treatment by sweating,
seems utterly irrelevant. See Melchiori, 'Dying of a
sweat: Falstaff and Oldcastle', *N&Q* ns 34 (1987),
210–11.

24–5 **Oldcastle ... man** This has been taken as a
belated apology possibly prompted by the successful
performance by the Admiral's Men late in 1599 of
*1 Sir John Oldcastle* by Munday, Drayton and others,
which, though mentioning Falstaff (MSR 1908,
1384–6 and 1416–19), vindicates Oldcastle in the
Prologue against his earlier presentation by the
Chamberlain's Men: 'It is no pamperd glutton we
present, / Nor aged Councellor to youthfull sinne, /
But one, whose vertue shone aboue the rest / ...let
faire Truth be grac'te, / Since forg'de inuention
former time defac'te'. But the mention of Oldcastle
here could be sarcastic (see C. G. Thayer,
*Shakespearean Politics*, 1983, p. 129), an oblique
reminder that the change from Oldcastle to Falstaff
was forced upon the company; in which case the
Admiral's play would be the answer to this ambiguous
allusion.

25 **when ... too** Announcing the beginning of the
jig; see 15.

# TEXTUAL ANALYSIS

There is only one quarto edition of *The Second Part of Henry IV*. The printer was Valentine Simmes, by all accounts a reputable workman, who was responsible for several other Shakespearean quartos, both good and bad.[1] It was printed for Andrew Wise and William Aspley in 1600 – close enough in time to the date of composition to suggest that the text was published with the full consent of the Chamberlain's Men, who had handed it over to the booksellers along with the text of *Much Ado About Nothing*, as the entry in the Stationers' Register for 23 August 1600 makes clear.[2] Both plays were set practically at the same time by a single compositor, whose habits have been extensively studied.[3] He has been accused of carelessness, and the accusation is borne out also by this text, notably by the omission in the first printing of a whole scene (3.1), which caused the replacement, in a second issue, of two leaves of quire E with a reset four-leaf quire (E3–6$^v$), to make room in it for the missing passage. This will be discussed later.

What matters is that, from a whole series of unequivocal signs – such as permissive stage directions, the presence of ghost characters, peculiar spellings, etc.[4] – it appears that Q was set from authorial manuscript (often called 'foul papers') and it should therefore reflect Shakespeare's original writing and composition more closely than most other texts in the canon. Besides, for all his vagaries and misreadings of words and punctuation, the compositor (more carefree than careless, as George Walton Williams put it)[5] was not the sort of person who would take it upon himself to 'improve' or alter substantially the spelling and capitalisation that he found in his copy: the quarto therefore offers a rare opportunity of speculating on Shakespeare's spelling habits, and its evidence is reinforced by some striking coincidences with the famous three pages in Hand D in the manuscript *Booke of Sir Thomas Moore*, the only document of any length in what is believed to be Shakespeare's handwriting.[6]

In view of these involuntary virtues of the quarto, it is the more disappointing to find that the text it prints is by no means wholly reliable. This is clear not only from the pitiful state of confusion into which the compositor falls whenever confronted with corrections,

[1] They are: *Richard II* (Q1, 1597, and Q2, 1598), *Richard III* (Q1, 1597), *First Part of the Contention* (bad Q2 of *2 Henry VI*, 1600), *Much Ado* (Q1, 1600), *Hamlet* (bad Q1, 1603 and Q3, 1611), *1 Henry IV* (Q4, 1604), *The Taming of a Shrew* (bad Q3, 1607).

[2] See p. 2 above.

[3] W. Craig Ferguson, 'The compositors of *Henry IV, Part 2, Much Ado About Nothing, The Shoemakers' Holiday*, and *The First Part of the Contention*', *SB* 13 (1960), 19–29.

[4] For a thorough listing and discussion of these features and of their significance see especially the textual Appendix to M. Shaaber's New Variorum Edition of *The Second Part of Henry the Fourth*, 1940, 'The copy for Q', pp. 488–94. Even the use of the name of the actor John Sincklo for the Beadle in 5.4 is no longer considered the work of the prompter, but is acknowledged as evidence of foul papers in the author's hand.

[5] 'The text of *2 Henry IV*: facts and problems', *S.St.* 9 (1976), 174.

[6] Apart from the well-known spelling 'scilens' for 'silence', another typical feature is the omission of medial full stops within verse lines; see here Induction 15, and Giorgio Melchiori, 'Hand D in "Sir Thomas More": an essay in misinterpretation', *S.Sur.* 38 (1985), 104–6.

deletions or insertions in his copy-text,[1] but also from a comparison with the next edition of the play in the Histories section of the First Folio of 1623, where it bears the head-title, on sig. f6ᵛ:

The Second Part of Henry the Fourth, / Containing his Death: and the Coronation / of King Henry the Fift.

The printing history of *Part Two* in the First Folio is not without accidents: there were difficulties in securing copy for the two first *Henry*s, so that the printers started setting *Henry V* first, and miscalculated the number of quires to be reserved for the later inclusion of the two parts of *Henry IV*. When they came to print them, they discovered that the 'overflow' of *Part Two* could not be contained even in a normal extra folio quire of three sheets; thus, they inserted between the quires designated with signatures g and h a larger one (gg) comprising four instead of three sheets. But the text of the play would fill only one of the two leaves of the extra sheet – a happy accident, in a way, allowing them to add the text of the Epilogue in large print on the recto and one of the rare lists of 'The Actors Names' on the verso of the spare leaf.[2] We can be sure that neither the list of actors nor the act and scene divisions introduced in the Folio (and adopted in the present text as more plausible than those in modern editions of the play)[3] are authorial. On the other hand, the Folio includes a number of variants worth discussion and, more to the point, no less than eight longer passages, totalling over 160 lines, which do not appear in the quarto but have an undoubted Shakespearean ring. A brief survey of the Folio printing and of the copy on which it seems to be based is in order at this point.

The printing process of the Folio and the work of the individual compositors in this section of it have been so thoroughly studied, notably by Charlton Hinman,[4] that it is unnecessary to go into them in detail. The Folio compositors are inordinately fond of capitalisation of common nouns, in contrast with the practice followed in the quarto where, apart from proper names, titles or other appellations, and collective nouns, capitals are reserved for abstract nouns used as personifications.[5] They are probably responsible also for some of the minor cuts of words and phrases and for the redistribution of lines of text. These were often caused by errors in 'casting off', as the practice of typesetting by formes frequently required the composition of whole pages in reverse order. There are, though, other omissions, alterations, and short additions, which cannot be imputed to the printers, but must depend on the copy from which the text was set. The most obvious case is the suppression of all oaths and mentions of the

---

[1] See especially the discussion of the passages not present in the quarto, pp. 192–8 below.
[2] The addition of a list of actors' names to *Timon* is the result of a similar printing accident. The other lists in the Folio are at the end of *Othello* and of four comedies, *The Tempest*, *Two Gentlemen of Verona*, *Measure for Measure* and *The Winter's Tale*, all of them set from fair copies made by the professional scribe Ralph Crane.
[3] The subdivision of 4.1 into three scenes (4.2 beginning at line 229 and 4.3 at line 352) was first introduced by Edward Capell in his 1768 edition. The Cambridge and Globe editors of 1864 are responsible for the division of 4.2 (renamed 4.4) at line 133, so that the act, in most subsequent editions, is divided, for ease of reference, though with several misgivings, into five scenes. The Oxford edition (1986), edited by S. Wells and G. Taylor, accepts only the new division at 4.1.352, and the act is therefore in three scenes.
[4] Charlton Hinman, *The Printing and Proof-Reading of the First Folio of Shakespeare*, 1963, II, 88–106.
[5] See Melchiori, 'Jealousy', pp. 327–30.

name of God (which is either omitted or replaced by 'Heaven');[1] this is of course connected with the Profanity Act of 1606, but it does not necessarily imply that the copy-text was based on a prompt-book used for the stage after that date. In spite of the fact that the Act did not apply to printed matter, it seems to have been the policy of the compilers of the Folio to avoid all possible offence of this kind in the plays included in it. There are also in the text of *Part Two* one or two cases of deliberate bowdlerisation[2] which can be attributed to editorial intervention. The most striking variants in the Folio are represented by the regularisation of colloquial forms such as 'a' for 'he', the replacement of single words and the addition of words and in several cases whole half-lines in order to regularise the metre.[3] These textual changes are certainly not compositorial, and must be attributed to the copy-text that went to the printers.

The nature of such copy has been studied by Eleanor Prosser,[4] who reached the conclusion that the text was prepared for the printer by a highly qualified scribe more experienced in the transcription of literary than of theatrical works. 'Using Qa as his copy, he consulted a supplementary manuscript, probably Shakespeare's foul papers, primarily to obtain copies for passages that are omitted in the Quarto'; the scribe, having a literary turn of mind, set out to improve and regularise the text by correcting what he considered metrical and formal faults. The theory of an intermediate transcript by an interfering scribe who had highly personal notions of what a play text should be like is inherently more plausible than the alternative suggestions that the Folio was based either on a hand-corrected copy of the quarto, or on a prompt-book of later date than the foul papers used as copy for the quarto, or, finally, on a transcript put together from actors' parts with the aid of the quarto.[5] The Folio text presents none of the features of a prompt-book, while the idea of a text assembled from actors' parts is highly improbable in itself, and unsupported by internal evidence: even if some of the words and sentences or half-lines added to the text can be construed as interpolations by actors, it is very unlikely that they should have taken the trouble of actually writing them into their parts. At all events, if this were the case, the interpolations should be disregarded as having no authorial sanction.

Even in the matter of regularising entrance stage directions, the Folio scribe does not

---

[1]  The words 'God' and 'the Lord' and expressions containing them are omitted or replaced in the Folio text no less than 70 times. The same procedure applies to 'Jesu', 'Mass' and, more surprisingly, 'faith', even in such current expressions as 'i'faith' or 'good faith'. The same kind of censorship applies to all interjections beginning with 'by', such as 'by this light' (2.2.49), 'by this hand' (2.2.34 and 2.4.123), and even 'by my troth', which is suppressed no less than ten times. 'Upon my soul' is replaced with 'upon my life' at 3.1.98 and 4.1.288, 'marry' disappears at 2.2.30 and 5.1.9 and the expression 'blessed are they' becomes 'happy are they' at 5.3.112. Whoever prepared the copy for the press seems to have been more scrupulous with this than with any of the other texts included in the Folio.

[2]  The omission in the Folio text of 1.2.168–73 is generally attributed to patriotic reasons, but those at 2.1.90–1, 2.2.19–22, 2.4.32, 44, 106–7, 115–16, and 3.2.254–8 concern passages with marked sexual innuendoes.

[3]  This occurs essentially in 4.2; see Commentary to lines 52, 120, 132, 179, 306, and 348; but the rearrangement of 204–5 may be part of the same process of regularisation, and the same is true of 1.1.96 and 4.1.345.

[4]  *Shakespeare's Anonymous Editors. Scribe and Compositor in the Folio Text of '2 Henry IV'*, 1981.

[5]  The arguments in favour of the latter theory are set out by P. H. Davison in the commentary and account of the text of his New Penguin edition of *The Second Part of King Henry the Fourth* (1977), especially pp. 292–5.

appear to be altogether reliable. Though rightly eliminating the 'ghost characters' that figure in several of the quarto directions,[1] he leaves out also some significant features of the original authorial directions, such as the description of Rumour's costume at Induction 0 SD (*painted full of tongues*), or the entrance of Lord Bardolph at 1.1. *at one door*. On the other hand, he occasionally includes in opening stage directions characters who come on stage much later – and this does not seem to be due to a mistaken notion of the scribal practice of 'massed entrances', but simply to a habit of running his eye down the speech headings in the rest of the scene before deciding who enters at the beginning, overlooking in so doing the later entrances of single characters; this accounts, for instance, for the presence of Colevile and Westmoreland in the opening direction of 4.1.[2]

In view of the nature of the copy, it appears that the Folio text has no real authority. The quarto readings should be preferred, except for the few cases in which the Folio corrects obvious mistakes in the quarto. This also implies that the addition in the Folio of words and sentences for the purpose of regularising the metre or 'improving' and correcting the language (the elimination of some typical Quicklyisms is significant)[3] should be ignored, while those passages that the Folio omitted because they might have appeared variously offensive to the eye and ear of the scribe[4] should be restored. The present edition, instead of accepting the uneasy compromise between the adoption of Folio and quarto readings followed by most modern editors, is firmly based on the quarto, and it not only accepts (frequently for the first time in a recent edition) nearly all the quarto readings whose adoption is recommended by Prosser,[5] but, at least in the case of Induction 16,[6] adds to them. All the same, there is no escaping the fact that the quarto itself is not exempt from mistakes and misreadings, and, more serious, that at least eight passages of some length do not appear in it.

The passages in question, present in the Folio and not in the quarto, are the following:

A  1.1.166–79  Part of a speech assigned to Morton recalling Northumberland to his responsibilities. My reasons for reassigning to Lord Bardolph the previous three lines, present also in the quarto, are connected with the discussion of 1.161, assigned by the quarto to *Vmfr.* and omitted by the Folio.[7]

B  1.1.189–209  Most of another speech of Morton, announcing the rebellion of the Archbishop of York and recalling the killing of Richard II.

---

[1] Notably *Fauconbridge* at 1.3.0, *Sir Iohn Blunt* at 3.1.31, *Bardolfe* (meaning Lord Bardolph) at 4.1.0, *Kent* at 4.2.0, *Westmerland* at 5.2.0, and *Blunt* at 5.2.41 – though the last can be justified (see Commentary to 5.2.41 SD). The case of *Sir Iohn Russel* at 2.2.0 is different, and is discussed at p. 13 above.

[2] See Commentary to 4.1.0 SD, and compare *Bardolfe, and Page* at 2.2.0, and *Pistoll* at 5.3.0.

[3] The regularisation of 'Wheeson' at 2.1.69, 'familiarity' at 2.1.77, 'debuty' at 2.4.68, 'Wedsday' at 2.4.69 and, more seriously, 'atomy' at 5.4.25 are cases in point. Throughout the Folio text the colloquial pronoun 'a' is always changed into 'he', and conditional 'and' into 'if', while all contractions, as Shaaber puts it, 'are remorselessly expanded'. He remarks that 'a systematic effort appears to have been made to divest Q of its ragged and homely garb and to fit it with a Sunday suit' (Shaaber, p. 503).

[4] See Prosser, *Anonymous Editors*, pp. 122–62.

[5] See Prosser, *Anonymous Editors*, Appendix C, pp. 191–4.

[6] See Commentary to the relevant line. Among recent editions, only the Oxford (1986) has restored the quarto reading in this case, though it had been suggested by Shaaber (p. 13), and by Berger–Williams, p. 241.

[7] Melchiori, 'Umfrevile', pp. 199–210.

C 1.3.21–4   Part of a short speech of Lord Bardolph, curiously recalling Rumour's words in the Induction.[1]

D 1.3.36–55   The first part of a speech of Lord Bardolph, developing elaborate metaphors from nature and architecture for the rebels' action.

E 1.3.85–108   A whole speech by the Archbishop justifying the rebels' action and evoking the death of Richard II and Bullingbrook's usurpation.

F 2.3.23–45   Part of Lady Percy's speech celebrating Hotspur.

G 4.1.55–79   Most of another speech by the Archbishop justifying to Westmoreland the rebels' position and evoking Richard II's death.

H 4.1.103–39   The debate between Westmoreland and Mowbray on the injuries suffered by the rebels at Bullingbrook's hands. This follows closely upon one of the most muddled and controversial passages in the play (4.1.93–6).

Most editors of the play have assumed that these passages were originally in Shakespeare's text, the foul papers on which the quarto is based. In the 1930s Alfred Hart advanced an explanation for the omission of the eight passages (as well as the omission of the whole of 3.1 from the first issue of the quarto) which enjoyed ample credit, albeit with slight adjustments of focus.[2] He separated the omissions into two groups: the reasons for omissions A, C, D and F were simply of a theatrical nature: those passages 'are of poetical or amplificatory rather than dramatic value', and therefore 'were struck out in order to shorten the play for the stage'. It should be noted that these cuts shorten the play by hardly more than 60 lines, just over a couple of minutes of playing time in the performance of a text that totalled over 3,300 lines. Omissions B, E, G and H are more substantial, totalling over 100 lines – or double that figure if we include 3.1 in the count. All these passages mention more strictly political matters, such as the death of Richard II, Bullingbrook's accession,[3] and the role of the Archbishop of York in the rebellion; it is logical to think that the cuts were due to some sort of censorial intervention, whether official or by the company itself, or even by the printers, in order to avoid possible trouble. Such interventions, though, would normally take place on a fair copy or prompt-book, rather than foul papers, such as were used for the quarto copy.

Very recently, in the course of their work on the new Oxford Shakespeare, John Jowett and Gary Taylor have totally reversed the accepted explanations by suggesting that to call 'omissions' the passages not appearing in the quarto is wrong. In their view, they were not in most cases omitted in the printing; rather, they are later authorial interpolations into the text.[4] Their starting point, as already noted in the Introduction (p. 2 above), is the insertion as a cancel in the second issue of the quarto (Qb) of a whole new scene, 3.1, which did not appear in the first issue (Qa). They correctly surmise that

[1] 1.3.23: 'Conjecture, expectation and surmise'; compare Induction 16, 'surmises, Jealousy's conjectures'. This supports the suggestion that the same actor was meant to double Rumour and Lord Bardolph; see Commentary to 1.1.0 SD.

[2] Alfred Hart, 'Was the Second Part of *King Henry the Fourth* censored?', in his *Shakespeare and the Homilies*, 1934, pp. 154–218.

[3] The only mention of Bullingbrook's name surviving in the quarto is at 3.1.70, in the scene missing from the first issue of the book, discussed in the next paragraph.

[4] Jowett–Taylor.

the scene must have filled the two sides of a separate leaf,[f] but instead of thinking, as most previous editors, that the leaf was not included in Qa because the compositor overlooked some sort of marginal mark in the foul papers directing him to insert the contents of the loose leaf in its right place, they maintain that the scene was actually an authorial afterthought. The entrance of Justice Shallow and Justice Silence (now scene 3.2) was meant to follow immediately upon the exit of the Hostess and Doll at the end of 2.4. In fact in Q, sig. E3ᵛ, Shallow's first speech seems to echo the Hostess's last words:

> *Hoſt.* O runne Doll, runne. runne good Doll, come, ſhee
> comes blubberd, yea? wil you come Doll? *exeunt*
>      *Enter Iuſtice Shallow, and Iuſtice Silens.*
>  *Sha.* Come on, come on, come on, giue me your hand ſir,
> giue me your hand ſir, an early ſtirrer, by the Roode: and how
> doth my good cooſin Silence?

Jowett and Taylor suggest (p. 39) that 'when he finished the rough draft of the play Shakespeare was apparently dissatisfied with the balance between its comic and serious material, and set out to expand the political plot ... We must therefore begin to suspect that some of the other material not present in Qa is absent from that text not because of interference by the censor, but because it had not yet been written when Shakespeare finished the foul papers which were eventually handed over to the printer.' In other words, the passages appearing only in F should in most cases be considered not as omissions for a variety of reasons from Q, but as expansions of the text originally delivered to Valentine Simmes. And they proceed to give the reasons for the different insertions. Those I have listed here as A, C, D, F – that is to say, passages that do not contain allusions which could have alarmed the censor – are, in their view, merely intended to reinforce the 'historical' sections of the play. But in the case of B and G they acknowledge that the two passages, of undoubted political relevance, must have been present in the copy handed to the printer. Valentine Simmes, who on other occasions had proved to be a cautious workman,[2] fearful of the allusions in them to the miserable end of Richard II, decided of his own accord not to print them. The other two 'political' passages (E and H) which do not appear in the quarto, however, are taken to be later amplifications of the text. They do acknowledge, though, that in these cases the quarto text presents possible traces of excision. In fact at 1.3.85 the last line of Hastings's speech in the quarto is incomplete and the next full line is assigned to the Archbishop instead of Mowbray as in the Folio.

The simplest explanation of this quarto peculiarity, though, is that the lengthy speech of the Archbishop, the first words of which complete Hastings's unfinished line, was

---

[1] From the addition in Hand D in the manuscript *Book of Sir Thomas More*, it appears that Shakespeare averaged some 49 lines per page, considerably fewer than any of the other contributors to that play. Taking into account the stage directions and divided lines, the 100-odd lines of 3.1, written out in Shakespeare's handwriting, would just about fill the two sides of a leaf.

[2] According to Jowett and Taylor ('Sprinklings of authority: the Folio text of *Richard II*', *SB* 38 (1985), 194–8) Simmes might have been responsible for the omission of the deposition scene from the 1597 quarto of *Richard II*, which he printed for Andrew Wise, while G. K. Hunter in his edition of John Marston's *The Malcontent*, 1957, pp. xxviii–xxxi, suggests that he probably omitted sensitive material from the 1604 quarto of that play, which he printed for William Aspley.

present but marked for omission in the copy that went to the printer. The quarto compositor set the speech heading *Bifh*, but then moved on directly to the first undeleted line, ignoring the fact that it was preceded by a different heading.

The case of passage H is more serious: in the quarto not only does Mowbray's speech at 4.1.99–103 end with an incomplete line, but Westmoreland's rejoinder beginning with the full line (140) 'But this is meere digression from my purpose' does not make sense, in so much as in that text there has been no digression from the main subject, which is the rebellion. The digression which he is referring to is obviously the discussion of the rights and wrongs of the Earl of Hereford's banishment by Richard II at Coventry, which appears only in the Folio text. Westmoreland's words have meaning only if we restore to the text the passage in the Folio (4.1.103–39).

But in at least these two cases there is even firmer evidence (ignored by most editors) of the manipulation or confusion of the copy that went to the printer of the quarto: only a few lines before each of these passages there are two of the most puzzling misunderstandings in the quarto text. At 1.3.78–80 the quarto reads (sig. C1):

> *Haft.* If he fhould do fo , French and Welch he leaues his
> back vnarmde, they baying him at the heeles neuer feare that.

It seems obvious that the manuscript read at this point:

> *Hast.* If he should do so, he leaves his back unarmed,
>      they baying him at the heels – never fear that.

and that somebody, possibly the author himself, finding unclear the pronoun 'they', which refers to 'one power against the French, And one against Glendower' at 71–2 above, decided to replace it with the words '[the] French and Welsh', and presumably interlined them; but the compositor misunderstood the correction ('they' into 'the' with three added words), an understandable confusion since it occurred on a page already heavily marked in order to delete the long speech of the Archbishop a few lines later (1.3.85–108).

A much more serious confusion occurs in the quarto only a few lines before the missing speeches of Westmoreland and Mowbray at 4.1.103–39. It is perhaps the most debated textual problem in the play,[1] and it is connected with the press corrections during the printing of the quarto, which presents two states. 4.1.90–6 read in the uncorrected state (sig. F4ᵛ):

> What peere hath beene fubornde to grate on you?
> That you fhould feale this lawleffe bloody booke
> Offorgde rebellion with a feale diuine,
> And confecrate commotions bitter edge.
>     *Bifhop* My brother Generall, the common wealth
> To brother borne an houfhold cruelty.
> I make my quarrell in particular.

---

[1]   Alice Walker, 'The cancelled lines in *2 Henry IV*, IV.i.93,95', *The Library* 5th ser. 6 (1951), 115–16, and *Textual Problems of the First Folio*, 1953, pp. 105–6, suggests that the lines were marked for cutting by the quarto proof-corrector in mistake for 101–3. Compare A. R. Humphreys in the introduction to his Arden edition of the play

In the corrected state of the quarto, however, lines 93 ('And conʃecrate commotions bitter edge') and 95 ('To brother borne an houʃhold cruelty') are altogether omitted, and the Folio follows suit. It is indeed difficult to make sense out of the Archbishop's speech in either state (see the Commentary to the relevant passage), but the deletion of the last line of the previous speech seems totally unjustified. As in the case of the passage at 1.3.78–80 that we saw before, the most reasonable explanation seems to be the following. The printer was confronted with a section of the manuscript heavily interfered with by a reviser who had deliberately set out to attenuate the justification offered by the rebels for their action. He marked for deletion 25 lines (55–79) of the Archbishop's speech at 53–87,[1] and 37 lines (103–39) out of the long debate between Mowbray and Westmoreland beginning at 99, and made excisions and corrections in the lines in between (88–98 – significantly Mowbray's speech at 99 begins without a capital, as if the speech heading had been moved there from a different position). The printer, confronted with copy in a fairly chaotic state, made it out as best he could; the proof-reader in turn, checking the sheet in its first state against the manuscript, interpreted as deletions the reviser's marks in it at lines 93 and 95 and proceeded accordingly. The omission of the two lines in the Folio as well is explained by the fact that the scribe who prepared the copy for it checked at this point the manuscript he was working from against a copy of the quarto containing the page in its corrected state.

The implication is, in both the cases examined, that the passages not figuring in the quarto were actually present in the manuscript that went to the printer; that the manuscript had been subjected before printing to some kind of revision; that at least one of the two passages (4.1.55–79) the presence of which in the manuscript is granted by Jowett and Taylor, was not necessarily suppressed by Simmes, but omitted as part of the general revision – and this of course holds good also for the other (Morton's speech at 1.1.189–209).[2] If we turn now to the other four passages (A, C, D, F) with no strong political implications that Jowett and Taylor consider as later additions in order to reinforce the historical aspects of the play, the state of the original editions reveals in these cases too confusions suggesting that these passages also were present in the original copy that went to the quarto printer, albeit marked for omission. The most notable is that occurring in the quarto at 1.1.161–5, immediately preceding the first major omission in the text. This will be discussed in a moment. However, in the case of Lord Bardolph's speech at 1.3.36–55, the confusion occurs in the first three lines, which appear only in the Folio: Shaaber's Variorum Edition lists over thirty different modern emendations of this inextricably tangled passage.[3] I take this to be a sign that the reviser

---

(1966), pp. lxxii–lxxiii, and see Gilian West, 'Scroop's quarrel: a note on *2 Henry IV*, iv.i.88–96', *ELN* 18 (1981), 174–5.

[1] It is the strongest plea for the rebels' cause, insisting on the theme of the diseased state, which links up with that of the king's illness.

[2] Discussing the absence in the quarto of 1.1.189–209 and 4.1.55–79, Jowett and Taylor remark (p. 41): 'We ought therefore reasonably to suspect ... that Q is defective at two points, and that in both places the missing material had to do with an Archbishop's initiation and defence of a rebellion against the King of England.' And (p. 43), 'We are therefore strongly inclined to regard them as an integral part of the play from its inception, excised in 1600 by the ecclesiastical censor or the printer because of their dangerous relevance to a contemporary political crisis.'

[3] Shaaber, pp. 92–5.

of the manuscript had marked the beginning of Lord Bardolph's speech so heavily for deletion that neither the transcriber of the prompt-book nor the literary-minded scribe who prepared the copy for the Folio was able to decipher the lines, and they patched them up as best they could.

It seems safe to conclude that all eight passages appearing only in the Folio were actually present in the foul papers used as copy by the quarto printer. Such foul papers, though, had undergone a thorough revision, presumably in view of their transcription by the person in charge of preparing the prompt-book for the early performances of the play: the reviser would take special care to mark in them the lines and speeches that the players had decided to omit or modify substantially, but relied on the prompter's ability in such matters as stage directions and speech headings, which had to be regularised at the moment of writing the prompt-book. There is little doubt that at least four of the omissions were decided upon in order to avoid further difficulties with the Master of the Revels, especially if the composition of *Part Two* followed the pattern I have outlined in the Introduction to this edition.[1] The reasons for the remaining four omissions may well have been mainly of a theatrical nature (though keeping in mind the general principle of weakening the case for the rebels),[2] but were perhaps not suggested merely by the need of shortening the play in performance. The section '*Part Two* on the stage' (pp. 31–6 above) connects these cuts with the practice of doubling.

In the case of omission A the issue is somewhat obscured by the state of the quarto, which reads at sig. B1 (161–5; 180–1):

> *Vmfr.* This ſtrained paſſion doth you wrong my lord.
> *Bard.* Sweet earle, diuorce not wiſedom from your honor,
> *Mour.* The liues of all your louing complices,
> Leaue on you health, the which if you giue ore,
> To ſtormy paſſion muſt perforce decay.
> *Bard.* We all that are ingaged to this loſſe,
> Knew that we ventured on ſuch dangerous ſeas,

The Folio instead (Histories, sig. g1ᵛ) omits the first of these lines and prints:

> And darkneſſe be the burier of the dead.          (Honor.
> *L.Bar.* Sweet Earle, diuorce not wiſedom from your
> *Mor.* The liues of all your louing Complices
> Leane-on your health, the which if you giue-o're
> To ſtormy Paſſion, muſt perforce decay.
> You caſt th'euent of Warre (my Noble Lord).

[This is the first of the fifteen lines appearing only in the Folio; after them the Folio proceeds with:]

> *L.Bar.* We all that are engaged to this loſſe,
> Knew that we ventur'd on ſuch dangerous Seas,

---

[1] See 'The Henriad as remake' and 'Rewriting the remake', pp. 9–15 above.          [2] See pp. 23–4 above.

Once again the quarto reflects at this point a manuscript copy which had been very heavily tampered with: the reviser, when crossing out the fifteen lines that the actors had decided to omit, corrected also the previous passage and tried to redistribute the speeches. The form of address 'my noble lord' in the first of the omitted lines shows that this was not the continuation of a speech already begun (as the Folio prints it), but the beginning of a new speech. In fact Morton uses practically the same form ('my most Noble Lord') in the first line of his next speech at 187. It appears that, having suppressed the whole of Morton's speech, the reviser intended to transfer from Lord Bardolph to him the preceding speech beginning with the words 'Sweet earl', otherwise there would have been two consecutive speeches by the same speaker. The comma instead of a full stop at the end of 162 shows that 162–5 were originally all one speech, and the familiar form of address 'sweet earl' indicates Lord Bardolph as the only possible speaker. But the reviser apparently made a very bad job of the crossing out and replacement of speech headings, which involved also 161, a one-line speech which could not originally have been spoken by Lord Bardolph since he began addressing the earl only in the next line, and which must therefore have been said by Morton. The compositor was faced with crossed-out speech headings at 161 and 162 and the scribbled words *Bard.* and *Mour.* more or less in the left margin of 162 and 163 respectively. He started then to look for the speaker of 161, a line which remained unassigned, and running his eye over the previous pages of his copy-text he found Sir John Umfrevile mentioned at 34 ('My lord, ſir Iohn Vmfreuile turnd me backe'); taking him to be a character in the scene, he introduced the heading *Vmfr.* at this point. In his turn, the scribe who prepared the copy for the Folio, finding some confusion in the manuscript, checked it against the quarto and decided to omit a line assigned to a non-existent character. In other words, the Folio text represents merely the fourth stage in a series of textual misunderstandings that I have traced elsewhere,[1] namely:

1. Shakespeare originally wrote this part of the scene assigning 161 to Morton, 162–5 to Lord Bardolph, 166–79 to Morton, 180–6 to Lord Bardolph, and 187–209 to Morton.

2. Following the decision to suppress Morton's speeches at 166–79 and 189–209, a reviser made the excisions in the foul papers and redistributed the surviving speeches: 161 to Lord Bardolph, 162–5 to Morton, 180–6 to Lord Bardolph, 187–8 to Morton.

3. The quarto compositor, misunderstanding the reviser's intentions, gave 161 to the non-existent *Vmfr.*, 162 to Lord Bardolph, 163–5 to Morton, 180–6 to Lord Bardolph, 187–8 to Morton.

4. The scribe who prepared the copy for the Folio, in restoring the two missing passages, omitted 161 altogether and gave 162 to Lord Bardolph, 163–79 to Morton, 180–6 to Lord Bardolph, and 187–209 to Morton.

The Folio arrangement of the speeches has no authority; its one merit is that of preserving the suppressed passages, which should therefore be restored to the text as originally written, since we can be sure that the omissions, though obviously accepted as a matter of theatrical expediency, were not intended by the author.

[1] Melchiori, 'Umfrevile'.

This leads us back to the question of the practice of doubling, not as the main but as a parallel reason for the omission of the passages without political relevance. It is notable that all four passages belong to speakers who figure only in one scene (Morton, Lady Percy) or at most two (Lord Bardolph). The quality of the verse suggests that it was meant for powerful speakers, not just walk-on players. Such actors could not be wasted in small parts, they had to be reutilised in other relevant roles in the course of the performance. Morton is a case in point: he is a fictional character introduced in the play more in the role of the historian, the chronicler of true events, than in that of the traditional messenger; the extent of his part goes well beyond what could be expected from a figure appearing only in the first scene. When political reasons suggested that his longest and most significant speech should be cut, it seemed appropriate to diminish also the rest of his role, by eliminating another speech that was merely a comment on the situation. In this way the actor had to memorise 42 instead of 77 lines[1] as Morton, and would be available to take on an exacting role in the later scenes, such as, for instance, that of the Archbishop of York (originally 148 lines, reduced to 99 after the cuts).

The likelihood that the spoken roles of Lord Bardolph and Lady Percy were reduced for the same reasons (from 88 to 64 lines and from 46 lines to 23 respectively) has already been put forward at pp. 32–3 above, and seems particularly strong in the case of the female role: one could not ask a young boy to learn too long a verse tirade if he also had to memorise for the same play Doll Tearsheet's difficult prose part.[2]

We can conclude not only that the eight major passages missing in the quarto were actually present in the foul papers on which the edition is based, but also that they were crossed out or otherwise marked for deletion by a reviser acting upon the players' instructions, with a view to preparing the copy for the book-keeper in charge of getting the prompt-book ready. The foul papers retained the typical signs of authorial inadvertency, such as unmarked exits, permissive or incomplete stage directions,[3] entrances for characters who never speak because the author has changed his mind about their presence in the scene.[4] A further token of Shakespeare's hand is the spelling 'Scilens' for 'Silence' which occurs nineteen times in 3.2 and 5.3 (including the abbreviated form 'Scil.'), a spelling which is found elsewhere only in the Shakespearean addition to the manuscript *Book of Sir Thomas More*.[5]

But another peculiarity of these foul papers has hardly been noticed: they included as well one or two pages or leaves left over from the earlier version of the Henry play, that written and presumably acted in 1596, which was objected to by the Brooke, Russell and Harvey families. The section 'The Henriad as remake' (pp. 12–13 above) provides the evidence for believing that at least 1.2.74–135 and 2.2.1–52 are such survivals, revealed

---

[1] Data based on the rearrangement of Morton's speeches suggested in the previous paragraphs.
[2] Boys' parts are generally in verse for ease of memorisation. The greater difficulty of memorising prose was propounded by the Italian tragic poet G. B. Della Porta in his treatise *L'arte di Ricordare* (1566, Latin translation 1602).
[3] For instance *Enter ... at one doore* at 1.1.0, *alone, with his page...* at 1.2.0, *an Officer or two* at 2.1.0, *Sir Iohn Russel, with other* at 2.2.0, *a Drawer or two* at 2.4.0, *Bardolfe, and one with him* at 3.2.44, *... and his armie* at 4.1.228, *Sincklo and three or foure officers* at 5.4.0.
[4] See p. 192 above, n. 1.
[5] See J. Dover Wilson, 'The new way with Shakespeare's text: an introduction for lay readers. III In sight of Shakespeare's manuscripts', *S.Sur.* 9 (1956), 69–80.

by the presence of the speech heading *Old.* at 1.2.96, and by the name of *ſir Iohn Ruſſel* in the entrance stage direction of 2.2. Owing to the price of paper – an imported commodity – the insertion into new manuscripts of those parts of the earlier versions which could be fitted into them with only essential corrections was far from rare. A study of the speech headings in the quarto version of 1.2 confirms this. The importance of the alternative speech headings for Falstaff and the Lord Chief Justice in establishing the nature of the copy for the quarto has been thoroughly discussed in terms of the play as a whole by George Walton Williams.[1] But a closer look at this particular scene may yield further information. The speech heading for Falstaff is *Iohn.* or *sir Iohn.* from the beginning of the scene till 70 and then again from 147 to the end; however, from 75 to 131 we find *Falſt.* except for one *sir Iohn.* at 82 and one *Old.* at 96. The Lord Chief Justice is designated in speech headings as *Iuſtice* or *Iuſt.* from his first speech at 45 to 130 while from 141 onwards he becomes *Lo.* or *Lord.* This change in the designation of the two main speakers in the scene suggests a different origin for the central part of it, roughly the section between 74 and 135, a section that, from what we know of Shakespeare's handwriting, would fill one side of a manuscript leaf.[2] Besides, the muddles occurring at 135–7 (set right in the Folio) suggest that the printer was put off by being confronted with an awkward transition from one kind of copy to another.[3] Since an interview between the Lord Chief Justice and the fat knight must have figured also in the original Oldcastle version of the play, it is reasonable to think that Shakespeare, in providing a new setting for it in the rewritten text with Falstaff replacing Oldcastle, decided to save paper and labour by inserting in the new manuscript the relevant page of the original with the necessary changes. The speech headings *Old.* in the original were systematically turned by the hand of a reviser into *Falſt.*, but the one at 96 was overlooked.

The same line of reasoning applies to the first section of 2.2, a dialogue between the prince and Poins which, from my tentative reconstruction of the ur-*Henry IV*,[4] seems to have occupied a different place in the earlier version of the play. In this instance the presence of *ſir Iohn Ruſſel* in the entrance stage direction is not a case of a 'ghost character' that the author later decided not to introduce into the scene, but a survival from the Oldcastle version in an odd page of it that the author had inserted in the new copy.

Other leaves or pages from the original Oldcastle version may have been incorporated with appropriate readjustments in the foul papers on which the quarto is based, especially as sections of 4.2, 5.2 and 5.5, but in the absence of solid evidence it is impossible to determine whether this was actually the case or whether such passages were merely transcribed onto the new copy.

A final anomaly in the printing of the quarto should be considered at this point: the cancel quire E3–6ᵛ containing 3.1, which replaced in the second issue of the book (Qb)

---

[1] 'The text of *2 Henry IV*', pp. 176–9.

[2] See p. 194 above, n. 1.

[3] The quarto makes nonsense of the sentence 'all the other gifts appertinent to man, as the malice of this age shapes them,' by misreading 'his' for 'this' and 'the one' for 'them', as well as omitting the comma after the last word.

[4] At pp. 12–13 above, and in Melchiori, 'The ur-*Henry IV*', pp. 69–70.

leaves E3–4$^v$ in the first issue (Qa), which did not include that scene. The reasons for the cancel are amply discussed at pp. 3, 12, 36 above. The omission of 3.1 from Qa can hardly be a simple case of inadvertency by the printers,[1] or of timidity on the part of Valentine Simmes, fearful of the extended political implications of it.[2] How could he be induced to go to the trouble of producing a cancel in this one instance when he had not reinstated the other passages omitted for political reasons? There is evidence instead that in writing *Part Two* as a sequel to the successful *History of Henrie the Fourth* Shakespeare did not at first contemplate the inclusion of 3.1 at this point.[3] But it is also unthinkable that, when he felt the need of breaking the sequence of comic scenes with the presentation of the distressed and sick state of the king and the kingdom, he wrote at very short notice these magnificent 107 lines. In fact they existed already as part of the discarded material in the ur-*Henry IV*. He simply decided at the last moment, when the printing of the foul papers was already at an advanced stage, to insert among them the recovered leaf containing the scene, as he had done with the pages of the earlier manuscript containing such passages as 1.2.76–135 or 2.2.1–52. The insertion was made when the reviser who had been at work on the rest of the foul papers had already completed his job, so that they escaped his attention.

The replacement of two leaves of quire E with the four of the cancel in order to accommodate 3.1 entailed the resetting of the last part of 2.4 (277–320) and of the beginning of 3.2 (1–85). The variants between the two printings have been thoroughly studied,[4] but, though very numerous, none of them seems particularly significant, except for the fact that the spelling 'Scilens' or 'Scil.' found three times in the first issue (71, 72, 74) is regularised in the second as 'Silens'. The same compositor is responsible for both settings, and the spelling 'Silens', abbreviated 'Si.' in speech headings, figures eleven times before line 44 in the first issue. The one variant of note is not between the two issues but between the uncorrected and the corrected state of the first issue. At 45–6 uncorrected Qa has two consecutive speeches both headed *Bardolfe*. In the corrected state (and in Qb) the first heading is omitted, so that the speech is continued to Silence, while in the Folio it is assigned to Shallow. This point and the suggested emendations are discussed in the Commentary, but there is no doubt that the line belongs to one of the Justices rather than Bardolph.

In conclusion, of the two early printings of the play (the later Folios merely reproduce the first, with some conjectural emendations and a few additional errors), the 1600 quarto is certainly very close to an authorial manuscript, to the point of revealing the nature of the manuscript itself. The 1623 Folio text, however, incorporates a number of would-be improvements and regularisations which are the result not of theatrical practice or even expediency (which would carry some weight with a dramatist like

---

[1] The point is discussed at pp. 3–5 above.
[2] Jowett and Taylor devote the first part of their paper to a well-argued rejection of these theories, especially Hart's in his *Shakespeare and the Homilies*, maintaining that it was firstly heavily abridged for theatrical reasons, and then omitted altogether to satisfy the censor.
[3] See pp. 193–4 above.
[4] Thomas L. Berger and George Walton Williams, 'Variants in the quarto of Shakespeare's *2 Henry IV*', *The Library* 6th ser. 3 (1981), 109–18.

Shakespeare) but of a misleadingly pedantic scribe and of an undistinguished compositor. The quarto is therefore to be preferred throughout, except in the case of the missing passages, which must be restored to the text because there is enough evidence in the quarto itself to show that they did exist in the original manuscript, and were not omitted by the author's wish, though perhaps – in view of pressing theatrical as well as political reasons – with his consent.

# APPENDIX 1: SHAKESPEARE'S USE OF HOLINSHED

There is no doubt that the *Chronicles* of Raphael Holinshed, in the much enlarged posthumous edition of 1586–7, are the main and practically only source of the strictly historical matter incorporated in the *Henry* plays. It is frequently forgotten, though, that, as Michael Tomlinson put it (*L&H* 10 (1984), 46–58), Shakespeare 'uses sources to supply little more than a factual framework, from which he constructs a completely new experience, embodying a new set of reflections and thought processes'. Some of the following extracts are intended to illustrate this point, showing how Holinshed suggested not only facts, but the introduction of the allegory of Rumour, as well as the adoption of some names, such as Sir John Russell and Umfrevile, which were destined to disappear in the final version of *Part Two*. References are to page/column/line of the 1587 edition of the third volume of the *Chronicles*. The marginal notes which serve to summarise the text ('A politike madnesse', 'The valiant dooings of the earle Dowglas') have been omitted.

Sir John Russell (see 2.2 headnote) and the unhouseled execution of Scroop (4.1.94–6)

[From the Reign of Richard II, 498/1/36 ff.] [When the Duke of York was advertised of the approach of Bullingbrook] he sent . . . for the lord treasuror William Scroope earle of Wiltshire, and other of the kings priuie councell, as Iohn Bushie, William Bagot, Henrie Greene, and Iohn Russell knights . . .
[498/2/63–499/1/3] [At Bristow] There were inclosed within the castell the lord William Scroope earle of Wiltshire and treasuror of England, sir Henrie Greene, and sir Iohn Bushie knights, who prepared to make resistance; but when it would not preuaile, they were taken and brought foorth bound as prisoners into the campe, before the duke of Lancaster. On the morow next insuing, they were arraigned before the constable and marshall, and found giltie of treason, for misgouerning the king and realme, and foorthwith had their heads smit off. Sir Iohn Russell was also taken there, who feining himselfe to be out of his wits, escaped their hands for a time.

Archbishop Scroop's 'brother born' (4.1.95)

[From the Reign of Henry IV, 1403, 522/1/15–18] The Persies to make their part seeme good, deuised certeine articles, by the aduise of Richard Scroope, archbishop of Yorke, brother to the lord Scroope, whome king Henrie had caused to be beheaded at Bristow . . .

The Battle of Shrewsbury (1.1.105–35)

[523/2/32–54] This battell lasted three long houres, with indifferent fortune on both parts, till at length, the king crieng saint George victorie, brake the arraie of his enimies, and aduentured so farre, that (as some write) the earle Dowglas strake him downe, & at that instant slue sir Walter Blunt, and three other, apparelled in the kings sute and clothing, saieng: I maruell to see so many kings thus suddenlie arise one in the necke of an other. The king in deed was raised, & did that daie manie a noble feat of armes, for as it is written, he slue that daie with his owne hands six and thirty persons of his enimies. The other on his part incouraged by his doings, fought valiantlie, and slue the lord Persie, called sir Henrie Hotspurre. To conclude, the kings enimies were vanquished, and put to flight, in which flight, the earle of Dowglas, for hast, falling from the crag of an hie mounteine, brake one of his cullions, and was taken, and for his valiantnesse, of the king frankelie and freelie deliuered.

There was also taken the earle of Worcester, the procuror and setter foorth of all this mischeefe.

### Glendower and Rumour (see Induction)

[1405. 525/1/46–52] All this summer, Owen Glendouer and his adherents, robbed, burned, and destroied the countries adioining neere to the places where he hanted, and one while by sleight & guileful policie, an other while by open force, he tooke and slue manie Englishmen, brake downe certeine castels which he wan, and some he fortified and kept for his owne defense...

[525/1/60–5] Also, the old countesse of Oxford, mother to Robert Veere late duke of Ireland, that died at Louaine, caused certeine of hir seruants, and other such as she durst trust, to publish and brute abroad, thorough all parts of Essex, that king Richard was aliue, and that he would shortlie come to light, and claime his former estate, honor, and dignitie.

[525/2/19–29] These forged inuentions caused manie to beleeue the brute raised by the countesse of Oxford, for the which they came in trouble, were apprehended and committed to prison. The countesse hir selfe was shut vp in close prison, and all hir goods were confiscat, and hir secretarie drawen and hanged, that had spred abroad this fained report, in going vp and downe the countrie, blowing into mens eares that king Richard was aliue, & affirming that he had spoken with him in such a place and in such a place, apparelled in this raiment and that raiment, with such like circumstances.

### Clarence and Kent in France (see 4.2.0 SD n.). The Gaultree episode (see 4.1.)

[1405. 529/1/46–530/2/43] Whilest such dooings were in hand betwixt the English and French, as the besieging of Marke castell by the earle of saint Paule, and the sending foorth of the English fleet, vnder the gouernance of the lord Thomas of Lancaster, and the earle of Kent, the king was minded to haue gone into Wales against the Welsh rebels, that vnder their cheefteine Owen Glendouer, ceassed not to doo much mischeefe still against the English subiects.

But at the same time, to his further disquieting, there was a conspiracie put in practise against him at home by the earle of Northumberland, who had conspired with Richard Scroope archbishop of Yorke Thomas Mowbraie earle marshall sonne to Thomas duke of Norfolke, who for the quarrell betwixt him and king Henrie had beene banished (as ye haue heard) the lords Hastings, Fauconbridge, Berdolfe, and diuerse others. It was appointed that they should meet altogither with their whole power, vpon Yorkeswold, at a daie assigned, and that the earle of Northumberland should be cheefteine, promising to bring with him a great number of Scots. The archbishop accompanied with the earle marshall, deuised certeine articles of such matters, as it was supposed that not onelie the commonaltie of the Realme, but also the nobilitie found themselues greeued with: which articles they shewed first vnto such of their adherents as were neere about them, & after sent them abroad to their freends further off, assuring them that for redresse of such oppressions, they would shed the last drop of blood in their bodies, if need were.

The archbishop not meaning to staie after he saw himselfe accompanied with a great number of men, that came flocking to Yorke to take his part in this quarrell, foorthwith discouered his enterprise, causing the articles aforesaid to be set vp in the publike streets of the citie of Yorke, and vpon the gates of the monasteries, that ech man might vnderstand the cause that mooued him to rise in armes against the king, the reforming whereof did not yet apperteine vnto him. Herevpon knights, esquiers, gentlemen, yeomen, and other of the commons, as well of the citie, townes and countries about, being allured either for desire of change, or else for desire to see a reformation in such things as were mentioned in the articles, assembled togither in great numbers; and the archbishop comming foorth amongst them clad in armor, incouraged, exhorted, and (by all meanes he could) pricked them foorth to take the enterprise in hand, and manfullie to continue in their begun purpose, promising forgiuenesse of sinnes to all them, whose hap it was to die in the quarrell: and thus not onelie all the citizens of Yorke, but all other in the countries about, that were able to beare weapon, came to the archbishop, and the earle marshall. In deed the respect that men had to the archbishop, caused them to like the better of the cause, since the grauitie of his age, his integritie of life, and incomparable learning, with the reuerend aspect of his amiable personage, mooued all men to haue him in no small estimation.

The king aduertised of these matters, meaning to preuent them, left his iournie into Wales, and marched with all speed towards the north parts. Also Rafe Neuill earle of Westmerland, that was not farre off, togither with the lord Iohn of Lancaster the kings sonne, being informed of this rebellious attempt, assembled togither such power as they might make, and together with those which were appointed to attend on the said lord Iohn to defend the borders against the Scots, as the lord Henrie Fitzhugh, the lord Rafe Eeuers, the lord Robert Umfreuill, & others, made forward against the rebels, and comming into a plaine within the forrest of Galtree, caused their standards to be pitched downe in like sort as the archbishop had pitched his, ouer against them, being farre stronger in number of people than the other, for (as some write) there were of the rebels at the least twentie thousand men.

When the earle of Westmerland perceiued the force of the aduersaries, and that they laie still and attempted not to come forward vpon him, he subtillie deuised how to quaile their purpose, and foorthwith dispatched messengers vnto the archbishop to vnderstand the cause as it were of that great assemblie, and for what cause (contrarie to the kings peace) they came so in armour. The archbishop answered, that he tooke nothing in hand against the kings peace, but that whatsoeuer he did, tended rather to aduance the peace and quiet of the common-wealth, than otherwise; and where he and his companie were in armes, it was for feare of the king, to whom he could haue no free accesse, by reason of such a multitude of flatterers as were about him; and therefore he mainteined that his purpose to be good & profitable, as well for the king himselfe, as for the realme, if men were willing to vnderstand a truth: & herewith he shewed foorth a scroll, in which the articles were written whereof before ye haue heard.

The messengers returning to the earle of Westmerland, shewed him what they had heard & brought from the archbishop. When he had read the articles, he shewed in word and countenance outwardly that he liked of the archbishops holie and vertuous intent and purpose, promising that he and his would prosecute the same in assisting the archbishop, who reioising hereat, gaue credit to the earle, and persuaded the earle marshall (against his will as it were) to go with him to a place appointed for them to commune togither. Here when they were met with like number on either part, the articles were read ouer, and without anie more adoo, the earle of Westmerland and those that were with him agreed to doo their best, to see that a reformation might be had, according to the same.

The earle of Westmerland vsing more policie than the rest: 'Well (said he) then our trauell is come to the wished end: and where our people haue beene long in armour, let them depart home to their woonted trades and occupations: in the meane time let vs drinke togither in signe of agreement, that the people on both sides maie see it, and know that it is true, that we be light at a point.' They had no sooner shaken hands togither, but that a knight was sent streight waies from the archbishop, to bring word to the people that there was peace concluded, commanding ech man to laie aside his armes, and to resort home to their houses. The people beholding such tokens of peace, as shaking of hands, and drinking togither of the lords in louing manner, they being alreadie wearied with the vnaccustomed trauell of warre, brake vp their field and returned homewards: but in the meane time, whilest the people of the archbishops side withdrew awaie, the number of the contrarie part increased, according to order giuen by the earle of Westmerland: and yet the archbishop perceiued not that he was deceiued, vntill the earle of Westmerland arrested both him and the earle marshall with diuerse other. Thus saith Walsingham.

But others write somwhat otherwise of this matter, affirming that the earle of Westmerland in deed, and the lord Rafe Eeuers, procured the archbishop & the earle marshall, to come to a communication with them, vpon a ground iust in the midwaie betwixt both the armies, where the earle of Westmerland in talke declared to them how perilous an enterprise they had taken in hand, so to raise the people, and to mooue warre against the king, aduising them therefore to submit themselues without further delaie vnto the kings mercie, and his sonne the lord Iohn, who was present there in the field with banners spred, redie to trie the matter by dint of sword if they refused this counsell: and therefore he willed them to remember themselues well: & if they would not yeeld and craue the kings pardon, he bad them doo their best to defend themselues.

Herevpon as well the archbishop as the earle marshall submitted themselues vnto the king, and to his sonne the lord Iohn that was there present, and returned not to their armie. Wherevpon their troops scaled and fled their waies: but being pursued, manie were taken, manie slaine, and manie spoiled of that that they had about them, & so permitted to go their waies. Howsoeuer the matter was handled, true it is that the archbishop, and the earle marshall were brought to Pomfret to the king, who in this meane while was aduanced thither with his power, and from thence he went to Yorke, whither the prisoners were also brought, and there beheaded the morrow after Whitsundaie in a place without the citie, that is to vnderstand, the archbishop himselfe, the earle marshall, sir Iohn Lampleie, and sir Robert Plumpton. Vnto all which persons though indemnitie were promised, yet was the same to none of them at anie hand performed. By the issue hereof, I meane the death of the foresaid, but speciallie of the archbishop, the prophesie of a sickelie canon of Bridlington in Yorkshire fell out to be true, who darklie inough foretold this matter, & the infortunate euent thereof in these words hereafter following, saieng:

*Pacem tractabunt, sed fraudem subter arabunt,*
*Pro nulla marca, saluabitur ille hierarcha.*

The archbishop suffered death verie constantlie, insomuch as the common people tooke it he died a martyr, affirming that certeine miracles were wrought as well in the field where he was executed, as also in the place where he was buried: and immediatlie vpon such bruits, both men and women began to worship his dead carcasse, whom they loued so much, when he was aliue, till they were forbidden by the kings freends, and for feare gaue ouer to visit the place of his sepulture. The earle marshalls bodie by the kings leaue was buried in the cathedrall church, manie lamenting his destinie; but his head was set on a pole aloft on the wals for a certeine space, till by the kings permission [after the same had suffered manie a hot sunnie daie, and manie a wet shower of raine] it was taken downe and buried togither with the bodie.

After the king, accordingly as seemed to him good, had ransomed and punished by greeuous fines the citizens of Yorke (which had borne armour on their archbishops side against him) he departed frō Yorke with an armie of thirtie and seuen thousand fighting men, furnished with all prouision necessarie, marching northwards against the earle of Northumberland. At his cōming to Durham, the lord Hastings, the lord Fauconbridge, sir Iohn Colleuill of the Dale, and sir Iohn Griffith, being conuicted of the conspiracie, were there beheaded. The earle of Northumberland, hearing that his counsell was bewraied, and his confederats brought to confusion, through too much hast of the archbishop of Yorke, with three hundred horsse got him to Berwike. The king comming forward quickelie, wan the castell of Warkewoorth. Wherevpon the earle of Northumberland, not thinking himselfe in suertie at Berwike, fled with the lord Berdolfe into Scotland, where they were receiued of Dauid lord Fleming.

### The end of Northumberland and Lord Bardolph (4.2.94–9)

[1408, 534/1/20–534/2/4] The earle of Northumberland, and the lord Bardolfe, after they had beene in Wales in France and Flanders, to purchase aid against king Henrie, were returned backe into Scotland, and had remained there now for the space of a whole yeare: and as their euill fortune would, whilest the king held a councell of the nobilitie at London, the said earle of Northumberland and lord Bardolfe, in a dismall houre, with a great power of Scots returned into England, recouering diuerse of the earls castels and seigniories, for the people in great numbers resorted vnto them. Heerevpon incouraged with hope of good successe, they entred into Yorkeshire, & there began to destroie the countrie. At their cōming to Threske, they published a proclamation, signifieng that they were come in comfort of the English nation, as to releeue the common-wealth, willing all such as loued the libertie of their countrie, to repaire vnto them, with their armor on their backes, and in defensible wise to assist them.

The king aduertised hereof, caused a great armie to be assembled, and came forward with the same towards his enimies: but yer the king came to Notingham, sir Thomas, or (as other copies haue) Rafe Rokesbie shiriffe of Yorkeshire, assembled the forces of the countrie to resist the earle and his power, comming to Grimbaut brigs, beside Knaresborough, there to stop them the passage; but they returning aside, got to Weatherbie, and so to Tadcaster, and finallie came forward vnto Bramham more, neere to Haizelwood, where they chose their ground meet to fight vpon. The shiriffe was as readie to giue battell as the earle to receiue it, and so with a standard of S. George spred, set fiercelie vpon the earle, who vnder a standard of his owne armes incountered his aduersaries with great manhood. There was a sore incounter and cruell conflict betwixt the parties but in the end the victorie fell to the shiriffe. The lord Bardolfe was taken, but sore wounded, so that he shortlie after died of the hurts. As for the earle of Northumberland, he was slaine outright: so that now the prophesie was fulfilled, which gaue an inkling of this his heauie hap long before; namelie,

   *Stirps Persitina periet confusa ruina.*

For this earle was the stocke and maine root of all that were left aliue called by the name of Persie; and of manie more by diuerse slaughters dispatched. For whose misfortune the people were not a little sorrie, making report of the gentlemans valiantnesse, renowne, and honour, and applieng vnto him certeine lamentable verses out of LUCANE, saieng;

   *Sed nos nec sanguis, nec tantùm vulnera nostri*
   *Affecere senis; quantum gestata per vrbem*
   *Ora ducis, quæ transfixo deformia pilo*
   *Vidimus.*

For his head, full of siluer horie heares, being put vpon a stake, was openlie carried through London and set vpon the bridge of the same citie: in like maner was the lord Bardolfes. The bishop of Bangor was taken and pardoned by the king, for that when he was apprehended, he had no armor on his backe. This battell was fought the ninteenth day of Februarie.


The death of Glendower (3.1.102) and the Chancellorship of Surrey (3.1.1 n.)

[1409, 536/1/1–14] The Welsh rebell Owen Glendouer made an end of his wretched life in this tenth yeare of king Henrie his reigne, being driuen now in his latter time (as we find recorded) to such miserie, that in manner despairing of all comfort, he fled into desert places and solitarie caues, where being destitute of all releefe and succour, dreading to shew his face to anie creature, and finallie lacking meat to susteine nature,

for meere hunger and lacke of food, miserablie pined awaie and died. This yeare
Thomas Beaufort earle of Surrie was made chancellor, and Henrie Scroope lord
treasuror.

The Umfreviles (see 1.1.34 and 161) and Sir John Oldcastle (see p. 000 above)

[1410, 536/2/65–7 and 537/1/10–20; 1412, 537/1/63–537/2/7] Moreouer this yeare
sir Robert Umfreuill vice-admeral of England, annoied the countries on the sea coasts of
Scotland . . .
  About foure years before this, he burnt the towne of Peples on the market daie,
causing his men to meat the cloathes which they got there with their bowes, & so to sell
them awaie, wherevpon the Scots named him Robert Mendmarket. Shortlie after his
returne from the sea now in this eleuenth yeare of king Henries reigne, he made a road
into Scotland by land, hauing with him his nephue yoong Gilbert Umfreuill earle of
Angus (commonlie called earle of Kime) being then but fourteene yeares of age, and this
was the first time that the said earle spread his banner.
  . . . the yoong duke of Orleance Charles, sonne to duke Lewes thus murthered, alied
himselfe with the dukes of Berrie and Burbon, and with the earles of Alanson &
Arminacke, whereby he was so stronglie banded against the duke of Burgognie, whome
he defied as his mortall fo and enimie, that the duke of Burgognie fearing the sequele of
the matter, thought good (because there was a motion of mariage betwixt the prince of
Wales & his daughter) to require aid of king Henrie, who foreseeing that this ciuill
discord in France (as it after hapned) might turne his realme to honor and profit, sent to
the duke of Burgognie, Thomas earle of Arundell, Gilbert Umfreuill earle of Angus
(commonlie called the earle of Kime) sir Robert Umfreuill, vncle to the same Gilbert, sir
Iohn Oldcastell lord Cobham, sir Iohn Greie, and William Porter, with twelue hundred
archers.

The dagger: Hal's first reformation – *1H4* 3.2 – echoed in the second (see 4.2.221 ff.)

[1412, 539/1/1–539/2/47] Whilest these things were a dooing in France, the lord
Henrie prince of Wales, eldest sonne to king Henrie, got knowledge that certeine of his
fathers seruants were busie to giue informations against him whereby discord might arise
betwixt him and his father: for they put into the kings head, not onelie what euill rule
(according to the course of youth) the prince kept to the offense of manie: but also what
great resort of people came to his house, so that the court was nothing furnished with
such a traine as dailie followed the prince. These tales brought no small suspicion into
the kings head, least his sonne would presume to vsurpe the crowne, he being yet aliue,
through which suspicious gelousie, it was perceiued that he fauoured not his sonne, as in
times past he had doone.
  The Prince sore offended with such persons, as by slanderous reports, sought not
onelie to spot his good name abrode in the realme, but to sowe discord also betwixt him
and his father, wrote his letters into euerie part of the realme, to reprooue all such
slanderous deuises of those that sought his discredit. And to cleare himselfe the better,

that the world might vnderstand what wrong he had to be slandered in such wise: about the feast of Peter and Paule, to wit, the nine and twentith daie of Iune, he came to the court with such a number of noble men and other his freends that wished him well, as the like traine had beene sildome seene repairing to the court at any one time in those daies. He was apparelled in a gowne of blew satten, full of small oilet holes, at euerie hole the needle hanging by a silke thred with which it was sewed. About his arme he ware an hounds collar set full of S S of gold, and the tirets likewise being of the same metall.

The court was then at Westminster, where he being entred into the hall, not one of his companie durst once aduance himselfe further than the fire in the same hall, notwithstanding they were earnestlie requested by the lords to come higher: but they regarding what they had in commandement of the prince, would not presume to doo in any thing contrarie there vnto. He himself onelie accompanied with those of the kings house, was streight admitted to the presence of the king his father, who being at that time greeuouslie diseased, yet caused himselfe in his chaire to be borne into his priuie chamber, where in the presence of three or foure persons, in whome he had most confidence, he commanded the prince to shew what he had to saie concerning the cause of his comming.

The prince kneeling downe before his father said: 'Most redoubted and souereigne lord and father, I am at this time come to your presence as your liege man, and as your naturall sonne, in all things to be at your commandement. And where I vnderstand you haue in suspicion my demeanour against your grace, you know verie well, that if I knew any man within this realme, of whome you should stand in feare, my duetie were to punish that person, thereby to remooue that greefe from your heart. Then how much more ought I to suffer death, to ease your grace of that greefe which you haue of me, being your naturall sonne and liege man: and to that end I haue this daie made my selfe readie by confession and receiuing of the sacrament. And therefore I beseech you most redoubted lord and deare father, for the honour of God, to ease your heart of all such suspicion as you haue of me, and to dispatch me heere before your knees, with this same dagger' [and withall he deliuered vnto the king his dagger, in all humble reuerence; adding further, that his life was not so deare to him, that he wished to liue one daie with his displeasure] 'and therefore in thus ridding me out of life, and your selfe from all suspicion, here in presence of these lords, and before God at the daie of the generall iudgement, I faithfullie protest clearlie to forgiue you.'

The king mooued herewith, cast from him the dagger, and imbracing the prince kissed him, and with shedding teares confessed, that in deed he had him partlie in suspicion, though now (as he perceiued) not with iust cause, and therefore from thencefoorth no misreport should cause him to haue him in mistrust, and this he promised of his honour. So by his great wisedome was the wrongfull suspicion which his father had conceiued against him remooued, and he restored to his fauour. And further, where he could not but greeuouslie complaine of them that had slandered him so greatlie, to the defacing not onelie of his honor, but also putting him in danger of his life, he humblie besought the king that they might answer their vniust accusation; and in case they were found to haue forged such matters vpon a malicious purpose, that then they might suffer some punishment for their faults, though not to the full of that they had deserued. The king seeming to grant his resonable desire, yet told him that he must tarrie a parlement, that such offendors might be punished by iudgement of their peeres: and so for that time he was dismissed, with great loue and signes of fatherlie affection.

Thus were the father and the sonne reconciled, betwixt whom the said pick-thanks had sowne diuision, insomuch that the sonne vpon a vehement conceit of vnkindnesse sproong in the father, was in the waie to be worne out of fauour. Which was the more likelie to come to passe, by their informations that priuilie charged him with riot and other vnciuill demeanor vnseemelie for a prince. Indeed he was youthfullie giuen, growne to audacitie, and had chosen him companions agreeable to his age; with whome he spent the time in such recreations, exercises, and delights as he fansied. But yet (it should seeme by the report of some writers) that his behauiour was not offensiue or at least tending to the damage of anie bodie; sith he had a care to auoid dooing of wrong, and to tender his affections within the tract of vertue, whereby he opened vnto himselfe a redie passage of good liking among the prudent sort, and was beloued of such as could discerne his disposition, which was in no degree so excessiue, as that he deserued in such vehement maner to be suspected.

### The prodigy of the three floods (4.2.125–8)

[1411, 540/1/45–9] In this yeare, and vpon the twelfth day of October, were three flouds in the Thames, the one following vpon the other, & no ebbing betweene: which thing no man then liuing could remember the like to be seene.

### Sir John Blunt (see 1.1.16 n.), the preparations for the crusade and the illness and death of Henry IV (4.2)

[1412–13, 540/2/46–541/2/45] In this meane while, the lord of Helie, one of the marshals of France, with an armie of foure thousand men, besieged a certeine fortresse in Guien, which an English knight, one sir Iohn Blunt kept, who with three hundred men that came to his aid, discomfited, chased, and ouerthrew the French power, tooke prisoners twelue men of name, and other gentlemen to the number of six score, and amongst other, the said marshall, who was sent ouer into England, and put in the castell of Wissebet, from whence he escaped, and got ouer into France, where seruing the duke of Orleance at the battell of Agincort he was slaine among other.

In this fourteenth and last yeare of king Henries reigne, a councell was holden in the white friers in London, at the which, among other things, order was taken for ships and gallies to be builded and made readie, and all other things necessarie to be prouided for a voiage which he meant to make into the holie land, there to recouer the citie of Ierusalem from the Infidels. For it greeued him to consider the great malice of christian princes, that were bent vpon a mischeefous purpose to destroie one another, to the perill of their owne soules, rather than to make war against the enimies of the christian faith, as in conscience (it seemed to him) they were bound. He held his Christmas this yeare at Eltham, being sore vexed with sicknesse, so that it was thought sometime, that he had beene dead; notwithstanding it pleased God that he somwhat recouered his strength againe, and so passed that Christmasse with as much ioy as he might.

The morrow after Candlemas daie began a parlement, which he had called at London, but he departed this life before the same parlement was ended: for now that his prouisions were readie, and that he was furnished with sufficient treasure, soldiers, capteins, vittels, munitions, tall ships, strong gallies, and all things necessarie for such a roiall iournie as he pretended to take into the holie land, he was eftsoons taken with a sore sickness, which was not a leprosie, striken by the hand of God (saith maister *Hall*) as foolish friers imagined; but a verie apoplexie, of the which he languished till his appointed houre, and had none other greefe nor maladie; so that what man ordeineth, God altereth at his good will and pleasure, not giuing place more to the prince, than to the poorest creature liuing, when he seeth his time to dispose of him this waie or that, as to his omnipotent power and diuine prouidence seemeth expedient. During this his last sicknesse, he caused his crowne (as some write) to be set on a pillow at his beds head, and suddenlie his pangs so sore troubled him, that he laie as though all his vitall spirits had beene from him departed. Such as were about him, thinking verelie that he had beene departed, couered his face with a linnen cloth.

The prince his sonne being hereof aduertised, entered into the chamber, tooke awaie the crowne, and departed. The father being suddenlie reuiued out of that trance, quicklie perceiued the lacke of his crowne; and hauing knowledge that the prince his sonne had taken it awaie, caused him to come before his presence, requiring of him what he meant so to misuse himselfe. The prince with a good audacitie answered; 'Sir, to mine and all mens iudgements you seemed dead in this world, wherefore I as your next heire apparant tooke that as mine owne, and not as yours.' Well faire sonne (said the king with a great sigh) what right I had to it, God knoweth. Well (said the prince) if you die king, I will haue the garland, and trust to keepe it with the sword against all mine enimies as you haue doone. Then said the king, 'I commit all to God, and remember you to doo well.' With that he turned himselfe in his bed, and shortlie after departed to God in a chamber of the abbats of Westminster called Ierusalem, the twentith daie of March, in the yeare 1413, and in the yeare of his age 46, when he had reigned thirteene yeares, fiue moneths and od daies, in great perplexitie and little pleasure [or fourteene yeares, as some haue noted, who name not the disease whereof he died, but refer it to sicknesse absolutelie, whereby his time of departure did approach and fetch him out of the world...

We find, that he was taken with his last sickenesse, while he was making his praiers at saint Edwards shrine, there as it were to take his leaue, and so to proceed foorth on his iournie: he was so suddenlie and greeuouslie taken, that such as were about him, feared least he would haue died presentlie, wherfore to releeue him (if it were possible) they bare him into a chamber that was next at hand, belonging to the abbat of Westminster, where they laid him on a pallet before the fire, and vsed all remedies to reuiue him. At length, he recouered his speech, and vnderstanding and perceiuing himselfe in a strange place which he knew not, he willed to know if the chamber had anie particular name, wherevnto answer was made, that it was called Ierusalem. Then said the king; 'Lauds be giuen to the father of heauen, for now I know that I shall die heere in this chamber, according to the prophesie of me declared, that I should depart this life in Ierusalem.'

Whether this was true that so he spake, as one that gaue too much credit to foolish prophesies & vaine tales, or whether it was fained, as in such cases it commonlie happeneth, we leaue it to the aduised reader to iudge. His bodie with all funerall pompe

was conueied vnto Canturburie, and there solemnlie buried, leauing behind him by the
ladie Marie daughter to the lord Humfrie Bohun earle of Hereford and Northampton,
Henrie prince of Wales, Thomas duke of Clarence, Iohn duke of Bedford, Humfrie
duke of Glocester, Blanch duchesse of Bauier, and Philip queene of Denmarke: by his
last wife Iane, he had no children. This king was of a meane stature, well proportioned,
and formallie compact, quicke and liuelie, and of a stout courage. In his latter daies he
shewed himselfe so gentle, that he gat more loue amongst the nobles and people of this
realme, than he had purchased malice and euill will in the beginning.

But yet to speake a truth, by his proceedings, after he had atteined to the crowne, what
with such taxes, tallages, subsidies, and exactions as he was constreined to charge the
people with; and what by punishing such as mooued with disdeine to see him vsurpe the
crowne (contrarie to the oth taken at his entring into this land, vpon his returne from
exile) did at sundrie times rebell against him, he wan himselfe more hatred, than in all his
life time (if it had beene longer by manie yeares than it was) had beene possible for him to
haue weeded out & remooued. And yet doubtlesse, woorthie were his subiects to tast of
that bitter cup, sithens they were so readie to ioine and clappe hands with him, for the
deposing of their rightfull and naturall prince king Richard, whose cheefe fault rested
onlie in that, that he was too bountifull to his freends, and too mercifull to his foes;
speciallie if he had not beene drawne by others, to seeke reuenge of those that abused his
good and courteous nature.

Gower's name (see 2.1.104 SD.2 n.)

[In the review of the most notable writers in the time of Henry IV, 541/2/64–542/1/10]
Iohn Gower descended of that worthie familie of the Gowers of Stitenham in Yorkeshire
(as Leland noteth) studied not onelie the common lawes of this realme, but also other
kinds of literature, and great knowledge in the same, namelie in poeticall inuentions,
applieng his indeuor with Chaucer, to garnish the English toong, in bringing it from a
rude vnperfectnesse, vnto a more apt elegancie: for whereas before those daies, the
learned vsed to write onelie in Latine or French, and not in English, our toong remained
verie barren, rude, and vnperfect; but now by the diligent industrie of Chaucer and
Gower, it was within a while greatlie amended, so as it grew not onelie verie rich and
plentifull in words, but also so proper and apt to expresse that which the mind conceiued,
as anie other vsuall language. Gower departed this life shortlie after the deceasse of his
deere and louing freend Chaucer; to wit, in the yeare 1402, being then come to great age,
and blind for a certeine time before his death. He was buried in the church of saint Marie
Oueries in Southwarke.

The prince's accession and reformation (5.2 and 5.5)

[The reign of Henry V, 1413, 543/1/1–12 and 543/1/47–543/2/50] Henrie prince of
Wales, son and heire to K. Henrie the fourth, borne in Wales at Monmouth on the riuer
of Wie, after his father was departed, tooke vpon him the regiment of this realme of
England, the twentith of March, the morrow after proclamed king, by the name of

Henrie the fift, in the yeare of the world 5375, after the birth of our sauior, by our account 1413 . . .

Such great hope, and good expectation was had of this mans fortunate successe to follow, that within three daies after his fathers deceasse, diuerse noble men and honorable personages did to him homage, and sware to him due obedience, which had not beene seene doone to any of his predecessors kings of this realme, till they had beene possessed of the crowne. He was crowned the ninth of Aprill being Passion sundaie, which was a sore, ruggie, and tempestuous day, with wind, snow and sleet, that men greatlie maruelled thereat, making diuerse interpretations what the same might signifie. But this king euen at first appointing with himselfe, to shew that in his person princelie honors should change publike manners, he determined to put on him the shape of a new man. For whereas aforetime he had made himselfe a companion vnto misrulie mates of dissolute order and life, he now banished them all from his presence (but not vnrewarded, or else vnpreferred) inhibiting them vpon a great paine, not once to approch, lodge, or soiourne within ten miles of his court or presence: and in their places he chose men of grauitie, wit, and high policie, by whose wise councell he might at all times rule to his honour and dignitie; calling to mind how once to hie offence of the king his father, he had with his fist striken the cheefe iustice for sending one of his minions (vpon desert) to prison, when the iustice stoutlie commanded himselfe also streict to ward, & he (then prince) obeied. The king after expelled him out of his priuie councell, banisht him the court, and made the duke of Clarence (his yoonger brother) president of councell in his steed. This reformation in the new king *Christ[opher] Okl[and]* hath reported, fullie consenting with this. For saith he,

> *Ille inter iuuenes paulo lasciuior antè,*
> *Defuncto genitore grauis constànsq: repentè,*
> *Moribus ablegat corruptis regis ab aula*
> *Assuetos socios, & nugatoribus acrem*
> *Pœnam (si quisquam sua tecta reuiserit) addit,*
> *Atq: ita mutatus facit omnia principe digna,*
> *Ingenio magno post consultoribus vsus, &c.*

But now that the king was once placed in the roiall seat of the realme, he vertuouslie considering in his mind, that all goodnesse commeth of God, determined to begin with some thing acceptable to his diuine maiestie, and therefore commanded the cleargie sincerelie and trulie to preach the word of God, and to liue accordinglie, that they might be the lanternes of light to the temporaltie, as their profession required. The laie men he willed to serue God, and obeie their prince, prohibiting them aboue all things breach of matrimonie, custome in swearing; and namelie, willfull periurie. Beside this, he elected the best learned men in the lawes of the realme, to the offices of iustice; and men of good liuing, he preferred to high degrees and authoritie. Immediatlie after Easter he called a parlement, in which diuerse good statutes, and wholesome ordinances, for the preserua-tion and aduancement of the common-wealth were deuised and established. On Trinitie sundaie were the solemne exequies doone at Canturburie for his father, the king himselfe being present thereat.

The end of Sir John Oldcastle (see pp. 9–13 above)

[1413, arrest, trial and escape: 541/1/17–55] Also in this first yeere of this kings reigne, sir Iohn Oldcastell, which by his wife was called lord Cobham, a valiant capteine and a hardie gentleman, was accused to the archbishop of Canturburie of certeine points of heresie, who knowing him to be highlie in the kings fauour, declared to his highnesse the whole accusation. The king first hauing compassion of the noble man, required the prelats, that if he were a straied sheepe, rather by gentlenes than by rigor to reduce him to the fold. And after this, he himselfe sent for him, and right earnestlie exhorted him, and louinglie admonished him to reconcile himselfe to God and to his lawes. The lord Cobham not onelie thanked him for his most fauorable clemencie, but also declared first to him by mouth, and afterwards by writing, the foundation of his faith, and the ground of his beliefe, affirming his grace to be his supreme head and competent iudge, and none other person, offering an hundred knights and esquiers to come to his purgation, or else to fight in open lists in defence of his iust cause.

The king vnderstanding and persuaded by his councell, that by order of the lawes of his realme, such accusations touching matters of faith ought to be tried by his spirituall prelats, sent him to the Tower of London, there to abide the determination of the clergie, according to the statutes in that case prouided, after which time a solemne session was appointed in the cathedrall church of saint Paule, vpon the three and twentith day of September, and an other the fiue and twentith daie of the same moneth, in the hall of the Blacke friers at London, in which places the said lord was examined, apposed, and fullie heard, and in conclusion by the archbishop of Canturburie denounced an heretike, & remitted againe to the Tower of London, from which place, either by helpe of freends, or fauour of keepers, he priuilie escaped and came into Wales, where he remained for a season.

[1417, pursuit: 560/1/57–66] The same time, the lord Cobham, sir Iohn Oldcastell, whilest he shifted from place to place to escape the hands of them, who he knew would be glad to laie hold on him, had conueied himselfe in secret wise into an husbandmans house, not farre from S. Albons, within the precinct of a lordship belonging to the abbat of that towne. The abbats seruants getting knowledge hereof, came thither by night, but they missed their purpose, for he was gone; but they caught diuerse of his men, whome they caried streict to prison.

[1417–18, capture and execution: 561/2/24–46] About the same season was sir Iohn Oldcastell, lord Cobham taken, in the countrie of Powes land, in the borders of Wales, within a lordship belonging to the lord Powes, not without danger and hurts of some that were at the taking of him: for they could not take him, till he was wounded himselfe.

At the same time, the states of the realme were assembled at London, for the leuieng of monie, to furnish the kings great charges, which he was at about the maintenance of his wars in France: it was therefore determined, that the said sir Iohn Oldcastell should be brought, and put to his triall, yer the assemblie brake vp. The lord Powes therefore was sent to fetch him, who brought him to London in a litter, wounded as he was:

herewith, being first laid fast in the Tower, shortlie after he was brought before the duke of Bedford, regent of the realme, and the other estates, where in the end he was condemned; and finallie was drawen from the Tower vnto saint Giles field, and there hanged in a chaine by the middle, and after consumed with fire, the gallowes and all.

# APPENDIX 2: SOME HISTORICAL AND LITERARY SOURCES

Besides Holinshed's *Chronicles*, Shakespeare consulted John Stow's *Annales of England* (1592) – not his *Chronicles* of 1580 – and was influenced by a number of other works of a more or less literary nature. Daniel's *Civil Wars* is half way between history and poetry, and in fact the dramatist got from it both historical incidents and stylistic suggestions; the contributions of *Ortho-epia Gallica* and of Harpsfield's manuscript *Life of Sir Thomas More* to the new creation of the characters of Pistol and Mistress Quickly respectively are essentially linguistic.

*THE ANNALES OF ENGLAND … from the first inhabitation vntill this present yeere 1592, by IOHN STOWE*

[The extracts are limited to passages markedly different from Holinshed's relation of the same episodes, though Shakespeare may have had Stow in mind also elsewhere – for example, in the Gaultree scene. I do not include the original version of the episode of the box on the ear of the Lord Chief Justice in Sir Thomas Elyot's *The Boke named the Gouernour* (1531) since Stow reports it verbatim. Texts and page numbers are from the 1592 edition (the 1580 *Chronicles* omits the Lord Chief Justice episode), with references to the play text.]

[545: see 4.2.221–351] In the time of whose languishing the king gaue to the prince his sonne diuers notable doctrines and insignements, that not onely of him, but of euery prince are to be holden and followed: among the which eruditions one is this: The king lieng greeuously diseased, called before him the prince his sonne, and said vnto him: My sonne, I feare me sore, after my departure from this life, some discord shall grow and arise betweene thee and thy brother Thomas duke of Clarence, whereby the realme may be brought to destruction and misery, for I know you both to be of great stomacke and courage. Wherefore I feare, that he through his high mind wil make some enterprise against thee, intending to vsurp vpon thee, which I know thy stomacke may not abide easily. And for dread hereof, as oft as it is in my remembrance, I sore repent me, that euer I charged my selfe with the crowne of this realm. To these words of the king the prince answered thus: Right redoubted lord and father, to the pleasure of God your grace shall long continue with vs, and rule vs both: but if God haueth so prouided that euer I shal succeed you in this realme, I shall honor & loue my brethren aboue al men, as long as they be to me true, faithfull and obedient, as to their soueraigne lord, but if any of them fortune to conspire or rebell against me, I assure you, I shall as soone execute iustice vpon one of them, as I shall vpon the worst and most simplest person within this your realme.

The king hearing this answere, was therewith maruellously reioyced in his mind, and said: My deere and welbeloued sonne, with this answere thou hast deliuered me of a great and ponderous agony: and I beseech thee, and vpon my blessing charge thee, that like as thou hast said, so thou minister iustice equally, and in no wise suffer not them that be oppressed long to call vpon thee for iustice, but redresse oppressions, and indif-ferently and without delay, for no perswasion of flatterers, or of them that be partiall, or such as do haue their hands replenished with gifts, deferre not iustice till tomorrow, if that thou mayest do iustice this day, lest (peraduenture) God do iustice on thee in the meane time, and take from thee thine authority: remember that the wealth of thy body, and thy soule, and of thy realme, resteth in the execution of iustice, and do not thy iustice so, that thou be called a tirant, but vse thy selfe meanely betwixt iustice and mercy in those things that belong to thee. And betweene parties do iustice truely and extremely, to the consolation of thy poore subiects that suffer iniuries, and to the punition of them that be extortioners and doers of oppressions, that other thereby may take example: and in thus doing, thou shalt obtaine the fauour of God, and the loue and feare of thy subiects, and therefore also thou shalt haue thy realme more in tranquillitie and rest, which shal be occasion of great prosperitie within thy realme, which Englishmen naturally doo desire: for so long as they haue wealth and riches, so long shalt thou haue obeysance: and when they be poore, then they be alwaies ready at euery motion to make insurrections, and it causeth them to rebell against their soue-[546]raigne lord: for the nature of them is such, rather to feare loosing of their goodes and worldly substance, then the ieoparding of their liues. And if thou thus keepe them in subiection mixed with loue and feare, thou shalt haue the most peaceable and fertile countrey, and the most louing, faithfull, and manly people of the world, which shall be cause of no small feare to thine aduersaries. My sonne, when it shall please God to call me the way decreede for euery worldly creature, to thee (as my sonne and heire) I must leaue my crowne and my realme, which I aduise thee not to take vainely, and as a man elate in pride, and reioyced in worldly honour, but thinke that thou art more oppressed with charge, to purueie for euery person within the realme, than exalted in vaine honour of the world. Thou shalt be exalted vnto the crowne, for the wealth and conseruation of the realme, and not for thy singular commoditie and auaile: My sonne, thou shalt be a minister to thy realme to keepe it in tranquillitie and defend it. Like as the hart in the middest of the body is principall and chiefe thing in the body, and serueth to couet and desire that thing that is most necessarie to euery of thy members, so (my sonne) thou shalt be amongst thy people as chiefe and principall of them to minister, imagine and acquire those things that may be most beneficiall for them. And then thy people shall be obedient to thee, to ayde and succour thee, and in all things to accomplish thy commandements, like as thy members labour, euery one of them in their office, to acquire and get that thing that the heart desireth, and as thy heart is of no force and impotent without the aide of thy members, so without thy people, thy raigne is nothing. My sonne, thou shalt feare and dread God aboue all things, and thou shalt loue, honour and worship him with all thy heart, thou shalt attribute and ascribe to him al things wherein thou seest thy selfe to be well fortunate, be it victorie of thine enemies, loue of thy friends, obedience of thy subiects, strength and actiuenesse of body, honor, riches, or fruitfull generations, or any other thing whatsoeuer it be that chanceth to thy pleasure. Thou shalt not imagine that any such thing should fortune to thee, by thine acte, nor by thy desert, but thou shalt thinke that all commeth onely of the goodnesse of the Lord. Thus thou shalt with all thine heart, prayse, honour, and thanke God for all his benefites that he giueth vnto thee. And in thy selfe eschew all vaineglorie and elation of heart, following the wholesome counsell of the Psalmist, which saieth, *Non nobis Domine, non nobis, sed nomini tuo da gloriam*, which is to say, Not vnto vs Lord, not vnto vs, but to thy holy name be giuen laud and praise. These and many other admonishments and doctrines this victorious king gaue vnto this noble prince his sonne, who with effect followed the same, after the death of his father: whereby hee obtained grace of our Lorde to attaine to great victories and many glorious and incredible conquests, through the helpe and succour of our Lorde, whereof he was neuer destitute. The king his father drawing to his end, after due thankes giuen, and supplications made to GOD, gaue [547] his benediction to the prince his son, and so yeelded to God his spirit, the xx. of March, *Anno* 1412. after the account of the church of England [i.e. 1413].

[King Henry the fift, 547; see 1.2.42–3, 5.2.67–110, and pp. 7–9 above] He liued somwhat insolently, insomuch that whilest his father liued, being accōpanied with som of his yong lords & gentlemen, he would wait in disguised aray for his owne receiuers, and distresse them of their mony: and sometimes at such enterprises both he and his company were surely beaten: and when his receiuers made to him their complaints how they were robbed in their comming vnto him, he would giue them discharge of so much mony as they had lost, and besides that, they shold not depart from him without great rewards for their trouble & vexation, especially they should be rewarded that best had resisted him and his company, and of whom he had receiued the greatest and most strokes, and for example sir Thomas Eliot writeth thus. The renowmed prince king Henry the fift, during the life of his father, was noted to be fierce, & of wanton courage. It hapned that one of his seruants, whom he fauored, was for felony by him committed, arraigned at the kings bench, whereof the prince being aduertised, and incensed by light persons about him, in furious rage [548] came hastily to the bar, where his seruant stood as prisoner, and commanded him to be vngiued and set at libertie, whereat all men were abashed, reserued the chiefe Iustice, who humbly exhorted the prince to be ordered according to the ancient laws of the realme, or if he would haue him saued from the rigor of the lawes, that he should obtaine if he might of the king his father, his gracious pardon, whereby no law or iustice should be derogate. With the which answere the prince nothing appeased, but rather more inflamed, indeuoured himselfe to take away his seruant. The Iudge, considering the perillous example and inconueniencie that might thereby ensue, with a valiant spirit & courage commanded the prince vpon his allegiance to leaue the prisoner, and to depart his way: with which commandement, the prince being set all in a fury, all chafed, and in a terrible maner came vp to the place of iudgement, men thinking that he would haue slaine the Iudge, or haue done to him some domage, but the Iudge sitting still, without moouing, declaring the maiestie of the kings place of iudgement, and with an assured bold countenance, had to the prynce these words following: Sir, remember your selfe, I keep here the place of the king your soueraigne lord and father, to whom you owe double obeisance, wherefore eftsoones in his name I charge you desist off your wilfulnes and vnlawfull enterprise, & from hencefoorth giue good example to those which hereafter shal be your proper subiects: and now for your contempt and disobedience, go you to the prison of the kings bench, wherevnto I commit you, and remain you there prisoner vntil the pleasure of the king your father be further known. With which words, being abashed, and also wondering at the maruellous grauitie of that worshipfull Iustice, the prince layeng his weapon apart, doing reuerence, departed, and went to the kings bench as he was commanded. Whereat his seruants disdaining, came & shewed the king all the whole affaire. Whereat he a while studieng, after, as a man all rauished with gladnes, holding his hands and eies towards heauen, abraid with a lowde voice: O mercifull God! how much am I bound to thy infinit goodnes, especially for that thou hast giuen me a Iudge, who feareth not to minister iustice, and also a sonne, who can suffer semblably and obey iustice. Now (saith Thomas Eliot) here a man may behold three persons worthy memory: first a Iudge, who being a subiect feared not to execute iustice on the eldest sonne of his soueraigne lord, and by the order of nature his successour. Also a prince, and sonne and heire of the K. in the middest of his folly, more considered his euill example, and the Iudges conscience in iustice, than his owne estate or wilfull appetite. Thirdly, a noble king and wise father, who contrary to the custome of parents, reioyced to see his sonne, and the heire of his crown, to be for his disobedience by his subiect corrected: wherfore I co[n]clude, that nothing is more honorable or to be desired in a prince, or noble man, than placability, as contrariwise nothing is so detestable, or to be feared in such a one as wrath & cruel malignitie.

[549, see 5.5.43–95] After which coronation, he called vnto him all those yoong lords and gentlemen that were the folowers of his yoong actes, to euery one of whom he gaue rich and bounteous gifts, and then commanded that as many as would change their maners as he intended to do, should abide with him in his court, and to all that would perseuer in their former light conuersation, he gaue expresse commandement vpon paine of their heads, neuer after that day to come in his presence.

Samuel Daniel, *THE FIRST FOWRE BOOKES OF THE CIUILE WARS BETWEEN THE TWO HOUSES OF LANCASTER AND YORKE.* 1595

[Extract from *The Third Booke*. Signatures in the 1595 edition and references to relevant passages in the play are provided in square brackets. Possibly the placing of Henry IV's deathbed scene immediately after the battle of Shrewsbury was reflected in the earlier one-play version of *Henry IV*.]

[R3ᵛ]    110    [See 1.1.105–35]
There lo that new-appearing glorious starre
Wonder of Armes, the terror of the field
Young *Henrie*, laboring where the stoutest are,
And euen the stoutest forces back to yeild,
There is that hand boldned to bloud and warre
That must the sword in woundrous actions weild:
But better hadst thou learn'd with others bloud
A lesse expence to vs, to thee more good.

111
Hadst thou not there lent present speedy ayd
To thy indaungerde father nerely tyrde,
Whom fierce incountring *Dowglas* ouerlaid,
That day had there his troublous life expirde:

Heroycall Couragious *Blunt* araid
In habite like as was the king attirde
And deemd for him, excusd that fate with his,
For he had what his Lord did hardly misse.

Which was sir
Walter Blunt.

112   [See 1.1.16]
For thought a king he would not now disgrace
The person then supposd, but princelike shewes
Glorious effects of worth that fit his place,
And fighting dyes, and dying ouerthrowes:
Another of that forward name and race
In that hotte worke his valiant life bestowes,
Who bare the standard of the king that day,
Whose colours ouerthrowne did much dismaie.

Another Blunt
which was the kings
Standard bearer.

[R4]   113
And deare it cost, and o much bloud is shed
To purchase thee this loosing victory
O trauayld king: yet hast thou conquered
A doubtfull day, a mightie enemy:
But ô what woundes, what famous worth lyes dead!
That makes the winner looke with sorrowing eye,
Magnanimous *Stafford* lost that much had wrought,
And valiant *Shorly* who great glory gote.

114   [See 1.1.49–50]
Such wracke of others bloud thou didst behold
O furious *Hotspur*, ere thou lost thine owne!
Which now once lost that heate in thine waxt cold,
And soone became thy Armie ouerthrowne;
And ô that this great spirit, this courage bold,
Had in some good cause bene rightly showne!
So had not we thus violently then
Have termd that rage, which valor should haue ben.

115   [See 3.1]
But now the king retires him to his peace,
A peace much like a feeble sicke mans sleepe,
(Wherein his waking paines do neuer cease
Though seeming rest his closed eyes doth keepe)
For ô no peace could euer so release
His intricate turmoiles, and sorrowes deepe,
But that his cares kept waking all his life
Continue on till death conclude the strife.

[R4ᵛ]   116   [See 4.2.117–20]
Whose harald sicknes, being sent before
With full commission to denounce his end,
And paine, and griefe, enforcing more and more,
Besiegd the hold that could not long defend,
And so consum'd all that imboldning store
Of hote gaine-striuing bloud that did contend,
Wearing the wall so thin that now the mind
Might well looke thorow, and his frailty find.

117

When lo, as if the vapours vanisht were,
Which heate of boyling bloud & health did breed,
(To cloude the sence that nothing might appeare
Vnto the thought, that which it was indeed)
The lightned soule began to see more cleere
How much it was abusd, & notes with heed
The plaine discouered falsehood open laid
Of ill perswading flesh that so betraid.

118

And lying on his last afflicted bed
Where death & conscience both before him stand,
Th'one holding out a booke wherein he red
In bloudie lines the deedes of his owne hand;
The other shewes a glasse, which figured
An ougly forme of fowle corrupted sand:
Both bringing horror in the hyest degree
With what he was, and what he straight should bee.

[SI]    119   [See 4.2.151–77]

Which seeing all confusd trembling with feare
He lay a while, as ouerthrowne in sprite,
At last commaunds some that attending were
To fetch the crowne and set it in his sight,
On which with fixed eye and heauy cheere
Casting a looke, *O God* (saith he) what right
I had to thee my soule doth now conceiue;
Thee, which with bloude I gote, with horror leaue.

120

Wert thou the cause my climing care was such
To passe those boundes, nature, and law ordaind?
Is this that good which promised so much,
And seemd so glorious ere it was attaind?
Wherein was neuer ioye but gaue a touch
To checke my soule to thinke, how thou were gaind,
And now how do I leaue thee vnto mine,
Which it is dread to keepe, death to resigne.

121

With this the soule rapt wholy with the thought
Of such distresse, did so attentiue weigh
Her present horror, whilst as if forgote
The dull consumed body senceles lay,
And now as breathles quite, quite dead is thought,
When lo his sonne comes in, and takes awaie
The fatall crowne from thence, and out he goes
As if vnwilling longer time to lose.

[SIᵛ]   122

And whilst that sad confused soule doth cast
Those great accounts of terror and distresse,
Vppon this counsell it doth light at last
How she might make the charge of horror lesse,

And finding no way to acquit thats past
But onely this, to vse some quicke redresse
Of acted wrong, with giuing vp againe
The crowne to whom it seem'd to appertaine.

123 [See 4.2.178–305]
Which found, lightned with some small ioy shee hyes,
Rouses her seruaunts that dead sleeping lay,
(The members of hir house,) to exercise
One feeble dutie more, during her stay:
And opening those darke windowes he espies
The crowne for which he lookt was borne awaie,
And all-agrieu'd with the vnkind offence
He causd him bring it backe that tooke it thence.

124
To whom (excusing his presumteous deed
By the supposing him departed quite)
He said: ô Sonne what needes thee make such speed
Vnto that care, where feare exceeds thy right,
And where his sinne whom thou shalt now succeed
Shall still vpbraid thy inheritance of might,
And if thou canst liue, and liue great from wo
Without this carefull trauaile; let it go.

[S2]    125
Nay father since your fortune did attaine
So hye a stand: I meane not to descend,
Replyes the Prince; as if what you did gaine
I were of spirit vnable to defend:
Time will appease them well that now complaine,
And ratefie our interest in the end;
What wrong hath not continuance quite outworne?
Yeares makes that right which neuer was so borne.

126 [See 4.2.306–47]
If so, God worke his pleasure (said the king)
And ô do thou contend with all thy might
Such euidence of vertuous deeds to bring,
That well may proue our wrong to be our right:
And let the goodnes of the managing
Race out the blot of foule attayning quite:
That discontent may all aduantage misse
To wish it otherwise then now it is.

127
And since my death my purpose doth preuent
Touching this sacred warre I tooke in hand,
(An action wherewithall my soule had ment
T'appease my God, and reconcile my land)
To thee is left to finish my intent,
Who to be safe must neuer idly stand;
But some great actions entertaine thou still
To hold their mindes who else will practise ill.

[s2ᵛ]   128
Thou hast not that aduantage by my raigne
To riot it (as they whom long descent
Hath purchasd loue by custome) but with payne
Thou must contend to buy the worlds content:
What their birth gaue them, thou hast yet to gaine
By thine owne vertues, and good gouernment,
And that vnles thy worth confirme the thing
Thou canst not be the father to a king.

129
Nor art thou born in those calm daies, where rest
Hath brought a sleepe sluggish securitie;
But in tumultuous times, where mindes adrest
To factions are inurd to mutinie,
A mischiefe not by force to be supprest
Where rigor still begets more enmitie,
Hatred must be beguild with some new course,
Where states are strong, & princes doubt their force.

130
This and much more affliction would haue said
Out of th'experience of a troublous raigne,
For which his high desires had dearly paide
Th'interest of an euer-toyling paine:
But that this all-subduing powre here staid
His faultring tongue and paine r'inforc'd againe,
And cut off all the passages of breath
To bring him quite vnder the state of death.

*The life and death of Sr Thomas Moore, knight, . . . written in the tyme of Queene Marie by Nicholas Harpsfield, L.D. (c. 1557)*

[In devising the new character of Pistol in *Part Two*, Shakespeare took as a model the person of the Braggart in John Eliot's recently published *Ortho-epia Gallica* (1593): reference should be made to J. W. Lever's 'Shakespeare's French fruits' (*S.Sur.* 6 (1953), 79–90) for full documentation on the subject. In the same way, when transforming the conventional character of the Hostess of *Part One* into the ageing Mistress Quickly of *Part Two*, at once shrewish, gullible and warm hearted, he must have remembered the pages containing a pen portrait of the shrewish and affectionate second Lady More in Sir Thomas's biography by Archdeacon Nicholas Harpsfield, circulating in manuscript in Catholic houses. Essential extracts (with page/line references) are from the edition based on the Emmanuel manuscript, by Elsie Vaughan Hitchcock (EETS, os 186, 1932).]

[93/13–94/12] After the death of his [More's] first wife, he maried a widowe, which continued with him till he suffred; whom he full entierly loued and most louingly vsed, though he had by her no children, and though she were aged, blunt and rude . . .

This wife, on a time after shrifte, bad Sir Thomas be merie. 'For I haue,' saith she, 'this day lefte all my shrewdnes, and will beginne afreshe.' Which merye conceyted talke, though nowe and then it proued true in verye deede, Sir Thomas More could well digest and like in her . . .

[95/18–96/25] When he was prisoner in the towre, and there had continued a good while, his saide wife obteyned licence to see him. Who, at the first comming, like a simple ignorant woman, and somewhat worldly too, with this maner of salutation bluntly saluted him:

'What the goodyere, Master More,' quoth she, 'I meruaile that you [that] haue beene alwayes hitherto taken for so wise a man, will nowe so play the foole to lye here in this close, filthy prison, and be content thus to shutt vp amonge mise and rattes; when you might be abrode at your libertie, with the fauour and good will both of the king and his counsaile, if you would but doo as all the Bisshops and best learned of this Realme haue done . . . I muse what a Gods name you meane here still thus fondlye to tarye.'

After he had a while quietly heard her, with a cheerefull countenaunce he saide vnto her:

'I praye thee, good mistris Als, tell me one thing.'

'What is that?' quoth she.

'Is not this house,' quothe he, 'as nigh heauen as mine owne?'

To whom she, after her accustomed homely fasshion, not lyking suche talke, aunswered: 'Tille valle, Tille valle.'

'Howe saye you, mistris Als?' quoth he, 'is it not so?'

'*Bone Deus*, *Bone Deus*, man, will this gere neuer be lefte?' quoth she.

[97/20–98/21] But among many other displeasures that for his sake she was sory for, one she lamented much in her minde, that he should haue the chamber doore vpon him by night made fast by the gayler that shoulde shett him in. 'For by my troth,' quoth she, 'if the doore should be shett vppon me, I would weene it would stopp vp my breth.'

# APPENDIX 3: *THE FAMOUS VICTORIES*

The peculiar relationship of the *Henry* plays to the text printed by Thomas Creede in 1598 under the title *The Famous Victories of Henry the fifth: Containing the Honourable Battell of Agincourt: As it was plaide by the Queenes Maiesties Players* has been discussed in the Introduction. The book seems to be a drastically cut memorial reconstruction of possibly two much earlier plays on Henry IV and Henry V, belonging to the Queen's Men. The section on 'The Henriad as remake' and that on 'Rewriting the remake' (pp. 9–13 above) suggest the process of transmission and transformation of the *Henry* plays of which *Famous Victories* is but a pale reflection. The following extracts reproduce from the 1598 quarto the sections relevant to *Part Two*, indicating the original signatures and adopting the scene divisions introduced in the Praetorius facsimile (introduction by P. A. Daniel, 1887).

[Scene iv: the Thief Cutbert Cutter has been brought before the Lord Chief Justice under the accusation of having robbed at Gad's Hill Derrick the carrier (the Clown).]

[B2ᵛ]  *Iudge.*  Well, what sayest thou, art thou guiltie, or not guiltie?
  *Theefe.*  Not guiltie, my lord.
  *Iudge.*  By whom wilt thou be tride?
[B3]  *Theefe.*  By my Lord the young Prince, or by my selfe whether you will.
   *Enter the young Prince, with Ned and Tom.*
  *Hen.5.*  Come away my lads, Gogs wounds ye villain, what make you heere?
   I must goe about my businesse my selfe, and you must stand loytering
   here.
  *Theefe.*  Why my Lord, they haue bound me, and will not let me goe.
  *Hen.5.*  Haue they bound thee villain, why how now my Lord?
  *Iudge.*  I am glad to see your grace in good health.
  *Hen.5.*  Why my Lord, this is my man,
   Tis maruell you knew him not long before this,
   I tell you he is a man of his hands.
  *Theefe.*  I Gogs wounds that I am, try me who dare[.]
  *Iudge.*  Your Grace shal finde small credit by acknowledging him to be your
   man.
  *Hen.5.*  Why my Lord, what hath he done?
  *Iud.*  And it please your Maiestie, he hath robbed a poore Carrier.
  *Der.*  Heare you sir, marry it was one *Dericke*,
   Goodman *Hoblings* man of *Kent*.
  *Hen.5.*  What wast you butten-breech?
   Of my word my Lord, he did it but in iest.
  *Der.*  Heare you sir, is it your mans qualitie to rob folks in iest? In faith, he
   shall be hangd in earnest.

*Hen.5.* Well my Lord, what do you meane to do with my man?

*Iudg.* And please your grace, the law must passe on him,
   According to iustice, then he must be executed.

[The last three speeches are erroneously repeated at this point.]

[B3ᵛ] *Hen.5.* Why then belike you meane to hang my man?

*Iudge.* I am sorrie that it falles out so.

*Hen.5.* Why my Lord, I pray ye who am I?

*Iud.* And please your Grace, you are my Lord the yong Prince, our King
  that shall be after the decease of our soueraigne, King *Henry* the fourth,
  whom God graunt long to raigne.

. *Hen.5.* You say true my Lord:
   And you will hang my man.

*Iudge.* And like your grace, I must needs do iustice.

*Hen.5.* Tell me my Lord, shall I haue my man?

*Iudge.* I cannot my Lord.

*Hen.5.* But will you not let him go?

*Iud.* I am sorie that his case is so ill.

*Hen.5.* Tush, case me no casings, shal I haue my man?

*Iudge.* I cannot, nor I may not my Lord.

*Hen.5.* Nay, and I shal not say, & then I am answered?

*Iudge.* No.

*Hen.5.* No: then I will haue him.
 *He giueth him a boxe on the eare.*

*Ned.* Gogs wounds my Lord, shal I cut off his head?

*Hen.5.* No, I charge you draw not your swords,
   But get you hence, prouide a noyse of Musitians,
   Away, be gone.     *Exeunt the Theefe* [*, Ned and Tom*].

*Iudge.* Well my Lord, I am content to take it at your hands.

*Hen.5.* Nay and you be not, you shall haue more.

*Iudge.* Why I pray you my Lord, who am I?

*Hen.5.* You, who knowes not you?
   Why man, you are Lord chiefe Iustice of England.

*Iudge.* Your Grace hath said truth, therfore in striking me in this place, you
  greatly abuse me, and not me onely, but also your father: whose liuely
  person here in this place I doo represent. And therefore to teach you
  what preroga[B4]tiues meane, I commit you to the Fleete, vntill we haue
  spoken with your father.

*Hen.5.* Why then belike you meane to send me to the Fleete?

*Iudge.* I indeed, and therefore carry him away.
          *Exeunt Hen.5. with the Officers.*

[Scene v parodies the previous action, with Derrick the Clown impersonating the
Prince and John Cobbler the Lord Chief Justice. It suggested the 'play acting' scene
in *1H4* 2.4, and may also have influenced the committing of Falstaff to the Fleet in
*Part Two*, 5.5.84–9.]

[B4]                              *Enter Dericke and Iohn Cobler.*

*Der.*  Sownds maisters, heres adoo,
         When Princes must go to prison:
         Why *Iohn*, didst euer see the like?

*Iohn.*  O *Dericke*, trust me, I neuer saw the like.

*Der.*  Why *Iohn* thou maist see what princes be in choller,
         A Iudge a boxe on the eare, Ile tel thee *Iohn*, O *Iohn*,
         I would not haue done it for twentie shillings.

*Iohn.*  No nor I, there had bene no way but one with vs,
         We should haue bene hangde.

*Der.*  Faith *Iohn*, Ile tel thee what, thou shalt be my Lord chiefe Iustice, and
         thou shalt sit in the chair,
         And ile be the yong prince, and hit thee a boxe on the eare,
         And then thou shalt say, to teach you what prerogatiues
         Meane, I commit you to the Fleete.

*Iohn.*  Come on, Ile be your Iudge,
         But thou shalt not hit me hard.

*Der.*  No, no.

*Iohn.*  What hath he done?

*Der.*  Marry he hath robd *Dericke*.

*Iohn.*  Why then I cannot let him go.

*Der.*  I must needs haue my man.

*Iohn.*  You shall not haue him.

*Der.*  Shall I not haue my man, say no and you dare:
         How say you, shall I not haue my man?

*Iohn.*  No marry shall you not.

[B4ᵛ]   *Der.*  Shall I not *Iohn*?

*Iohn.*  No *Dericke*.

*Der.*  Why then take you that till more come,
         Sownes, shall I not haue him?

*Iohn.*  Well I am content to take this at your hand,
         But I pray you, who am I?

*Der.*  Who are thou, Sownds, doost not know thy self?

*Iohn.*  No.

*Der.*  Now away simple fellow,
         Why man, thou art *Iohn* the Cobler.

*Iohn.*  No, I am my Lord chiefe Iustice of England.

*Der.*  Oh *Iohn*, Masse thou saist true, thou art indeed.

*Iohn.*  Why then to teach you what prerogatiues mean I commit you to the
         Fleete.

*Der.*  Wel I will go, but yfaith you gray beard knaue, Ile course you.
                              *Exit. And straight enters again.*
         Oh *Iohn*, Come, come out of thy chair, why what a clown weart thou, to
         let me hit thee a box on the eare, and now thou seest they will not take

me to the Fleete, I thinke that thou art one of these Worenday Clownes.

[The scene ends with Derrick the Clown's decision to leave the profession of carrier and to go and stay at John the Cobbler's. Scene vi, the prince's first repentance, is relevant not only to *1H4* 3.2, but also to *Part Two*, 2.2.1–52 and 4.2.221 ff.]

[c1]                              *Enter the yoong Prince, with Ned and Tom.*

*Hen.5.*  Come away sirs, Gogs wounds *Ned*,
          Didst thou not see what a boxe on the eare
          I tooke my Lord chiefe Iustice?
*Tom.*  By gogs blood it did me good to see it,
          It made his teeth iarre in his head.
                              *Enter sir Iohn Old-Castle.*
*Hen.5.*  How now sir *Iohn Old-Castle*,
          What newes with you?
*Ioh.Old.*  I am glad to see your grace at libertie,
          I was come I, to visit you in prison.
*Hen.5.*  To visit me, didst thou not know that I am a Princes son, why tis
          inough for me to looke into a prison, though I come not in my selfe, but
          heres such adoo now a-dayes, heres prisoning, heres hanging, whip-
          ping, and the diuel and all: but I tel you sirs, when I am King, we will
          haue no such things, but my lads, if the old king my father were dead,
          we would be all kings.
*Ioh.Old.*  Hee is a good olde man, God take him to his mercy the sooner.
*Hen.5.*  But *Ned*, so soone as I am King, the first thing I wil do, shal be to put
          my Lord chiefe Iustice out of office, And thou shalt be my Lord chiefe
          Iustice of England.
*Ned.*  Shall I be Lord chiefe Iustice?
          By gogs wounds, ile be the brauest Lord chiefe Iustice
          That euer was in England.
*Hen.5.*  Then *Ned*, ile turne all these prisons into fence Schooles, and I will
          endue thee with them, with landes to [c1ᵛ] maintaine them withall: then
          I wil haue a bout with my Lord chiefe Iustice, thou shalt hang none but
          picke purses and horse stealers, and such base minded villaines, but
          that fellow that will stand by the high way side couragiously with his
          sword and buckler and take a purse, that fellow giue him commenda-
          tions, beside that, send him to me and I will giue him an anuall pension
          out of my Exchequer, to maintaine him all the dayes of his life.
*Ioh.*  Nobly spoken *Harry*, we shall neuer haue a mery world til the old king
          be dead.
*Ned.*  But whither are ye going now?
*Hen.5.*  To the Court, for I heare say, my father lies verie sicke.
*Tom.*  But I doubt he wil not die.
*Hen.5.*  Yet will I goe thither, for the breath shal be no sooner out of his
          mouth, but I wil clap the Crowne on my head.

*Iockey.* Wil you goe to the Court with that cloake so full of needles?

*Hen.5.* Cloake, ilat-holes, needles, and all was of mine owne deuising, and therefore I wil weare it.

*Tom.* I pray you my Lord, what may be the meaning thereof?

*Hen.5.* Why man, tis a sign that I stand vpon thorns, til the Crowne be on my head.

*Ioc.* Or that euery needle might be a prick to their harts that repine at your doings.

*Hen.5.* Thou saist true *Iockey*, but thers some wil say, the yoong Prince will be a well toward yoong man and all this geare, that I had as leeue they would breake my head with a pot, as to say any such thing, but we stand prating here too long, I must needs speake with my father, therfore come away.

*Porter.* What a rapping keep you at the Kings Court gate?

[C2]   *Hen.5.* Heres one that must speake with the King.

*Por.* The King is verie sick, and none must speak with him.

*Hen.5.* No you rascall, do you not know me?

*Por.* You are my Lord the yong Prince.

*Hen.5.* Then goe and tell my father, that I must and will speake with him.

*Ned.* Shall I cut off his head?

*Hen.5.* No, no, though I would helpe you in other places, yet I haue nothing to doo here, what you are in my fathers Court.

*Ned.* I will write him in my Tables, for so soone as I am made Lord chiefe Iustice, I wil put him out of his Office.          *The Trumpet sounds.*

*Hen.5.* Gogs wounds sirs, the King comes,
        Lets all stand aside.
            *Enter the King, with the Lord of Exeter.*

*Hen.4.* And is it true my Lord, that my sonne is alreadie sent to the Fleete? now truly that man is more fitter to rule the Realme then I, for by no meanes could I rule my sonne, and he by one word hath caused him to be ruled. Oh my sonne, my sonne, no sooner out of one prison, but into an other, I had thought once whiles I had liued, to haue seene this noble Realme of England flourish by thee my sonne, but now I see it goes to ruine and decaie.                              *He wepeth.*
            *Enters Lord of Oxford.*

*Ox.* And please your grace, here is my Lord your sonne,
        That commeth to speake with you,
        He saith, he must and wil speake with you.

*Hen.4.* Who my sonne *Harry*?

*Oxf.* I and please your Maiestie.

*Hen.4.* I know wherefore he commeth,
        But looke that none come with him.

[C2ᵛ]   *Oxf.* A verie disordered company, and such as make
        Verie ill rule in your Maiesties house.

*Hen.4.*  Well let him come,
    But looke that none come with him.                    *He goeth.*
*Oxf.*  And please your grace,
    My Lord the King, sends for you.
*Hen.5.*  Come away sirs, lets go all togither.
*Oxf.*  And please your grace, none must go with you.
*Hen.5.*  Why I must needs haue them with me,
    Otherwise I can do my father no countenance,
    Therefore come away.
*Oxf.*  The King your father commaunds
    There should none come.
*Hen.5.*  Well sirs then be gone,
    And prouide me three Noyse of Musitians.        *Exeunt knights.*
    *Enters the Prince with a dagger in his hand.*
*Hen.4.*  Come my sonne, come on a Gods name,
    I know wherefore thy comming is,
    Oh my sonne, my sonne, what cause hath euer bene,
    That thou shouldst forsake me, and follow this vilde and
    Reprobate company, which abuseth youth so manifestly:
    Oh my sonne, thou knowest that these thy doings
    Wil end thy fathers dayes.                    *He weepes.*
  I so, so, my sonne, thou fearest not to approach the presence of thy sick
father, in that disguised sort, I tel thee my sonne, that there is neuer a
needle in thy cloke, but it is a prick to my heart, & neuer an ilat-hole, but
it is a hole to my soule: and wherefore thou bringest that dagger in thy
hande I know not, but by coniecture.                    *He weepes.*
*Hen.5.*  My cŏscience accuseth me, most soueraign Lord, and welbeloued
father, to answere first to the last point, [C3] That is, whereas you
coniecture that this hand and this dagger shall be armde against your
life: no, know my beloued father, far be the thoughts of your sonne,
sonne said I, an vnworthie sonne for so good a father: but farre be the
thoughts of any such pretended mischiefe: and I most humbly render it
to your Maiesties hand, and liue my Lord and soueraigne for euer: and
with your dagger arme show like vengeance vpon the bodie of that your
sonne, I was about say and dare not, ah woe is me therefore, that your
wilde slaue, tis not the Crowne that I come for, sweete father, because I
am vnworthie, and those vilde & reprobate company, I abandon, &
vtterly abolish their company for euer. Pardon sweete father, pardon:
the least thing and most desire[d]: and this ruffianly cloake, I here teare
from my backe, and sacrifice it to the diuel, which is maister of al
mischiefe: Pardŏ me, sweet father, pardon me: good my Lord of *Exeter*
speak for me: pardon me, pardŏ good father, not a word: ah he wil not
speak one word: A *Harry*, now thrice vnhappie *Harry*. But what shal I
do? I wil go take me into some solitarie place, and there lament my

sinfull life, and when I haue done, I wil laie me downe and die. *Exit.*
*Hen.4.* Call him againe, call my sonne againe.
*Hen.5.* And doth my father call me again? now *Harry*,
    Happie be the time that thy father calleth thee againe.
*Hen.4.* Stand vp my son, and do not think thy father,
    But at the request of thee my sonne I wil pardon thee,
    And God blesse thee, and make thee his seruant.
*Hen.5.* Thanks good my Lord, & no doubt but this day,
    Euen this day, I am borne new againe.
*Hen.4.* Come my son and Lords, take me by the hands.    *Exeunt omnes.*


[After a brief scene in which the Clown complains of the shrewish behaviour of John Cobbler's wife, scene viii presents the taking of the crown and the king's death, serving as model for 4.2.]

[c3ᵛ]                      *Enter the King with his Lords.*
*Hen.4.* Come my Lords, I see it bootes me not to take any physick, for all
the Phisitians in the world cannot cure me, no not one. But good my
Lords, remember my last wil and Testament concerning my sonne, for
truly my Lordes, I doo not thinke but he wil proue as valiant and
victorious a King, as euer raigned in England.
*Both.* Let heauen and earth be witnesse betweene vs, if we accomplish not
thy will to the vttermost.
*Hen.4.* I giue you most vnfained thãks, good my Lords,
    Draw the Curtaines and depart my chamber a while,
    And cause some Musicke to rocke me a sleepe.
                                 *He sleepeth.Exeunt Lords.*

[c4]                          *Enter the Prince.*
*Hen.5.* Ah *Harry*, thrice vnhappie, that hath neglect so long from visiting
thy sicke father, I wil goe, nay but why doo I not go to the Chamber of
my sick father, to comfort the melancholy soule of his bodie, his soule
said I, here is his bodie indeed, but his soule is, whereas it needs no
bodie. Now thrice accursed *Harry*, that hath offended thy father so
much, and could not I craue pardon for all. Oh my dying father, cursed
be the day wherin I was borne, and accursed be the houre wherin I was
begotten, but what shal I do? if weeping teares which come too late, may
suffice the negligence neglected too soone [to some: Q], I wil weepe day
and night vntil the fountaine be drie with weeping.     *Exit.*
            *Enter Lord of Exeter and Oxford.*
*Exe.* Come easily my Lord, for waking of the King.
*Hen.4.* Now my Lords.
*Oxf.* How doth your Grace feele your selfe?
*Hen.4.* Somewhat better after my sleepe,

> But good my Lords take off my Crowne,
> Remoue my chaire a litle backe, and set me right,

*Ambo.* And please your grace, the crown is takē away.

*Hen.4.* The Crowne taken away,
> Good my Lord of *Oxford*, go see who hath done this deed:
> No doubt tis some vilde traitor that hath done it,
> To depriue my sonne, they that would do it now,
> Would seeke to scrape and scrawle for it after my death.

> > *Enter Lord of Oxford with the Prince.*

*Oxf.* Here and please your Grace,
> Is my Lord the yong Prince with the Crowne.

*Hen.4.* Why how now my sonne?
> I had thought the last time I had you in schooling,
> I had giuen you a lesson for all,
> And do you now begin againe?
> Why tel me my sonne,

[c4ᵛ]      Doest thou thinke the time so long,
> That thou wouldest haue it before the
> Breath be out of my mouth?

*Hen.5.* Most soueraign Lord, and welbeloued father,
> I came into your Chamber to comfort the melancholy
> Soule of your bodie, and finding you at that time
> Past all recouerie, and dead to my thinking,
> God is my witnesse: and what should I doo,
> But with weeping tears lament yᵉ death of you my father,
> And after that, seeing the Crowne, I tooke it:
> And tel me my father, who might better take it then I,
> After your death? but seeing you liue,
> I most humbly render it into your Maiesties hands,
> And the happiest man aliue, that my father liue:
> And liue my Lórd and father, for euer.

*Hen.4.* Stand vp my sonne,
> Thine answere hath sounded wel in mine eares,
> For I must need confesse that I was in a very sound sleep,
> And altogither vnmindful of thy comming:
> But come neare my sonne,
> And let me put thee in possession whilst I liue,
> That none depriue thee of it after my death.

*Hen.5.* Well may I take it at your maiesties hands,
> But it shal neuer touch my head, so lõg as my father liues.

> > *He taketh the Crowne.*

*Hen.4.* God giue thee ioy my sonne,
> God blesse thee and make thee his seruant,

And send thee a prosperous raigne.
For God knowes my sonne, how hardly I came by it,
And how hardly I haue maintained it.
*Hen.5.* Howsoeuer you came by it, I know not,
But now I haue it from you, and from you I wil keepe it:
And he that seekes to take the Crowne from my head,
Let him looke that his armour be thicker then mine,
Or I will pearce him to the heart,

[DI]     Were it harder then brasse or bollion.
*Hen.4.* Nobly spoken, and like a King.
Now trust me my Lords, I feare not but my sonne
Will be as warlike and victorious a Prince,
As euer raigned in England.
*L.Ambo.* His former life shewes no lesse.
*Hen.4.* Wel my lords, I know not whether it be for sleep,
Or drawing neare of drowsie summer of death,
But I am verie much giuen to sleepe,
Therefore good my Lords and my sonne,
Draw the Curtaines, depart my Chamber,
And cause some Musicke to rocke me a sleepe.    *Exeunt omnes.*
*The king dieth.*

[Scene ix opens with the knights' rejoicing for the death of the king (see 5.3)
immediately followed by the rejection.]

*Enter the Theefe.*
*Theefe.* Ah God, I am now much like to a Bird
Which hath escaped out of the Cage,
For so soone as my Lord chiefe Iustice heard
That the old King was dead, he was glad to let me go,
For feare of my Lord the yong Prince:
But here comes some of his companions,
I wil see and I can get any thing of them,
For old acquaintance.
*Enter the Knights raunging.*
*Tom.* Gogs wounds, the King is dead.
*Ioc.* Dead, then gogs blood, we shall be all kings.
*Ned.* Gogs wounds, I shall be Lord chiefe Iustice
Of England.
*Tom.* Why how, are you broken out of prison?
*Ned.* Gogs wounds, how the villaine stinkes.
*Ioc.* Why what will become of thee now?
Fie vpon him, how the rascall stinkes.
*Theef.* Marry I wil go and serue my maister againe.

*Tom.*  Gogs blood, doost think that he will haue any such
  Scab'd knaue as thou art? what man he is a king now.

*Ned.*  Hold thee, heres a couple of Angels for thee,
  And get thee gone, for the King wil not be long
  Before he come this way:
  And hereafter I wil tel the king of thee.   *Exit Theefe.*

*Ioc.*  Oh how it did me good, to see the king
  When he was crowned:
  Me thought his seate was like the figure of heauen,
  And his person like vnto a God.

*Ned.*  But who would haue thought,
  That the king would haue changde his countenance so?

*Ioc.*  Did you not see with what grace
  He sent his embassage into *France*? to tel the French king
  That *Harry* of England hath sent for the Crowne,
  And *Harry* of England wil haue it.

*Tom.*  But twas but a litle to make the people beleeue,
  That he was sorie for his fathers death.  *The Trumpet sounds.*

*Ned.*  Gogs wounds, the king comes,
  Lets all stand aside.
  *Enter the King with the Archbishop, and the Lord of Oxford.*

*Ioc.*  How do you my Lord?

*Ned.*  How now *Harry*?
  Tut my Lord, put away these dumpes,
  You are a king, and all the realme is yours:
  What man, do you not remember the old sayings,
  You know I must be Lord chiefe Iustice of England,
  Trust me my lord, me thinks you are very much changed,
  And tis but with a little sorrowing, to make folkes beleeue
  The death of your father greeues you,
  And tis nothing so.

*Hen.5.*  I prethee *Ned*, mend thy maners,
  And be more modester in thy tearmes,
  For my vnfeined greefe is not to be ruled by thy flattering
  And dissembling talke, thou saist I am changed,
  So I am indeed, and so must thou be, and that quickly,
  Or else I must cause thee to be chaunged.

*Ioc.*  Gogs wounds how like you this?
  Sownds tis not so sweete as Musicke.

*Tom.*  I trust we haue not offended your grace no way.

*Hen.5.*  Ah *Tom*, your former life greeues me,
  And makes me to abandō & abolish your company for euer
  And therfore not vpō pain of death to approch my presence
  By ten miles space, then if I heare wel of you,

It may be I wil do somewhat for you,
Otherwise looke for no more fauour at my hands,
Then at any other mans: And therefore be gone,
We haue other matters to talke on.          *Exeunt Knights.*
Now my good Lord Archbishop of *Canterbury*,
What say you to our Embassage into *France*?

[The scene continues with the Archbishop arguing the English right to the French crown, immediately followed by the arrival of the French ambassador delivering a tun of tennis balls, and the decision to wage war in France (see *H5* 1.2); then the new king calls for the Lord Chief Justice (*Part Two* 5.2).]

[D3ᵛ]          Now my Lords, to Armes, to Armes,
For I vow by heauen and earth, that the proudest
French man in all *France*, shall rue the time that euer
These Tennis balles were sent into England.
My Lord, I wil yᵗ there be prouided a great Nauy of ships,
With all speed, at *South-Hampton*,
For there I meane to ship my men,
For I would be there before him, if [it: Q] it were possible,
Therefore come, but staie,
I had almost forgot the chiefest thing of all, with chafing
With this French Embassador.
Call in my Lord chiefe Iustice of England.
[D4]                    *Enters Lord chiefe Iustice of England.*
*Exe.*  Here is the King my Lord.
*Iustice.*  God preserue your Maiestie.
*Hen.5.*  Why how now my lord, what is the matter?
*Iustice.*  I would it were vnknowne to your Maiestie.
*Hen.5.*  Why what aile you?
*Iust.*  Your Maiestie knoweth my griefe well.
*Hen.5.*  Oh my Lord, you remember you sent me to the Fleete, did you not?
*Iust.*  I trust your grace haue forgotten that.
*Hen.5.*  I truly my Lord, and for reuengement,
I haue chosen you to be my Protector ouer my Realme,
Vntil it shall please God to giue me speedie returne
Out of *France*.
*Iust.*  And if it please your Maiestie, I am far vnworthie
Of so high a dignitie.
*Hen.5.*  Tut my Lord, you are not vnworthie,
Because I thinke you worthie:
For you that would not spare me,
I thinke wil not spare another,
It must needs be so, and therefore come,
Let vs be gone, and get our men in a readinesse.     *Exeunt omnes.*

[Scene x anticipates the enrolment scene (3.2), especially Mouldy's pleading for the sake of his 'dame', while the allusion to 'two shirts' recalls the plight of Poins at 2.2.]

*Enter a Captaine, Iohn Cobler and his wife.*

*Cap.* Come, come, there's no remedie,
        Thou must needs serue the King.
*Iohn.* Good maister Captaine let me go,
        I am not able to go so farre.
*Wife.* I pray you good maister Captaine,
        Be good to my husband.
*Cap.* Why I am sure he is not too good to serue y^e king,
*Iohn.* Alasse no: but a great deale too bad,
        Therefore I pray you let me go.
*Cap.* No, no, thou shalt go.
[D4^v]   *Iohn.* Oh sir, I haue a great many shooes at home to Cobble.
*Wife.* I pray you let him go home againe.
*Cap.* Tush I care not, thou shalt go.
*Iohn.* Oh wife, and you had beene a louing wife to me,
        This had not bene, for I haue said many times,
        That I would go away, and now I must go
        Against my will.                                    *He weepeth.*

                    *Enters Dericke.*
*Der.* How now ho, *Basillus Manus*, for an old codpeece,
        Maister Captaine shall we away?
        Sownds how now *Iohn*, what a crying?
        What make you and my dame there?
        I maruell whose head you will throw the stooles at,
        Now we are gone.
*Wife.* Ile tell you, come ye cloghead,
        What do you with my potlid? heare you,
        Will you haue it rapt about your pate?
                                    *She beateth him with her potlid.*
*Der.* Oh good dame,                            *Here he shakes her.*
        And I had my dagger here, I wold worie you al to peeces –
        That I would.
*Wife.* Would you so, Ile trie that.            *She beateth him.*
*Der.* Maister Captaine will ye suffer her?
        Go too dame, I will go backe as far as I can,
        But and you come againe,
        Ile clap the law on your backe thats flat:
        Ile tell you maister Captaine what you shall do?
        Presse her for a souldier, I warrant you,
        She will do as much good as her husband and I too.
                    *Enters the Theefe.*
        Sownes, who comes yonder?

  *Cap.* How now good fellow, doest thou want a maister?
[EI]  *Theefe.* I truly sir.
  *Cap.* Hold thee then, I presse thee for a souldier,
    To serue the King in *France*.
  *Der.* How now Gads, what doest knowes [?] thinkest?
  *Theefe.* I, I knew thee long ago.
  *Der.* Heare you maister Captaine?
  *Cap.* What saist thou?
  *Der.* I pray you let me go home againe.
  *Cap.* Why what wouldst thou do at home?
  *Der.* Marry I haue brought two shirts with me,
    And I would carry one of them home againe,
    For I am sure heele steale it from me,
    He is such a filching fellow.
  *Cap.* I warrant thee he wil not steale it from thee,
    Come lets away.
  *Der.* Come maister Captaine lets away,
    Come follow me.
  *Iohn.* Come wife, lets part louingly.
  *Wife.* Farewell good husband.
  *Der.* Fie what a kissing and crying is here?
    Sownes, do ye thinke he wil neuer come againe?
    Why *Iohn* come away, doest thinke that we are so base
    Minded to die among French men?
    Sownes, we know not whether they will laie
    Vs in their Church or no: Come M. Captain, lets away.
  *Cap.* I cannot staie no longer, therefore come away.

               *Exeunt omnes.*

# APPENDIX 4: TARLTON AND THE LORD CHIEF JUSTICE

A collection of anecdotes concerning the famous clown Richard Tarlton, who died in 1588, was published under the title *Tarltons Iests: drawn into these three parts* in 1638, though it had been entered in the Stationers' Register in 1609. The best-known item is the following.

### An excellent iest of Tarltons suddenly spoken

At the Bull at Bishops-gate, was a play of Henry the fift, wherein the iudge was to take a box on the eare; & because he was absent that should take the blowe, Tarlton himselfe, euer forward to please, took vpon him to play the same iudge, besides his owne part of the clowne: and Knel [William Knell of the Queen's Men] then playing Henry the fift, hit Tarlton a sounde boxe indeed, which made the people laugh the more because it was he, but anon the iudge goes in, and immediately Tarlton in his clownes cloathes comes out, and askes the actors what newes: O saith one hadst thou been here, thou shouldest haue seene Prince Henry hit the iudge a terrible box on the eare: What, man, said Tarlton, strike a iudge? It is true, yfaith, said the other. No other like, said Tarlton, and it could not be but terrible to the iudge, when the report so terrifies me, that me thinkes the blow remaines still on my cheeke, that it burnes againe. The people laught at this mightily: and to this day I have heard it commended for rare ...

Though *Famous Victories* was presented as a play of the Queen's Men (Tarlton's company), it has been maintained that the anecdote refers to another play on the subject, since, in the text we have, the Clown and the Justice are present on the stage together, preventing the possibility of one actor doubling both parts. As a matter of fact, it is far from uncommon, even today, for the sudden absence of an actor to force the players to modify the script in performance: in this case the decision was to act the 'serious' box-on-the-ear scene leaving out the small clown part in it, in order to give him full scope instead in the following clowning scene. The first speech quoted in the anecdote is typical of such forced improvisations: 'hadst thou been here' implies 'in other performances the clown is present in the scene which has just been enacted'. The Tarlton anecdote is evidence that *Famous Victories* is in fact a garbled summary version of a play or plays on Henry V acted to popular audiences in London by the Queen's Men before 1588.

# READING LIST

This list includes books and articles which are particularly useful for a study of Shakespeare's histories with special regard to the present play. It should be complemented with the works mentioned in the List of Abbreviations and Conventions at pp. xii–xv above, and with some of those discussed in the Introduction, Commentary and Textual Analysis in connection with specific points of less general interest.

Alvis, John. 'A little touch of the night in Harry: the career of Henry Monmouth', in *Shakespeare as Political Thinker*, ed. J. Alvis and T. G. West, 1981, pp. 95–126

Baldini, Gabriele. 'Lord Bardolph e sir John Umfrevile nell' "Enrico IV" di Shakespeare', *Belfagor* 5 (1952), 1–9

Beck, Richard J. *Shakespeare: Henry IV*, 1965

Berry, E. I. 'The rejection scene in *2 Henry IV*', *SEL* 17 (1977), 201–18

Bevington, David M. *Tudor Drama and Politics: A Critical Approach to Topical Meaning*, 1968

(ed.). *Henry the Fourth Parts 1 and 2: Critical Essays*, 1986 (an ample selection of essays, ranging from 1744 to 1983, supplementing Hunter's *Casebook*)

Blanpied, John W. *Time and the Artist in Shakespeare's English Histories*, 1983

Bradbrook, Muriel C. 'King Henry IV', in *Artist and Society in Shakespeare's England*, 1985, pp. 121–32

Brockbank, J. Philip. 'Shakespeare: his histories, English and Roman', in the *Sphere History of English Literature*, ed. Christopher Ricks, vol. 3, 1971

Calderwood, James L. *Metadrama in Shakespeare's Henriad*, 1979

Campbell, Lily B. *Shakespeare's Histories: Mirrors of Elizabethan Policy*, 1947

Chambers, E. K. *William Shakespeare: A Study of Facts and Problems*, 2 vols., 1930

Champion, Larry S. *Perspectives in Shakespeare's English Histories*, 1980

David, Richard. *Shakespeare in the Theatre*, 1978

'Shakespeare's history plays: epic or drama', *S.Sur.* 6 (1953), 129–39

Dessen, Alan C. *Shakespeare and the Late Moral Plays*, 1986

Empson, William. 'They that have power', in *Some Versions of Pastoral*, 1935, pp. 89–118

'Falstaff', in *Essays on Shakespeare*, 1986, pp. 29–78

Greenblatt, Stephen. *Shakespearean Negotiations*, 1988, pp. 95–126

Greg, W. W. *The Editorial Problem in Shakespeare*, 3rd edn, 1954

Hart, Alfred. 'Was the second part of *King Henry the Fourth* censored?', in *Shakespeare and the Homilies*, 1934, pp. 154–218

Hawkins, Sherman H. '*Henry IV*: the structural problem revisited', *SQ* 33 (1982), 279–301

Hibbard, George R. 'Henry IV and Hamlet', *S.Sur.* 30 (1977), 1–12

Hinman, Charlton. *The Printing and Proof-Reading of the First Folio of Shakespeare*, 2 vols., 1963

Holmes, Martin. *Shakespeare and His Players*, 1972, pp. 44–57

Honigmann, Ernst A. J. *Shakespeare: 'The Lost Years'*, 1985

Howard Hill, Trevor (ed.). *Henry IV Part II. A Concordance to the Text of the First Quarto of 1600*, 1971

Hunter, George K. (ed.). *Henry IV Parts I and II: A Casebook*, 1970 (includes influential essays by Maurice Morgann (1977), A. C. Bradley (1909), H. B. Charlton (1929), J. I. M. Stewart (1949), William Empson (1953), Harold Jenkins (1956), W. H. Auden (1959), C. L. Barber (1959) and Paul A. Jorgensen (1960))

'Shakespeare's politics and the rejection of Falstaff', *CQ* 1 (1959), 229–36

'*Henry IV* and the Elizabethan two-part play', in *Dramatic Identities and Cultural Tradition*, 1978, pp. 303–18

Jorgensen, Paul A. 'The "dastardly treachery" of Prince John of Lancaster', *PMLA* 76 (1961), 488–92

Knights, Lionel C. 'Time's subjects: the Sonnets and *King Henry IV, Part II*', in *Some Shakespearean Themes*, 1959, pp. 45–64

Law, Robert Adger. 'Structural unity in the two parts of *Henry IV*', *SP* 24 (1927), 223–42

'The composition of Shakespeare's Lancastrian trilogy', *TSLL* 3 (1961–2), 321–7

Leech, Clifford. 'The unity of 2 *Henry IV*', *S.Sur.* 6 (1953), 16–24

Lever, J. Walter. 'Shakespeare's French fruits', *S.Sur.* 6 (1953), 79–90

Long, John H. *Shakespeare's Use of Music: The Histories and the Tragedies*, 1971

McFarland, Thomas. *Shakespeare's Pastoral Comedy*, 1972, Appendix, pp. 177–211

McLuhan, Herbert Marshall, '*Henry IV*, a mirror for magistrates', *UTQ* 3 (1948), 152–9

Melchiori, Giorgio. 'Dying of a sweat: Falstaff and Oldcastle', *N&Q* ns 34 (1987), 210–11

Mendilow, A. A. 'Falstaff's death of a sweat', *SQ* 9 (1958), 479–83

Morgan, A. E. *Some Problems of Shakespeare's 'Henry the Fourth'*, 1924

Palmer, D. J. 'Casting off the old man: history and St Paul in "Henry IV"', *CQ* 12 (1970), 267–83

Prior, Moody E. 'Comic theory and the rejection of Falstaff', *S.St.* 9 (1976), 159–71

Rabkin, Norman. *Shakespeare and the Problem of Meaning*, 1981

Reese, M. M. *The Cease of Majesty: A Study of Shakespeare's History Plays*, 1961

Ribner, Irving. *The English History Play in the Age of Shakespeare*, 1957

Saccio, Peter. *Shakespeare's English Kings: History, Chronicle, and Drama*, 1977

Sahel, Pierre. *La pensée politique dans les drames historiques de Shakespeare*, Paris, 1984

Salingar, Leo. 'Falstaff and the life of shadows' (1980), in *Dramatic Form in Shakespeare and the Jacobeans*, 1986, pp. 32–52

Scoufos, Alice-Lyle. *Shakespeare's Typological Satire: A Study of the Falstaff–Oldcastle Problem*, 1979

Shaaber, Matthias A., 'The unity of *Henry IV*', *John Quincy Adams Memorial Studies*, 1948, pp. 217–27

Shanker, Sidney. *Shakespeare and the Uses of Ideology*, The Hague, 1975

Siegel, Paul N. *Shakespeare's English and Roman History Plays: A Marxist Approach*, 1986

Somerset, J. A. B. 'Falstaff, the prince, and the pattern of 2 *Henry IV*', *S.Sur.* 30 (1977), 35–46

Spencer, Benjamin T. '2 *Henry IV* and the theme of Time', *UTQ* 13 (1944), 394–9

Thayer, C. G. *Shakespearean Politics. Government and Misgovernment in the Great Histories*, 1983

Tillyard, E. M. W. *Shakespeare's History Plays*, 1944

Tomlinson, Michael. 'Shakespeare and the chronicles reassessed', *L&H* 10 (1984), 46–58

Trafton, Dain A. 'Shakespeare's Henry IV: a new prince and a new principality', in *Shakespeare as Political Thinker*, ed. J. Alvis and T. G. West, 1981, pp. 83–94

Traversi, Derek A. *Shakespeare: From Richard II to Henry V*, 1957

Vickers, Brian. *The Artistry of Shakespeare's Prose*, 1968

Waith, E. M. (ed.). *Shakespeare: The Histories, A Collection of Critical Essays*, 1965

Wharton, T. F. *Henry the Fourth Parts 1 & 2: Text and Performance*, 1983

Wilders, John. *The Lost Garden: A View of Shakespeare's English and Roman History Plays*, 1978

Williams, George Walton. 'Fastolf or Falstaff', *ELR* 5 (1975), 308–12
  'Second thoughts on Falstaff's name', *SQ* 30 (1979), 82–4

Wilson, John Dover. *The Fortunes of Falstaff*, 1943

Winny, J. *The Player King: A Theme of Shakespeare's Histories*, 1968

Young, D. P. (ed.). *Twentieth Century Interpretations of Henry IV, Part Two*, 1968